HANDBOOK OF DIAGNOSIS AND TREATMENT OF DSM-5 PERSONALITY DISORDERS

Since the publication of the acclaimed second edition of the *Handbook of Diagnosis and Treatment of DSM-IV-TR Personality Disorders*, much has changed in how the personality disorders are understood and treated. However, like its previous editions, this new edition is a hands-on manual of the most current and effective, evidence-based assessment and treatment interventions for these challenging disorders. The beginning chapters describe several cutting-edge trends in the diagnosis, case conceptualization, and treatment of them. Then, specific chapters focus on evidence-based diagnosis and treatment interventions for each of the ten DSM-5 personality disorders. Emphasized are the most recent developments from Cognitive Behavior Therapies, Dialectical Behavior Therapy, Cognitive Behavior Analysis System of Psychotherapy, Pattern-Focused Psychotherapy, Mindfulness, Schema Therapy, Transference Focused Psychotherapy, and Mentalization-Based Treatment. As in previous editions, extensive case material is used to illustrate key points of diagnosis and treatment.

Len Sperry, MD, PhD, is a professor of mental health counseling and director of clinical training at Florida Atlantic University, and clinical professor of psychiatry at the Medical College of Wisconsin. For more than three decades he has treated and taught courses and workshops on the personality disorders. Among his 1000+ professional publications are several articles, book chapters, and books on these disorders, including the recently published *Cognitive Behavior Therapy of DSM-5 Personality Disorders*.

"Len Sperry has been a leader in the treatment of personality disorders for over twenty-five years. This third edition of his Handbook provides treatment strategies informed by recent research and updates from DSM-5. Sperry is the top contemporary clinical scholar of personality disorders with his integration of empirical science, human development, and a synthetic understanding of different treatment approaches. If you are going to purchase one book on personality disorders, get this one."—**Steven J. Sandage, PhD, LP**, Professor of Psychological & Brain Sciences, Boston University

"As a much needed antidote to the one-size fits all of current cognitive therapy, be it for Axis I or Axis II, Dr. Sperry has presented a much needed series of evidence- based and tailored interventions that effectively treat the gamut of personality disorders that are so prevalent today."—**Nicholas A. Cummings, PhD, ScD**, Former President, American Psychological Association

"The *Handbook of Diagnosis and Treatment of DSM-5 Personality Disorders: Assessment, Case Conceptualization, and Treatment, Third Edition* is a must read for any practicing mental health clinician working with personality disordered clients. It is remarkably practical, user friendly, updated, and helpful to assist both professionals and trainees alike stay up-to-date on the thoughtful evidence based strategies for understanding and treating personality disorders. This is one of those books that should be on the shelf of all mental health professionals. Dr. Sperry, as usual, has offered the profession a terrific update to his now classic text." —**Thomas G. Plante, PhD, ABPP**, Professor of Psychology, Santa Clara University

"Len Sperry's third edition of the *Handbook of Diagnosis and Treatment of DSM-5 Personality Disorders* offers both the experienced clinician and student a concise overview and description of the range of personality disorders, as well as presenting the essential elements of comprehensive diagnosis and treatment. Sperry understands the world of the clinician, distilling the theoretical and pragmatic advances in clinical science that offer hope for identifying, conceptualizing and more importantly influencing the course of change for these ubiquitous and challenging disorders."—**Jeffrey J. Magnavita, PhD, ABPP**, independent practice and Lecturer in Psychiatry, Yale University

"Sperry's third edition of this benchmark handbook makes it the instant standard on the assessment and treatment of personality disorders. Evidence-based yet delightfully reader-friendly, Sperry's guide blends a scientist's mastery of the evidence with a healer's empathy for the pain and disruption that stalk the lives of the personality impaired. Jam-packed with case examples and practitioner-oriented recommendations, this is a must-read for the competent clinician."—**W. Brad Johnson, PhD**, Professor of Psychology, U.S. Naval Academy & Johns Hopkins University

"To provide effective short-term and enduring treatment, it is necessary to diagnose and treat the personality of the client. Len Sperry MD, PhD, provides the insight and guidelines to make this once considered impossible task, likely. The book is chocked full of practical suggestions and tools that aid the diagnosis, conceptualization, and treatment of personality disorders following the DSM-5 guidelines. The third edition of the *Handbook of Diagnosis and Treatment of DSM-5 Personality Disorders* belongs on every clinician's bookshelf. If you read only one professional book this year, this is the one!"—**Jon Carlson, PsyD, EdD, ABPP**, Distinguished Professor of Adlerian Psychology, Adler University, Chicago

"Unlike many writers who help the reader understand personality disorders, Sperry helps the reader understand personality disorders and, more importantly, how to help those who struggle with them. With the changes in the DSM-5 related to the understanding and treatment of personality disorders, Sperry's work is cutting edge and a must-read for all clinicians."—**Craig S. Cashwell, PhD**, Professor of Counseling, University of North Carolina at Greensboro

"The third edition of Dr. Sperry's Handbook demonstrates the strengths of the previous edition: it is clearly written, comprehensive, up-to-date, and jargon-free. Its biopsychosocial approach to the personality disorders is realistically optimistic, while adhering to evidence-based treatments. Finally, Dr. Sperry is clearly dedicated to 'listening with the third ear,' which is essential in working with personality-disordered patients."—**Ronald W. Pies, MD**, Professor of Psychiatry, Lecturer on Bioethics & Humanities, SUNY Upstate Medical University

"Personality disorders are the most misunderstood and misdiagnosed of all the DSM-5/ICD 10 mental disorders. Here, in this easy-to-read handbook, Len Sperry presents the most user-friendly guide available to personality disorders coupled with a completely integrative model to case conceptualization: A book for every graduate psychopathology course in the nation."—**James Robert Bitter, EdD**, Professor of Counseling and Human Services, East Tennessee State University

"There's an old myth that personality disorders are equivalent to a life sentence to psychotherapy. Len Sperry uses scientific evidence and logical analysis to systematically bust this myth. If you're interested in working with clients with personality disorders, this book is indispensable. Not only does Sperry offer hope and optimism for positive outcomes, he also deftly summarizes many evidence-based approaches that can transform your optimism to clinical reality."—**John Sommers-Flanagan, PhD**, Professor of Counselor Education at the University of Montana

"Len Sperry MD, PhD, is a brilliant writer who with his psychology and psychiatry background is able to capture nuances in cognitions, and affective and interpersonal styles of individuals with personality disorders in a way that crystalizes the concept for the reader. The wonderful case examples and understanding the parental injunctions and worldview perspectives of the patient were especially helpful for me. This book is an incredible manual and reference book—I still have one of Dr Sperry's first books on personality disorders and still reference it to this day."—**Jon A. Lehrmann, MD**, Chairman and Charles E. Kubly Professor of Psychiatry and Behavioral Medicine, Medical College of Wisconsin

"A tremendous resource, including the latest DSM-5 descriptions, cross-theoretical conceptualizations, and integrative treatment approaches for all of the identified personality disorders, under one cover. Sperry neatly addresses the 'categorical vs. dimensional' assessment dilemma by expertly contrasting each personality disorder with its corresponding sub-clinical personality 'style.' Sperry's captivating clinical vignettes combine with his presentation of empirical evidence to create a most satisfying volume for the interested scientist-practitioner."—**Cory F. Newman, PhD, ABPP**, Professor of Psychology, in Psychiatry, Perelman School of Medicine, University of Pennsylvania

HANDBOOK OF DIAGNOSIS AND TREATMENT OF DSM-5 PERSONALITY DISORDERS

Assessment, Case Conceptualization, and Treatment

Third Edition

Len Sperry, MD, PhD

Routledge
Taylor & Francis Group

NEW YORK AND LONDON

Third edition published 2016
by Routledge
711 Third Avenue, New York, NY 10017

and by Routledge
2 Park Square, Milton Park, Abingdon, Oxon, OX14 4RN

Routledge is an imprint of the Taylor & Francis Group, an informa business

© 2016 Taylor & Francis

First edition published by Brunner/Mazel 1995

Second edition published by Routledge 2003

Library of Congress Cataloging in Publication Data
Names: Sperry, Len, author.
Title: Handbook of diagnosis and treatment of DSM-5 personality disorders: assessment, case conceptualization, and treatment / Len Sperry.
Description: Third edition. | New York, NY : Routledge, 2016.
Includes bibliographical references and index.
Identifiers: LCCN 2015040215| ISBN 9780415841900 (alk. paper) | ISBN 9780415841917 (alk. paper) | ISBN 9780203763728 (alk. paper)
Subjects: LCSH: Personality disorders--Handbooks, manuals, etc.
Classification: LCC RC554 .S68 2016 DDC 616.85/81—dc23
LC record available at http://lccn.loc.gov/2015040215

ISBN: 978-0-415-84190-0 (hbk)
ISBN: 978-0-415-84191-7 (pbk)
ISBN: 978-0-203-76372-8 (ebk)

Typeset in Bembo
by Florence Production Ltd, Stoodleigh, Devon, UK

Printed in Canada

CONTENTS

FOREWORD

As a new graduate student in psychology at New York University in 1964, I took the required course in psychopathology. The instructor quoted liberally from a volume he called the "Diagnostic and Statistical Manual," or DSM, published by the American Psychiatric Association in 1952. We immediately asked if we could purchase the thin, spiral-bound book at the bookstore, but the instructor told us that access was limited to *psychiatrists*, and that only they could use it to diagnose a patient. He had clearly gotten the volume under false pretenses or through some subterfuge. While we did not think that that was fair, as new graduate students we recognized the pecking order in mental health. The psychiatrist was at the top and psychologists were not ordained to read or use the holy words of the DSM. This first edition was not labeled as DSM-I, simply DSM, with no portent of what was ahead. In DSM-I, all mental disorders were divided into two major groups: "(1) those in which there is a disturbance of mental function resulting from, or precipitated by a primary impairment of the function of the brain, generally due to a diffuse impairment of brain tissue; and (2) those which are the result of a more general difficulty in adaptation of the individual, and in which any associated brain function disturbance is secondary to the psychiatric disorder" (p. 9). The DSM, as might be expected of the zeitgeist, was suffused with the contemporary perspective of psychoanalysis. The descriptions were brief and still left a great deal of room for clinician interpretation and creativity.

It was not until 1968, with the publication of the second edition of DSM, labeled DSM-II, that there was a sequencing of editions noted. The only place that we could get the DSM-II was at the Medical School bookstore. We gave one of our graduate cohort the money and they did a DSM-II run and got copies for all of us. We never asked what lies he had to tell to get by the eagle-eyed cashiers at the bookstore.

By 1980, I was a practicing licensed clinical psychologist when I was confronted by the most horrible event I had yet encountered in my career. The third edition, DSM-III, was published. The sheer weight and size of this new volume had me thinking that I needed to leave clinical psychology. There was no way that I could learn all of this new information or become knowledgeable in this new diagnostic format. The diagnostic descriptions in DSM-I ran to 31 pages (pp. 12–43). For DSM-II there was an increase to 38 pages in length. Now, in DSM-III, the diagnostic descriptions ran to 300 pages. Who were these people to do this to the field? Who amongst us could master this tenfold increase in material? By 1980, psychologists could obtain the DSM and use it for diagnoses. There were some excellent additions, including the idea of a multiaxial diagnosis. In the good old days, one could make up one's own diagnosis with some impunity using mixed formulations, including dynamic, behavioral, and mythical ideas. By 1980, however, there were established limits to what we could use as diagnostic statements. Some of us were troubled by these strictures; others were comforted by the boundaries. If a patient did not meet criteria for a particular diagnosis, they could not be diagnosed with that disorder. If, however, the patient met the minimum criteria, whether the clinician liked it or not the patient could earn that diagnosis. As I taught my students, "If it looks like a duck, walks like a duck, and quacks like a duck, it is likely a duck, not a dog that has learned a foreign language." A critical change in DSM-III was the idea of diagnosing an individual on five separate and distinct axes. This multiaxial diagnosis allowed the clinician to identify and code "aspects of the environment, and areas of functioning that might be overlooked if the focus was on assessing a single presenting problem" (p. 23). The five axes were:

Axis I   Clinical Syndromes
Axis II   Personality Disorders
            Specific Developmental Disorders
Axis III   Physical Disorders and Medical/Health Problems
Axis IV   Severity of Psychosocial Stressors
Axis V   Highest Level of Adaptive Functioning in the Past Year.

A non-axial category would be used when conditions are not attributable to a mental disorder but were still the focus of attention or treatment (e.g. Occupational Problems, Marital Problems). These were coded as "V" codes.

In 1994, the fourth edition of DSM was published (DSM-IV), where the definition of terms had swelled to an astounding 650 pages. The description of Antisocial Personality Disorder was the same, though some criteria differed from DSM-III-R.

DSM-IV-TR was published in 2000. The criteria sets were generally unchanged but there was a substantial revision of the descriptions, features, cultural factors, age, and gender differences, associated features, prevalence, course of the disorder, familial pattern, and differential diagnosis. The definition of terms now covered 703 pages, almost 23 times the number of definitional pages in DSM-I.

Finally, the long-awaited and much-heralded publication of DSM-5 occurred in 2013. Definitions now take 775 pages—again, an almost 10 percent increase. There have been changes in many realms, but few (if any) changes in the criteria and descriptions of the personality disorders. Given that the patients with personality disorders are often among the most difficult to treat, and take more work and energy on the part of the therapist, all without the same treatment success, they can take a major share of the therapist's time and focus.

While there has been disagreement with the categorical approach taken by DSM and ICD because of its "labeling" or "pigeonholing" potential, these volumes represent the commonly used diagnostic schema for the range and breadth of mental disorders. The approach of DSM has been criticized as cumbersome and even of driving medical students from considering a career in psychiatry. It is not our goal to argue the value of the DSM, the dispensing with the multiaxial system, or the accuracy of criteria. In our view, probably a far greater issue in the use of both DSM and ICD is the lack of operational definitions in both of these diagnostic schemes. A reading of both volumes would find that many terms are self-evident and need little explication, e.g. the first criterion in DSM-5 for Borderline Personality Disorder states, "Frantic efforts to avoid real or imagined abandonment." The words "effort," "avoid," "real," and "imagined" need relatively little clarification. The terms "frantic" and "abandonment" are, however, quite vague and open to interpretation. Given the lack of agreement on all terms, it should also be noted that over 200 combinations of criteria can be used to meet the required number of criteria to arrive at a diagnosis of any personality disorder.

To add to the diagnostic confusion, the International Classification of Diseases (ICD) published by the World Health Organization is presently preparing its 11th edition. Plus, the Psychodynamic Diagnostic Manual (PDM), a collaborative effort of the American Psychoanalytic Association, the International Psychoanalytical Association, the Division of Psychoanalysis of the American Psychological Association, the American Academy of Psychoanalysis and Dynamic Psychiatry, and the National Membership Committee on Psychoanalysis in Clinical Social Work was published in 2006. According to the overview offered by the authors, the PDM is "a diagnostic framework that attempts to characterize an individual's full range of functioning—the depth as well as the surface of emotional, cognitive, and social patterns" (p. 1).

Given the lack of coherence, the confusion regarding diagnostic entities, and the issues regarding cohesiveness, what has become a necessity is a single volume that can explain and put the pieces in order. To do this requires a clear vision of what a personality disorder is, how it can potentially impact on an individual and that individual's family and cultural system. It requires a clinical understanding of multiple treatment models, and the ability to apply the diagnostic understanding into clinical practice. It requires the author to be able to engage the reader on several different levels: the diagnostic, the theoretical, the strategic, and the technical. The third edition Len Sperry's *Handbook of Diagnosis and Treatment of DSM-5 Personality Disorders: Assessment, Case Conceptualization, and Treatment*, has all of this and more.

The first two chapters need to be included in a bound monograph that would be required reading for every graduate course in psychopathology. Chapter 1, on the diagnosis and treatment of personality disorders, offers not only the historical perspective of personality disorders, but addresses the development and maturation of the clinical view of the disorders and the treatment of the individuals whose behavior, mood, and style have earned them membership in this small but important group. After reviewing the changes that have gone into the current revision of DSM, Sperry introduces the clinician/reader to the diagnostic scheme that has become the required model. Sperry describes the substantive issues of comorbidity, heterogeneity, and an understanding of the construct of personality. We can easily recognize that individuals have personal styles that may be emblematic of how they respond both interactively and intra-psychically. It is when the style impairs function or results in maladaptive behavior that the style becomes a disorder. Of value to the novice and the experienced clinician, of whatever stripe, the discussion of the alternative model of personality disorders is of special value. The constructs of personality functioning and personality traits are viewed dimensionally as levels of impairment, from no impairment, to mild impairment, moderate impairment, severe impairment, and extreme impairment.

The discussion of personality styles and disorders in regard to the individual's attachment style is of great use for both diagnosis and treatment planning. Most clinicians view the patient in regard to their *phenotype*—how the patient looks to others and how their behavior is described via the criteria sets. Sperry makes the case for the importance of the *genotype*, the temperament and neuroscientific base; but also describes the patient's *sociotype,* their cultural and family attachment style.

The review of the various empirically supported models for treatment offers the reader a survey of what is available. This alone is worth the price of admission. The discussion of Sperry's Pattern-Focused Psychotherapy is an excellent combination of several models, but sets itself aside by its strong allegiance to a DSM-5 understanding of the personality patterns and styles. Sperry's broad-based scholarship includes his discussion of Transference Focused Psychotherapy, Mentalization-Based Treatment, Schema Therapy, and Development Therapy.

In Chapter 2, Sperry tackles what is the most sophisticated and difficult part of the overall treatment process, the assessment and conceptualization of the style and disorders. The best therapists are quite a bit like Sherlock Holmes. They are well versed in several theories (not that they have to practice them all), they understand the historical issues for the client/patient, they work to develop an understanding that includes the patient's cultural experience, and can build a coherent model of the patient that they can then "test" with micro-interventions.

The sequence of data collection and conceptualization are areas in which Sperry excels. He takes the clinician on a step-by-step journey that ends in the clinician actually understanding why one set of interventions has a greater likelihood of working, as opposed to another set of technical interventions. His clinical examples give clarity and substance to his discussions of treatment and give the reader insight into Sperry's clinical thinking. Few texts give such a clear and substantive discussion of this complex (and essential) behavior. In his discussions of each of the disorders, Sperry uses the same template for each chapter, which makes it an easier read for the reader and of maximum use to the clinician.

In my therapy work, I am a strong believer and user of story, parable, metaphor, and myth. In reading through the manuscript for this text, I realized that there was a character dancing at the back of my mind. I finally realized who it was. A story retold by the Brothers Grimm was about the character named Rumpelstiltskin. He had the ability to spin straw into gold. That is, in effect, what Sperry has done with this tour de force volume. Len Sperry has taken the diagnostic straw of 60-plus years of DSM, ICD, and PDM and has spun it into clinical gold!

Art Freeman
Co-editor, *Cognitive Therapy of Personality Disorders, Third Edition*

PREFACE

Today, some 50 percent of those evaluated in clinical settings meet criteria for a personality disorder (Zimmerman, Rothschild, & Chelminski, 2005), as do 10 percent of the general public (Torgersen, 2009). These disorders can greatly disrupt an individual's work, family, and social relationships. Personality disorders are associated with high rates of family conflict, separation, divorce, child custody proceedings, job termination, homelessness, substance abuse, violence, and criminal behavior. Such disorders complicate co-occurring medical conditions, as well as the prognosis of other mental disorders. They are associated with poor treatment compliance, increased use of medical and psychiatric services, and the likelihood of relapse and premature termination (Skodol, Bender, Gunderson, & Oldham, 2014). Arguably, treating these disorders can be extraordinarily challenging, and sometimes exasperating, for clinicians.

The first edition of *Handbook of Diagnosis and Treatment of DSM-IV Personality Disorders* (Sperry, 1995a) broke new ground as the first single authored text to address the diagnosis, case conceptualization, and treatment of the DSM personality disorders. It differed from other personality disorder books by offering a brief but thorough, user-friendly resource for clinicians and trainees in planning and implementing effective treatment of these disorders. The second edition of *Handbook of Diagnosis and Treatment of DSM-IV-TR Personality Disorders* (2003) incorporated additional resources for diagnosing, planning and implementing effective clinical interventions. This third edition of *Handbook of Diagnosis and Treatment of DSM-5 Personality Disorders* promises to continue this tradition of user-friendliness and clinical utility.

In the 13 years since the second edition was released, several changes involving mental health have occurred, not the least of which was the publication of DSM-5. Major changes were expected in how DSM-5 would characterize the personality disorders. However, when it appeared in May 2013, the same disorders and criteria from the previous edition were retained. The few specific DSM-5 changes involving the personality disorders, including an Alternative Model for Personality Disorders, are discussed in Chapter 1. Despite these minimal changes in involving the personality disorders in DSM-5, clinical practice and the demands on clinicians have changed significantly since the first edition of Handbook appeared.

Among these changes are several exciting developments in both research and in clinical practice. Many of these represent highly effective evidence-based practices. The timing of these developments could not be better. They coincide with the peak of the accountability era wherein therapists are increasingly expected to provide evidence-based treatment to all their clients and patients, including those who are personality-disordered. Fortunately, research increasingly demonstrates that focused psychotherapeutic interventions are effective in the treatment of these disorders. In the past decade, several new treatment interventions and strategies for effecting changes with these disorders are available to clinicians.

Whereas it was once assumed that treatment even of milder personality disorders required years of intensive psychotherapy, published case reports and even prospective studies are indicating that shorter-term treatment can be effective with even severe disorders, including borderline personality. Still, some clinicians remain convinced that most personality disorders are untreatable. A recently published prospective study greatly challenges that belief (Zanarini, Frankenburg, Reich, & Fitzmaurice, 2010). It followed nearly 300 individuals diagnosed and treated for Borderline Personality Disorder over a 10-year period. The main results were that 87 percent achieved symptom remission and 50 percent achieved total recovery. This means that these individuals no longer met diagnostic criteria for this disorder and were functioning reasonably well in daily life!

Other clinicians are more optimistic, yet are not aware or do not utilize the best available evidence-based interventions that are proven to be effective. It has been observed that "(t)herapeutic nihilism has yielded to widespread, but very inconsistent, use of the spectrum of potentially valuable treatment modalities" (Skodol, Bender, Gunderson, & Oldham, 2014, p. 868). In contrast, clinicians who are aware of and do utilize the best available evidence-based treatments increase the likelihood of successful treatment among individuals with these disorders.

This book describes the most recent developments in the treatment of personality disorders. It focuses on how clinicians can increase their effectiveness and efficacy in working with personality-disordered individuals by adopting a focused and tailored treatment strategy. A basic premise underlying this book is that the most effective treatment is tailored treatment that addresses the underlying maladaptive pattern as well as the degree of severity of the disorder.

This new edition emphasizes the increasing applicability and effectiveness of a variety of evidence-based interventions with personality-disordered individuals.

These include Cognitive Behavior Therapies, Dialectical Behavior Therapy, Cognitive Behavior Analysis System of Psychotherapy, Pattern-Focused Psychotherapy, Mindfulness, Schema Therapy, Structured Treatment Interventions, Transference Focused Psychotherapy, Mentalization-Based Treatment, and Developmental Therapy—all of which are highlighted in this book.

The book is intended as a reader-friendly, "hands-on" manual for practicing clinicians as well as for clinicians-in-training. It offers clinicians a hopeful perspective on the treatability of these disorders and provides highly effective diagnostic and treatment interventions for achieving positive treatment outcomes. My hope is that it will make a difference in the lives of those who are afflicted with these disorders.

Len Sperry

ACKNOWLEDGMENTS

It is important to publicly acknowledge those individuals who have greatly influenced me and encouraged my development as a clinician. One of the great pioneers in the personality disorders field was the late Theodore Millon. Ted was both a mentor and colleague. Our relationship began in 1984, when I was beginning a fellowship at the University of Wisconsin Medical School and he was a visiting professor. Over the years he was gracious and generous with his time and feedback. I am forever appreciative of his back cover endorsement for the first edition of this book, which appeared in 1995, and for the Foreword he wrote for the second edition, which appeared in 2003. The expectation was that he would write a Foreword for this third edition. Unfortunately, he passed away before this revision was completed. Words cannot adequately express my appreciation for his influence and encouragement.

I am also most grateful to my colleagues at the Medical College of Wisconsin for their friendship and wonderful feedback and support over the years. They include Harry Prosen, MD, and Laura Roberts, MD, past chairs, and Jon Lehrmann, MD, current chair of the Department of Psychiatry and Behavioral Medicine. All of you have enriched my career and supported my research and writing. I want to also recognize my colleague and friend, Paul R. Peluso, PhD at Florida Atlantic University.

As always, a big thanks to George Zimmar, PhD, my longtime publisher and friend at Routledge/Taylor & Francis for encouraging me to complete this third edition. Finally, I need to acknowledge the efforts of George Stoupas, one of my doctoral students, who assisted in the final phase of this revision.

1

DIAGNOSIS AND TREATMENT OF PERSONALITY DISORDERS TODAY

The first chapter of the first edition of *Handbook of Diagnosis and Treatment of DSM-IV Personality Disorders* (Sperry, 1995a) likened the paradigm shift occurring with the personality disorders beginning the early 1990s to the paradigm shift that already had occurred with the depressive disorders. Until the mid-1970s, many clinicians felt relatively ineffective in treating depressive disorders, and until the early 1990s this same sentiment was shared by many clinicians about treating personality disorders. I insisted that such a paradigm shift involving the personality disorders would require a major change in the way clinicians conceptualize, assess, and treat these disorders. I predicted that while such a change in attitude and practice patterns might be resisted by some, most clinicians would respond to the challenge. Such a shift would mean relinquishing the then prevailing view that the personality disorders were essentially "untreatable" conditions. With some trepidation, I ended the chapter with a quote conveying the sentiment that clinicians might even come to consider that personality-disordered patients would "become our most welcome clients in the new century, clients who are deeply troubled, but whom we can help with confidence" (*Clinical Psychiatry News*, 1991, p. 26).

Some 20 years and two editions later, much has changed in clinician attitudes and practice patterns. Indeed, the paradigm has shifted. While not every clinician believes that they can help every personality-disordered individual "with confidence," there is, nevertheless, an increasing consensus among clinicians that many patients can be helped with current treatment interventions, even those meeting DSM-5 criteria for Borderline Personality Disorder.

This chapter provides an introduction and overview to the diagnosis and treatment of the personality disorders. It begins with a description of changes in DSM-5, emphasizing those involving the personality disorders, particularly the

"Alternative DSM-5 Model of Personality Disorders" and the Levels of Personality Functioning Scale. Following this is a brief description and illustration of the Psychodynamic Diagnostic Manual, another alternative way of conceptualizing personality disorders. The main part of this chapter details several exciting, cutting-edge trends—in both diagnosis and treatment—that are further effecting this paradigm shift. Prior to detailing these trends, the chapter begins by explaining the nature of the paradigm shift underway in the diagnosis and treatment of the personality disorders. Finally, the chapter concludes with an overview of the structure of Chapters 3–12.

DSM-5 and the Personality Disorders

The DSM diagnostic system has undergone some major changes since the second edition of this book was published in 2003. Most of these changes have involved adding or removing diagnoses and criteria. However, there are also some major changes in the structure of the DSM-5 (*American Psychiatric Association, 2013*), and these are briefly noted here.

DSM-5: General Changes

The most obvious change in DSM-5 is the return to a single-axis diagnosis, as it was in DSM-I and DSM-II. The multiaxial (5-axes) system was introduced in DSM-III and continued through DSM-IV-TR. Of particular relevance for the personality disorders were Axis II and Axis V. Axis II was added for the coding of personality disorders, while Axis V was added for coding the individual's current level of functioning and impairment on the Global Assessment of Functioning Scale. There were several reasons for eliminating the multiaxial system. Among these was an unexpected drawback to adding Axis II. Although it was not the intent of earlier editions of DSM, the opportunity to specify a diagnosis of a personality disorder became problematic for many clinicians. Out of concern that the diagnosis of a personality disorder would stigmatize an individual, some clinicians refused to specify an Axis II diagnosis when it was present. This was complicated by the mistaken notion among therapists and third party payers that personality disorders were untreatable. As a result, some individuals who were diagnosed with personality disorders encountered problems securing treatment. Today, however, individuals who met the criteria for a personality disorder diagnosis may now find it easier to navigate mental health treatment, since they are less likely to be viewed as having a diagnosis that is more difficult to treat than of other disorders.

By eliminating Axis V, the Global Assessment of Functioning (GAF) score is gone. GAF was the numeric measure used by clinicians to rate an individual's social, occupational, and psychological functioning and well-being. It is a subjective measure of the degree of adaptivity (well-being) or maladaptivity (impaired functioning) an individual demonstrates in dealing with various problems-in-living. In place of this largely unreliable measure of functioning and impairment, DSM-5 encourages the use of the World Health Organization Disability Assessment Schedule 2.0 (WHODAS 2.0). Nevertheless, GAF continues to be used by some clinicians. It provides a continuum (1–lowest, to 100–highest) on which to rate overall functioning and well-being. Clinicians can also utilize the Level of Psychological Functioning Scale (LPFS), which is described below.

DSM-5 Section on Personality Disorders

While there were a number of significant changes in many diagnoses in DSM-5, there were very few changes involving the personality disorders. Retained in DSM-5 was the earlier DSM definition of a personality disorder as an "enduring pattern of inner experience and behaviors that deviates markedly from the expectations of the individual' s culture, is pervasive and inflexible . . . is stable over time, and leads to distress or impairment" (American Psychiatric Association, 2013, p. 645). While DSM-IV-TR diagnostic criteria have been retained, there has been some updating of descriptions of the various disorders. However, there is one notable change. The diagnosis of Personality Disorder Not Otherwise Specified (NOS) has been replaced with Other Specified Personality Disorder (301.89) and Unspecified Personality Disorder (301.9).

Despite the efforts of the DSM-5 Personality Disorders Work Group to effect major change, the 10 "official" personality disorder diagnoses remain unchanged from DSM-IV-TR. The Work Group proposed that a "dimensional" model replace the existing "categorical" model due to its numerous and significant problems. However, that proposal was ultimately rejected by the Board of Directors of the American Psychiatric Association. Instead, it was relegated to "Section III: Emerging Measures and Models" of the DSM-5 manual. The new dimensional model developed by the Work Group is referred to as the "Alternative DSM-5 Model for Personality Disorders," in contrast to the DSM-IV-TR Model of Personality Disorders, also known as the categorical model.

Categorical Model of Personality Disorders

So why replace the categorical model? Three major concerns with the DSM-IV-TR Personality Disorder model involve comorbidity, heterogeneity, and the construct of personality.

The concern about comorbidity is that individuals can simultaneously meet criteria for more than one disorder. For instance, it was estimated that the modal number of personality disorder diagnoses possible for an individual who meets criteria for at least one DSM personality disorder is 3–4 diagnoses (Gunderson, 1996). Arguably, this is problematic for case conceptualization and planning tailored interventions: if there are 3 diagnoses, which one should be the initial focus of treatment, and why? The Alternative DSM-5 Personality Disorder model solves this problem through the diagnosis of Personality Disorder-Trait Specified (PD-TS). If the client is not a good match to a specific DSM-5 Personality Disorder (e.g., Narcissistic Personality Disorder), the clinician records PD-TS and details the client's clinically important personality features. For example, a client may have features of Narcissistic, Histrionic, Antisocial, and Borderline Personality Disorder. Instead of recording all four diagnoses, the clinician can record PD-TS and note the mix of grandiose, attention-seeking, antagonistic, and emotional lability.

The other concern involves heterogeneity. The premise of the DSM-IV-TR Personality Disorder model was that articulating specific personality disorder categories would facilitate accurate diagnoses. Unfortunately, individuals' personality and psychopathological features seldom fit such a categorical model. For example, individuals meeting DSM-IV-TR criteria for Borderline Personality Disorder are a highly heterogeneous group. In fact, there are six distinctive subgroups of clients who met these criteria and these subgroups differed markedly with regard to therapeutic concerns such as past suicide attempts, antisocial behavior, and self-injury (Wright et al., 2013). The Alternative DSM-5 Personality Disorder model greatly reduces this heterogeneity problem, because relevant heterogeneity is specified as part of the diagnostic process. For example, a client may meet the general Borderline Personality Disorder profile but also presents with other clinically significant personality features, such as unusual beliefs and experiences. In this case, the diagnosis of Borderline Personality Disorder can be given, while also recording the unusual beliefs and experiences.

The third concern is with the very nature of categorical diagnosis. As a categorical model it is expected to accurately determine whether an individual has or does not have a personality disorder. In many respects, such a model is not well suited for diagnosing personality disorders since personality is a continuous, multi-faceted dimension. To illustrate, consider the trait of grandiosity, a characteristic trait of the Narcissistic Personality Disorder. On a continuum from healthy self-esteem to self-centered entitlement, where does a clinician distinguish between health and disorder with regard to this trait? Utilizing a categorical model with a continuous dimension like grandiosity is akin to trying to force a round peg into a square hole.

Given these concerns, it is not surprising that many clinicians did not find the DSM-IV-TR Personality Disorder model to be very clinically useful. As a result they often deferred making meaningful personality description in clients' charts. Many also viewed DSM-IV-TR Personality Disorders as highly stigmatized conditions, leading to further reluctance to characterize personality disorder features accurately in clinical practice.

Presumably, the Alternative Model can solve these problems. A survey of 337 psychiatrists and psychologists found the Alternative Model to be considerably more useful than the DSM-IV-TR Personality Disorders model (Morey, Skodol,

& Oldham, 2014). As clinicians become more familiar with the Alternative Model, clients are likely to receive more accurate assessments and diagnoses, which can lead to improved clinical care.

Alternative DSM-5 Model for Personality Disorders

So what is this alternative model? Recognizing the many limitations of the categorical model of DSM-IV, the DSM-5 Personality Disorders Work Group proposed a dimensional model to replace the categorical model. That dimensional model has two primary criteria: personality functioning and pathological personality traits (*American Psychiatric Association, 2013*).

Personality Functioning. Four elements of personality functioning are identified. There are two indicators of self-functioning: Identity and Self-direction. There are also two indicators of interpersonal functioning: Empathy and Intimacy. Impairment in these four elements of personality functioning is rated along a continuum from 0 to 4. Assessment of such impairment can be accomplished with the *Levels of Personality Functioning Scale*, which is provided below.

Pathological Personality Traits. Five broad trait domains are specified in a dimensional or continuous fashion. These traits are derived from the Five-Factor Model of Personality and Personality Psychopathology (*American Psychiatric Association, 2013, p. 773*). These trait domains contain 25 specific personality trait facets. These domains and facets can be assessed with several psychometric tests. They are: Negative Affectivity vs. Emotional Stability; Detachment vs. Extraversion; Antagonism vs. Agreeableness; Disinhibition vs. Conscientiousness; and Psychoticism vs. Lucidity. In the Alternative Model, only six specific personality disorders are listed, compared to the current 10. These are Antisocial Personality Disorder, Avoidant Personality Disorder, Borderline Personality Disorder, Narcissistic Personality Disorder, Obsessive-Compulsive Personality Disorder, and Schizotypal Personality Disorder. Due to lack of research evidence to support their inclusion, the remaining four are not included: Dependent Personality Disorder, Histrionic Personality Disorder, Paranoid Personality Disorder, and Schizoid Personality Disorder.

With this dimensional method, it is now possible to diagnose a personality disorder based on traits. The designation: "Personality Disorder—Trait Specified" is used. Another useful feature of the Alternative Model is that it can be used to assess personality functioning and traits, irrespective of whether or not a personality disorder is present. This increases the clinical utility of the Alternative Model, because it assists clinicians to identify clients' strengths in addition to deficits.

This model is expected to become the "official" diagnostic approach for personality disorders at some point in the future. In the meantime, clinicians may wish to familiarize themselves with it. They can also choose to use the dimensional model now.

Levels of Personality Functioning Scale

Besides assessing client functioning with the World Health Organization Disability Assessment Schedule 2.0 (WHODAS 2.0), clinicians can also utilize the Level of Psychological Functioning Scale (LPFS). This scale is included on pages 775–778 in Section III of DSM-5 (*American Psychiatric Association, 2013*). The LPFS is an objective measure for quickly and accurately determining the presence of a personality disorder. It assesses the four components of personality functioning in the Alternative DSM-5 Personality Disorders model: identity, self-direction, empathy, and intimacy (Bender, Morey, & Skodol, 2011). Impairment in these four elements of personality functioning is rated along a continuum of five levels of functioning and impairment where 0 = little to no impairment; 1 = some impairment; 2 = moderate impairment; 3 = severe impairment; and 4 = extreme impairment. Moderate or greater impairment is required for diagnosis of a personality disorder. Table 1.1 summarizes these levels of functioning and impairment.

Psychodynamic Diagnostic Manual

This section briefly describes another clinically valuable alternative to DSM-5 which an increasing number of clinicians utilize in planning and implementing treatment with personality-disordered individuals. *The Psychodynamic Diagnostic Manual* (PDM) (PDM Task Force, 2006) is a diagnostic framework that characterizes individuals in terms of both their psychodynamics as well as their emotional, cognitive, and social functioning. The purpose of the PDM is to complement the *Diagnostic and Statistical Manual of Mental Disorders* (DSM) with psychodynamically based descriptions of patterns of personality, global functioning, and symptom formation. It also emphasizes motivational factors that commonly underlie the emergence of particular personality disorders and symptom disorders (depressive disorders) and the ways individuals with these disorders are likely to experience them. While the DSM provides a behavioral description and diagnostic criteria of a specific disorder, the PDM identifies the influences and causes or etiology that underlies that disorder. The PDM attempts to explain how and why those influences are emerging in the present and causing symptoms, and the role of early environment, developmental factors, current stressors, and internal psychological factors. In short, unlike the DSM, the PDM provides a more individualized, dimensional, and motivationally based understanding as well as a therapeutic strategy for working with such individuals.

The PDM was published in 2006 as a collaborative effort of five psychoanalytic organizations. It was authored by a task force consisting of Stanley Greenspan, Nancy McWilliams, Robert Wallenstein, and an interdisciplinary group of 37 other task force members and consultants. Despite the considerable clinical value of the PDM, it seems unlikely that the PDM will replace the DSM. There are

TABLE 1.1 Levels of Personality Functioning

0. **No Impairment.**
These individuals functionally optimally in all spheres of life. They have a well-integrated sense of self and of the world. They experience a mostly positive and appropriately regulated emotional life. They are goal-directed and possess the capacity to function productively in society. They easily empathize with others, and can form mutually reciprocating and satisfying relationships.

1. **Mild Impairment.**
These individuals have a relatively intact sense of self and of the world and a lessened clarity about boundaries in the face of strong emotions or mental distress. They may be overly goal-directed or goal-inhibited, or have somewhat unrealistic personal standards. They tend to have some difficulty appreciating and understanding others' perspectives, and may not consistently be aware of the effect of their behavior on others. Although they can form intimate and reciprocal relationships, they may be somewhat limited in their ability to respect and to cooperate with others.

2. **Moderate Impairment.**
These individuals have a compromised sense of self and of the world, along with some difficulty maintaining boundaries. Their self-appraisal tends to be inflated or deflated, and can experience difficulty in emotional regulation. Threats to self-esteem may engender strong emotions such as rage and shame. Goals are more often a means of gaining external approval than self-generated, and thus may lack coherence and stability. Their capacity for empathy is somewhat limited. While they can form relationships, they are superficial and not always reciprocal. They cooperate with others primarily for personal gain.

3. **Severe Impairment.**
These individuals have an impoverished sense of self. Their self-appraisal ranges from self-loathing to self-aggrandizing. They have considerable difficulty in emotional regulation. They have a weak sense of autonomy, and may experience a lack of identity, or emptiness. Boundaries are poorly defined or rigid. They have difficulty establishing and achieving personal goals. Their ability to reflect upon and understand their inner experiences is quite limited, and their capacity for empathy is limited. Their relationships are unstable and are viewed as means of meeting their needs. Cooperative efforts are often disrupted due to the perception of slights from others.

4. **Extreme Impairment.**
These individuals have a greatly impoverished, disorganized, weak, ineffective, and/or conflicted sense of self. They have a propensity to negative and significantly dysregulated emotions. Their capacity for empathy is significantly limited, and they cannot consider alternative perspectives, or are threatened by different perspectives. They lack the capacity for adaptive and cooperative interpersonal functioning and social behavior.

many reasons for this, not the least of which is that it does not yet have the established reliability necessary to warrant its widespread adoption. Overall, the PDM complements DSM by providing a valuable framework for planning and implementing clinical treatment.

While DSM-5 describes 10 personality disorders, the PDM describes several additional personality disorders that are common in clinical practice but may not have the research base that is required of those described in DSM-5. Among these are the Depressive Personality Disorder, the Anxious Personality Disorder, the Dissociative Personality Disorder, the Sadistic and Sadomasochistic Personality Disorder, and the Passive-Aggressive Personality Disorder. Following is an illustration of how the PDM conceptualizes a relatively common clinical presentation that no longer appears in the recent versions of the DSM: the Passive-Aggressive Personality Disorder.

Passive-Aggressive Personality Disorder

PDM conceptualizes the passive-aggressive pattern as a variant of Dependent Personality Disorder. Typically, individuals with this disorder define themselves in reference to others, but with a negative valence, e.g., "I'm the wife of that SOB." Like those with paranoid personalities, these individuals preemptively attack in anticipation of being attacked by others, but they do so indirectly. Like those with masochistic personalities, they expect mistreatment, but they fight back, but cunningly. While they have core narcissistic concerns, they tend to be more interpersonally engaged than those with narcissistic personalities. Their central preoccupation is getting revenge while tolerating mistreatment of others, and their main affects are anger, resentment, and pleasure in hostile enactments. Their main ways of defending themselves are projection of negativity onto others, denial, externalization, and rationalization. Their self-view is that feeling worthwhile requires sabotaging the achievements of others. Related to this, their view of the world and others is that everyone wants them to conform to their rules.

Because they are predisposed to oppose others' agendas, they find it difficult to conceive of and to pursue their own personal and professional goals. Accordingly, one of the main tasks of therapy is to increase their sense of identity and their capacity to accept themselves as active rather than just passive responders and reactors. Not surprisingly, it can be therapeutically challenging to connect with those who reach out with aggression or respond aggressively to others' efforts to relate to them.

> The therapist needs a sense of humor as counterpoise to the feelings of irritation and impatience the patient is likely to evoke. Negative feelings emerge quickly in treatment, and power struggles are a risk to avoid. Sometimes stunningly naïve about the hostility they exude, passive-aggressive patients need help naming their negative feelings and

differentiating verbal from behavioral expressions of anger. To avoid feeding into their oppositionalism, therapists should not seem to be overinvested in their progress. Instead, clinicians need to take their provocations and inconsistencies in stride, keeping the therapy focused on the price the patient pays for passive-aggressive acts.

(PDM Task Force, 2006, p. 53)

Trends in the Diagnosis of Personality Disorders

This section describes a number of cutting-edge clinical and research trends that are and will continue to impact the assessment and diagnosis of personality disorders. These include: attachment styles, temperament, culture, emotional abuse and neglect, and functional impairment.

Attachment Styles and Personality Disorders

Attachment refers to the emotional bond that develops between child and parent or caregiver and subsequently influences the child's capacity to form mature intimate relationships in adulthood. It is an inborn system of the brain that influences and organizes motivational, emotional, and memory processes that involve caregivers. The impact of the process of attachment on development cannot be underestimated since the "patterning and organization of attachment relationships during infancy is associated with characteristic processes of emotional regulation, social relatedness, access to autobiographical memory, and the development of self-reflection and narrative" (Siegel, 1999, p. 67).

Attachment researchers insist that early life relational deficits lead to both neurophysiological brain deficits as well as psychological deficits (Siegel, 1999). A sensitive and responsive parent helps grow the connections in the orbitofrontal cortex of the infant's brain by communicating—or "collaborating"—with the baby, via eye contact, facial expression, gestures, tone of voice, and so on. The gurgling, smiling infant is picked up and "answered" by the parent with a smiling and joyful expression and words. Or, the baby cries in pain or frustration and the parent soothes and consoles it, or calms down the overexcited child at bedtime. These routine and continuous interactions serve to stimulate the growth of synapses in the orbitofrontal cortex of the brain which enable children to modulate their frustration, rage, and fear, and to respond flexibly to others. Research indicates that securely attached children develop neural pathways for resilience. Even when their parents are upset or impatient, their brain's wiring "knows" from experience that they won't be abandoned and will reconnect after the storm has passed. Unfortunately, children with insecure attachment styles do not experience such reciprocal parental attention, and consequently they tend to be more vulnerable to emotional assaults, i.e., they are less able to modulate rage and aggressive affects, calm and soothe their anxieties and sadness, as well as tolerate high levels of pleasure and excitement (Ainsworth et al., 1978). Needless to say, they are also less likely to correctly interpret others' social cues because of deficits in their orbitofrontal cortex which further complicates interpersonal relationships.

Types of Attachment Styles

Distinct patterns or styles of attachment in early life tend to persist into adulthood (Bartholomew & Horowitz, 1991; Hazen & Shaver, 1987; Main & Solomon, 1990). Reflecting Bowlby's (1973) concept of working models of self and others, Bartholomew (1990) developed a four-category system of adult attachment that organizes a person's working models along two dimensions: (1) the distinction between self and others; and (2) valence—positive vs. negative evaluation. Based on these dimensions, Bartholomew derived four prototypical styles of adult attachment: The four attachment styles are: **secure** (positive view of self and others), **preoccupied** (negative view of self and others), **dismissing** (positive view of self, negative view of others), and **fearful** (negative view of self and others).

Subsequently, based on clinical experience, an additional style, the **disorganized** (fluctuating positive and negative views of self and others) style was added (Main, Goldwyn, & Hesse, 1998; Main & Solomon, 1990).

Accordingly, personality disorders can be viewed as the outcome of insecure working models that have become self-confirmatory. These working models of self and other have become relatively inflexible and closed to new information, and as a result the individual experiences significant distress in social, occupational, and relational functioning. It is possible to characterize the various personality disorders in terms of this dimensional model of self and others. It should be noted that Bartholomew (1990) does not assume that "all individuals are expected to exhibit a single attachment style" (p. 162). Instead, these attachment styles are conceptual prototypes and, thus, it is more appropriate to view adult attachment in a multidimensional way, with individuals exhibiting one or more style types as predominant. Accordingly, the DSM-IV personality disorders can be categorized in the following adult attachment style designations (Lyddon & Sherry, 2001).

Preoccupied attachment style. The preoccupied attachment dimension is characterized by a sense of personal unworthiness and a positive evaluation of others. These individuals tend to be very externally oriented in their self-definitions. Personality disorders that seem to exemplify this adult attachment style include the Dependent, Obsessive-Compulsive, and Histrionic personality disorders.

Fearful attachment style. Individuals with a fearful attachment style exhibit a sense of personal unworthiness combined with an expectation that other people will be rejecting and untrustworthy. They trust neither their own internal cognitions or feelings nor others' intentions. While they believe themselves to be special and different from others, they guard against threats and unexpected circumstances, since they cannot trust that others will protect them. The personality disorder most characteristic of such a fearful adult attachment style is the Paranoid Personality Disorder.

Dismissing attachment style. Individuals with a dismissing attachment style are characterized by a sense of self that is worthy and positive, as well as a low and negative evaluation of others which typically manifests as mistrust of others. Because they believe they are emotionally self-sufficient while others are emotionally unresponsive, they dismiss the need for friendship and contact with others. The personality disorder most characteristic of such a preoccupied and fearful adult attachment style is the Schizoid Personality Disorder.

Preoccupied-fearful attachment style. Individuals with a self-view that is negative and an other-view that vacillates between positive and negative exhibit a composite preoccupied and fearful style of attachment. Their avoidance is based on the desire to be liked and accepted by others, while at the same time fearing rejection and abandonment. The personality disorder most characteristic of such a preoccupied and fearful adult attachment style is the Avoidant Personality Disorder.

Fearful-dismissing attachment style. Individuals with a view of others that is negative and a self-view that vacillates between positive and negative exhibit a composite fearful-dismissing style of attachment. They tend to view themselves as special and entitled, but are also mindful of their need for others, who can potentially hurt them. Accordingly, they use others to meet their needs while being wary and dismissive of them. Personality disorders that are characterized by such a fearful-dismissing adult attachment style are the Antisocial, Narcissistic, and Schizotypal personality disorders.

Disorganized attachment style. Individuals with vacillating views of both self and others exhibit the disorganized attachment style: "Disorganized attachment develops from repeated experiences in which the caregiver appears frightened or frightening to the child" (Siegel, 1999, p. 117). This style is associated with dissociative symptomatology, which increases their proneness to posttraumatic stress disorder. The Borderline Personality Disorder is characterized by unstable personality structure that seems to shift among the various insecure attachment styles, creating a disorganized profile.

Temperament and Personality Disorders

Like attachment, temperament is a construct that appears to have both research and clinical utility. Temperament refers to "the characteristic phenomena of an individual's emotional nature, including his susceptibility to emotional stimulation, his customary strengths and speed of response, the quality of his prevailing moods, and the peculiarities and fluctuation and intensity of moods; these phenomena being regarded as dependent on constitutional makeup and therefore largely hereditary in origin" (Allport, 1937, p. 54). Although proposed over 60 years ago, Allport's definition is remarkably consistent with many contemporary formulations of the construct. Reflecting the clinician's view that temperament and attachment styles are related, temperament is viewed as "a filter of personality through which information is processed, attachments evolve, and emotions are experienced and expressed" (Graybar & Boutilier, 2002, p. 156).

While clinicians seem convinced that temperament influence attachment—and vice versa—researchers are still trying to clarify the exact nature of the relationship between the two constructs. This is largely because both constructs represent different origins and different research agendas. While temperament represents a biological determinant of personality (nature), attachment style represents an environmental determinant of personality (nurture). As in other nature-nurture discussions, the relationship is seldom "either-or" but usually "both-and." Currently, the research consensus seems to be that attachment and temperament are *modestly* related and that "both will influence the formation and expression of personality and self-concept as these are assembled during early childhood" (Vaughn & Bost, 1999, p. 221).

Temperamental traits and patterns are evident from birth. For instance, while some infants are quite sensitive to light and loud sounds, others are not; while some are calm and placid, others are very active or very fussy. Three main temperament pattern styles have been observed in infants: *easy* (usually predictable and in a good mood), *slow to warm* (more likely to be resistant to attention and moody), and *difficult* (typically unpredictable and with irritable moods) (Thomas & Chess, 1977). A child's temperament tends to be reflected in adult patterns. For example, optimism and consistency of effort are more common in adults who have easy temperaments, while negativity and suspiciousness are associated with the "difficult" temperament, and passivity and overdependency with the "slow to warm up" temperament. Several other temperament traits or descriptors have been identified in adults, including: impulsivity, irritability, hypersensitivity to stimulation, reactivity, emotional lability, inhibition, reflectivity, mood constriction, hypervigilance, and intensity.

Before 1980, personality disorders were typically conceptualized in "character language," such as the oral character or obsessive character. Although there was a biological tradition in the study of personality that emphasized temperament, the psychological tradition that emphasized character was in vogue for most of the 20th century. Descriptions of personality disorders in DSM-I and DSM-II reflected this emphasis on character and psychodynamics. Within the psycho-analytic community, character reflected specific defense mechanisms. Accordingly, from a character perspective, the obsessive-compulsive personality would be characterized by the defenses of isolation of affect, intellectualization, and rationalization.

Currently, personality disorders are conceptualized in a broader perspective that include both character *and* temperament (Cloninger, 2004; Stone, 1993). **Character** refers to the learned, psychosocial influences on personality. Character forms largely because of the socialization process, particularly regarding cooperativeness, and the mirroring process that promotes the development of self-concept and a sense of purpose in life (i.e., self-transcendence and self-responsibility).

Temperament refers to the innate, genetic, and constitutional influences on personality. Whereas character and schema reflect the psychological dimension of personality, temperament or trait (or style, as it is used synonymously in this book) reflects the biological dimension of personality. Cloninger (2004) contends that temperament has four biological dimensions (novelty-seeking, harm-avoidance, reward-dependence, and persistence), whereas character has three quantifiable dimensions (self-directedness or self-responsibility, cooperativeness, and self-transcendence). Other researchers would describe impulsivity and aggressivity as additional dimensions of temperament (Costello, 1996). Another widely known temperament-based model is the Five Factor Model with its trait dimensions of neuroticism, extraversion, openness, agreeableness, and conscientiousness (Costa & McCrae, 1990). Section III of the DSM-5 provides a dimensional approach to the personality disorders that is based on these and other models. It consists of five temperament domains: negative affectivity, detachment, antagonism, disinhibition, and psychoticism (American Psychiatric Association, 2013). Accordingly, from a temperament perspective, the obsessive-compulsive personality would be characterized by inhibited emotional expression, behavioral inhibition, cognitive rigidity, and overconscientiousness.

Temperament and character can be assessed by interviews and self-report instruments. The relevance of distinguishing character and temperament for treatment planning is significant. Whereas insight-oriented psychotherapy might be focused on the character dimensions, psychotherapy can have little or no impact on temperament dimensions. However, the addition of focused skill training may sufficiently regulate or modulate temperament or style features such as emotional dysregulation, impulsivity, and distress intolerance.

Attachment, Temperament, Culture, and Personality Disorders

As already indicated, research strongly suggests that insecure attachment influences the development of personality disorders (Brennan & Shaver, 1998). But what about the influence of temperament and culture on the development of personality and personality disorders? Brennan and Shaver (1998) believe that the same environmental conditions that contribute to the development of insecure attachments, and subsequently personality disorders, also interact with an individual's temperament: "In addition, cultural variations in the extent to which particular traits (e.g. independence, eccentricity) are sxpressed are also likely to result in cross-cultural differences in the expression of personality" (p. 868).

Unfortunately, there is currently little research on the cultural aspects of personality disorders to offer specific guidelines for clinical practice (Mulder, 2012). Nevertheless, DSM-5 does offer some general guidelines regarding diagnosis. It states that personality disorders "should not be confused with problems associated with acculturation following immigration or with the expression of habits, customs, or religious and political values professed by the individual's culture of origin. It is useful for the clinician, especially when evaluating someone from a different background, to obtain additional information from informants who are familiar with the person's cultural background" (American Psychiatric Association, 2013, p. 648).

Trends in the Treatment of Personality Disorders

In comparison to the previous approach of utilizing conventional psychotherapy in the treatment of personality disorders, treatment methods today tend to be considerably more focused and structured, with the clinician taking a more active role. Many of these treatment approaches and intervention strategies are theory-based and have been researched in clinical trials in comparison with other treatment approaches and modalities. These include the Cognitive Behavior Therapies, Dialectical Behavior Therapy, Cognitive Behavior Analysis System of Psychotherapy, Pattern-Focused Psychotherapy, Mindfulness, Schema Therapy, Structured Treatment Interventions, Transference Focused Psychotherapy, Mentalization-Based Treatment, and Developmental Therapy. A useful framework for understanding the recent trends in treatment comes from the neurosciences, and it begins this discussion.

Neurosciences and the Treatment Processes

One of the outcomes of recent neuroscience investigations regarding the treatment of personality disorders is the conceptualization of treatment as either "top-down" or "bottom-up" strategies. This conceptualization is useful in understanding efforts to normalize the expression of overmodulated maladaptive personality traits with various psychotropic and behavioral interventions (Fawcett, 2002). "*Top-down*" refers to treatment efforts that are primarily focused on cortical structures and neural tracts (top) which also can influence subcortical circuits, particularly in the limbic system (down). Similarly, "*bottom-up*" refers to the treatment efforts that are largely focused on limbic circuits which also can produce changes in cortical circuits. Of particular promise are recent efforts to normalize the expression of under- and overmodulated maladaptive personality traits with psychotropic and behavioral interventions. For example, top-down treatment strategies typically utilize psychotherapies and behavioral interventions, i.e., cognitive behavior therapy, to enhance cortical influences on limbic circuits. The goal is to undo negative learning, particularly maladaptive schemas, and to increase the modulating or normalizing effects of emotional responses. Bottom-up treatment strategies typically involve the use of psychotropic medication in order to modulate harmful personality traits and emotional states by normalizing the activity of limbic structures. Besides medications, it appears that skill-training interventions function as bottom-up treatments.

Cognitive Behavior Therapies

Since the mid-1980s, Behavior Therapy, Cognitive Therapy, and CBT have been the treatment of choice for the psychosocial treatment of the personality disorders. While research did not consistently support the efficacy of these traditional approaches, it has for newer, more focused approaches such as Dialectic Behavior Therapy (DBT), Cognitive Behavior Analysis System of Psychotherapy (CBASP), and Mindfulness-Based Cognitive Therapy (MBCT). Interestingly, DBT, CBASP, and MBCT constitute what is being called the "third wave" of behavior therapy (Hayes, Follette, & Linehan, 2004).

The first wave refers to traditional behavior therapy, which endeavors to replace problematic behaviors with constructive ones through counterconditioning and reinforcement. Cognitive therapy is the second wave of behavior therapy. It works to modify problem behaviors by changing the thoughts that cause and perpetuate them. In the third wave, treatment tends to be more experiential and indirect and utilizes techniques such as mindfulness, dialectics, acceptance, values, and spirituality. More specifically, third wave approaches are characterized by "letting go of the attempts at problem solving, and instead standing back to see what it feels like to see the problems through the lens of non-reactivity, and to bring a kindly awareness to the difficulty" (Segal, Williams, Teasdale, & Williams, 2004, p. 55). Unlike the first and second wave, third wave approaches emphasize second-order change, i.e., basic change in structure and/or function, and are based on contextual assumptions, including the primacy of the therapeutic relationship. These approaches appear to be particularly germane to treating personality disorders.

Dialectical Behavior Therapy

Originally developed for the treatment of borderline personality disorder (Linehan, 1993a), Dialectical Behavior Therapy (DBT) has been modified and extended for use with other personality disorders, as well as Axis I or symptom disorders such as mood disorders, anxiety disorders, eating disorders, and substance use disorders (Lynch & Cuper, 2012; Marra, 2005). DBT is an outgrowth of behavior therapy but is less cognitive than traditional CBT, since DBT assumes that cognitions, per se, are less important than affect regulation. Accordingly, DBT places more emphasis on emotion regulation rather than maladaptive thought processes. While it recognizes that cognitions are a factor in behavior, they are not a necessary mediating factor. Rather, cognitions are more likely to serve to make sense of behavior and emotional events after the fact (Marra, 2005).

Theory. There are numerous similarities between DBT and traditional CBT, particularly cognitive therapy. Both require a collaborative stance between client and therapist. Both utilize learning principles, analyze triggers and environmental prompts, explore schemas and emotions, and utilize modeling, homework, and imagery. Furthermore, both recognize the importance of empathic responding.

There are a number of differences between cognitive therapy and DBT in the treatment of personality disorders. Essentially, cognitive therapy posits that the same techniques used in eliciting and evaluating automatic thoughts during depression or anxiety disorders are used in treating personality disorders (Beck, Davis, & Freeman, 2015). While cognitive therapy contends that dysfunctional feelings and behaviors are due to schemas that produce consistently biased judgments and a tendency to make cognitive errors through attributional bias, DBT focuses instead on how schemas are initially formed. Accordingly, therapists utilizing DBT explore schemas and the underlying dialectic conflicts that produced them rather than performing "collaborative experiments" to prove their limited usefulness. Rather than utilizing cognitive restructuring, the DBT therapist attempts to connect belief systems to underlying affect and need, and then to assist clients to reinterpret their belief systems based upon greater awareness of their feelings and needs.

Instead of utilizing "guided discovery" to dispute and revise maladaptive beliefs, DBT analyzes both the affective and cognitive inference processes to determine how the schema was formed in the first place. This involves identifying deprivational emotional states in early development that could have produced fixation or perseveration and attentional constriction that could serve as protection from threatening internal or external cues, as well as broadly examining the effects of negative reinforcement through emotional escape and avoidance strategies or inadequate psychological coping skills that could have been rewarded through the partial reinforcement effect (Marra, 2005, p. 141).

Finally, DBT differs from the cognitive therapy of personality disorders by adopting a nonpejorative interpretation of pathology. Instead, the DBT therapist sees behavior and strategy as operant behavior. Like others, the personality-disordered client is attempting to avoid harm and seek pleasure but has difficulty successfully obtaining the desired outcome due to the emotional vulnerability. Nevertheless, the DBT therapist assumes that inadequate compromises between competing and contradictory needs and desires form the basis of their personality structure and helps them achieve their needs in a non-pejorative way.

Treatment. Linehan (1993a, 2015) specified four primary modes of treatment in DBT: individual therapy; skills training in a group, telephone contact, and therapist consultation (Linehan, 1993a, 2015). Whilst keeping within the overall model, group therapy and other modes of treatment may be added at the discretion of the therapist, providing the targets for that mode are clear and prioritized. The individual therapist is the primary therapist and the main work of therapy is carried out in the individual therapy sessions. Between sessions the client should be offered telephone contact with the therapist, including out-of-hours telephone contact, although the therapist has the right to set clear limits on such contact. The purpose of telephone contact is not psychotherapy but rather to give help and support to clients to find ways of avoiding self-injury as well as for relationship repair where the client feels that she has damaged her relationship with her therapist and wants to put this right before the next session. To avoid reinforcing self-injury, calls after the client has injured herself are not acceptable and, after ensuring her immediate safety, no further calls are allowed for the next 24 hours. DBT therapists are encouraged to participate regularly in therapist consultation groups. These groups provide both emotional support for therapists dealing with difficult clients, as well as for ongoing training in DBT methods.

Skills training is usually carried out in a group context, ideally by someone other than the individual therapist. In the skills training groups, clients are taught skills considered relevant to the particular problems of personality-disordered individuals. There are four groups of skills: core mindfulness skills, interpersonal effectiveness skills, emotion modulation skills, and distress tolerance skills (Linehan, 2015).

Stages of treatment. Following an initial period of pre-treatment involving assessment, commitment and orientation to therapy, DBT consists of four stages of treatment (Linehan, 2015). Stage 1 focuses on "severe behavioral dyscontrol." The goal of this stage is to increase behavioral control and it targets suicidal behaviors, self-harm, and severe therapy interfering like substance abuse. Stage 2 focuses on "quiet desperation," with the goal of increasing emotional experiencing in those dealing with issues like posttraumatic stress and other residual disorders not addressed in Stage 1. Stage 3 focuses on "problems of living." The goal of this stage is to work through concerns of ordinary happiness and unhappiness. Stage 4 focuses on "incompleteness," where the work is on increasing the capacity for joy, freedom, and spiritual fulfillment. The targeted behaviors of each stage are brought under control before moving on to the next phase. Therapy at each stage is focused on the specific targets for that stage, which are arranged in a definite hierarchy of relative importance.

Core strategies. The core strategies in DBT are "validation" and "problem solving." Attempts to facilitate change are surrounded by interventions that validate clients' behavior and responses in relation to the clients' current life situation and that demonstrate an understanding of their difficulties and suffering. Problem solving focuses on the establishment of necessary skills. Other treatment modalities include contingency management, cognitive-therapy exposure-based therapies, and medication.

Practicing DBT. The provision of DBT therapy is easier to accomplish in an inpatient, partial hospitalization or residential treatment setting rather than in outpatient practice. The reason is that, as described by Linehan (1993a), DBT is best implemented with a treatment team in which one therapist provides psychosocial skill training, another provides individual therapy, others can provide a consultation function, and the therapists have access to a therapist consultation group for support. Recently, Marra (2005) has offered suggestions for adapting DBT treatment in private practice settings. While he recommends that skills training be provided by another therapist, he offers guidelines when that is not possible. Nevertheless, he encourages any private practice clinician who anticipates utilizing DBT to have access to a psychotherapy consultant if involvement in a therapist consultation group is not possible.

Research support. Finally, empirical support exists for the effectiveness of DBT. Several randomized controlled trials that evaluate the overall effectiveness of a comprehensive DBT treatment have been published (Linehan et al., 1991, 2002, 2006). When evaluated against treatment-as-usual control conditions, DBT was superior. While most of this research focused on borderline personality disorders in females, some studies modified DBT for use in other populations and in various settings. These include studies with adolescents and adults in inpatient and forensic settings with various disorders, including binge eating disorder, bulimia, anorexia nervosa, chronic depression, and other personality disorders. However, there is very little research on the use of DBT with males or minorities (Lynch & Cuper, 2012).

Cognitive Behavior Analysis System of Psychotherapy

Cognitive Behavior Analysis System of Psychotherapy (CBASP) is a form of CBT that was developed by McCullough (2000) and further elaborated (McCullough, Schramm & Penberthy, 2015). Basic to this approach is a situational analysis which combines behavioral, cognitive, and interpersonal methods to help clients focus on the consequences of their behavior and to use problem solving for resolving both personal and interpersonal difficulties. CBASP was initially targeted for the treatment of clients with chronic depression. A national, multisite study launched CBASP as an effective treatment. Clients who met criteria for chronic unipolar depression, usually meeting criteria for both major depressive disorder and dysthymic disorder, were randomly assigned to one of three treatment groups: medication only (nefazodone with the, trade name of Serzone), psychotherapy (CBASP) only, or a combination of medication and CBASP. While clients in all three treatment conditions improved significantly, those receiving the combined treatment improved the most. Over the 12-week study period, 55 percent of the medication-only group reported a positive response, and 52 percent of the CBASP-only group experienced a treatment response, whereas 85 percent of those who took both medication and received CBASP had a positive response to treatment (Keller et al., 2000).

Theory. A basic assumption of CBASP is that clients can learn to analyze specific life situations and then manage daily stressors on their own. The basic premise of CBASP is simple and straightforward: a therapist assists clients to discover why they did not obtain a desired outcome by evaluating their problematic thoughts and behaviors. In short, therapists assist clients in determining which thoughts and behaviors have gotten in the way of achieving what they wanted. Since there is often a mismatch between what a client wants and what actually occurs in the client's life, the CBASP approach can be utilized with a variety of distressing problems and presentations ranging from child behavior problems and couples conflict to anxiety disorders and personality disorders, including Borderline Personality Disorder (Driscoll, Cukrowicz, Reardon, & Joiner, 2004). Interestingly, McCullough (2002) noted his reservations to utilizing CBASP with adults with severe Borderline Personality Disorder, particularly those with comorbid chronic depression.

Treatment. The overall goal of CBASP treatment is to identify the discrepancy between what clients want to happen in a particular situation and what has happened or is actually happening. By examining their specific circumstances, clients gradually discover problematic themes and patterns in their lives as well as ways in which they can achieve what is desired.

There are two phases in CBASP treatment: elicitation and remediation. The elicitation phase consists of six steps, which are framed by specific questions: How would you describe the situation? How did you interpret the situation? Specifically, what did you do and what did you say? What did you want to get out of the situation, i.e., what was your desired outcome?

What was the actual outcome of this situation? And, finally: Did you get what you wanted?

During the remediation phase, behaviors and interpretations or cognitions are targeted for change and revised so that the client's new behaviors and cognitions will contribute and result in the desired outcome. First, each of the client's interpretations of the situation is assessed to determine whether it helped or hindered the achievement of the desired outcome. Next, each of the client's behaviors is similarly analyzed to determine whether or not it helped or hindered in the attainment of the desired outcome (Driscoll et al., 2004).

A modified version of this approach (Sperry, 2006b, 2014) is particularly useful in working with personality-disordered individuals, particularly those who are assessed as low in learning from experiences. Such individuals have not had sufficient experience in learning from their mistakes because they, too, often engage in emotional thinking rather than in consequential thinking. This modified intervention strategy works by increasing consequential thinking. It focuses the individual's attention on the link between how their negative or self-defeating thoughts and behaviors result in the negative consequence (actual outcome) they end up with instead of the desired outcome that they really want. The strategy includes nine steps, which begin with a cognitive and a behavioral analysis and proceed to process their interpretations and behaviors in terms of their desired outcome or consequence.

Pattern-Focused Psychotherapy

Pattern-Focused Psychotherapy was developed by Len Sperry (Sperry, in press). It is derived from Biopsychosocial Therapy which emphasizes pattern identification and pattern change (Sperry, 1998, 2000, 2006b), Cognitive Behavioral Analysis System of Psychotherapy (CBASP) (McCullough, 2000), and Motivational Interviewing (MI) (Miller & Rollnick, 2002). Both CBASP and MI are identified as empirically supported treatments by the Society of Clinical Psychology (Division 12) of the American Psychological Association.

Theory. Pattern is the predicable, consistent, and self-perpetuating style and manner in which individuals think, feel, act, cope, and defend themselves (Sperry, 2006b; Sperry, Brill, Howard, & Grissom, 1996). Patterns can be maladaptive or adaptive. Maladaptive patterns tend to be inflexible, ineffective, and inappropriate, and cause symptoms, impairment in personal and relational functioning, and chronic dissatisfaction (Sperry, 2010). If such a pattern is sufficiently distressing or impairing, it can be diagnosed as a personality disorder. In contrast, an adaptive pattern reflects a personality style that is flexible, appropriate, and effective, and is reflective of personal and interpersonal competence (Sperry & Sperry, 2012).

Pattern-Focused Psychotherapy is based on four premises. The first is that individuals unwittingly develop a self-perpetuating, maladaptive pattern of functioning and relating to others. Subsequently, this pattern underlies the client's presenting issues. The second premise is that pattern change is an essential component of evidence-based practice. The third is that effective treatment involves a change process in which the client and practitioner collaborate to identify the maladaptive pattern, break it, and replace it with a more adaptive pattern. At least two outcomes result from this change process: resolution of the client's presenting issue and increased well-being (Sperry & Sperry, 2012). The fourth premise is that *replacing* non-productive thinking and behaviors with more productive ones is likely to effectively and quickly lead to therapeutic change that might otherwise occur with directly *restructuring* cognitions or *modifying* behavior.

Practice. Pattern-Focused Psychotherapy begins with establishing a collaborative relationship and educating the client in the basic premises of this approach. Central to the assessment and case conceptualization process is the identification of the maladaptive pattern, and then planning treatment that focuses on pattern change. Other key factors considered in planning treatment are level of readiness for change, severity, skill deficits, and strengths and protective factors.

A basic therapeutic strategy in the change process is to analyze problematic situations reported by clients in terms of their maladaptive pattern. Clients are first asked to describe the situation and their resulting interpretations (thoughts) and behaviors. Then, they are queried about their expected outcome in contrast to the actual one that resulted. As therapy begins, clients inevitably report that they did not achieve their expected outcome. They are then asked about their interpretation and if each *helped or hurt* them in getting what they expected. If not, they are asked what alternative interpretations would have helped them achieve. Their reported behaviors are analyzed as to whether they helped or hurt in achieving their expected outcome. If not, the focus is on identifying alternative behavior which could achieve that end. Finally, the client's *level of importance* of changing the maladaptive pattern and *level of confidence* in doing so are assessed and therapeutically processed. Not surprisingly, a marker of therapeutic change is that clients increasingly achieve their expected outcome as a result of shifting to a more adaptive pattern.

In short, this therapeutic strategy focuses on identifying and changing a maladaptive pattern to a more adaptive one primarily by *replacing* the nonproductive interpretations and behaviors that underlie the maladaptive pattern. Other modalities, including cognitive restructuring, behavioral activation, exposure, skills training, reframing, interpretation, etc., might also be employed as adjunctive treatments.

Mindfulness

Mindfulness is a form of awareness in which an individual can focus on thoughts, feelings, and experiences in the present moment with an attitude of acceptance and without analysis or judgment. The practice of mindfulness can diffuse negativity, aggression, and compulsivity without suppressing emotions or indulging them (Marlatt & Kristeller, 1999). While mindfulness derives from the Buddhist tradition, it has recently been incorporated into medicine and psychotherapy. Since it is associated with developing an awareness of alternative perspectives and reducing habitual response patterns, mindfulness has been proposed as a common factor across various therapeutic systems (Martin, 1997). Linehan (2015) describes the application of mindfulness techniques as a way of integrating acceptance into psychotherapy, emphasizing its association with intentional rather than automatic information processing as well as the nonjudging, nonevaluative nature of mindfulness attention. Not surprisingly, mindfulness is included in Linehan's dialectical behavior therapy of borderline personality disorder. Recently, mindfulness approaches have been incorporated in several cognitive and cognitive behavioral treatment interventions, including depression (Segal, Williams & Teasdale, 2002; Teasdale et al., 2000), substance abuse (Marlatt, 1994), Borderline Personality Disorder (Linehan, 1994), panic disorder (Kabat-Zinn et al., 1992), binge eating (Kristeller & Hallet, 1999), generalized anxiety disorder (Roemer & Orsillo, 2002), and obsessive compulsive disorder (Schwartz & Begley, 2002). There is mounting research evidence that mindfulness is effective in these disorders as well as medical conditions such as stroke and Tourette's syndrome (Schwartz & Begley, 2002). The extent to which mindfulness has become the core strategy in Teasdale's approach to depression and other disorders is reflected in the name of his approach: "mindfulness-based cognitive therapy "(Teasdale et al., 2000). It is also interesting to note that Young's Schema Therapy (Young, Klosko, & Weishaar, 2003) has incorporated mindfulness as a key strategy in the treatment of personality disorders.

Schema Therapy

Schema Therapy is an elaboration of cognitive therapy that has been developed by Young (1990, 1999; Young et al., 2003) specifically for personality disorders, and other difficult individual and couples problems. It integrates elements of Adlerian psychology, behavior therapy, object relations, and Gestalt therapy into a systematic approach to treatment. Recently, it has incorporated mindfulness for clients sensitive to the spiritual dimension.

The most basic concept in Schema Therapy is an Early Maladaptive Schema. Schemas are defined as broad, pervasive themes regarding one's view of self and of others that were developed during childhood and elaborated throughout one's lifetime. They are enduring and self-defeating patterns that typically begin early in life—although they can also form in adulthood, cause negative/dysfunctional thoughts and feelings, and interfere with accomplishing goals and meetings one's needs. These schemas are perpetuated behaviorally through the coping styles of schema maintenance, schema avoidance, and schema compensation (Young, 1999).

Young (1999; Young et al., 2003) has identified 18 schemas. They develop in childhood from an interplay between the child's innate temperament and the child's ongoing damaging experiences with parents, siblings, or peers, and because they begin early in life, schemas become familiar and thus comfortable. We distort our view of the events in our lives in order to maintain the validity of our schemas, which may remain dormant until they are activated by situations relevant to that particular schema.

These schemas are arranged into five broad developmental categories of schemas called schema domains. Each of these domains represents an important component of a child's core needs. Schemas interfere with the child's attempts to get the core needs met within each domain.

Table 1.2 provides a capsule description of these schemas and domains.

Schema Therapy involves identifying maladaptive schemas, deciding on the appropriate level of change, and planning interventions to effect this level or degree of change. Differing levels of schema change are noted: schema reconstruction, schema modification, interpretation and schema camouflage. Schema reconstruction—i.e., maladaptive replacing the schema with a more functional one—is the most extensive level of transformation and often involves long-term treatment, whereas schema camouflage is the least extensive and may be a more appropriate goal in shorter-term treatment (Young, 1999; Young et al., 2003).

TABLE 1.2 Maladaptive Schemas and Schema Domains

Disconnection and Rejection

- **Abandonment/Instability:** The belief that significant others will not or cannot provide reliable and stable support.
- **Mistrust/Abuse:** The belief that others will abuse, humiliate, cheat, lie, manipulate, or take advantage.
- **Emotional Deprivation:** The belief that one's desire for emotional support will not be met by others.
- **Defectiveness/Shame:** The belief that one is defective, bad, unwanted, or inferior in important respects.
- **Social Isolation/Alienation:** The belief that one is alienated, different from others, or not part of any group.

Impaired Autonomy and Performance

- **Dependence/Incompetence:** The belief that one is unable to competently meet everyday responsibilities without considerable help from others.
- **Vulnerability to Harm or Illness:** The exaggerated fear that imminent catastrophe will strike at any time and that one will be unable to prevent it.
- **Enmeshment/Undeveloped Self:** The belief that one must be emotionally close with others at the expense of full individuation or normal social development.
- **Failure:** The belief that one will inevitably fail or is fundamentally inadequate in achieving one's goals.

Impaired Limits

- **Entitlement/Grandiosity:** The belief that one is superior to others and not bound by the rules and norms that govern normal social interaction.
- **Insufficient Self-Control/Self-Discipline:** The belief that one is incapable of self-control and frustration tolerance.

Other-Directedness

- **Subjugation:** The belief that one's desires, needs, and feelings must be suppressed in order to meet the needs of others and avoid retaliation or criticism.
- **Self-Sacrifice:** The belief that one must meet the needs of others at the expense of one's own gratification.
- **Approval-Seeking/Recognition-Seeking:** The belief that one must constantly seek to belong and be accepted at the expense of developing a true sense of self.

Overvigilance and Inhibition

- **Negativity/Pessimism:** A pervasive, lifelong focus on the negative aspects of life while minimizing the positive and optimistic aspects.
- **Emotional inhibition:** The excessive inhibition of spontaneous action, feeling, or communication—usually to avoid disapproval by others, feelings of shame, or losing control of one's impulses.
- **Unrelenting Standards/Hypercriticalness:** The belief that striving to meet unrealistically high standards of performance is essential to be accepted and to avoid criticism.
- **Punitiveness.** The belief that others should be harshly punished for making errors.

Structured Treatment Interventions

Unlike schemas which reflect the psychological dimension of personality, temperament—i.e., the innate, genetic, and constitutional aspect of personality—reflects its biological dimension. Temperament plays an important role in the regulation and dysregulation of an individual's affective, behavioral, and cognitive styles (Sperry & Sperry, 2016). While research shows that medication can modulate or normalize dysregulated behaviors, a similar modulating effect has also been noted for social skills training (Lieberman, DeRisi, & Mueser, 1989). Thus, it appears that social skills training is a relatively potent bottom-up treatment strategy for normalizing such limbic system mediated behaviors as impulsivity, aggressivity, and mood lability, to name a few. Sperry (2015) contends that personality-disordered individuals typically exhibit significant skill deficits, and that structured skill training interventions are useful and necessary in successful treatment of moderate to severe personality disorders. Skill deficits can be reversed by the acquisition of requisite skills in individual and group sessions through practice via modeling, coaching, role-playing, and graded task assignment. Sixteen structured intervention strategies for modifying a personality-disordered individual's affective, behavioral, and cognitive temperament styles are described and illustrated in *Cognitive Behavior Therapy of DSM-5 Personality Disorders, Third Edition* (Sperry & Sperry, 2016). Table 1.3 lists these interventions.

Transference-Focused Psychotherapy

Transference Focused Psychotherapy (TFP) was developed by Otto Kernberg, MD and associates (Clarkin, Yeomans, & Kernberg, 2015) for the treatment of personality disorder, but initially for Borderline Personality Disorder. It is a highly structured, manualized, evidence-based treatment approach.

TFP emerged in response to the failure of psychoanalysis to treat personality disorders. While psychoanalysis benefited some individuals, it was not helpful for those with severe personality disorders. In fact, many with personality disorders appeared to worsen with psychoanalysis. Instead of concluding that the treatment method itself might be the cause, many concluded that personality disorders were untreatable. The developers of TFP challenged this belief and went on to modify and tailor the traditional psychoanalytic methods to severe personality disorders.

TFP is based on object relations theory, which contends that infants form internal representations of themselves ("self") and others ("objects"). Typically, these "objects" are early caregivers. These early self-object representations are connected to each other through a dominant affect. In early stages of infant development, it is posited that positively toned, self-object representations develop separately from negative-toned representations. According to Kernberg, healthy

TABLE 1.3 Structured Treatment Interventions

1. Anger Management Training
2. Anxiety Management Training
3. Assertiveness Training
4. Distress Tolerance Training
5. Emotional Regulation Training
6. Empathy Training
7. Impulse Control Training
8. Interpersonal Skills Training
9. Limit Setting
10. Mindfulness Training
11. Problem-Solving Training
12. Radical Openness Skills Training
13. Self-Management Training
14. Sensitivity Reduction Training
15. Symptom Management Training
16. Thought Stopping

adult personality development requires these split-off, positively and negatively toned object representations to become integrated into a single, cohesive whole. On the other hand, when good and bad representations remain split off and separate, a disintegrated personality organization, or personality disorder, is likely to result.

Once formed, these object relationship pairs (dyads) serve as a map or template by which later relationships can be understood and enacted. Such internalized object relations are thought to later play out in the individual's life in important relationships. To the extent that an individual has an accurate map or template, a healthy and accurate understanding of future relationships is available. In contrast, when the individual has an inaccurate, "split-off," and polarized map or template, interpersonal problems result. This also applies to the relationship with a therapist. Accordingly, the therapist is able to identify the nature of the problem and its repair.

In transference-focused psychotherapy (TFP) the relationship that forms between the therapist and patient is the mechanism of change. This means that the therapeutic relationship itself provides the means to identify and then correct the problematic personality structure. The goal is to provide patients with a corrected template of relationships. This correction becomes possible through the process of "transference," which occurs because the patient draws upon the faulty relationship template formed during childhood. As transference occurs during therapy sessions, the therapist uses this experience as a framework for identifying, understanding, and updating these internal representations or templates. As TFP therapists recognize this transference, they assist patients to understand and to modify these internal representations.

The primary goal of TFP is to assist patients in achieving a corrective emotional experience by means of the therapeutic relationship. The therapist seeks to create an empathic and soothing relational climate that enables patients to directly experience painful, contradictory, and ambivalent feelings toward the therapist. In this safe and comforting setting, patients learn to confront and tolerate the disturbing feelings that emerge when the chaotic and split-off, self-object representations are activated. This ability to tolerate these highly uncomfortable feelings was not possible as an infant or child. The purpose of this process is to assist the patient to integrate split-off representations of self-and-other into a cohesive whole. The ultimate goal of TFP is identity integration.

TFP differs from the traditional psychoanalytic treatment, in several ways. For one, there is a very specific agenda and therapy contract. The contract addresses the boundaries of the treatment, such as frequency and duration of sessions, phone calls, and procedures when crises arise. The therapist is not simply a passive listener, but instead takes on a very active role in the therapy, asking pointed, clarifying questions, and challenging self-destructive or other negative behaviors. Of particular note is that the focus of treatment is on here-and-now, relational problems. Such a focus helps patients make connections between their present relationship with the therapist, and the current problems they experience with other relationships in their life. Furthermore, patients are expected to develop a meaningful and productive life outside of therapy by finding a job, engaging in volunteer work, or continuing in school. Typically, therapy sessions are 45 minutes long and meet twice weekly. When indicated, group treatment or involvement in a 12-step program may be recommended.

Mentalization-Based Treatment

Mentalization-Based Treatment (MBT) was developed by Anthony Bateman and Peter Fonagy (Bateman & Fonagy, 2007, 2009) for the treatment of personality disorders, particularly for Borderline Personality Disorder. MBT is primarily based on attachment theory, wherein the basic premise is that infants have an inborn need to seek closeness with their caregiver. When distressed, an infant's attachment behaviors (e.g., smiling, clinging, crying) are activated in an order to elicit the response of soothing from a caregiver. How the caregivers respond greatly influences the development of the child's basic sense of security. Over time, children develop an internal working model of relationships based on their interactions with caregivers, and this model influences other important relationships later in life.

To the extent caregivers respond appropriately in soothing and comforting the child, a secure attachment is formed. As a result of secure attachments, children learn to self-soothe and self-regulate their emotions as they model their caregiver's comforting responses. To the extent the caregivers fail to respond appropriately, an insecure attachment is formed, and the child is less likely to engage in self-soothing and self-regulating behaviors.

Mentalization is the ability to reflect upon, and to understand, one's own state of mind. It is the insightful understanding of what and why one is feeling. Mentalization develops by means of the caregiver's empathic and insightful response to a child's distress. It is learned through the experience of a secure attachment.

Mentalization is a critical coping skill necessary for effective emotional regulation. For all practical purposes, mentalizing is like hitting the "pause" button. For example, the experience of a powerful negative feeling is usually coupled with an intense urge to act or respond. The ability to tolerate briefly that powerful feeling, and to reflect on it, can effectively deter one from acting on that intense urge. Since the defining characteristic of a personality disorder is relational difficulties, personality-disordered individuals typically have deficits in this critical skill. A basic premise of MBT is that mentalization must be learned to correct relational difficulties. Accordingly, a basic goal of MBT therapy is to increase the capacity for mentalization, a necessary skill.

Typically, this is how MBT therapy works. It begins with the development of a warm and empathic therapeutic alliance which provides the context for learning this skill of mentalization. Then, the therapist actively encourages the patient to reflect upon current relational interactions. This includes interactions within therapy sessions. The mind of the patient becomes the focus of treatment in that patients come to know and understand what their minds are thinking. They also learn to identify and label the feelings associated with what they are thinking. They learn to evaluate errors and misjudgments in themselves and others that have led to negative consequences. Usually, sessions for individuals are scheduled on a weekly basis, as are group sessions in which group members learn from one another.

Developmental Therapy

As increasing numbers of individuals seek or demand that psychotherapy help them to improve personal, relational, or professional performance—in other words, to become more fully functioning—therapists and focused therapies will rise to the occasion. The developmental focus in psychotherapy that began to emerge in the 1960s and 1970s (Blocher, 1974; Shostrum, 1976), and was subsequently eclipsed, is now being retrieved (Blocher, 2000; Cortright, 1997; Sperry, 2002). Such a developmentally focused approach conceptualizes an individual's needs and concerns on a continuum ranging from pathological states to growth states.

The developmental perspective is particularly compatible with the treatment of personality disorders, in that it conceptualizes problem-oriented and growth-oriented needs and views in dimensional rather than in categorical terms, i.e., on a continuum from the low to high level of functioning: disordered, adequate, and optimal functioning (Sperry, 2002). Such a developmental-dimensional perspective is superior to the current DSM-5 categorical distinction between pathological functioning vs. normal functioning or optimal functioning. While

TABLE 1.4 Developmental Levels of Personality: Optimal, Adequate, and Disordered

OBSESSIVE	
Optimal	Conscientious but spontaneous individuals who balance personal integrity with generosity, hopefulness, and kindness.
Adequate	Less perfectionism and rigidity in tasks and relationships, with some degree of emotional involvement.
Disordered	Perfectionism and feeling avoidance that interferes with task completion and relationships; overly rigid thinking and attitudes; pessimistic and stingy.
HISTRIONIC	
Optimal	Having found the love they seek within themselves, they are altruistic and giving without expecting reciprocity.
Adequate	While fun-loving and often impulsive, they can delay gratification and be emotionally appropriate much of the time.
Disordered	Uncomfortable in situations in which they are not the center of attention.
NARCISSISTIC	
Optimal	Energetic and self-assured without expecting special treatment or privilege.
Adequate	Confident, yet emotionally vulnerable, they favor special treatment or privilege.
Disordered	Manifest a grandiose sense of self-importance and demand special privilege.
AVOIDANT	
Optimal	While sensitive to interpersonal cues and possessing a keen intuition about others, they are nonetheless respectful and compassionate toward others.
Adequate	Maintain a reserved demeanor around others, because they are sensitive and concerned about others' opinion of them.
Disordered	Avoid social and work-related activities that involve significant interpersonal contact because of fear of criticism, disapproval, or rejection.
SCHIZOID	
Optimal	Deeply grounded in themselves, they are emotionally connected to the world.
Adequate	Reasonably comfortable being around others, provided there are limited demands for intimacy or emotional connectedness.
Disordered	Neither desire nor enjoy close relationships.

TABLE 1.4 *continued*

DEPENDENT

Optimal
May seek out the opinions and advice of others when making major decisions, but the decisions they make are ultimately their own.

Adequate
Have the capacity to be responsible and make decisions, but still seek out and rely on others for help and advice.

Disordered
Need others to assume responsibility for most major areas of their life.

ANTISOCIAL

Optimal
Have the gift of gab and easily befriend others, although they may not offer much depth to these relationships.

Adequate
Earn respect by acting honorably and with compassion, by using power constructively and by promoting worthwhile causes.

Disordered
Exhibit aggressive, impulsive, self-serving, and irresponsible behavior.

BORDERLINE

Optimal
Sensitive, introspective, and impressionable individuals who are very comfortable with their feelings and inner impulses.

Adequate
They quickly and easily engage in relationships and are sometimes hurt and rejected in the process.

Disordered
Display frantic efforts to avoid real or imagined rejection and abandonment.

SCHIZOTYPAL

Optimal
Possess the unique capacity to view situations and life differently so as to benefit others.

Adequate
Immersed in the unique and unusual, irrespective of whether it has any socially redeeming value.

Disordered
Exhibit odd, eccentric, or peculiar behavior, thinking, and speech.

PARANOID

Optimal
Highly observant and discerning, they can defend themselves without losing control or becoming aggressive.

Adequate
Thin-skinned, they are rather sensitive to and hurt by criticism.

Disordered
Suspicious, without sufficient basis, that others are exploiting, harming, or deceiving them.

---

it is true that third party payers may not easily be convinced that it is immediately in their best interest to reimburse for therapy that focuses on optimal functioning, such a developmental-dimensional conceptualization can serve to not only guide therapists' decisions for optimizing treatment but also to guide outcomes research on the cost-effectiveness of such treatment. A brief overview of these three levels of functioning for each of the 10 personality disorders is presented in Table 1.4.

A protocol for conducting developmental therapy focused on increasing optimal functioning is described by Sperry (2002). Other developmental approaches for fostering optimal functioning have been described by Cortright (1997) and Blocher (2000).

Medication Strategies

Traditionally, the use of medication in the treatment of personality disorders was viewed as limited. Medication tended to be utilized only for a concurrent clinical disorder such as Bipolar Disorder or a target symptom like insomnia. This view is rapidly changing. Today, a growing number of psychopharmacologists believe that psychopharmacological treatment can and should be directed to basic dimensions that underlie the personality. Psychopharmacological research on treatment of selected personality disorders has grown rapidly in the past few years (Reich, 2002; Sperry, 2003). Until recently, medication treatment of personality-disordered individuals has been largely empirical, that is, largely trial and error. The reason is that there are still no specific drug treatments for DSM-5 personality disorders except for Avoidant and Borderline Personality disorders (Black, Zanarini, Romine, Shaw, Allen, & Schulz, 2014; Silk & Feurino, 2012).

Combined Treatment

There is growing consensus, among all segments of the mental health community, that effective treatment of the personality disorders involves combining treatment modalities and integrating treatment approaches (Sperry, 2006a). In many treatment centers, this means individual therapy is combined with group therapy or psychoeducation groups, and it may include medication or other modalities. Combining medication with individual and group modalities tends to increase effectiveness. Such efforts to integrate various approaches, as well as to combine treatment modalities, would have been considered heretical just a few years ago. Now, integrating and combining treatments is an emerging consensus that reflects the immensity of the "paradigm shift" that is occurring (Beitman, 2003; Sperry, 2003).

Structure of Subsequent Chapters

Each chapter is divided into five major sections: overview, description, case conceptualization, assessment, and treatment. The overview section provides a brief historical sketch of the disorder including its evolution in DSM. It also reports an incidence/prevalence data on the disorder.

The section on Description provides an extensive discussion of the particular personality disorder in biopsychosocial terms. Emphasized are aspects of temperament such as cognitive style, affective style, behavioral style, and interpersonal style. To assist the clinician in both establishing whether the presentation is one of disorder or style, and what the profile of successful treatment of the disorder would look like, descriptions, characteristic features, and case examples of both the personality style and disorder are provided. Included are DSM-5 descriptions, prototypic descriptions, and prevalence data. Case conceptualizations can be thought of in terms of diagnostic, clinical, cultural, and treatment formulations (Sperry, Gudeman, Blackwell, and Faulkner, 1992; Sperry & Sperry, 2012). This section represents a diagnostic formulation of the disorder.

The next section contains five different case conceptualizations of the disorder. The five dominant clinical formulations are psychodynamic, the biosocial—represented largely by Millon (1981, 1990; Millon & Everly, 1985); the cognitive-behavioral in which the cognitive is represented largely by Beck and Freeman (1990) and the behavioral which is represented by Turkat (1990); the interpersonal—described by Benjamin (1993); and the integrative or biopsychosocial—described by Sperry (1990, 2010a, 2015).

The section on Assessment describes typical interview behavior manifested by the personality-disordered patient and the ease or difficulty of establishing rapport. It also describes characteristic response patterns common for this personality disorder on such psychological tests as the MMPI-I, the MCMI-II, which is based on Millon's (1981, 1990) biosocial formulation and research data; and two common projective tests, the Rorschach and the Therapeutic Apperception Test (TAT). Since psychological testing can be particularly useful in clarifying a dimensional characterization of the patient's personality, i.e. where more than one personality disorder or clusters of traits are present, this section may be clinically relevant to psychologists and others who utilize psychological assessment. The following section on case conceptualization can be quite useful in understanding the origins of these disorders.

Three general approaches most commonly utilized in the individual Treatment of the disorder are detailed. They are the psychodynamic, the cognitive-behavioral, and the interpersonal approaches. The psychodynamic approach usually includes a description of the ways the traditional analytic method has been modified for this disorder in terms of expressive-supportive terms. The cognitive therapy of personality disorder approach of Beck, Davis, and Freeman (2015) is highlighted, and complemented with the research-based behavioral approach of Turkat (1990) and others. Furthermore, Benjamin's (1993, 2007) protocol for interpersonal treatment is presented.

Other modalities of treatment relevant to the disorder are explored, along with relevant research on theory indications and efficacy. A unique feature of this book is the discussion of group, marital and family, and psychopharmacology modalities for each disorder. The group treatment modality can be either homogeneous or heterogeneous, and structured and time-limited, or less structured and ongoing. Heterogeneous refers to the composition group being diverse in terms of

TABLE 1.5 Chapter Format

I.	**Overview and Background**
II.	**Description**

    1.   Defining Characteristics

         a.   Style vs. Disorder
         b.   Triggering Event
         c.   Behavioral Style
         d.   Interpersonal Style
         e.   Cognitive Style
         f.   Affective Style
         g.   Attachment Style
         h.   Optimal Diagnostic Criterion

    2.   Prototypic Description
    3.   DSM-5 Description
    4.   Prevalence

III. **Case Conceptualization**

    1.   Psychodynamic
    2.   Biosocial
    3.   Cognitive-Behavioral
    4.   Interpersonal
    5.   Integrative

IV. **Assessment**

    1.   Interview Behavior and Rapport
    2.   Psychological Testing Data

         a.   MMPI-2
         b.   MCMI-IV
         c.   TAT/Rorschach

V. **Treatment Approaches and Interventions**

    1.   Treatment Considerations
    2.   Individual Psychotherapy

         a.   Psychodynamic Approaches
         b.   Cognitive-Behavioral Approaches
         c.   Interpersonal Approaches

    3.   Group Therapy
    4.   Marital and Family Therapy
    5.   Medication
    6.   Combined/Integrative Approaches

functioning. Homogeneous refers to the group composition being similar in terms of personality types and level of functioning (Frances, Clarkin, & Perry, 1984). Homogeneous groups lend themselves to being structured, and time-limited. Finally, specific suggestions for combining modalities and integrating or blending treatment approaches, round out this section and the book.

Chapters 3 to 12 follow the same general format or chapter outline as noted in Table 1.5.

Defining Characteristics of Personality Disorders

A key to providing effective treatment of the personality disorders is an in-depth understanding of how and why personality disorder pathology develops as well how it is experienced by the both personality-disordered individual and related others. Although the narrative of each chapter—in the Description section—provides a detailed description of a given personality disorder, a table providing a *capsule summary* of these defining characteristics is included in each chapter. Its purpose is to facilitate both initial learning about the disorder and to serve as a subsequent reference source. Table 1.6 lists these characteristics. This is followed by a brief description of each these 12 characteristics.

Triggering event(s). The characteristic and predictable situations, circumstances, or other stimuli that initiate a characteristic maladaptive response—in family or intimate relations, in social situations, or in work settings (Othmer & Othmer, 2002)—are reflected in the individual's behavioral, interpersonal, cognitive, and affective styles. Triggering events can be intrapersonal, such as failing an exam, or interpersonal, for instance a narcissistic injury.

Behavioral style. The characteristic way in which an individual reacts personally to a triggering event. Examples include: self-centeredness, impatience, defensiveness, arrogance, etc.

TABLE 1.6 Defining Characteristics of a Personality Disorder

• Triggering Event(s)
• Behavioral Style
• Interpersonal Style
• Cognitive Style
• Affective Style
• Temperament
• Attachment Style
• Parental Injunction
• Self-Other Schema
• Maladaptive Core Schemas
• Optimal Diagnostic Criterion

Interpersonal style. The characteristic way in which an individual relates to others. Examples include: exploitive, disdainful, socially facile without empathy, pleasing, clinging, blaming, condescending, etc.

Cognitive style. The characteristic way in which an individual perceives and thinks about a problem and then conceives and implements a solution. Examples of such styles include analytic, methodical, global or thematic, cautious, careless, etc.

Affective style. The characteristic way in which an individual responds with various types and intensities of affects. Examples of such styles include anger, rage, elation, and mood lability.

Temperament. An inborn, characteristic response pattern reflecting an individual's energy level, emotional makeup, intensity, and tempo of response which serve as "a filter of personality through which information is processed, attachments evolve, and emotions are experienced and expressed" (Graybar & Boutilier, 2002, p. 156). Examples of such styles include: inhibited, impulsive, reflective, and aggressive.

Attachment style. The pattern of adult relating reflecting the emotional bond between parent and infant which influences affect regulation, psychological resilience, access to autobiographical memory, and the development of self-reflection and narrative. Styles are either secure or insecure (Ainsworth et al., 1978; Erdman & Caffery, 2003). Examples of insecure styles noted in personality-disordered individuals include preoccupied, fearful, dismissing, and disorganized styles.

Parental injunction. An expressed or implied parental expectation for what a child should be or how they should act. Examples of such injunctions are: "You can't do it by yourself," "You must be better to be worthwhile," "Never make mistakes."

Self-other schema. This schema involves self-view and view of others. An individual's self-view or personal conception of self includes a self-evaluation of abilities, personal worth, potential, and goals. Examples of such self-convictions include: "I am defective," "I need the attention of others to feel important and worthwhile," "I am special and entitled" (Sperry, 2015).

An individual's evaluative conception of others includes beliefs about human nature, the world, and other people. Examples of such convictions include: "life is a struggle," "people can't be trusted," "other are here to take care of me" (Sperry, 2015).

Maladaptive core schemas. Schemas are enduring and self-defeating patterns regarding one's view of self and of the world and others that are developed during childhood and elaborated throughout one's lifetime. They cause negative thoughts and feelings, and interfere with accomplishing goals and meetings one's needs (Young et al., 2003). Examples of such schemas include: defectiveness, social isolation, approval-seeking, self-sacrifice.

Optimal diagnostic criterion. It's believed that if clinicians can remember one key criterion for each personality disorder, they "could then test for the presence or absence of that criterion and quickly diagnose the personality disorder" (Allnutt & Links, 1996, p. 22). An optimal criterion is derived from three characteristics: its protypicality, i.e., having a high correlation with the sum of all criteria for that disorder; an apt behavioral description; and a high positive predictive value, i.e., the probability the individual has the criteria of the target disorder. Data on protypicality and predictive value were derived from research with the *Structured Interview for Diagnosing Personality—Revised* (Allnutt & Links, 1996)

Concluding Note

At the outset of this new millennium, clinicians are considerably more confident and effective in working with personality-disordered individuals than at any time in the history of psychiatry and the mental health sciences. Whereas 20 years ago many, if not most, clinicians believed these disorders to be untreatable, now clinicians can point to both clinical experience and research evidence that indicate that personality-disordered individuals, including those with Borderline Personality Disorder, can be helped to increase their functioning and well-being. As chronicled in the first edition of this book, the emerging shift in the treatment paradigm of the personality disorders is now fully underway and promises to be as exciting and far-ranging as was the earlier paradigm shift in diagnosing and treating the depressive disorders.

This chapter has previewed a number of cutting-edge developments involving the conceptualization, assessment and diagnosis, and treatment of the DSM-5 personality disorders. Many of these developments in diagnosis and treatment are incorporated in subsequent chapters. My hope is that this revised edition will further foster an attitude of confidence and a measure of competence in clinicians when working with personality-disordered individuals.

2

CASE CONCEPTUALIZATION AND THE EFFECTIVE TREATMENT OF PERSONALITY DISORDERS

In this age of accountability, effective clinical practice presumes that clinicians will conduct a focused clinical assessment and develop a compelling case conceptualization based on it. The case conceptualization then becomes the basis for making informed clinical decisions about treatment tailored to the individual's circumstances and level of functioning. In other words, the case conceptualization is central to achieving effective treatment outcomes with difficult-to-treat individuals, particularly those with personality disorders.

This chapter describes the clinical value of an integrative case conceptualization. It defines and describes case conceptualization and its components and elements, making the case for the centrality of the case conceptualization as the bridge that links assessment with treatment, and particularly in informing treatment goals and interventions. It is argued that effective case conceptualizations are those with high levels of explanatory power and predictive power, and which focus on replacing maladaptive patterns with more adaptive ones. Examples of case conceptualizations for three of the most common personality disorders in clinical practice today are presented. Case material illustrates the discussion, beginning with the interactive cases in the next section.

Clinical Illustrations

This is an interactive section which aims to involve you directly in the learning process. It begins with this question: How do you make clinical decisions in working with personality-disordered individuals? Read the following two cases and consider how you would approach them in terms of assessment, case conceptualization, and interventions.

Case of Kiera

Kiera is a 33-year-old, never-married female who was first diagnosed with Borderline Personality Disorder after some 20 years of psychotherapy and drug treatment. During this time she experienced mood instability, unstable relationships, and life-threatening behaviors which led to several hospitalizations and ongoing outpatient therapy. She began full-scale Dialectical Behavior Therapy (DBT) approximately two years ago, which consisted of individual DBT therapy, phone consultations with her therapist during times in which she experienced crises, and group psychoeducation.

The following developmental history was elicited. As a child she describes herself as overly sensitive and emotionally dysregulated. Reportedly, her childhood was marked by demanding, critical, and emotionally distant parents. Her parents divorced when she was about 4 years old, presumably because of her father's alcoholism. Her mother is described as "invalidating," meaning that she denied, disregarded, and erratically responded to Kiera's concerns and experiences. Kiera was also blamed for not meeting her mother's high expectations and standards for achievement and propriety. Over the years, she has been involved in several intense, short-term relationships as well as many jobs, all of short duration.

She also reports a history of sexual abuse, initially by a babysitter at age 6, which may be related to her hypersexuality throughout her adolescence and early adulthood. Her first suicide attempt was at age 12, leading to the first of many hospitalizations. Since then she has engaged in various self-harming behaviors, including wrist-cutting. She began substance use at age 14 which escalated until her early 20s. Reportedly, she has been sober for 10 years with ongoing AA and NA involvement. Kiera describes being involved in "every form of therapy" with several therapists for nearly 20 years for moodiness, substance abuse, and self-harmful behavior before beginning individual and group DBT.

What other pertinent information might you need to complete your assessment? What is your case conceptualization, diagnosis, and intervention plan? We'll return to the case of Kiera and these questions near the end of this chapter.

Case of Aimee

Aimee is a 30-year-old single mother of two boys, aged 12 and 11. She's currently employed as a limousine driver and attends graduate school part-time. Her stated reason for seeking therapy was to learn to deal with anger and resentment toward her mother. She describes herself as passive and hides her anger and resentment, but she displays these feelings "by beating myself up, running myself ragged," which means she continually focuses on meeting the needs of others and not relaxing nor enjoying life. Aimee is very careful and circumspect in talking with her mother, fearful she will hurt her mother's feelings. Essentially,

Aimee was abandoned by her mother as a child, and raised by her maternal grandmother. She indicated that she was, and is, very close to her grandmother, and remains much closer to her father.

She also reported that her ex-husband had been verbally and physically abusive to her and that he is being released from prison soon. In anticipation of his release, she worries for her safety and that of her children. Aimee reports that she remains very close to her father but quite emotionally distant from her mother. On the intake form she stated, "I have very angry feelings about her." No current medical problems are reported, although she does report having somewhat severe headaches, anxiety, depression, trouble with sleeping, and bad dreams. Psychological testing reveals a high need to please and being a victim. She reports that her greatest worry is being alone. While Aimee had been involved in therapy previously, she indicated that, while she understood her situation better, no positive changes occurred.

What other pertinent information might you need to complete your assessment? What is your case conceptualization, diagnosis, and intervention plan? We'll return to the case of Aimee and these questions near the end of this chapter.

Case Conceptualization

While the term "case conceptualization" is relatively new, clinicians and researchers have used "case formulation" for more than 50 years (Tarrier, 2006). Common to most case conceptualization models, including the analytic, constructivist, interpersonal, psychodynamic, cognitive behavioral, and systemic approaches, is the element of "pattern." This is not to suggest that all approaches to case conceptualization are the same. However, while there are elements that are unique in every approach, there are also some elements, such as pattern, that are common among nearly all approaches (Eells, 2007, 2010). The remainder of this chapter describes an integrative approach to case conceptualization that emphasizes common elements and can incorporate unique elements as well (Sperry & Sperry, 2012).

Case Conceptualization: Definition and Components

A case conceptualization is a way of summarizing diverse information in a brief, coherent manner for the purpose of better understanding and treating of the individual. Furthermore, a case conceptualization consists of four components: the diagnostic formulation, clinical formulation, cultural formulation, and treatment formulation (Sperry, 2010; Sperry & Sperry, 2012).

Diagnostic Formulation. A diagnostic formulation is a descriptive statement about the nature and severity of the individual's psychiatric presentation. The diagnostic formulation aids the clinician in reaching three sets of diagnostic conclusions: whether the patient's presentation is primarily psychotic, characterological, or neurotic; whether the individual's presentation is primarily organic or psychogenic in etiology; and whether the individual's presentation is so acute and severe that it requires immediate intervention. In short, diagnostic formulations are descriptive, phenomenological, and cross-sectional in nature. They answer the "What happened?" question. For all practical purposes the diagnostic formulation lends itself to being specified with DSM-5 criteria.

Clinical Formulation. A clinical formulation, on the other hand, is more explanatory and longitudinal in nature, and attempts to offer a rationale for the development and maintenance of symptoms and dysfunctional life patterns. Clinical formulations answer the "Why did it happen?" question. Just as various theories of human behavior exist, so also do various types of clinical formulations: psychoanalytic, Adlerian, cognitive, behavioral, biological, family systems, biopsychosocial, or some combination. In this book, Cognitive Behavioral case conceptualizations are emphasized.

Cultural Formulation. A cultural formulation is a systematic review and explanation of cultural factors and dynamics that are operative in the presenting problems. It answers the "What role does culture play?" question. More specifically, it describes the client's cultural identity and level of acculturation. It provides a cultural explanation of the client's condition, as well as the impact of cultural factors on the client's personality and level of functioning. Furthermore, it addresses cultural elements that may impact the relationship between the individual and the therapist, and whether cultural or culturally sensitive interventions are indicated.

Treatment Formulation. A treatment formulation follows from the diagnostic, clinical, and cultural formulations and serves as an explicit blueprint governing treatment interventions. Rather than answering the "What happened?" or "Why did it happen?" questions, the treatment formulation addresses the "What can be done about it, and how?" question.

The most useful and comprehensive case conceptualizations are integrative ones that encompass all four components: diagnostic, clinical, cultural, and treatment formulations (Sperry & Carlson, 2014; Sperry & Sperry, 2012). The format of the following chapters of this book will highlight integrative conceptualizations. The diagnostic formulation will emphasize DSM-5 criteria; the clinical formulation will emphasize Cognitive Behavioral explanations; while the treatment formulation will suggest Cognitive Behavioral treatment goals and methods.

Basic Premises and Elements

In the opinion of many clinicians and researchers, case conceptualization is one of the most challenging clinical competencies to master (Eells, 2010; Sperry & Sperry, 2012). The perceived difficulty in developing an effective case conceptualization may be one reason why many therapists neither develop nor use case conceptualizations, or they lack confidence in their ability to conceptualize cases.

My experience is that both experienced therapists and trainees can easily and confidently begin to master this competency in as little as two to three hours of formal training. The training approach involves learning an integrated model of case conceptualization based on common and distinctive elements, and which emphasizes the element of pattern, i.e., maladaptive pattern. Two basic premises underlie this integrative model.

Maladaptive Pattern. The first premise is that individuals unwittingly develop a self-perpetuating, maladaptive pattern of functioning and relating to others. Inevitably, this pattern underlies the individual's presenting issues. Effective treatment always involves a change process in which the client and therapist collaborate to identify this pattern, break it, and replace it with a more adaptive pattern. At least two outcomes result from this change process: increased well-being and resolution of the client's presenting issue.

Pattern Recognition and Change. The second premise is that pattern recognition and pattern change is at the heart of the case conceptualization process. Pattern is the predictable, consistent, and self-perpetuating style and manner in which individuals think, feel, act, cope, and defend themselves (Sperry, 2005; Sperry et al., 1996). Pattern change involves three processes: (1) identify the maladaptive pattern, (2) relinquish the maladaptive pattern and replace it with a more adaptive pattern, and (3) maintain the adaptive pattern (Beitman & Yue, 1999).

Case Conceptualization: Elements

The integrative case conceptualization described in this chapter comprises 17 elements, which are identified in Table 2.1 (Sperry & Sperry, 2012). Identifying these elements is considered essential in conceptualizing cases involving individuals who meet the criteria for one or more personality disorders (Sperry & Sperry, 2016).

Case Conceptualization: Strengths and Protective Factors

This integrative case conceptualization model accounts for strengths and protective factors as well as deficits, and risk factors (Sperry, 2014). The influence of client strengths and protective factors—specified as one aspect of predisposition—is of considerable clinical value in a case conceptualization, because it both "balances" strengths and protective factors with deficits and risk factors, and provides a tangible basis for estimating prognosis.

Case Conceptualization: Full-Scale vs. Concise Case Conceptualizations

Full-scale case conceptualizations include all or most of these 17 elements. As such, a full-scale case conceptualization represents all four formulations: diagnostic,

TABLE 2.1 Elements of an Integrative Case Conceptualization

Presentation	presenting problem and characteristic response to precipitants
Precipitant	triggers that activates the pattern resulting in presenting problem
Pattern: maladaptive	inflexible, ineffective manner of perceiving, thinking, acting
Predisposition	factors fostering adaptive or maladaptive functioning, including **protective factors**, strengths, and risks factors
Perpetuants	triggers that activate one's pattern, resulting in presentation
Cultural identity	sense of belonging to a particular ethnic group
Culture: acculturation and acculturative stress	level of adaptation to the dominant culture; stress-rooted acculturation including psychosocial difficulties
Cultural explanation	beliefs regarding cause of distress, condition, or impairment
Culture vs. personality	operative mix of cultural and personality dynamics
Treatment pattern	flexible, effective manner of perceiving, thinking, acting
Treatment goals	stated short- and long-term outcomes of treatment
Treatment focus	central therapeutic emphasis providing directionality to treatment that is keyed to the adaptive pattern
Treatment strategy	action plan and vehicle for achieving a more adaptive pattern
Treatment interventions	specific change techniques and tactics related to the treatment strategy for achieving treatment goals and pattern change
Treatment obstacles	predictable challenges in the treatment process anticipated from the maladaptive pattern
Treatment—cultural	incorporation of cultural intervention, culturally sensitive therapy or interventions when indicated
Treatment prognosis	prediction of the likely course, duration, and outcome of a mental health condition with or without treatment

clinical, cultural, and treatment formulations. In contrast, a concise case conceptualization includes fewer elements. At a minimum, a concise case conceptualization should include presentation, precipitant, pattern, treatment goal(s), and treatment intervention(s). To the extent that a concise case conceptualization is clinically useful, it must provide a reasonably compelling explanation for an individual's behavior and level of functioning. Because of its explanatory power, a case conceptualization, no matter how brief, cannot be considered merely a case summary.

Case Conceptualizations: Explanatory, Tailoring, and Predictive Power

A clinically useful case conceptualization has three characteristics. First, it provides a high level of *explanatory power*, which means that the case conceptualization provides a compelling explanation for the presenting problem that answers the question of why the individual acted the way he or she did. Second, it provides a high level of *tailoring power*, which refers to the selection of treatment interventions that are the "best fit" to the individual's style and functional profile, and extent of symptom severity, level of functioning, and whether it is an internalizing or externalizing disorder. The selected interventions must also match the presenting problem and the clinical, diagnostic, and cultural formulations and have a high likelihood of being successful for effecting change. Third, a clinically useful case conceptualization also provides a high level of *predictive power*—the anticipation of both the most likely obstacles and facilitators to treatment success (Sperry & Sperry, 2012). All three are essential for effectively and competently planning and guiding the treatment process.

Case Conceptualization: Case Example

The process of constructing an integrative case conceptualization is illustrated here. Following background information, there is an integrative assessment section that identifies key information. This is followed by a table summarizing the 17 elements from the diagnostic, clinical, cultural, and treatment formulations for the case. Then, a full-scale case conceptualization statement is provided that integrates this information in a coherent narrative. The first paragraph reports the diagnostic and clinical formulation, the second paragraph reports the cultural formulation, and the third reports the treatment formulation. A concise case conceptualization statement is also provided.

Case of Geri

Geri is a 35-year-old, African-American female who works as an administrative assistant. She is single, lives alone, and was referred by her company's human resources director for evaluation and treatment following three weeks of depression and social isolation. Her absence from work prompted the referral. Geri's symptoms began soon after her supervisor told her that she was being considered for a promotion. As a child, she reports isolating and avoiding others when she was criticized and teased by family members and peers. She is highly acculturated, and believes that her depression is a result of work stress and a "chemical imbalance" in her brain.

Integrative Assessment

Besides diagnostic assessment information, the following biopsychosocial information was elicited. Her family history suggests a biological vulnerability to depression. Geri recalls her parents talking about her maternal aunt being prescribed antidepressants. Besides moderate obesity, she reports reasonably good health. She denies the use of medication, alcohol, or recreational drugs. Her developmental and social history reveals demanding, critical, and emotionally distant parents who reportedly provided her little emotional support and favored her younger brother. In addition, she was regularly teased and criticized by her peers in the neighborhood and at school. There is a lifelong history of social isolation, rejection sensitivity, and avoidance of others, instead of fighting backing or neutralizing the criticism and teasing of others. She reports no best friends as a child and only one coworker with whom she feels comfortable being around. Besides a paternal aunt, she has limited contact with her family. It is noteworthy that, despite the experience of being a college graduate and working for several years in an office setting, she continues to have significant skill deficit in assertive communications, friendship skills, and problem-solving skills. Furthermore, she lacks confidence in being around others whom she cannot fully trust. She meets criteria for Major Depressive Disorder, Single Episode and for Avoidant Personality Disorder with Obsessive-Compulsive traits. Table 2.2 summarizes the elements of an integrative case conceptualization in the case of Geri (Sperry & Sperry, 2012).

Full-Scale Case Conceptualization

Geri's increased social isolation and depressive symptoms (**presentation**) seem to be her reaction to the news of an impending job transfer and promotion, given her history of avoiding situations in which she might be criticized, rejected, and feel unsafe (**precipitant**). Throughout her life, she found it safer to avoid others when possible and conditionally relate to them at other times; as a result she lacks key social skills and has a limited social network (**pattern**). This is a mild-to-moderate internalizing pattern designated as "moderate impairment" on the *Levels of Personality Functioning Scale* (LPFS). Her reaction and pattern can be understood in light of demanding, critical, and emotionally unavailable parents,

TABLE 2.2 Integrative Conceptualization Elements: Case of Geri

Presentation	increased social isolation and depressive symptoms
Precipitant	talk of job promotion and transfer out of her close-knit work group
Pattern: maladaptive	avoid and disconnect from others when feeling unsafe
Predisposition	*Biological*—family history of depression
	Psychological—shy, avoidant, non-assertive; rejection sensitive
	Social—current: avoids critical and demanding people; past: demanding, critical, emotionally, unavailable parents; teasing, taunting, critical peers
	Protective factors / strengths—one trustworthy friend; strong religious convictions against suicide; likely to qualify for a return-to-work accommodation (ADA) re: psychiatric disability
Presentation	increased social isolation and depressive symptoms
Perpetuants	maintained by her shyness, living alone, and generalized social isolation
Cultural identity	middle-class African American with limited ethnic ties
Acculturation and acculturative stress	highly acculturated; no obvious acculturative stress
Cultural explanation	sadness results from job stress and chemical brain imbalance
Culture vs. personality	personality dynamics are significantly operative
Treatment pattern	connect with others while feeling safer
Treatment goals	reduce depressive symptoms; increase socialization; return to work
Treatment focus	troublesome situations triggered or exacerbated by vulnerabilities
Treatment strategy	target social vulnerabilities and foster adaptive functioning; medication; support; replacement; skill training
Treatment interventions	medication evaluation/ monitoring; supportive and cognitive-behavioral interventions; psychoeducation group; collaborate work supervisor
Treatment obstacles	"test" practitioners; likely to resist group therapy; overdependence on clinicians; difficulty with termination
Treatment—cultural	gender may be an issue, so consider assigning supportive female clinicians
Treatment prognosis	good, if increased social connections, skills, and returns to work

strong parental injunctions against making personal and family disclosure to others, and the teasing and criticism of peers. Her family history of depression may biologically predispose her to sadness and social isolation, as did the underdevelopment of relational skills (*predisposition*). This pattern is maintained by her shyness, the fact that she lives alone, her limited social skills, and that she finds it safer to socially isolate (*perpetuants*).

She identifies herself as a middle-class African American but has little interest and no involvement with the African-American community (*cultural identity*). She is highly acculturated, as are her parents, and there is no obvious acculturative stress (*culture: acculturation*). She believes that her depression is the result of stress at work and a "chemical imbalance" in her brain (*cultural explanation*). There are no obvious cultural factors that are operative. Instead, it appears that Geri's personality dynamics are significantly operative in her current clinical presentation (*culture vs. personality*).

The challenge for Geri is to function more effectively and feel safer in relating to others (*treatment pattern*). The goals of treatment include reducing depressive symptoms, increasing interpersonal and friendship skills, returning to work, and increasing her social network (*treatment goals*). Treatment that is focused on interpersonal relatedness will keep the treatment goals in the forefront of therapy (*treatment focus*). The basic strategy for treatment is to target her vulnerabilities while fostering a more adaptive pattern and functioning. Specific treatment strategies include medication, support, replacement, and skill training (*treatment strategy*). Initially, reducing her depressive symptoms will be addressed with medication, support, and behavioral activation in an effort to sufficiently energize her to accomplish daily routines and responsibilities. Next, cognitive and behavior replacement interventions will target her rejection sensitivity and isolation from others. Then, social skills training in a group therapy setting will emphasize assertive communication, trust, and friendship skill. It is very likely that Geri will be eligible for a work accommodation under the American for Disabilities Act (ADA). Presumably, she can return to the safety of her former work setting with a promotion and/or raise. Accordingly, this treatment goal can be facilitated by the therapist consulting with her work supervisor and human resources director about such an accommodation. Treatment will be sequenced with medication management by her physician (in consultation with the clinic's psychiatrist), in addition to supportive and cognitive behavioral interventions beginning immediately in an individual treatment format which will prepare her to transition into a group treatment mode (*treatment interventions*). Some obstacles and challenges to treatment can be anticipated. Given her avoidant personality structure, ambivalent resistance is likely. It can be anticipated that she would have difficulty discussing personal matters with practitioners, and that she would "test" and provoke practitioners into criticizing her for changing or canceling appointments at the last minute, being late, and that she might procrastinate, avoid feelings, and otherwise "test" the practitioner's trustability. Once trust in the practitioner is achieved, she is likely to cling to the practitioner and treatment and thus termination may be difficult unless her social support system outside therapy is increased. Furthermore, her pattern of avoidance is likely to make entry into and continuation in group therapy and support groups difficult. Therefore, individual sessions can serve as a transition into group, including having some contact with the group practitioner, who will presumably be accepting and nonjudgmental. This should increase Geri's feeling safe and making self-disclosure in a group setting less difficult. Transference enactment is another consideration. Given the extent of parental and peer criticism and teasing, it is anticipated that any perceived impatience and verbal or nonverbal indications of criticalness by the practitioner will activate this transference. Finally, because of her tendency to cling to others whom she trusts, increasing her capacity to feel more confident in functioning with greater independence and increasing time between the last four or five sessions can reduce her ambivalence about termination (*treatment obstacles*).

Concise Case Conceptualization

Geri's increased social isolation and depressive symptoms seem to be her reaction to the news of an impending job transfer and promotion. Throughout her life, she found it safer to avoid others when possible and conditionally relate to them at other times. This is mild-to-moderate internalizing pattern of "moderate impairment" on the *Levels of Personality Functioning Scale*. Her pattern can be understand in light of demanding, critical, and emotionally unavailable parents, strong parental injunctions against making personal and family disclosure to others, the teasing and criticism of peers, and schemas of defectiveness and social isolation. As a result she lacks key social skills and has a limited social network. Her family history of depression may biologically predispose her to sadness and social isolation, as did the underdevelopment of relational skills. This pattern is maintained by her shyness, the fact that she lives alone, her limited social skills, and that she finds it safer to socially isolate. A more adaptive pattern is for her feeling safe and connecting with others who are trustworthy. Initial treatment goals were to reduce her depressive symptoms and return to work. A longer-term goal is to increase social connections, which would reflect a more adaptive pattern.

Clinical Illustrations—Continued

Case of Kiera—Continued

When this case was first presented, you were asked some questions: What else would you need to complete your assessment? What is your case conceptualization, diagnosis, and intervention plan? Here is the way I answered these questions.

Additional Assessment Information. Despite several risk factors that seemed to fuel her distress and self-mutilation, there have also been some protective factors. These include the validation and financial and emotional support of Raymond, her mother's ex-boyfriend, and a consistent and supportive work environment during the course of DBT therapy, both of which appear to have been significant factors in her recovery. Kiera's description of her relational pattern as a cycle of accusing, arguing, crying, and further accusation was quite useful in framing the case conceptualization.

Diagnosis. Her DSM-5 diagnoses were Borderline Personality Disorder, Other Specified Depressive Disorder, and Substance Related Disorders, in sustained emission. On the *Levels of Personality Functioning Scale* (American Psychiatric Association, 2013), her impairment was assessed as 3—severe impairment—which would be equivalent to 43 on the *Global Assessment of Functioning* (GAF) scale.

Case Conceptualization. The following case conceptualization is offered. Kiera presented with mood instability, unstable relationships, and life-threatening behaviors, which were her reaction to feeling victimized or jealous or in anticipation of being abandoned. Her relationship difficulties involve the cycle of accusing, arguing, crying, and then more accusing. This reflects a maladaptive pattern of driving others away with unrealistic demands for closeness. It is a strong externalizing pattern designated as "severe impairment" on the *Level of Personality Functioning Scale*. The origins of this pattern include her oversensitivity to distress and emotional dysregulation, her demanding, critical, and emotionally distant parents, and particularly her mother's "invalidating" response to her. She views herself as helpless and vulnerable and views others as dangerous and uncaring. When under increased stress, she is most likely to experience feelings of abandonment. She is particularly sensitive and finds it very difficult to tolerate such negative emotional states. She is also biologically vulnerable to substance abuse, distress intolerance, and impulsivity. Dialectical Behavior Therapy with group skills training in mindfulness, emotion regulation, distress tolerance, and interpersonal effectiveness are interventions that, together with individual DBT therapy and telephone consultation, are aimed at decreasing her distress intolerance and increasing her sense of self-control, emotional balance, and resilience.

Intervention Plan. The dynamics of this case strongly suggest that full-scale DBT is the treatment of choice. This would include twice-weekly individual therapy, telephone consultation, and group psychoeducation. Four specific goals were established to focus treatment. They were: (1) decrease her suicidal and self-harming behaviors and achieve safety; (2) work through her emotional and traumatic experiences and learn to survive them; (3) work through problems of daily living and maintain gainful employment; and (4) increase her capacity for experiencing a fulfilling life and sustaining relationships. These treatment goals directly reflect a more adaptive pattern of more effectively relating to others without self-harm.

Clinical Outcome. Despite few, if any, reported treatment gains in her previous 20 years of therapy, Kiera did respond positively to a full course of DBT and continuing care. An intensive course of twice-weekly individual and group DBT were effective in ending to her distress, mood instability, unstable relationships, and life-threatening behaviors. After one year she was in remission of her personality disorder, and over the next two years she increasingly began to experience a more fulfilling life.

Kiera's story is an actual case, reported in Kiera Van Gelder's autobiography, *The Buddha and the Borderline: A Memoir* (Van Gelder, 2010). This engaging book provides readers a firsthand account of the development of the Borderline Personality Disorder and her response to a full course of DBT.

Case of Aimee—Continued

When this case was first presented, you were asked some questions: What else would you need to complete your assessment? What is your case conceptualization, diagnosis, and intervention plan? Here is the way I answered those questions.

Additional Assessment Information. There were some key strengths and protective factors. Among these were the fact that she bonded to a caring maternal grandmother, who effectively raised her when her own abusive mother was absent for long periods of time. Although it was quite difficult, Aimee was able to leave her abusive husband knowing that her father would protect her from him. She is also articulate, hard-working, and perfectionistic. She also has notable skill deficits in assertiveness and self-empowerment.

Diagnosis. Her DSM-5 diagnoses were Dependent Personality Disorder, Obsessive-Compulsive Personality traits, and Other Specified Depressive Disorder. On the *Levels of Personality Functioning Scale* (American Psychiatric Association, 2013), her impairment was assessed as 2—moderate impairment—which would be equivalent to 59 on the *Global Assessment of Functioning* (GAF) scale.

Case Conceptualization. The following case conceptualization is offered. Aimee presented with depression, fatigue, insomnia, anger at her mother, and worries about her children and ex-husband, which were her reactions to the increased demands to care for others and the anticipation of her ex-husband's release from prison. Her maladaptive pattern involves focusing on meeting others' needs in a perfectionistic and overly conscientious manner while ignoring her own needs. Doing so allowed her to feel needed and worthwhile. This is a mild to moderate internalizing pattern designated as "moderate impairment" on the *Level of Personality Functioning Scale*. The origins of this pattern include an upbringing in which her parents were self-centered, highly critical, and overly demanding while emotionally absent; as well as skill deficits in assertive communication and self-care. It also included maladaptive beliefs about herself as being nice but deficient, and a view of the world as demanding, critical, and conditional. Initially, treatment was focused on decreasing symptoms of depression, fatigue, and insomnia. The longer-term goal was to balance meeting the needs of others and her own needs in a reasonably conscientious manner, which was a more adaptive and life-giving pattern.

Intervention Plan. Three goals were specified as the focus of six planned treatment sessions. They were: (1) decrease her presenting symptoms; (2) increase her sense of empowerment; (3) take better care of herself. These treatment goals directly reflect a more adaptive pattern of caring for others and also caring for herself. In the process of achieving these goals she effectively dismantled her maladaptive behavior. Several intervention strategies were seamlessly combined to achieve this new pattern and four treatment goals.

Clinical Outcome. This planned six-session treatment was provided by Dr. Jon Carlson and is available as a DVD in the American Psychological Association's "Psychotherapy Over Time" series (Carlson, 2006). In the last session, treatment gains are discussed and Aimee indicates that she achieved all her specified treatment goals. In a subsequent interview seven years after therapy was completed, Aimee reflects on the impact of this time-limited therapy. She indicates that she not only maintained the treatment gains but also extended these gains to other areas of her life (Sperry & Carlson, 2014).

Like the case of Kiera, the case of Aimee is also an actual case, and is reported in detail in *How Master Therapists Work: Effecting Change from the First to the Last Session and Beyond* (Sperry & Carlson, 2014). Besides additional case history the book contains session transcriptions, and commentaries on each therapy session.

Commentary on the Cases

It may be useful to step back and reflect on the successful outcomes of these two cases.

Like many individuals presenting for psychological treatment with personality disorder diagnoses, both Kiera and Aimee experienced considerable early childhood abuse and neglect.

Both also had troubling symptoms and skill deficits. However, both also had notable protective factors and strengths that were not only recognized but also "incorporated" as therapeutic adjuncts to the treatment process by those therapists who were most effective. For Kiera the support and validation of Raymond, and supportive coworkers, appear to have been important and, presumably, necessary factors in her recovery. Similarly, having the experience of being raised by a caring grandmother and then later leaving her abusive marriage were obvious strengths and protective factors for Aimee.

The focused nature of the therapeutic interventions was obvious in both cases. These case conceptualization-informed interventions were effective, whereas previous therapeutic efforts for both Kiera and Aimee had not been effective.

In the case of Aimee, a focused form of talk therapy along with some skill training (assertive communication) was a good "fit" for her, largely because her cognitive, emotional, and behavioral styles—i.e., temperament—were reasonably well modulated. In the case of Kiera, however, her cognitive, emotional, and behavioral styles were so overly modulated that 20 years of talk therapy had little effect. It was not until Kiera developed sufficient DBT skill mastery in emotional regulation, distress tolerance, mindfulness, and interpersonal effectiveness that she was able to profit from focused psychotherapy.

When clinicians inform their therapy with case conceptualizations that have high levels of explanatory power and predictive power, and they recognize and "incorporate" strengths and predictive factors, positive therapeutic outcomes are likely. Of course, clinician expertise is also a factor. While not every clinician would be able to complete therapy with Aimee in only six sessions, it would not be unreasonable for most therapists—including interns—to have similar results in 20 sessions. This assumes that they followed the case conceptualization's focus on replacing Aimee's maladaptive pattern with a more adaptive pattern, as Dr. Carlson did with Aimee.

Concluding Note

Competency in working effectively with individuals diagnosed with personality disorders is increasingly expected of psychotherapists today, and competency in case conceptualization is perhaps the most important competency for effective clinical outcomes. This chapter has highlighted the value of an integrative case conceptualization that effectively links assessment with treatment and informs treatment goals and interventions. Case conceptualizations with high levels of explanatory power, tailoring power, and predictive power are ones that focus on replacing maladaptive patterns with more adaptive ones. Case conceptualizations for three of the most common personality disorders in clinical practice today—Avoidant, Borderline, and Dependent personality disorders—were presented. Case material on two actual cases illustrated key points.

3

ANTISOCIAL PERSONALITY DISORDER

Individuals with antisocial personalities commonly present with assaultiveness, impulsivity, hedonism, promiscuity, unreliability, and drug and alcohol abuse. Criminality may be involved. These individuals fail at work, change jobs frequently, tend to receive dishonorable discharges from the military, are abusing parents and neglectful spouses, have difficulty maintaining intimate relationships, and may be convicted and spend time in prison. This disorder is similar but different from the psychopathic personality disorder, which is also known as psychopathy, and sociopathy (Hare, Neumann, & Widiger, 2012).

This chapter describes a framework for the assessment and effective treatment of this disorder. It includes sections on diagnosis, psychological assessment, case conceptualization, and treatment interventions. It begins with background information on the disorder as well as a DSM-5 description and a prototypic description of this disorder. The section on case conceptualization provides five common clinical formulations of this disorder: psychodynamic, biosocial, cognitive-behavioral, interpersonal, and an integrative conceptualization of this disorder. Several treatment approaches, modalities, and intervention strategies are also described. These include individual psychotherapy, group therapy, marital and family therapy, medication, and integrative and combined treatment.

Description of the Antisocial Personality Disorder

Antisocial Personality Disorder can be recognized by the following descriptors and characteristics: styles vs. disorders, triggering event, behavioral styles, interpersonal styles, cognitive styles, affective styles, attachment style, and optimal criterion.

Style vs. Disorder. The antisocial personalities can be thought of as spanning a continuum from healthy to pathological, wherein the antisocial personality style is on the healthy end, and the Antisocial Personality Disorder is on the pathological end. Table 3.1 compares and contrasts the antisocial personality style and disorder.

The following two cases further illustrate differences between the Antisocial Personality Disorder (Juan G.) and the antisocial personality style (Gordon J.).

TABLE 3.1 Comparison of Antisocial Personality Style and Disorder

Personality Style	Personality Disorder
Prefer freelancer living, and live well by their talents, ingenuity, and wits.	Unable to sustain consistent work behavior.
Tend to live by their own internal code of values and not much influenced by social norms, yet live within the law.	Fail to conform to social norms with regard to lawful behavior, performing acts that are grounds for arrest.
As adolescents were usually high-spirited hellraisers and mischief makers.	Irritable and aggressive as indicated by physical fights or assaults.
Can be responsible and meet financial obligations.	Irresponsible and fail to meet financial obligations.
Tend to be wanderlusts, but are able to make plans and commitments	Fail to plan ahead, or act impulsively.
Reasonably truthful, albeit gifted in using words and making friends.	Have little regard for the truth, and lie, use aliases, or "con" others for personal profit.
Tend to be courageous, physically bold, and tough; will stand up to those who take advantage of them.	Reckless regarding their own and others' personal safety, as indicated by driving while intoxicated or recurrent speeding.
Tend not to worry too much about others, expecting others to be responsible for themselves.	If a parent or guardian lacks the ability to function as a responsible parent.
Have strong libido and, while may desire several partners, can remain monogamous.	Have never sustained a totally monogamous relationship for extended periods of time.
Tend to live in the present and seldom experience much guilt.	Lack remorse and feel justified in having hurt, mistreated, or stolen from another.

Because individuals with Antisocial Personality Disorder, Psychopathic Personality Disorder, and Sociopathic Personality Disorder can engage in criminal behavior, some clinicians use the three terms interchangeably. Because research indicates some notable differences in behavior and in etiology, others prefer to differentiate psychopathy and sociopathy (Hare et al., 2012; Walsh & Wu, 2008).

CASE STUDY: ANTISOCIAL PERSONALITY DISORDER

Juan G. is a 28-year-old Cuban male who presented late in the evening to the emergency room at a community hospital complaining of a headache. His description of the pain was vague and contradictory. At one point he said the pain had been present for three days, while at another point it was "many years." He indicated that the pain led to violent behavior and described how, during a headache episode, he had brutally assaulted a medic while he was in the Air Force. He gave a long history of arrests for assault, burglary, and drug dealing. Neurological and mental status examinations were within normal limits, except for some mild agitation. He insisted that only Darvon—a narcotic—would relieve his headache pain. The patient resisted a plan for further diagnostic tests or a follow-up clinic appointment, saying unless he was treated immediately, "something really bad could happen."

CASE STUDY: ANTISOCIAL PERSONALITY STYLE

Gordon J. is the 38-year-old president of a rapidly expanding manufacturing company. He has taken over the small business that his uncle had founded after the Second World War and Gordon had greatly increased production, added new product lines and formed a marketing and sales group, which he personally supervised in the nine years he had run the company. Prior to taking over the company, Gordon had become the youngest member of the million-dollar club for selling real estate for the firm that he had worked for for just three years. His father had died in a freak skiing accident when Gordon was 11, but that didn't seem to stop him from pursuing his fascination with scuba diving and hang-gliding. Gordon was invited to join the Young President's Organization (YPO) in his region soon after turning his uncle's corporation into a highly profitable enterprise. He was quite popular in the group given his magnetic personality, visionary outlook, and captivating stories of his various exploits. He had been married for nearly five years before divorcing. Since then he has not remarried, but has maintained ongoing relationships with two women.

Psychopathic Personality Disorder

Psychopathic personality disorder—also referred to as psychopathy—is a mental disorder characterized by amoral behavior, extreme self-centeredness, and interpersonal deficits, such as grandiosity, arrogance, and deceitfulness, and global lack of empathy. Affective deficits such as lack of guilt and remorse are also noted. According to the *Psychodynamic Diagnostic Manual* (PDM) (PDM Task Force, 2006), this disorder is diagnosable by the following criteria: individuals exhibit high threshold for emotional stimulation and aggressiveness; they are preoccupied with manipulating others; their basic emotions tend to be rage and envy; their view of themselves is that they are omnipotent, in that they believe that they can make anything happen and control everything; and their view of others is that everyone is selfish, manipulative, or dishonorable.

Furthermore, their basic way of defending themselves is by attempting to control everything around them. Psychopaths are not common in corporate settings and may engage in and elude criminal prosecution by cleverly exploiting loopholes in regulations (Babiak & Hare, 2007).

The diagnosis of Psychopathic Personality Disorder has not appeared in the DSM since the first edition; however, it reappears as a specifier: "with psychopathic features" for Antisocial Personality Disorder in the "Alternative DSM-5 Model for Personality Disorders" (American Psychiatric Association, 2013).

Sociopathic Personality Disorder

Sociopathic personality—also known as sociopathy—is a mental disorder characterized by amoral and criminal behavior and a diminished sense of moral responsibility. Individuals with this disorder tend to spontaneously act out in inappropriate ways without thinking through the consequences. They may be nervous, easily agitated, and quick to display anger. They will lie, manipulate, and hurt others, but will often avoid doing so to the select few individuals they care about. Most often they are able to form attachments and loyalties to others. This means that they are likely to experience guilt and remorse when should they end hurt someone they care about. While they are capable of committing heinous crimes, they are unlikely to commit crimes against family or friends. Unlike the psychopathic personality, which research suggests has more genetic loading, the sociopathic personality appears to be more influenced by environmental factors such as poverty, exposure to violence, and overly permissive or neglectful parenting (Stout, 2005). The Sociopathic Personality Disorder only appeared in DSM-II.

Triggering Event. The typical situation, circumstance, or event that most likely triggers or activates the characteristic maladaptive response of the Antisocial Personality Disorder (Othmer & Othmer, 2002), as noted in behavioral, interpersonal, cognitive, and affective styles, is "social standards and rules."

Behavioral Style. The behavioral style of antisocial personalities is characterized by impulsivity, irritability, and aggressiveness. They are likely to be irresponsible in honoring work commitments and financial obligations. Rule-breaking is typical. Antisocial personality-disordered individuals are also noted for their impulsive anger, deceitfulness, and cunning. They tend to be forceful individuals who regularly engage in risk-seeking and thrill-seeking behavior.

Interpersonal Style. Their interpersonal style is characterized by antagonism and reckless disregard of others' needs and safety. They tend to be highly competitive and distrustful of others and often poor losers. Their relationships may at times appear to be "slick" as well as calculating. These behaviors can characterize the successful businessperson, politician, lawyer, medical professional, as well as the criminal. They tend to develop superficial relationships that involve few, if any, lasting emotional ties or commitments. Furthermore, they tend to be callous toward the pain and suffering of others.

Cognitive Style. The cognitive style of the antisocial personality is described as impulsive and cognitively inflexible as well as externally oriented. They tend to be keenly aware of social cues and may be quite adept at "reading" people and situations. Because they are contemptuous of authority, rules, and social norms, they easily rationalize their own behavior. Impulsivity, irritability, and aggressivity predispose them to argumentation and even assaultive action. Recent research indicates that there tends to be significant neuropsychological impairment in individuals diagnosed with this disorder. In particular, there is likely to be impairment in executive functioning tasks of planning ability and set shifting (Dolan & Park, 2002).

Affective Style. Their emotional or affective style is characterized as shallow and superficial. They avoid "softer" emotions such as warmth and intimacy, because they regard these as signs of weakness. Guilt is seldom, if ever, experienced. They are unable to tolerate boredom, depression, or frustration and subsequently are sensation-seekers. Finally, they may show little guilt, shame, or remorse over their own deviant actions.

Attachment Style. Individuals with a view of others that is negative and a self-view that vacillates between positive and negative exhibit a composite fearful-dismissing style of attachment. They tend to view themselves as special and entitled, but are also mindful of their need for others, who can potentially hurt them. Accordingly, they use others to meet their needs while being wary and dismissive of them. The fearful-dismissing attachment style is associated with the Antisocial Personality Disorder.

Optimal Diagnostic Criterion. Of all the diagnostic criteria for the Antisocial Personality Disorder, one has been found to be the most useful in diagnosing this disorder. The belief is that, by beginning with this criterion, the clinician can test for the presence or absence of the criterion and more quickly diagnose the personality disorder (Allnutt & Links, 1996). The optimal criterion for this disorder is criminal, aggressive, impulsive, irresponsible behavior.

DSM-5 Description

Individuals with this personality disorder are characterized by an unremitting pattern of disregarding and violating the rights of others. They disrespect and disregard laws and social norms, and regularly engage in acts that are grounds for arrest. These individuals lie, are deceitful, and will take advantage of others for pleasure or for personal profit. They are impulsive and fail to plan ahead. They are also irritable and aggressive, which results in physical fights or assaults. It is not surprising that these individuals disregard the safety of others as well as themselves. Their irresponsibility is demonstrated by their failure to engage in consistent work behavior and failure to meet financial obligations. Furthermore, their lack of remorse is shown by their indifference in having hurt, mistreated, or stolen from others (American Psychiatric Association, 2013).

The "Alternative DSM-5 Model for Personality Disorders" provides another description of this disorder (American Psychiatric Association, 2013). It is described as a failure to conform to legal and ethical norms, along with deceitfulness, manipulativeness and risk-taking. Characteristic difficulties are noted in identify, self-direction, empathy, and intimacy, as well as impulsivity and irresponsibility.

Prototypic Presentation

A prototype is a brief description that captures the essence of how a particular disorder commonly presents. Prototypic descriptions are useful and convenient and clinicians commonly rely on them rather than lists of behavioral criteria or core beliefs (Westen, 2012). Here is a common prototypic description of the Antisocial Personality Disorder: These individuals displayed symptoms of Conduct Disorder from early childhood, engaged in delinquent behavior as adolescents, and turned into selfish, manipulative, and ruthless adults. Their primary interest in others is what they can get from them. They manipulate, lie, cheat, and steal and have no remorse or empathy for the harm they inflict on others. They are reckless, impulsive, and engage in criminal behavior. This disorder is common among criminals and is a predictor of violence. Fortunately, by middle age these individuals can outgrow this pattern.

Prevalence

Prevalence of this disorder has been estimated at between 0.2 and 3.3 percent in the general population. However, it is greater than 70 percent in males with alcohol and substance use disorders in clinics, prison, and other forensic settings (American Psychiatric Association, 2013).

Conceptualizations of the Antisocial Personality Disorder

Psychodynamic Case Conceptualizations

Psychoanalytic writers describe the antisocial personality as similar to the narcissistic personality. While both form a pathological grandiose self, the antisocial individual's self is based on an aggressive introject, called the "stranger self-object" (Meloy, 1988). This self-object reflects an experience of the parent as a stranger who cannot be trusted and who harbors bad will toward the infant. Not surprisingly, this threatening internalized object derives from experiences of parental neglect or cruelty. Combined with an absence of a loving maternal object is a lack of basic trust and a fixation in the separation-individuation process so that object constancy does not occur. Since the mother is experienced as a stranger or predator, the infant's emotional attachment to her is derailed, leading to a detachment from all relationships and affective experiences, as well as sadistic attempts to bond with others through destructive and controlling behaviors.

As a result the antisocial individuals do not perceive others as separate individuals. Hence, they cannot develop the capacity for guilt and depressive anxieties based on how their actions hurt others. A corollary is that they are incapable of true depression. Kernberg (1984) notes that these antisocial individuals are similarly stunted in superego development, except for sadistic superego precursors manifest by cruel and sadistic behaviors. Higher functioning antisocial individuals are noted to have some development of consciousness with circumscribed areas—called superego lacunae—where their superego does not seem to function. Furthermore, antisocial individuals show little interest in rationalizing or morally justifying behavior, or adherence to a value system other than the exploitive, aggressive exercise of power (Kernberg, 1984; Meloy, 1988).

Biosocial Case Conceptualization

There is mounting evidence that biological factors influence the development of the antisocial personality. Low levels of the neurotransmitter serotonin have been noted in individuals prone to aggressive and impulsive behavior. Meloy (1988) suggests that antisocial individuals often have histories of childhood abuse or neglect. They are likely to have had a difficult infant temperament (Thomas & Chess, 1977), meaning they were difficult to soothe and comfort, which may have interfered with the normal attachment process, further increasing the probability of childhood abuse or neglect. Millon and Everly (1985) suggest that low thresholds for limbic system stimulation are likely in antisocial individuals. Meloy (1988) adds that antisocial individuals have been found to be autonomically hyperactive, possibly because of their inability to learn from experience, and thus manifest less anticipatory anxiety to deter them from ill-advised behavior.

Environmental factors such as parental hostility, deficient parental role modeling, and reinforcement of vindictive behavior appear to interact with these biological predisposing factors. Parental hostility may result from the child's disruptiveness with the parents, from the perception that these children are ill-tempered, or because these children are used as a scapegoat for the parents' or family's frustration. They often have had little or no parental guidance or the absence of an authority figure in the home. Without such an authority figure to model, and feeling abandoned or rejected, these children often become streetwise and hardened to the world around them. Out of these experiences they learn that "the end justifies the means," "it's a dog-eat-dog world," and "you've got to be strong and crafty to survive." Not surprisingly, this defiant behavior is met with social disapproval, which further reinforces their self-reliance and hardened outlook. As a result they learn not to trust others and, anticipating that others intend to exploit or humiliate them, they strike out at others with vindictive behaviors.

This personality pattern is self-perpetuated through consistent perceptual distortion, a demeaning attitude toward affection and cooperation, and antagonistic and vindictive behavior that breeds antagonism in return. Further, this pattern is perpetuated by their fear of being used and forced into an inferior, dominated position (Millon & Everly, 1985).

Cognitive-Behavioral Case Conceptualizations

According to Beck (2015), the behavior of individuals with this disorder is persistently irresponsible. They hold various core, conditional, and instrumental beliefs. Their *core beliefs* are that they must look out for themselves and be aggressive so as not to be victimized by others. They also believe they are entitled to break rules. They believe that their thoughts and feelings are always accurate, and that their choices are always right and good. In addition, they believe that feelings make facts which means they are in the right because they feel right about their actions. Their *conditional belief* is that if they don't manipulate, exploit, or attach others, they will never get what they deserve. Their *instrumental belief* is to get others before they get you, and take what you need since you deserve it. Underlying these various beliefs are their beliefs about self and the world (Mitchell, Tafrate, & Freeman, 2015).

These individuals tend to view themselves as strong, clever, self-sufficient, and invulnerable. They tend to view others as either weak and vulnerable, or stupid and exploitable. Accordingly, they have two strategies: they will openly attack, defraud, and victimize others; or they will more subtly "con," deceive, and manipulate them (Beck, 2015). Furthermore, they are likely to dismiss unsolicited counsel from others as irrelevant to their purposes. Finally, they tend to be present-oriented, with absolutely no concern for future outcomes.

From a more behavioral perspective, Turkat (1990) describes three subtypes of this disorder: the clear sociopath—meaning the individual clearly and obviously meets DSM-5 criteria; the clever sociopath—wherein this individual feigns psychological symptoms usually to avoid legal responsibility for their actions; and the hurting sociopath—who meets the DSM criteria but is sincerely and genuinely distressed. For all three types, the core behavioral deficits are in managing impulses and anger. Of the three, only the hurting sociopath is considered amenable to behavior therapy.

Interpersonal Case Conceptualization

For Benjamin (2003a), persons with Antisocial Personality Disorders typically have developmental histories of harsh, neglectful parenting. The adult consequence of this is that the antisocial individual neglects and is insensitive to others' needs, or exploits others. This unpredictable pattern of parenting tends to result in undermodulated parental control and blaming. The result is that, as an adult, the antisocial individual fiercely protects their autonomy. Furthermore, this pattern of inept parental caring can be internalized by the antisocial individual as substance abuse, criminal behavior, or parental dereliction of duty. The antisocial-to-be is likely to "take over" parental responsibilities, since no one else did. As a consequence of this inappropriate parental role-taking, the antisocial individual is likely to continue controlling others as an end in itself, without emotionally bonding with those being controlled. In short, a sustained pattern of inappropriate and unmodulated desire for control of others is prominent. There is also a strong need for independence, and for resisting being controlled by others, who are typically held in contempt. Unbridled aggressivity is frequently utilized to sustain control and independence. Finally, antisocial-disordered individuals may present friendly and sociable, albeit somewhat detached, since they have little regard for others.

Integrative Case Conceptualization

The following integrative formulation provides a biopsychosocial explanation for how this personality is likely to have developed and how it is maintained. Biologically, antisocial personalities manifested "difficult child" temperaments (Thomas & Chess, 1977). As such their patterns were unpredictable, tended to withdraw from situations, showed high intensity and had a fairly low, discontented mood. This ill-tempered infantile pattern has been described by Millon (1981) as resulting, in part, from a low threshold for limbic stimulation and a decrease in inhibitory centers of the central nervous system. Their body types tend to be endomorphic (lean) and mesomorphic (muscular) (Millon, 1981).

Psychologically, these individuals have a unique view of themselves, others, and the world. They tend to view themselves with some variant of the theme

"I am cunning and entitled to get whatever I want." In other words, they see themselves as strong, competitive, energetic, and tough. Their view of life and the world is variant of the theme "Life is devious and hostile, and rules keep me from fulfilling my needs." Not surprisingly their life's goal has a variant of the theme "Therefore, I'll bend or break these rules because my needs come first, and I'll defend against efforts to be controlled or degraded by others." Acting out and rationalization are common defense mechanisms used by the antisocial personality.

Socially, predictable parenting styles and environmental factors can be noted for this disorder. Typically, the parenting style is characterized by hostility and deficient parental modeling. Or, the parents might have provided such good

TABLE 3.2 Characteristics of Antisocial Personality Disorder

Triggering Event(s)	Social standards and rules
Behavioral Style	Self-reliant, cunning, and forceful Risk-taking and thrill-seeking Glib and shallow
Interpersonal Style	Deceitful Irritable and aggressive Reckless disregard for others Lacks empathy Distrustful of others
Cognitive Style	Impulsive Externally oriented and realistic
Affective Style	Avoids "softer" emotions which connote weakness Shows little guilt, remorse, or shame
Temperament	Ill-tempered infantile pattern and an aggressive, impulsive adult pattern
Attachment Style	Fearful and dismissing
Parental Injunction	"The end justifies the means"
Self-View	"I'm cunning and I'm entitled to get what I want."
World-View	"Life is devious and hostile and rules keep me from fulfilling my needs. Therefore, I'll bend or break them because my needs come first and I'll defend any efforts to be controlled or degraded."
Maladaptive Schemas	Mistrust/abuse; entitlement; insufficient self-control; defectiveness; emotional deprivation; abandonment; social isolation
Optimal Diagnostic Criterion	Criminal, aggressive, impulsive, irresponsible behavior

modeling that the child could not, or refused to, live up to high parental standards. The parental injunction is that "The end justifies the means." Thus, vindictive behavior is modeled and reinforced. The family structure tends to be disorganized and disengaged. The antisocial pattern is confirmed, reinforced, and perpetuated by the following individual and systems factors: the need to be powerful and the fear of being abused and humiliated leads to a denial of "softer" emotions plus uncooperativeness. This, along with the tendency to provoke others, leads to further reinforcement of antisocial beliefs and behaviors (Sperry, 2015; Sperry & Mosak, 1996).

Table 3.2 summarizes the characteristics of this disorder.

Assessment of Antisocial Personality Disorder

Several sources of information are useful in establishing a diagnosis and treatment plan for personality disorders. Observation, collateral information, and psychological testing are important adjuncts to the patient's self-report in the clinical interview. This section briefly describes some characteristic observations that the clinician makes and the nature of the rapport likely to develop in initial encounters with specific personality-disordered individuals. Characteristic response patterns on various objective (i.e. MMPI-2 and MCMI-IV) and projective tests (i.e. Rorschach and TAT) are also described.

Interview Behavior and Rapport

Interviewing an individual with Antisocial Personality Disorder can be particularly challenging. While it is easy to communicate with them as long as the clinician plays along, they become angry and critical when the clinician resists their manipulations. It is very difficult to have them focus on their impulsivity, irresponsibility, or the negative consequences of their actions. Such lack of genuineness and sincerity limits rapport. Nevertheless, these individuals crave attention, and the clinician can stimulate discussion by encouraging them to display their accomplishment (Ackley, Mack, Beyer, & Erdberg, 2011). By avoiding a judgmental or accusatory tone, the clinician may be able to encourage cooperation and explore the negative consequences of their actions. When they are unwilling to cooperate, answer questions, or adopt a complaining or hostile posture, the clinician does well to display indifference or initiate termination of the interview. Both of these strategies may quickly reverse their behavior. However, while they are seldom remorseful about their deceit and mistreatment of others, they can be made to realize that things are going poorly for them and they are ruining their lives. The clinician can establish rapport and review their difficulties free of distortions and lies by showing empathy for the consequences of their behavior and failures. Only when they perceive the clinician as a non-punitive ally who will support their constructive goals and shows understanding of their inability to follow social forms, can they begin to form a therapeutic alliance (Othmer & Othmer, 2002).

Psychological Testing Data

The Minnesota Multiphase Personality Inventory (MMPI-2), the Millon Clinical Multiaxial Inventory (MCMI-IV), the Rorschach Psychodiagnostic Test, and the Thematic Apperception Test (TAT) can be useful in diagnosing Antisocial Personality Disorder, as well as the antisocial personality style or trait (Groth-Marnat, 2009).

On the MMPI-2, the 4–9/9–4 (Psychopathic Deviant-Hypomania) profile is considered the classic profile of the Antisocial Personality Disorder. While the 9 represents the activator energizer of acting-out behavior, the 4 represents the cognitive component of the psychopathy (Graham, 2012). Two patterns of antisocial personality or psychopathology have been noted (Megargee and Bohn, 1979). The primary psychopath is easily provoked to violence, and thus a spike on scale 4 (Psychopathic Deviant), with elevators on 6 (Paranoid) and 8 (Schizophprenia), is likely. The 4–9/9–4 profile is more suggestive of secondary psychopathy as is the 2–4/4–2 (Depression-Psychopathic Deviant) profile (Meyer, 1995).

On the MCMI-IV elevations on scale 5 (Narcissistic) and 6 A (Antisocial) are most likely (Millon, Millon, Grossman, Boice, & Sinsabaugh, 2015). Because alcohol and drug abuse are common in antisocial individuals, elevations in B (Alcohol use disorder) and/or T (Drug use disorder) are expected. Since Antisocial individuals are usually not highly distressed, elevations on A (Generalized anxiety disorder), D (Dysthymia disorder) and H (Somatic symptom disorder) are not common (Choca & Denburg, 1997).

Projective techniques can be very helpful in assessing the antisocial patient's object relations and superego development. Although these individuals are more likely to deceive a clinician during a clinical interview by simulating guilt or remorse, they are less likely to do so with ambiguous stimuli such as Rorschach blots, where there are no "correct" answers (Gabbard, 2000).

On the Rorschach, antisocial individuals tend to produce only a low to average number of responses, and they even reject cards that they could clearly handle cognitively. There is often a delayed reaction to the color cards, but then they may respond with C (Pure Color) responses in a fairly primitive and impulsive manner. They tend to give a high number of A (Animal) and P (Popular) responses, and a low number of M (Human Movement) and W (Whole) response. An absence of shading (Y, YF, and FY) and a low Form plus (F+%) response is common (Wagner & Wagner, 1981).

On the TAT, their stories tend to be juvenile and sophomoric. And, while the protagonist may be caught in a negative act, there is usually no mention of the consequences of the negative act (Bellak, 1997).

Treatment Approaches and Interventions

Treatment Considerations

This diagnosis is reserved for individuals with a history of disregarding and violating the rights of others since the age of 15. The differential diagnosis for Antisocial Personality Disorder includes other personality disorders, such as the Narcissistic Personality Disorder, the Paranoid Personality Disorder, and the Borderline Personality Disorder, where it tends to be misdiagnosed in females. The most common symptom disorders associated with it are Substance Use Disorders, Bipolar Disorder, Delusional Disorders, and Factitious Disorders.

In terms of treatment goals, these individuals are usually not interested in presenting for treatment or are resistant to treatment if they are forced by the courts, employers, or other agencies. This is probably because they appear to suffer little or no personal distress, see little wrong with their behavior or attitudes, and consent to treatment only if it is in their best interest, such as when it might improve their chances when seeking parole or probation (Hare et al., 2012).

Individual therapy, in and of itself, has proved to be remarkably ineffective with these individuals. This is particularly the case when therapy is insight-oriented or focuses on developing empathy, conscience, or interpersonal skills. However, special residential treatment programs have shown some promise (Harris & Rice, 2006). If the antisocial personality is able to engage in psychotherapy, a clear sign of progress is noted with the appearance of depressive features (Sperry, 2015).

Individual Psychotherapy

Hatchett (2015) recently conducted an in-depth literature review regarding treatment options for Antisocial Personality Disorder. While he concluded that there does seem to be some benefit to psychosocial interventions to remediate antisociality and reduce criminal recidivism, the picture is muddy and complex. Research has not yet identified any interventions that clearly meet the standard for treatment efficacy in his analysis. Because of this, he concludes that there is no basis to support the clinical utility for any psychosocial intervention for the treatment of this disorder. However, this doubt is not universally held. This section reviews the psychodynamic, cognitive-behavioral, and interpersonal approaches of individual psychotherapy with Antisocial Personality-Disordered individuals.

Psychodynamic Psychotherapy Approach

There is relatively little literature on successful treatment outcomes of individual dynamic psychotherapy with Antisocial Personality-Disordered individuals. In fact, there is widespread pessimism that dynamic psychotherapy can change the antisocial pattern (Valliant & Perry, 1985). A number of explanations have been offered for this seeming failure. These explanations involve both patient selection and therapeutic stance and interventions.

Gabbard (1990) indicates that the clinician's task at the outset of treatment is to determine which patients are "worth" the time, energy, and money required by a long-term therapy process with an uncertain outcome. Meloy (1988) has identified five contraindications for psychotherapy with antisocial patients. They are: a history of sadistic, violent behavior toward others; total absence of remorse for such behavior; a long-standing incapacity to develop emotional attachments; high or low intelligence that can thwart the therapeutic process; and the clinician's intense countertransference fear for their personal safety. In short, the more the patient resembles the dynamic profile of the pure psychopath, the less likely they are to respond to dynamic psychotherapy.

On the other hand, antisocial patients with narcissistic features may be somewhat more amenable to psychotherapy. They may reveal some dependency in the transferences, and their internal "ideal object" may be somewhat less aggressive than in the pure psychopath (Meloy, 1988). The presence of major depression may reflect amenability to psychotherapy (Woody et al., 1985). Turkat (1990) notes that the "hurting sociopath," who is sincerely and genuinely distressed, has potential for profiting from psychotherapy. However, the most important predictor of treatment success is the ability to form a therapeutic alliance. Gertsley et al. (1989) showed a significant association between the ability to form a therapeutic alliance and treatment outcome in their study of 48 methadone-maintained male opiate addicts who meet criteria for Antisocial Personality Disorder.

Parenthetically, a study of sex difference in treatment recommendations for antisocial personality is thought-provoking. A survey was undertaken involving 119 clinical psychologists who responded to case histories depicting either a male or female with Antisocial Personality Disorder and somatization. Results showed that clinicians were less likely to diagnose Antisocial Personality Disorder correctly for female than for male patients. Females were consistently given better prognosis and more likely to be recommended for insight-oriented psychotherapy than males who were given poorer prognoses and more likely to be recommended for group therapy and legal constraints (Fernbach, Winstead, & Derlega, 1989).

Therapeutic stance and intervention strategy and techniques are other important factors in the treatment outcome equation. The traditional dynamic stance of neutrality is contraindicated. Gabbard (2000) contends that neutrality is tantamount to silent endorsement or collusion with the antisocial patient's actions. Instead, the recommended therapeutic stance is active and confrontative. The clinician will need to repeatedly confront the patient's minimization and denial of antisocial behavior. Furthermore, confrontation must focus on here-and-now behavior rather than analyzing unconscious material from the past.

From a dynamic perspective, it is crucial for the clinician to assist the patient in linking actions with internal states. Finally, the clinician's expectation for therapeutic change must be starkly realistic. Gabbard (1994) cautions that antisocial patients take delight in thwarting the clinician's wishes for them to change.

Needless to say, countertransference issues are important in working with antisocial patients. Two common forms are disbelief and collusion (Symington, 1980). Disbelief involves the clinician's rationalization that the patient is not really "that bad." Collusion is perhaps the most problematic type of countertransference. Gabbard insists that the clinician be stable, persistent, and thoroughly incorruptible, as these patients will do whatever necessary to corrupt the clinical into dishonest or unethical behavior. Through simulated tearfulness, sadness, or remorse, they can manipulate the clinician into empathizing with them.

As noted previously, there are studies of dynamic treatment with antisocial patients. One study of severe personality disordered individuals, including those with Antisocial Personality Disorder, found that significant split self-representation was present in the 27 patients studied. Relaxation exercises and a merging intervention were utilized to reduce the amnestic barriers that maintained this compartmentalization. Results showed the 24 patients responded with reduced resistance, increased treatment compliance, and improved daily functioning (Glantz & Goisman, 1990).

Meloy and Yakeley (2010) point out that many of the more recent therapeutic approaches to antisocial individuals have been largely behavioral in nature. These include relapse prevention classes, social skills groups, and other such efforts at changing surface behaviors and symptoms, while overlooking the changes to antisocial individuals' internal mental states. One exception to this trend is Bateman and Fonagy's mentalization-based treatment (McGauley, Yakeley, Williams, & Bateman, 2011). Sometimes referred to as "mentalizing," this is the process by which individuals interpret their own subjective cognitions, behaviors, and emotions, as well as those of others. Many antisocial individuals exhibit deficits in this ability, particularly with respect to reflecting the feelings of others. This rudimentary capacity for mentalization is combined with difficulty tolerating internal states of anxiety, resulting in the type of aggressive behavior that is a hallmark of this disorder. Malancharuvil (2012) also provides a psychodynamic formulation for empathy deficit in Antisocial Personality Disorder. It is important to note that developing the capacity to mentalize without also increasing empathy may serve to make the antisocial individual a more effective predator rather than achieving the treatment's intended goal.

Cognitive Therapy Approach

Beck, Freeman, Davis, and associates (2004) provide an extended discussion of the cognitive therapy approach to Antisocial Personality-Disordered individuals. They note that it is particularly difficult to develop a collaborative working relationship with these patients. These patients are difficult to work with because they are likely to distrust the therapist, are uncomfortable accepting help, and have little motivation because of the therapist's countertransference. Establishing rapport requires the therapist to avoid, or disengage from, positions of control or power struggles with them, as well as to admit vulnerability to their manipulativeness. Since these individuals are likely to lie, the therapist can avoid entrapment in the role of being arbiter of truth by admitting that it could happen. To avoid premature termination, it is suggested that the therapist work gradually to establish trust, explicitly acknowledge the antisocial individual's strengths and capabilities, and refrain from pressing the individual to acknowledge weaknesses. Premature termination also may occur if the individual's distress, i.e., depression or anxiety symptoms, are quickly alleviated. In such instances Beck et al. suggest pointing out that continuing in therapy is in the individual's best interest and identifying any remaining distress that the individual may be denying or minimizing.

Mitchell, Tafrate, and Freeman (2015) note that, contrary to the dramatic and confrontational depictions of therapy with antisocial individuals found in popular media, a more collaborative approach is needed. Confrontation leads to loss of momentum and premature termination. Therapist qualities like warmth, empathy, and the willingness to reward are especially important with this population. Techniques such as Motivational Interviewing (Miller & Rollnick, 2013), reviewing signs and symptoms of the disorder to raise awareness of potential consequences and offer the choice to change, and focusing on the patient's strengths and values are specific ways to engage antisocial individuals in treatment. Selecting appropriate treatment goals can be challenging with this disorder, and considerable time must be spent exploring these with this population. For those who experience negative symptoms of anxiety or depression, symptom relief is a primary motivator. They see themselves as suffering, and the consequence of not acting is harmful to them alone. On the other hand, those who do not experience negative symptoms may see their antisocial behavior as rewarding and egosyntonic. In this case, motivation for change is minimal or outright resistant, as it is others who suffer and not the individual. Regardless of the individual's preferences, reducing criminal behavior should remain an overarching goal of treatment because of the harm caused to others and society as a whole.

After treatment goals have been agreed upon, focusing on specific problem situations with problem-solving and behavioral strategies is suggested. If impulse control, acting out, or inappropriate expression of anger are treatment targets, impulse control and anger management strategies are advised. As these individuals become better able to control impulses and anticipate consequences of their actions, shifting the therapeutic focus to automatic thoughts and underlying schemas is possible. This transition from a largely behavioral focus to a more cognitive one gradually allows these individuals to become less vulnerable and more comfortable in disclosing thoughts and feelings. As planned termination of treatment approaches, the focus shifts to the social pressures the individual faces to continued antisocial behavior. Relapse prevention strategies are useful in sensitizing these patients to people, places, and circumstances that are potential triggers for antisocial thinking and behaviors. Presuming that the individual has learned sufficient social skills and can engage in therapeutic group work, the likelihood of effective coping in the face of social pressures is increased. Beck et al. (2004) note that group and family therapy can be useful adjunct to individual treatment.

Furthermore, Freeman et al. (1990) believe that cognitive therapy can be effective, not only in reducing antisocial behavior, but also in assisting the individual to adopt a more prosocial lifestyle. They caution that these individuals often terminate treatment prematurely unless they experience sufficient distress from an Axis I condition, which provides an incentive for continuing to work in treatment.

An exploratory randomized controlled trial of cognitive behavioral therapy for violent men with Antisocial Personality Disorder was conducted by Davidson and colleagues (2009). Fifty-two adult men with acts of aggression within the past six months were randomized to treatment as usual (TAU) plus CBT or TAU alone. Twelve-month followup indicated that there were no significant outcome differences in the two groups. Both groups reported decreased frequency of aggressive acts; however, trends in the data favored CBT in the areas of problematic drinking, social functioning, and beliefs about others. Reflections about working with this population and this study may be found in Davidson et al. (2010).

Schema Therapy. Schema Therapy is an elaboration of cognitive therapy that has been developed by Young (1994, 1999) specifically for personality disorders and other difficult individual and couples problems. Schema Therapy involves identifying maladaptive schemas and planning specific strategies and interventions. Four main strategies are: cognitive, experiential, behavioral, and the therapeutic relationship itself. Cognitive restructuring, modification of maladaptive schemas, is an important cognitive strategy, but is combined with imagery exercises, empathic confrontation, homework assignments, and "limited reparenting," i.e., a form of corrective emotional experience (Young, 1999).

Maladaptive schemas typically associated with Antisocial Personality Disorder are: *mistrust/abuse*—the belief that others will abuse, humiliate, cheat, lie, manipulate, or take advantage; *entitlement*—the belief that one is superior to others and not bound by the rules and norms that govern normal social interaction; *insufficient self-control*—the belief that one is incapable of self-control and frustration tolerance; *defectiveness*—the belief that one is defective, bad, unwanted, or inferior in important respects; *emotional deprivation*— the belief that one's desire for emotional support will not be met by others; *abandonment*— the belief that significant others will not or cannot provide reliable and stable support; and *social isolation*—the belief that one is alienated, different from others, or not part of any group (Bernstein, 2002).

Interpersonal Approach

For Benjamin (2003a), psychotherapeutic interventions with Antisocial Personality-Disordered individuals can be planned and evaluated in terms of whether they enhance collaboration, facilitate learning about maladaptive patterns and their roots, block these patterns, enhance the will to change, and effectively encourage new patterns.

Benjamin notes that antisocial individuals do not respond well to individual psychotherapy alone. She echoes the sentiments of others by cautioning that the kind and attentive therapist, as well as those who mistakenly believe they are firmly in control, may be "taken for a ride" by these individuals. Conversely, Benjamin notes that the opposite approach of being harsh and unsympathetic will only serve to reconfirm the antisocial individual's belief that they cannot trust those who claim to care. This pattern of "hostile autonomy" guarantees that these individuals are denied benevolent contact with those around them. The therapist's challenge is to break through this barrier and develop a bond with these deeply alienated clients. While individual therapy may be problematic, when combined with other modalities, such as milieu therapy, positive treatment outcome may be possible. The goal of the collaborative phase of treatment is to establish a bonding and some degree of interdependence. Since collaboration in individual psychotherapy cannot be coerced and is seldom chosen by antisocial individuals, Benjamin suggests joining the individual in their initial hostile position and then progressively moving toward collaboration.

Other ways of eliciting collaboration suggested by Benjamin are utilizing sports heroes as role models. The antisocial individual may respond to a story about an athlete's warmth and benevolent power by internalizing these qualities, particularly in conduct-disordered adolescents. Another strategy for cultivating warmth may be to allow the antisocial individual the opportunity to occupy a nurturant position, such as providing kittens to prison inmates or teaching kids to play basketball— all while under supervision, of course. Wilderness survival training is another potential modality. In these instances, nurturance and bonding could be facilitated. Carefully managed group therapy can provide opportunities for bonding and control. Family therapy can likewise lead to positive change, but family collusion in maintaining problem patterns must be considered.

Once bonding and interdependence begin, the preconditions for collaboration have been met. Next, the antisocial individual is helped to recognize and understand the self-destructive features of their exploitive lifestyle and pattern. Benjamin believes that these individuals can then begin to develop needed self-management and social skills such as self-care, delay of gratification, and empathy for others. Unfortunately, she offers little discussion and few suggestions for facilitating change for individuals with this disorder.

Group Therapy

Group therapy for Antisocial Personality Disorder is commonly considered to be more effective than individual therapy because it offers antisocial individuals the ability to connect with the experiences of others in a less direct manner than individual therapy. This modality also enables these patients to see their behavior through the eyes of others. Structured forms of group therapy may be quite effective with Antisocial Personality-Disordered individuals. Open, exploratory, and nondirective groups (Yalom, 1985) with heterogeneous composition are easily disrupted by antisocial patients; therefore such groups are not advisable for these patients (Liebowitz et al., 1986).

Three types of group treatment have been utilized with these patients: psychoeducational, psychotherapy, and support groups (Walker, 1992). Psycho-educational groups combine didactic presentation by the clinician, which is then processed by group members. Content and agenda is structured, as is patient participation. The group is composed of antisocial patients who meet given criteria for participation, and are chosen by the clinician. The groups are time-limited and meet weekly for 90 minutes. Because of the complexity of these patients' interpersonal and other problems, these groups have limited utility for antisocial patients.

Psychotherapy groups have somewhat less structure than psychoeducational groups, but make use of cohesive themes relevant to these patients. Group membership is determined by the clinician who is in charge of both content and process. These groups tend to be long term, meet weekly for 90 minutes, and are limited to nine or ten patients. Because a group of ten antisocial patients can be quite formidable, two clinician group therapists are recommended.

Two group therapists serve to diminish the group's potential for acting out against the group leaders, as one clinician is an easy target for isolation, as well as attack or dismissal, by group members. Two group leaders also offer patients more opportunity for constructive identification because of differences in personality and therapeutic style of therapists. Furthermore, it allows for a "good guy-bad guy" routine, and allows "lateral passes" by the leaders, who may find themselves unable to handle a particular issue or patient (Walker, 1992).

Support groups for antisocial patients are useful for individuals who have had intensive inpatient or outpatient group psychotherapy. While they are based on a self-help model, they are led by a clinician. The main focus of these ongoing groups with open membership is relapse prevention and the development of peer support.

Walker (1992) described some useful guidelines for setting up these three different types of groups. He also described a number of rules and specific procedures for doing group work with antisocial patients.

Meloy and Yakeley (2010) describe the group process for Antisocial Personality Disorder from a psychodynamic perspective. They note that the therapy group acts as a container for the antisocial individual's projections, as well as a collective auxiliary ego that can reflect on behalf of the individual. This gradually moves the patient to healthier ego functioning.

Therapeutic Community. An extension of group treatment in an inpatient or residential setting in which the milieu is a medium of change is the therapeutic community (TC). Recent research indicates that drug-addicted individuals with Antisocial Personality Disorder can benefit significantly from therapeutic community treatment, provided they complete the treatment program and continue with aftercare in the community. Treatment completion was found to be the most important factor in reducing recent drug use and post-discharge arrests (Messina, Wish, Hoffman, & Nemes, 2002).

Marital and Family Therapy

There are a considerable number of studies on the family dynamics and treatment of the antisocial patient, mostly involving delinquent youths (Glueck & Glueck, 1950; Minuchin et al., 1967). A few studies suggest that short term family therapy can also be effective with delinquent adolescents (Alexander & Parsons, 1973; Parsons & Alexander, 1973). Harbir (1981) notes that antisocial patients are seldom motivated to engage in family therapy, but to the extent that the clinician is able to engage the patient's parents or spouse, the more likely therapeutic change is possible. Since the antisocial patient tends to precipitously leave outpatient treatment when difficult and anxiety-provoking issues are faced, it is incumbent on the clinician to maximize therapeutic leverage. Specifically, this means establishing a consistent therapeutic alliance and involving the family at the outset, usually at the beginning of hospital treatment, as a part of a court stipulation or as a required adjunct to residential treatment.

A major treatment goal is to help family members, or the spouse in couples therapy, set limits on the patient. Typically, family members and spouses have minimized, ignored, or acted inconsistently in the face of the patient's antisocial behavior. As the family or spouse consistently sets and enforces limits, the patient's pathological behavior reduces, and sometimes treatment-amenable symptoms like depression emerge. This suggests the patient is beginning to change and is more motivated to stop destructive behaviors. As family treatment proceeds, changes in destructive communication patterns can be achieved systematically (Parsons & Alexander, 1973).

Nichols (1996) describes the marital interactional patterns and symptomatology of individuals with Antisocial Personality Disorder and Histrionic Personality Disorder in close interpersonal relationships, as well as a suggested treatment plan protocol and strategies for dealing with such couples in a therapeutic context.

Medication

Currently, there are no psychotropic medications specifically indicated for treating individuals with this disorder. However, there is some evidence that those with this disorder have responded to SSRIs (Silk & Feurino, 2012). For this reason, these medications are used to target specific troubling symptoms, particularly anxiety. Generally, they are used as an adjunct to psychotherapy and skills training. Because troubling symptoms often respond to medications sooner than most psychological interventions, medications are usually prescribed at the onset of treatment (Sperry, 1995b). Unfortunately, there is limited research evidence to provide guidelines for the use of SSRIs for other indications or for the use of other medications (Silk & Feurino, 2012).

Combined/Integrative Treatment Approaches

Despite widespread pessimism about the treatability of this disorder, there is reason for cautious optimism provided that treatment is combined or multimodal and tailored to the particular needs and circumstances of the individual. There is clear evidence that time itself is the most effective treatment modality. In other words, the intensity of antisocial behaviors tends to dissipate with age (Regier et al., 1988); purportedly that is due to the cumulative effects of personal, social, legal, and financial repercussions of antisocial behavior. The next most effective modality is specialized treatment, therapeutic communities, or a wilderness program that provides firm limits and structure, group work with peers and a structured work program (Woody et al., 1985). To the extent that sufficient therapeutic leverage is present in outpatient settings, treatment outcomes for antisocial patients can be at least guardedly optimistic.

As with Borderline Personality Disorder, most agree that pharmacotherapy should not be the only treatment for Antisocial Personality Disorder (Gunderson, 1986). Kellner (1986) suggests that treatment often begins with a psychotherapeutic modality, after which a trial of medication may be considered for a specific target symptom such as impulsivity, aggressivity, explosiveness, and violence. Treatment, in many cases, will be long because of the patient's unwillingness or inability to persevere. It may consist of a few sessions interspersed with long intervals without any therapeutic work, or for medication monitoring only. In any case, the clinician must attempt to establish a therapeutic relationship while maintaining firm limits. Psychoeducation, whether in an individual or group format, is usually necessary. Kellner (1986) notes that data supports the use of sustained treatment that invariably involves psychotherapies—individual, group, and family, behavior therapy, and psychoeducation—aimed at teaching self-control and postponement of gratification as well as the use of medication. Though such interventions are exceedingly complex and difficult, Kellner believes they can make a substantial difference in the life and adjustment of these patients.

Many of the studies about combined treatment focus on the treatment of co-occurring Antisocial Personality Disorder and substance use disorders. Ogloff, Talevski, Lemphers, Wood, and Simmons (2015) investigated the relationship between mental illness, substance use disorders, Antisocial Personality Disorder, and offending in a sample of 130 males in a forensic mental health service facility in Australia. They found that the majority of these individuals met the criteria for multiple disorders, highlighting the need for an integrative treatment approach. Havens et al. (2007) investigated a case management intervention on admission to substance abuse treatment for injection drug users with and without Antisocial Personality Disorder. They found that injection drug users with Antisocial Personality Disorder were 3.51 times more likely to enter substance abuse treatment after spending time with a case manager. Messina, Farabee, and Rawson (2003) examined the effectiveness of four different types of treatment for cocaine-dependent patients with Antisocial Personality Disorder. These were: cognitive-behavioral therapy (CBT); contingency management (CM); combined CBT and CM; and methadone maintenance. They found that patients with Antisocial Personality Disorder were more likely to abstain from cocaine use during treatment than those without this disorder, an effect that was significantly related to the contingency management condition.

4

AVOIDANT PERSONALITY DISORDER

Individuals with avoidant personalities tend to be shy, lonely, hypersensitive individuals with low self-esteem. Although they are desperate for interpersonal involvement, they avoid personal contact with others because of their heightened fear of social disapproval and rejection sensitivity (Sanislow, da Cruz, Gianoli, & Reagan, 2012). While treatment of such individuals involves a number of unique therapeutic challenges, it can be highly effective and successful.

This chapter describes a framework for the assessment and effective treatment of this disorder. It includes sections on diagnosis, psychological assessment, case conceptualization, and treatment interventions. It begins with background information on the disorder as well as a DSM-5 description and a prototypic description of this disorder. The section on case conceptualization provides five common clinical formulations of this disorder: psychodynamic, biosocial, cognitive-behavioral, interpersonal, and an integrative conceptualization of this disorder. Several treatment approaches, modalities, and intervention strategies are also described. These include individual psychotherapy, group therapy, marital and family therapy, medication, and integrative and combined treatment.

Description of the Avoidant Personality Disorder

The Avoidant Personality Disorder can be recognized by the following descriptors or characteristics: style vs. disorder, triggering event(s), behavioral style, interpersonal style, cognitive style, affective style, attachment style, and optimal diagnostic criterion.

Style vs. Disorder. The avoidant personality can be thought of as spanning a continuum from healthy to pathological, with the avoidant personality style on the healthy and the Avoidant Personality Disorder on the pathological end. Table 4.1 compares and contrasts differences between the avoidant style and disorder.

Triggering Event(s). The typical situation, circumstance or event that triggers or activates the characteristic maladaptive response of the Avoidant Personality Disorder (Othmer & Othmer, 2002), as noted in behavioral, interpersonal, cognitive, and affective styles, is: "demands for close interpersonal relating and/or social and public appearances."

Behavioral Style. The behavioral style of avoidant personalities is characterized by chronic tenseness and self-consciousness. Their behavior and speech are controlled, and they appear apprehensive and awkward. They also tend to be self-critical and devalue their achievements.

Interpersonal Style. Interpersonally, they are rejection-sensitive. Even though they desire acceptance by others, they keep distance from others and require unconditional approval before being willing to "open up." They guardedly "test" others to determine who can be trusted to like them.

Cognitive Style. The cognitive style of such individuals can be described as hypervigilant, meaning that they scan the environment looking for clues of potential threat or acceptance. Their thoughts are often distracted by their hypersensitivity. Not surprisingly, they have low self-esteem because of their devaluation of their own achievements and their overemphasis of their own shortcomings.

TABLE 4.1 A Comparison of Avoidant Personality Style vs. Disorder

Personality Style	Personality Disorder
Comfortable with habit, repetition, and routine. Prefer the known to the unknown.	Exaggerates the potential difficulties, physical dangers, or risks involved in doing something ordinary but outside their usual routine.
Close allegiance with family and/or a few close friends; tend to be homebodies.	Has no close friends or confidants—or only one—other than first degree relatives; avoids activities that involve significant interpersonal contact.
Sensitive and concerned about what others think of them.	Unwilling to get involved with others unless certain of being liked; easily hurt and worriers.
Very discrete and deliberate in dealing with others.	Fears being embarrassed by blushing, crying or showing signs of anxiety in front of other people.
Tend to maintain a reserved, self-restrained demeanor around others.	Reticent in social situations because of a fear of saying something inappropriate or foolish, or of being unable to answer a question.
Tend to be curious and can focus considerable attention on hobbies, and avocations; however, a few engage in counterphobic coping behaviors.	Tend to be underachievers, and find it difficult to focus on job tasks or hobbies.

Affective Style. Their emotional or affective style is marked by a shy and apprehensive quality. Because they are seldom able to attain unconditional approval from others, they routinely experience sadness, loneliness, and tenseness. At times of increased distress, they will describe feelings of emptiness and depersonalization.

Attachment Style. Individuals with a self-view that is negative and an other-view that vacillates between positive and negative exhibit a composite preoccupied and fearful style of attachment. Their avoidance is based on the desire to be liked and accepted by others, while at the same time fearing of rejection and abandonment. The Preoccupied-Fearful Attachment Style adult attachment style is common in individuals with Avoidant Personality Disorder (Lyddon & Sherry, 2001).

Optimal Diagnostic Criterion. Of the various criteria for the Avoidant Personality Disorder, one has been found to be the most useful in diagnosing this disorder. The belief is that by beginning with this criterion the clinician can test for the presence or absence of the criterion and quickly diagnose the personality disorder (Allnutt & Links, 1996). The "optimal criterion" for this disorder is: "avoids occupational activities that involve significant interpersonal contact, fearing criticism, disapproval or rejection."

The following two case examples illustrate the differences between the avoidant personality style—Dr. Q and the Avoidant Personality Disorder—Ms. A.

CASE STUDY: AVOIDANT PERSONALITY STYLE

Peter Q. is a 31-year-old eye surgeon who had recently been hired by a large HMO hospital and clinic. He had recently completed residency training, and being new, good–looking, and single was quickly noticed by the female staff. His specialty was laser surgery for which he was exquisitely skilled and respected by his patients. Although courteous, he was somewhat emotionally distant and shy. Dr. Q seldom participated in staff get-togethers, and if he did make an appearance he would politely excuse himself after his beeper sounded—which seemed all the time—and he wouldn't return. His social life seemed to be a mystery, and he had little contact after hours with his male colleagues, except for one. Dr. S. had run into Peter at a civil war convention in another city, and to his surprise learned of Peter's long-standing hobby and collection of civil war books and memorabilia. In time the two became very good friends, spending considerable time together. Although he had his own apartment, Peter spent much of his free time at home with his parents. Dr. S. soon became a regular guest at the Q. home and initially was surprised at how warm, cordial, and comfortable Peter was in this small setting as compared to the hospital.

CASE STUDY: AVOIDANT PERSONALITY DISORDER

Ms. A. is a 27-year-old female student who contacted the University Counseling Center for help with "difficulty concentrating." She indicated that the problem started when Ms. A's roommate of two years precipitously moved out to live with her boyfriend. Ms. A. described herself as being "blown away and hurt" by this. She noted that she had no close friends and described herself as being shy and having had only one date since high school. Since then, she avoided attempts by men to date her because of being rejected when she was a freshman by a guy who had dated her for a month and never contacted her again. On examination, she had poor eye contact with the admissions counselor and appeared very shy and self-conscious.

DSM-5 Description

DSM-5 emphasizes specific behaviors for this disorders. Individuals who meet criteria for this diagnosis are characterized by an unremitting pattern of being socially inhibited, feeling inadequate, and overly sensitive to the negative evaluations of others. This is typically because they view themselves as socially inept, unappealing, or inferior to others. They consistently avoid work activities that require close interpersonal contact for fear of being criticized or rejected. They will not get involved with others unless they are certain of being accepted. Fearing they will be shamed or ridiculed, they are uncomfortable and act with restraint in intimate relationships. In anticipation of shame or ridicule, they are uncomfortable, and are hesitant in intimate relationships. Similarly, they experience feelings of inadequacy and inhibition in new interpersonal situations. Not surprising, they refuse to take personal risks or engage in activities that may prove embarrassing (American Psychiatric Association, 2013).

Prototypic Description

A prototype is a brief description that captures the essence of how a particular disorder commonly presents. Prototypic descriptions are useful and convenient and clinicians commonly rely on them rather than lists of behavioral criteria or core beliefs (Westen, 2012). Here is a common prototypic description of the Avoidant Personality Disorder: These individuals are frightened and interpersonally awkward. They are also extremely sensitive to criticism and rejection. Just the idea of meeting someone new engenders fear of being humiliated or embarrassed. So, it is much easier to avoid any new work or social relationship that could threaten their personal sense of security and safety. Still, they crave connection with others that they have come to trust. Accordingly, they may have a friend or a relative with whom they can relax and feel safe (Frances, 2013).

Prevalence

Prevalence of this disorder has been estimated at 2.4 percent in the general population (American Psychiatric Association, 2013). In clinical settings, estimates are that it is found in 5.1 to 55.4 percent, which is the most frequently occurring personality disorder in three epidemiological studies (Torgersen, 2012).

Table 4.2 summarizes these characteristics.

TABLE 4.2 Characteristics of Avoidant Personality Disorder

Triggering Event(s)	Demands for close interpersonal relating and/or social and public appearances
Behavioral Style	Chronically tense and self-conscious Aloof, controlled, and underactive behavior Self-critical and devalue their achievements
Interpersonal Style	Avoids interpersonal contacts fearing rejection Cautious to get involved with others Restrained intimacy for fear of ridicule Preoccupied with social criticism or rejection Inhibited in new interpersonal situations Reluctant to take social risks
Cognitive Style	Hypervigilant Thinking is easily distracted by their hypersensitivity
Affective Style	Shy and apprehensive Feelings of emptiness and depersonalization
Attachment Style	Preoccupied and fearful
Temperament	Irritable
Parental Injunction	"We don't accept you, and probably nobody else will either."
Self-View	"I'm inadequate and frightened of rejection."
World-View	"Life is unfair, people reject and criticize me, but I want someone to like me. Therefore, be vigilant, demand reassurance, and, if all else fails, fantasize and daydream."
Maladaptive Schemas	Defectiveness, social isolation, approval-seeking, self-sacrifice
Optimal Diagnostic Criteria	Avoids occupational activities that involve significant interpersonal contact, fearing criticism, disapproval, or rejection

Conceptualizations of the Avoidant Personality Disorder

Psychodynamic Case Conceptualization

Shyness, shame, and avoidant behaviors are conceptualized as defenses against embarrassment, humiliation, rejection, and failure (Gabbard, 1990). Shame and fear of exposure of the self to others are interconnected. Individuals with avoidant personalities tend to feel ashamed about their self-perceptions as weak, unable to compete, physically or mentally defective, or disgusting and unable to control bodily function (Wurmser, 1981). Shame evolves from many different developmental experiences throughout the early childhood years. These developmental experiences, plus a constitutional predisposition to avoid stressful situations, tend to be reactivated in the avoidant patient upon exposure to individuals who matter a great deal to the patient (Gabbard, 1994). Psychodynamic theorists conceptualize the behavior of those with avoidant personality as being motivated by shame for not living up to their ego ideal (Eskedal & Demetri, 2006). This poor self-image results in numerous behaviors intended to protect avoidant individuals, including misreading others' neutral and positive reactions as negative and restricting social experiences to avoid situations where their perceived inadequacies may be revealed.

Biosocial Case Conceptualization

Millon (1981), Millon and Everly (1985), and Millon and Davis (1996, 2000) believe that the etiology and development of this personality disorder represents an interactive constellation of biogenic environmental factors. They hypothesize that the vigilance characterizing this personality reflects functional dominance of the sympathetic nervous system with a lowered autonomic arousal threshold. This could allow irrelevant impulses to intrude on logical association, diminish control and direction of thought and memory processes resulting in marked interface with normal cognitive processes. Research cited by Kagan, Resnick, and Snidman (1988) suggests that the trait of shyness is of genetic-constitutional origin, which requires specific environmental experiences to develop into a full-blown pattern of timidity and avoidance.

Parental and peer group rejection are two critical and prevalent environmental influences. The amount of parental rejection appears to be particularly intense and/or frequent. When peer group rejection reinforces parental rejection the child's sense of self-worth and self-competence tends to be severely eroded, and result in self-critical attitudes. As a result these individuals restrict their social experiences, are hypersensitive to rejection, and become excessively introspective. By restricting their social environment, they subsequently fail to develop social competence, which tends to evoke the ridicule of others for their asocial behavior. Because of their hypersensitivity and hypervigilance, they are prone to interpret minor rebuffs as principal indicators of rejection, where no rejection was intended. Finally, because of their excessive introspection, they are forced to examine the painful condition they have created for themselves. Not surprisingly, they conclude that they do not deserve to be accepted by others.

Cognitive-Behavioral Case Conceptualizations

According to Beck (2015) individuals with avoidant personality are fearful of initiating relationships as well as fearful of responding to others' attempts to relate to them because of their overriding belief that they will be rejected. For them, such rejection is unbearable, so they engage in social avoidance. Furthermore, they engage in cognitive and emotional avoidance by not thinking about things which could cause them to feel dysphoric. Because of their low tolerance for dysphoria, they further distract themselves from their negative cognitions. Underlying these avoidance patterns are maladaptive schemas or long-standing dysfunctional beliefs about self and others. They tend to view themselves as inept socially and incompetent academically and vocationally. They typically view others as critical, demeaning, and uninterested in them. Schemas about self include themes of being different, inadequate, defective, and unlikable. Schemas about others involve themes of uncaring and rejection.

These individuals are likely to predict and interpret the rejection as caused solely by their personal deficiencies. This prediction of rejection results in dysphoria. Finally, avoidant individuals do not have internal criteria to judge themselves in a positive manner. Thus, they must rely on their perception. They tend to misread a neutral or positive reaction as negative, which further compounds their rejection-sensitivity and social emotional and cognitive avoidance. In short, they hold negative schemas which lead them to avoid solutions where they could interact with others. They also avoid tasks that could engender uncomfortable feelings, and avoid thinking about matters that produce dysphoria. Because of their low tolerance for discomfort, they utilize distractions, excuse-making, and rationalizations when they begin to feel sad or anxious (Padesky & Beck, 2015).

Turkat (1990) describes this disorder as primarily anxiety-based, and characterized by timidity and anxiety concerning evaluation, rejection, and/or humiliation. He notes that the disorder is very responsive to behavioral interventions, particularly anxiety management desensitization methods where the hierarchy is based on fear of rejection, criticism, and/or evaluation.

Interpersonal Case Conceptualization

According to Benjamin (2003a), persons diagnosed with Avoidant Personality Disorder tended to begin their development sequence with appropriate nurturance and social bonding. As a result, they continued to desire social contact and nurturance. Unfortunately, these individuals were subject to relentless parental control with regard to creating an impressive social image. Visible flaws were cause for great embarrassment and humiliation, particularly for the family. Besides exhortations to be admirable, they experienced degrading mockery for failures, personal imperfections, or shortcomings. The adult consequence is that avoidant individuals are socialized to perform adequately and manage an appropriate impression while avoiding occasions for embarrassment or humiliation. Typically, this humiliation was associated with exclusion, banishment, or rejection. As a result they anticipate rejection and thus socially isolate themselves. Because they are well bonded, they crave relationships and social contact but are absolutely convinced there is little or no risk of rejection or dejection.

Furthermore, although they experienced rejection and ridicule from their families, they also internalized the belief that family is their source of support. Thus, they have intense family loyalty, while harboring equally intense fears of outsiders. In short, avoidant individuals exhibit intense fear of humiliation and rejection. To avoid this, they socially withdraw and restrain themselves, while prying for love and acceptance. They can become very intimate with a select few who pass their highly stringent safety test. Occasionally, they can lose control and explode with rageful indignation.

Integrative Case Conceptualizations

The following integrative formulation provides a biopsychosocial explanation for how this personality is likely to have developed and how it is maintained. Biologically, these individuals commonly were hyperirritable and fearful as infants, and they most likely exhibited the "slow to warm" temperament (Thomas & Chess, 1977). Individuals with this personality pattern are also likely to have experienced various maturational irregularities as children. There irregularities and their hyperirritable pattern are attributed a low arousal threshold of their autonomic nervous system (Millon & Everly, 1985).

Psychologically, those with Avoidant Personalities typically view themselves as "See, I am inadequate and frightened of rejection." They are likely to view the world as some variant of the theme: "Life is unfair—people reject and criticize me—but, I still want someone to like me." As such, they are likely to conclude: "Therefore, be vigilant, demand reassurance, and if all else fails, fantasize and daydream about the way life could be." A common defense mechanism of the avoidant personality is fantasy. Thus, it is not surprising that avoidant personalities are major consumers of romance novels and soap operas.

Socially, predictable patterns of parenting and environmental factors can be noted for the avoidant personality disorder. The avoidant personality is likely to have experienced parental rejection and/or ridicule. Later, siblings and peers will likely continue this pattern of rejection and ridicule. The parental injunction is likely to have been: "We don't accept you, and probably no one else will, either."

They may have had parents with high standards and worried that they may not have or would not meet these standards and therefore would not be accepted.

This avoidant pattern is confirmed, reinforced, and perpetuated by the following individual and systems factors: a sense of personal inadequacy and a fear of rejection leads to hypervigilance, which leads to restricted social experiences. These experiences, plus catastrophic thinking, lead to increased hypervigilance and hypersensitivity, leading to self-pity, anxiety and depression, which leads to further confirmation of avoidant beliefs and styles (Sperry, 2015).

Assessment of Avoidant Personality Disorder

Several sources of information are useful in establishing a diagnosis and treatment plan for personality disorders. Observation, collateral information, and psychological testing are important adjuncts to the patient's self-report in the clinical interview. This section briefly describes some characteristic observations that the clinician makes and the nature of the rapport likely to develop in initial encounters with specific personality-disordered individuals. Characteristic response patterns on various objective (i.e. MMPI-2 and MCMI-III) and projective tests (i.e. Rorschach and TAT) are also described.

Interview Behavior and Rapport

In the initial interview, Avoidant Personality Disordered individuals tend to be monosyllabic, circumstantial, and guarded. Some may even appear suspicious or quite anxious, but all are hypersensitive to rejection and criticism. Reluctance and guardedness should be approached with empathy and reassurance. The clinician does well to avoid confrontation, which likely will be interpreted as criticism. Instead, empathic responses which encourage sharing of past pain and anticipatory fears should be used. When these individuals feel that the clinician understands their hypersensitivity and will be protective of them, they are willing to trust and cooperate with treatment. After feeling safe and accepted, the character of the interview can change dramatically. Rapport has been achieved, and they feel relieved when they can describe their fears of being embarrassed and criticized, and sensitivity to being misunderstood. They may experience these fears of being embarrassed as silly or foolish. If the clinician fails to respond empathically, they are likely to feel ridiculed and withdraw again (Othmer & Othmer, 2002).

Psychological Testing Data

The Minnesota Multiphase Personality Inventory (MMPI-2), the Million Clinical Multiaxial Inventory (MCMI-IV), and the Rorschach Psychodiagnostic Test can be useful in diagnosing the Avoidant Personality Disorder as well as the Avoidant Personality Style or trait (Groth-Marnat, 2009).

On the MMPI-2 a 2–7/7–2 (Depression-Psychasthenia) profile is typical. This profile reflects depression about assumed rejection, as well as apprehension and self-doubt about relating to others (Graham, 2012). When social withdrawal is also present, a high score on 0 (Social Introversion) is likely, as well as a lowered 9 (Hypomania) scale. When social withdrawal and self-rejection lead to decreased functioning, an elevation on scale 8 (Schizophrenia) may occur (Meyer, 1995).

On the MCMI-IV, an elevation of 85 or above on scale 2B (Avoidant) along with low scores on 4 (Histrionic) and 7 (Compulsive) are likely. Moderate elevators on scales 8B (Masochistic-Self-Defeating) and C (Borderline) may also be present (Millon et al., 2015). The higher S (Schizotypal) is elevated, the more likely decompensation has occurred (Choca & Denburg, 1997).

On the Rorschach, blocked or relatively inactive M (Human Movement) responses are likely. A high number of P (Popular) responses occurs, and C (Contrast) often involves passive animals such as deer and rabbits—sometimes being maimed or killed—or passive interactions in the M responses (Meyer, 1995).

Treatment Approaches and Interventions

Treatment Considerations

Basically, the overall goals of treatment with avoidant personality-disordered individuals are to increase their capacity to tolerate feedback from others and become more selectively trusting of others. That means that instead of automatically assuming that others intend to criticize, reject, or humiliate them, or reflexively "testing" the trustworthiness of others, avoidant individuals will be able to take some measured risks in relating to others. This might mean assertively communicating their needs and wants, or it might mean taking the risk of requesting some feedback from others who previously have been supportive of them.

Avoidant individuals already know how to relate to a small and select number of individuals, often relatives. If the clinician simply becomes one of them, the individual's basic pattern of avoidance may remain unchanged. It is only when these individuals learn to recognize the impact of their pattern on others and take risks in new relationships that they can change.

Although individual therapy can help avoidant individuals recognize and analyze their pattern of avoidance and withdrawal, couples therapy and group therapy permit both clinician and individual to observe the impact of this pattern on others, and for the individual to risk new behaviors. If the individual is married or in a long-term relationship, triangular patterns are often present. For instance, the avoidant individual may be married to a spouse who travels extensively and makes few if any emotional demands on their avoidant partner, providing the avoidant partner the opportunity for a secret extramarital affair. This triangular pattern provides some degree of intimacy as well as protection from public humiliation, while also insuring interpersonal distance (Sperry & Sperry, 2016).

Individual Psychotherapy

Psychodynamic Psychotherapy Approaches

Both expressive and supportive aspects of psychodynamic psychotherapy can be most effective in the treatment of the Avoidant Personality-Disordered individual (Gabbard, 1994). The supportive aspect involves an empathic appreciation of the humiliation and embarrassment associated with exposure to fearful interpersonal circumstances and the pain connected with rejection. The supportive aspect also involves the clinician's prescription of exposure to the feared situation. Needless to say, firm encouragement must accompany this prescription. More of their fantasies and anxieties will be activated in the actual situation of exposure rather than in their defensive posture of withdrawal. Explaining this fact will further encourage avoidant patients to seek out fearful situations.

The expressive aspect of therapy focuses on exploring the underlying causes of shame as related to past developmental experiences. To the extent the patient is willing to risk confronting the feared circumstance, the expressive aspect of therapy is greatly enhanced. Initial exploratory efforts can be frustrating in that avoidant individuals may be somewhat uncertain about who it is they fear. They tend to provide vague and global explanations such as "rejection" and "shyness" rather than specific fantasies. Thus, the clinician does well to explore specific fantasies within the context of the transference.

These individuals tend to have a considerable degree of anxiety about the psychotherapeutic requirement to openly share thoughts and feelings. Accordingly, when they nonverbally react, i.e. blush, about something that has been verbalized, the clinician might ask them to share their embarrassment and what they imagine the clinician could be thinking and feeling. By pursuing the details of specific situations, these patients can develop a greater awareness of the correlates of the shame affect (Gabbard, 1994).

Interpretive techniques are also useful as either the primary intervention or as adjunctive to behavioral and interpersonal approaches. The basic strategy involves interpretive unconscious fantasies that their fear or impulses will become uncontrollable and harmful to self and others. Not surprisingly, their avoidant behavior maintains a denial of unconscious wishes or impulses (Mackinnon & Michels, 1971). Furthermore, these patients tend to have harsh superegos and subsequently project their own unrealistic expectations of themselves onto others. In doing so, they evade expected criticism and embarrassment by avoiding relationships with others. A complete interpretation, then, identifies the unconscious impulse and the fear, and traces the resulting avoidant defensive pattern in early life experiences, in outside relationships, and in the transference (Fenichel, 1945).

Compared to other personality disorders, there has been relatively little formal study of the effectiveness of long-term psychodynamic treatment for this disorder. Svartberg, Stiles, and Seltzer (2004) conducted a randomized trial of 40 sessions of cognitive therapy versus psychodynamic therapy with 50 participants who met the criteria for Cluster C personality disorders. Thirty-one of them qualified for a diagnosis of Avoidant Personality Disorder. Results indicated that both forms of therapy led to significant positive changes; however, only the psychodynamic therapy group showed significant decreases in symptom distress at the end of treatment. Porcerelli, Dauphin, Ablon, Leitman, and Bambery (2007) conducted a five-year case study of a 50-year-old male computer technician who received psychoanalysis four times per week. Later sessions after year two included elements of cognitive-behavioral and interpersonal therapies. Results indicated that long-term psychoanalysis resulted in clinically significant reductions in symptom severity and relational pathology, with gains being maintained at the one-year follow up.

Cognitive-Behavioral Therapy Approaches

Beck et al. (2015) provide an in-depth discussion of the Cognitive Therapy approach with Avoidant Personality-Disordered individuals. Avoidant individuals are often difficult to engage in treatment given their basic strategy of avoidance and their hypersensitivity to perceived criticism. The therapist must work diligently yet carefully at building trust. Trust tests are common in the early stage of treatment and can include a pattern of cancelling appointments or having difficulty scheduling regular appointments. It is important not to prematurely challenge automatic thoughts, as such challenges can be viewed as personal criticism. Only after these individuals are solidly engaged in treatment should the therapist use cognitive interactions to test their expectancies in social situations. To the extent the therapist utilizes collaboration rather than confrontation and guided discovery rather than direct disputation, these individuals are more likely to view therapy as constructive and are likely to remain in treatment.

Since these individuals often experience high levels of interpersonal anxiety, it is useful to employ anxiety management interventions early in the course of treatment. Because these individuals work at avoiding not only unpleasant affects but also avoid thinking about matters that elicit unpleasant feelings, it is useful to work in increasing emotional tolerance with desensitization methods and reframing. Furthermore, since these individuals may not have learned the basics of social interaction, structured social skills training may need to be incorporated.

Later in therapy, when these individuals have achieved some of their short-term treatment goals and developed sufficient trust in the therapist, efforts to challenge automatic thoughts and restructure maladaptive schemas are appropriate. Issues involving risk of developing close relationships and intimacy are central. Typically, it is necessary to decatastrophize disapproval and rejection. To the extent these individuals have developed sufficient self-efficacy and have experienced enough success on a variety of levels of relationships, they are more receptive to entertaining the notion that disapproval in a close relationship does not equal rejection or devastation. Adding group therapy has a place in the treatment of this disorder, so that they can learn new attitudes and practice new skills in a socially benign and accepting environment. Padesky and Beck (2015) suggest three primary treatment goals: target emotional avoidance in and between sessions to help the patient become aware of how this pattern contributes to problems; build self-reflection and interpersonal skills such as self-expression, assertion, and conflict negotiation; and develop alternative cognitions that allow for both intimacy and assertiveness in relationships.

In summary, the cognitive therapy approach to this disorder recognizes the significant challenge of engaging the avoidant individual in treatment and utilizes several efforts to build trust, reduce social anxiety, and cognitive and emotional avoidance. It then proceeds to correcting social skills deficits with behavioral methods before turning to cognitive analysis and disputation of automatic thoughts and schemas and provides a safe environment to try out socially proactive behavior.

From a behavioral perspective, management of the avoidant pattern is relatively straightforward (Turkat, 1990). Anxiety-management procedures, assertiveness and social skills training through role-playing, direct instruction, and modeling are effective in developing confident social behavior. However, graded exposure is the single most effective behavioral intervention strategy for extinguishing avoidant behavior and anxiety intolerance (Greist & Jefferson, 1992).

Paradoxical intention may also prove useful, particularly with avoidant patients who are also oppositional. With this strategy, the patient seeks rejection in a way that is both predictable, and under the patient's control. For instance, a single male with a fear of dating agrees to an experiment requiring that he be rejected for dates by two women in the coming week. If one of the women approached accepted his offer, he could go out with her, on the condition that he had asked out an additional woman who rejected him. In other words, being rejected becomes a treatment goal. This intervention reduces rejection sensitivity. Use of such a paradoxical intervention may work with the appositionally avoidant patient by accentuating the patient's need to defeat the clinician by doing the opposite of what is suggested or prescribed (Haley, 1978; Weeks & L'Abate, 1982).

Regarding treatment involving comorbid Avoidant Personality Disorder and social phobia, Brown et al. (1995) found that individuals with both generalized and nongeneralized social phobia treated with cognitive behavior therapy improved similarly to those with the more generalized form of social phobia but remained more impaired after treatment. Curiously, the presence of Avoidant Personality Disorder was not predictive of treatment outcome; however, several individuals who met criteria for this diagnosis before treatment no longer met criteria after treatment. Similarly, Osterbaan, van Balkom, Spinhoven, de Meij, and van Dyck (2002) found that individuals with social phobia and comorbid Avoidant Personality Disorder had a poorer response to treatment and remained more impaired in the short term compared to those with the comorbidity. Nevertheless, after 15 months, those with comorbid Avoidant Personality Disorder showed similar progress in the long term.

Schema Therapy. Schema Therapy is an elaboration of cognitive therapy that has been developed by Young (Young et al., 2003) specifically for personality disorders, and other difficult individual and couples problems. Schema Therapy involves identifying maladaptive schemas and planning specific strategies and interventions. Four main strategies are cognitive, experiential, behavioral, and the therapeutic relationship itself. Cognitive restructuring, modification of maladaptive schemas, is an important cognitive strategy, but is combined with imagery exercises, empathic confrontation, homework assignments, and "limited reparenting," i.e., a form of corrective emotional experience (Young et al., 2003).

Maladaptive schemas typically associated with Avoidant Personality Disorder include: *defectiveness*: i.e., the belief that one is defective, bad, unwanted, or inferior in important respects; *social Isolation*, i.e., the belief that one is alienated, different from others, or not part of any group; *self-sacrifice, i.e.,* the belief that one must meet the needs of others at the expense of one's own gratification; and *approval-seeking , i.e.,* the belief that one must constantly seek to belong and be accepted at the expense of developing a true sense of self (Bernstein, 2002).

Interpersonal Approach

For Benjamin (2003a) psychotherapeutic interventions with Avoidant Personality-Disordered individuals can be planned and evaluated in terms of whether they enhance collaboration, facilitate learning about maladaptive patterns and their roots, block these patterns, enhance the will to change, and effectively encourage new patterns.

Fortunately, avoidant individuals already know how to relate to a select few individuals and thus a supportive therapist can easily provide a safe haven for them. Avoidant individuals respond favorably to accurate empathy and warm support. Gradually, as they share intimacies and feelings of inadequacy, guilt, or shame, they begin to increase self-acceptance. Only then can they realistically begin exploring maladaptive patterns. Since they are exquisitely sensitive to criticism, premature confrontation must be avoided.

General reconstructive changes will occur only if these individuals understand and appreciate the impact of their maladaptive patterns in a way that helps them decide to change. Benjamin advocates couples therapy for avoidant individuals in marriages of long-term relationships. Typically, these relationships are characterized by intimacy that assures interpersonal distance and safety for the avoidant partner. Such a pattern of hiding on the margins of relationships is often rooted in unconscious loyalty to the family mandate that avoidant individuals remain isolated and safe. In couples therapy, the clinician would block attempts of partners to humiliate or thrash each other which previously justified that avoidant individual's withdrawal. The most difficult therapeutic task for avoidant individuals is deciding to sacrifice the benefits of their maladaptive patterns and accept the risk of developing new ones. Insight into their humiliation and loyalty to abusive parents or siblings is insufficient. However, Benjamin believes that steady reassurance in a context of competent, protective instruction fosters this change.

Fiore, Dimaggio, Nicolo, Giuseppe, Semerari, and Carcione (2008) reported a case study using metacognitive interpersonal therapy to treat a 48-year-old male computer manager with Obsessive-Compulsive Personality Disorder and Avoidant Personality Disorder. He completed both individual and group therapy to accomplish goals of modulating perfectionism, reducing avoidance behaviors and acknowledging suppressed desires. Following one year of treatment, this individual no longer met the full criteria for any personality disorder. Gilbert and Gordon (2012) likewise reported the case of a 24-year-old female graduate student being treated with interpersonal therapy for Avoidant Personality Disorder and depression. Following two years of twice-monthly IPT and skills training (a total of 44 sessions), the participant experienced improvements in the areas of self-confidence, somatic complaints, worry, anxiety, and depression.

Group Therapy

Avoidant Personality-Disordered patients typically fear group therapy in the same way they fear other new and socially demanding situations. It is for this very reason that group therapy may be specifically and especially effective for the avoidant patients who can be persuaded and role-induced to undertake the exposure (Yalom, 1975). Empathetic group therapy can assist these individuals in overcoming social anxieties and developing interpersonal trust and rapport. Group therapy presents avoidant individuals an opportunity to belong and feel wanted, which challenges their previously held negative beliefs about themselves. Other group members may provide positive feedback about behavior in group that counteracts the avoidant individual's self-image, and the therapist can reinforce this feedback in individual therapy (Fiore et al., 2008). Benjamin (2003a) maintains that safe group therapy, in which the therapist blocks negative or abusive behavior ("trashing") from other members, can have enormous benefits in the areas of self-acceptance and social skills development.

A combination of cognitive therapy and social skills training appears effective. Alden (1989) included aspects of cognitive therapy in the group process. These were: (1) identifying underlying fears, (2) increasing awareness of the anxiety related to fears, and (3) shifting attentional focus from fear-related thinking to behavioral action. Didactic information, modeling, and the practice of role-playing were basic techniques incorporated into the sessions. Stravynski, Grey and Elie (1987) found that a briefer course of group therapy centered on social skills training can be highly effective in ameliorating social skills deficits that exacerbate anxiety about social relatedness.

This type of individual tends to avoid activities that involve significant interpersonal contact for fear of being exposed or ridiculed. Therefore, it takes them longer to adapt to a group setting and begin to actively participate in treatment. The group therapist's role in pacing the avoidant patient's disclosure and engagement within the group can be very important (Cramer Azima, 1983). Rennenberg et al.(1990) found clients with this disorder so extremely anxious and avoidant that processing directly to social skills training and behavioral rehearsal was unproductive. Stravynski, Grey, and Elie (1987) suggest beginning with progressive relaxation training and systematic desensitization. Behavioral reversal was used in the group for exposure, itself an effective treatment for social phobia (Stravynski, Marks, & Yule, 1982). Turner used communication and social skills training during behavioral rehearsal as well.

Structured activities will help the avoidant individuals organize how they think and act so they are more efficient in therapy. Alden (1989) established specific goals for patients to accomplish between sessions in order to enhance generalization from treatment sessions to daily life. The patients selected several social tasks to try, beginning with easier situations and progressing to more difficult ones. In the group setting, she also introduced interpersonal skills training. The process of friendship formation was presented and clients were encouraged to incorporate these skills into their weekly social tasks. Four sets of behavioral skills that facilitate relating to others were described, modeled by therapists, and discussed and practiced by group members. They included listening/attending skills, empathic sensitivity, appropriate self-disclosure, and respectful assertiveness.

Rennenberg et al. (1990) found that treatment gains through group intervention were stable over one year; however, most patients continued with individual therapy after completing group treatment. It is quite possible that the continued therapy served to reinforce and maintain gains made during the group treatment program. Clinically important changes were reported by patients themselves or their individual therapists. Treated subjects reported decreases in their social reticence, less interference due to social anxiety at work and in social situations, fewer symptoms of social anxiety, and greater satisfaction with social activities (Alden, 1989). Wilberg, Karterud, Urnes, Pedersen, and Friis (1999) measured the effectiveness of cognitive behavioral therapy groups for individuals with personality disorders, most of whom were classified as avoidant. They found significant improvements for those who participated in the groups compared to those who did not. Harper (2004) found that avoidant individuals who completed a 10-week behavioral group program showed greater improvement in a number of areas than did the control group.

Marital and Family Therapy

Although avoidant individuals need to recognize how their current dysfunctional patterns were developed, they need to focus on their current interpersonal experiences with significant others in their life. As Avoidant Personality-Disordered individuals generally provide clinicians with vague descriptions of their interpersonal experiences, others may be helpful in filling in the important gaps of information. Couple and family treatments may be indicated in order to establish a family structure that allows more room for interpersonal exploration outside the tightly closed family circle (Gurman & Kniskern, 1991). Benjamin (2003a) advocates couples therapy for avoidant individuals in marriages or long-term relationships, as typically these are characterized by intimacy that assures interpersonal distance and safety for the avoidant partner. She also notes that those with avoidant personality disorder may likely feel disloyal discussing any humiliation or abuses experienced in the family of origin, which may create an obstacle to family participation in therapy. If they do agree to participate, family members may make matters worse by mocking the therapist, the treatment, or the individual's desire for change.

Medication

Currently, there are no psychotropic medications specifically indicated for treating the Avoidant Personality Disorder (Silk & Feurino, 2012). Nevertheless, medications are used that target specific troubling symptoms associated with the disorder, such as depression, anxiety, or sleep problems. Generally, these medications are used as an adjunct to psychotherapy and skills training. Because troubling symptoms often respond to medications sooner than most psychological interventions, medications are usually prescribed at the onset of treatment. Unfortunately, there is little research evidence to provide guidelines for the use of such medications. However, because of the comorbidity of this disorder to social anxiety disorder, it was speculated that this personality disorder might respond well to medications with anxiety-reducing effects such as selective serotonergic reuptake inhibitors (SSRIs). There is now evidence from a randomized controlled trial that individuals with avoidant personality disorder do respond to low doses of sertraline (Zoloft), an SSRI medication (Silk & Feurino, 2012).

Combined and Integrated Treatment Approaches

Clinical experience reveals that many Avoidant Personality-Disordered individuals are often unable to focus on the patient-clinician relationship to the extent necessary to work with a purely dynamic therapy. Millon and Davis (2000) suggest an overall poor prognosis for Avoidant Personality Disorder precisely because the problem features of this disorder are the antithesis of what makes psychotherapy successful, such as an open, trusting relationship. Similarly, many have difficulty fully utilizing cognitive-behavioral interventions in the interpersonal context of therapy. Thus, an integrative treatment strategy may be required. Alden (1992) describes an integration of the cognitive and the psychodynamic-interpersonal approaches. The cognitive is, of course, based on Beck, Freeman, and associates (1990) and the psychodynamic-interpersonal is based on the Time-Limited Dynamic Psychotherapy approach developed by Strupp and Binder (1984).

The cognitive-interpersonal patterns that characterize the avoidant personality are dysfunctional beliefs of being different or biologically defective, as well as beliefs that these defects and feelings are visible to others who will react with disgust, disapproval, or dismissal. These individuals tend to protect themselves by looking to the clinician to provide direction and by understating or even withholding feelings and reactions of what they fear the clinician will disapprove. Thus, the clinician's primary task is to work collaboratively with the patient to modify their cognitive-interpersonal style. Alden (1992) describes four steps in the integrative approach. The first step is recognition of treatment process issues. The clinician must quickly recognize that these patients tend to withhold or understate information that is clinically relevant. Clinicians should expect these patients to respond to direct questions with "I'm not sure" or "I don't know." Such evasive and avoidant responses characterize the thought process and prevent these patients from encoding details about social encounters.

Unfortunately, clinicians may find themselves interpreting "resistance" or focusing on global and vague interpersonal beliefs and behavior as treatment targets. In either instance, both clinician and patient will experience discouragement and treatment outcomes will be limited. Furthermore, clinicians must recognize the avoidant patient's infectious "hopelessness" and depression largely due to their inability to process positive information, lack of attentiveness, and their firmly established negative beliefs and schemas.

The second step is increased awareness of cognitive-interpersonal patterns. Patients need to be encouraged to observe their interpersonal encounters outside sessions by means of self-monitoring and diary-keeping. Alden notes four components of the interpersonal pattern: their beliefs and expectancy of the other person; the behavior that arises from these beliefs; the others' reaction to them; and the conclusion they draw from the experience. As this process of self-observation and analysis proceeds, these patients come to realize their mutual understanding of their interpersonal problem is incomplete and a common pattern emerges. The clinician's role is to draw attention to the beliefs that underlie self-perception that leads to self-protective behaviors.

Step three focuses on alternative strategies. As patients recognize and understand these cognitive-interpersonal pattern and style, the clinician can increase their motivation to try new behavior by helping them recognize that old and new views of self are in conflict and that this conflict can be reconciled.

Helping patients integrate their current beliefs with their earlier interpersonal experiences helps them understand that their social fears and expectations resulted in part from their temperament and parenting. As the patient continues to identify and understand their cognitive-interpersonal patterns they begin to try new strategies, either on their own or at the clinician's prompting.

Step four involves behavioral experimentation and cognitive evaluation. These therapeutic strategies are discussed in detail by Beck, Freeman, and associates (1990), to which the reader is referred. Friendship formation and assertive communication are the two basic interpersonal skills that avoidant patients must increase. Role-playing and directed assignments are particularly useful in this regard. In addition, Zimbardo's (1977) social skills training exercises have been extremely useful in treating avoidant patients. Patients are gently guided through exercises to develop assertive communication skills. As a matter of fact, the entire book is an invaluable adjunct in the treatment of the avoidant personality.

Combined/Integrative Treatment Approaches

The basic premise of this book is that a single treatment modality like psychotherapy may well be effective for the highest functioning personality-disordered individual, but less effective for moderate functioning, and largely ineffective for more severely dysfunctional individuals. These lower functioning patients tend to be more responsive to combined treatment modalities. Combined modalities include integrative psychotherapeutic intervention with medication and/or group treatment such as group therapy or support groups. As noted in the section on group therapy, avoidant patients have considerable difficulty with any kind of group. Ideally, lower functioning avoidant patients should be involved in both individual and group therapy concurrently. When this is not possible, time-limited skill-oriented group training sessions or a support group may be sufficient. Aware that their pattern of avoidance and social inhibition makes entry into and continuation with therapeutic groups distressing, individual sessions should be focused on transitioning the patient into the group.

Medication is often necessary in the early stages of treatment, and can be particularly useful in reducing distress and self-protective behavior during the transition into concurrent group treatment.

The co-occurrence between personality disorders and substance use disorders is very common, with some estimating that a personality disorder is present in 90 percent of those being treated for polyvalent addiction (Rentrop, Zilker, Lederle, Birkhofer, & Horz, 2014). Dimaggio et al. (2015) conducted a case study of a 43-year-old male musician with comorbid avoidant personality disorder and substance use disorder (heroin). Treatment progressed according to stages, as follows: drug therapy to manage the symptoms of abstinence from heroin; forming a therapeutic bond; fostering awareness of emotions and triggers;

exploring maladaptive interpersonal schemas; understanding the link between interpersonal events and substance use; acquiring distance from maladaptive schemas; and using adaptive coping skills instead of resorting to substance use.

To overcome the difficulty of treating those with avoidant personality due to their social, emotional, and cognitive avoidance, some novel treatments have been explored. Eikenaes, Gude, and Hoffart (2006) reported on a quasi-experimental study integrating traditional inpatient treatment with a wilderness program, with positive results.

5

BORDERLINE PERSONALITY DISORDER

Individuals with borderline personality tend to lack a sense of self, as a result of which they experience fears of abandonment and feelings of emptiness. They are also likely to experience intense but unstable relationships, emotional instability, outbursts of anger and violence, and impulsivity. Suicidal threats and acts of self-harm are also common.

Of all the personality disorders, the Borderline Personality Disorder (BPD) is of most concern for clinicians. Specifically, many clinicians believe that this disorder is untreatable, and this belief persists despite research evidence to the contrary. In fact, more research has been published on this disorder than any other personality disorder, and increasingly it indicates that this disorder is quite treatable. For example, Zanarini and colleagues (Zanarini et al., 2010) followed nearly 300 individuals prospectively over a 10-year period. They found that one half these individuals achieved total recovery. That meant that they no longer met diagnostic criteria for this disorder, and also attained reasonable social and occupational functioning. The good news of this important prospective study is that for individuals with this disorder treatment can be quite successful.

This chapter describes a framework for the assessment and effective treatment of this disorder. It includes sections on diagnosis, case conceptualization, psychological assessment, and treatment interventions. It begins with background information on the disorder as well as a DSM-5 description and a prototypic description of this disorder. The section on case conceptualization provides five common clinical formulations of this disorder: psychodynamic, biosocial, cognitive-behavioral, interpersonal, and an integrative conceptualization of this disorder. Several treatment approaches, modalities, and intervention strategies are also described. These include individual psychotherapy, group therapy, marital and family therapy, medication, and integrative and combined treatment.

TABLE 5.1 Comparison of the Borderline Personality Style and Disorder

Personality Style	Personality Disorder
Maintenance of stable interpersonal relationships in which negative and positive perceptions of another are integrated rather than polarized.	Pattern of intense and unstable relationships marked by alternating between devaluation and overidealization.
Low levels of impulsivity that fall within the normal range of culturally approved indulgence and do not cause devastation to self or others.	Impulsive behavior that can be self-damaging, such as spending, sex, substance abuse, shoplifting, reckless driving, or binge eating
Affective stability with tolerable levels of negative emotions.	Affective instability marked shifts from baseline mood to depression, irritability, or anxiety, usually lasting a few hours and only rarely more than a few days.
Ability to manage and diffuse anger in ways appropriate to the context in which they occur.	Inappropriate and intense anger or lack of control of anger, e.g.,frequent displays of temper, constant anger, recurrent physical fights.
Sense of connection to self, body, and place in the world.	Persistent feelings of boredom or emptiness.
Possessing an accurate sense of self that is consistent over time without being overly inflexible or overly malleable.	Marked and persistent identity disturbance with uncertainty about at least two of the following: self-image, sexual orientation, long-term goals or career choice, type of friends desired, preferred values.
Ability to tolerate and manage experiences of loss; capacity to realistically assess abandonment/loss.	Frantic efforts to avoid imagined or actual experiences of abandonment.
Absence of suicidal behavior, gestures and threats (excludes suicidal ideation), self-mutilating behavior.	Repeated suicidal gestures, behavior, threats, or self-mutilating behavior.
Capacity to manage stressful situations and stay cognitively and physically present.	Brief, stress-related paranoid ideation or severe dissociative symptoms.

Description of the Borderline Personality Disorder

The Borderline Personality Disorder can be recognized by the following descriptors and characteristics: styles vs. disorders, triggering event, behavioral style, interpersonal style, cognitive style, affective style, attachment style, and optimal diagnostic criterion.

Styles vs. Disorders. The borderline personality can be thought of as spanning a continuum from healthy to pathological, wherein the borderline personality style is on the healthy end, and the Borderline Personality Disorder is on the pathological end. Table 5.1 compares and contrasts the antisocial personality style and disorder.

The following case examples further illustrate the differences between the Borderline Personality Disorder—Mr. J—and the borderline personality style—Ms. B.

CASE STUDY: BORDERLINE PERSONALITY DISORDER

Mr. J is a 31-year-old unemployed male who was referred to the hospital emergency room by his therapist at a community mental health center after two days of sustained suicidal gestures. He appeared to function adequately until his senior year in high school, when he became preoccupied with Transcendental Meditation. He had considerable difficulty concentrating during his first semester of college and seemed to focus most of his energies on finding a spiritual guru. At times, massive anxiety and feelings of emptiness swept over him, which he found would suddenly vanish if he lightly cut his wrist enough to draw blood. He had been in treatment with his current therapist for 18 months and became increasingly hostile and demanding as a patient, whereas earlier he had been quite captivated with his therapist's empathy and intuitive sense. Lately, his life seemed to center on these twice-weekly therapy sessions. Mr. J's most recent suicidal thoughts followed the therapist's disclosure that he was moving out of the area.

CASE STUDY: BORDERLINE PERSONALITY STYLE

Janice P. is a 29-year-old graduate student in Oriental Literature. She had completed her undergraduate degree at the university in business and management with honors and had planned on starting her MBA that fall. A summer tour of Japan and China dramatically changed her life. She fell in love with the Orient: the people, the food, the customs, the ambience, but especially a literature professor at a Tokyo university she met. She fell madly in love with him the first time she met him, and spent the next two weeks before her flight back to the United States totally engrossed with his poetry, his stories, and his life. Although he was married, his wife was on a holiday alone. Janice was conflicted about returning home even though he broke off the relationship. Janice was crushed that he would not leave his wife. Nevertheless, she returned to the university with an ardent desire to immerse herself in the study of Oriental literature. But, she had fantasies of returning to Tokyo as a visiting professor and working alongside the love of her life, with the goal of eventually having him all to herself. Yet, even though she was doing well in her classes, she occasionally got in touch with the anger and hurt she had experienced that summer. Midway in her first semester in grad school she met a stunning Oriental graduate student, with whom she instantly fell in love.

Triggering Event. The typical situation, circumstance, or event that most likely triggers or activates the characteristic maladaptive response of the Borderline Personality Disorder Personality Disorder (Othmer & Othmer, 2002), as noted in behavioral, interpersonal, cognitive, and affective styles, is: "frantic efforts to avoid real or imagined abandonment."

Behavioral Style. Behaviorally, borderlines are characterized by physically self-damaging acts such as suicide gestures, self-mutilation, or the provocation of fights. Their social and occupational accomplishments are often less than their intelligence and ability warrant. Of all the personality disorders, they are more likely to have irregularities of circadian rhythms, especially of the sleep-wake cycle. Thus, chronic insomnia is a common complaint.

Interpersonal Style. Interpersonally, borderlines are characterized by their paradoxical instability. That is, they fluctuate quickly between idealizing and clinging to another individual to devaluing and opposing that individual. They are exquisitely rejection-sensitive, and experience abandonment depression following the slightest of stressors. Millon and Davis (1996) consider separation anxiety as a primary motivator of this personality disorder. Interpersonal relationships develop rather quickly and intensely, yet their social adaptiveness is rather superficial. They are extraordinarily intolerant of being alone and they go to great lengths to seek out the company of others, whether in indiscriminate sexual affairs, late-night phone calls to relatives and recent acquaintances, or late-night visits to hospital emergency rooms with a host of vague medical and/or psychiatric complaints.

Cognitive Style. Their cognitive style is described as inflexible and impulsive (Millon, 1981). Inflexibility of their style is characterized by rigid abstractions that easily lead to grandiose, idealized perceptions of others, not as real people, but as personifications of "all good" or "all bad" individuals. They reason by analogy from past experience and thus have difficulty reasoning logically and learning from past experiences and relationships. Because they have an external locus of control, the borderlines usually blame others when things go wrong. By accepting responsibility for their own incompetence, borderlines believe they would feel even more powerless to change circumstances. Accordingly, their emotions fluctuate between hope and despair, because they believe that external circumstances are well beyond their control (Shulman, 1982). Their cognitive style is also marked by impulsivity, and just as they vacillate between idealization and devaluation of others their thoughts shift from one extreme to another: "I like people, no I don't like them"; "Having goals is good, no it's not"; "I need to get my life together, no I can't, it's hopeless." This inflexibility and impulsivity complicate the process of identity formation. Their uncertainty about self-image, gender identity, goals, values, and career choice reflects this impulsive and flexible stance. Gerald Adler (1985) suggested that borderlines have an underdeveloped evocative memory, such that they have difficulty recalling images and feeling states that could structure and soothe them in times of turmoil. Their inflexibility and impulsivity are further noted in their tendency toward "splitting," the inability to synthesize contradictory qualities, such that the individual views others as all good or all bad and utilizes "projective identification," that is, attributing his or her own negative or dangerous feelings to others. Their cognitive style is further characterized by an inability to tolerate frustration. Finally, micropsychotic episodes can be noted when these individuals are under a great deal of stress. These are ill-defined, strange thought processes especially noted in response to unstructured rather than structured situations and may take the form of derealization, depersonalization, intense rage reactions, unusual reactions to drugs, and intense brief paranoid episodes. Because of difficulty in focusing attention and subsequent loss of relevant data, borderlines also have a diminished capacity to process information.

Affective Style. The emotional style of individuals with this disorder is characterized by marked mood shifts from a normal or euthymic mood to a dysphoric mood. In addition, inappropriate and intense anger and rage may easily be triggered. On the other extreme are feelings of emptiness, a deep "void," or boredom.

Attachment Style. Individuals with vacillating views of both self and others exhibit the disorganized attachment style; "Disorganized attachment develops from repeated experiences in which the caregiver appears frightened or frightening to the child" (Siegel, 1999, p. 117). This style is associated with dissociative symptomatology which increases their proneness to posttraumatic stress disorder. The Borderline Personality Disorder is characterized by unstable personality structure that seems to shift among the various insecure attachment styles creating a disorganized profile, called the disorganized attachment style (Lyddon & Sherry, 2001).

Optimal Diagnostic Criterion. Of all the criteria for the Borderline Personality Disorder, one has been found to be the most useful in its diagnosis.

The belief is that, by beginning with this criterion, the clinician can test for the presence or absence of the criterion and quickly diagnose this disorder. The optimal criterion for this disorder is: frantic efforts to avoid real or imagined abandonment (Allnutt & Links, 1996).

   Childhood Abuse and Etiology. There is increasing research evidence that a history of early abuse or neglect is common in adults with personality disorders, particularly Borderline Personality Disorder (Van der Kolk, Perry, & Herman, 1989; Zanarini et al., 2010). Bernstein (2002) indicates that childhood histories of *severe* emotional abuse are noted in adults diagnosed with Borderline Personality Disorder. Data on sexual abuse among individuals with this disorder are troubling, in that the odds of such an individual attempting suicide in adulthood is over 10 times that of those who were never sexually abused (Soloff, Lynch, & Kelly, 2002).

   Many clinicians have come to assume that this disorder is caused by such childhood abuse. Research largely supports this presumption. Nevertheless, it does not suggest that abuse is the primary cause of all cases of Borderline Personality Disorder. But exactly how prevalent is such trauma in those presenting for treatment? A recent meta-analytic study (Fossatti, Madeddu, & Maffei, 1999) indicates that in individuals diagnosed with Borderline Personality Disorder, the prevalence rates of abuse are in the range of 60–80 percent. This means that 20–40 percent of these individuals do *not* report such histories. Presumably, such individuals are more likely to be the so-called "higher functioning" borderlines. In other words, while there are traumatic pathways in the development of personality disorders, there are also nontraumatic pathways. An important treatment implication is that such clients, who were not traumatized but rather may have been otherwise wounded as children in their efforts to meet emotional needs, may be responsive to a broader range of therapeutic interventions than more focused approaches such as Dialectical Behavior Therapy. These other interventions might include exploratory, uncovering, and abreactive interventions, which are less likely to be regressive or iatrogenic than they would be with clients with trauma histories (Graybar & Boutilier, 2002).

DSM-5 Description

Individuals with this personality disorder are characterized by an unremitting pattern of unstable relationships, emotional reactions, identity, and impulsivity. They engage in frantic efforts to avoid abandonment, whether it is real or imagined. Their interpersonal relationships are intense, unstable, and alternate between the extremes of idealization and devaluation. They have chronic identity issues and an unstable sense of self. Their impulsivity can result in self-damaging actions such as reckless driving or drug use, binge eating, or high-risk sex. These individuals engage in recurrent suicidal threats, gestures, acting out, or self-mutilating behavior. They can exhibit markedly reactive moods, chronic feelings of emptiness, emotional outbursts, and difficulty controlling their anger. They may also experience brief, stress-related paranoid thinking or severe episodes of dissociation (American Psychiatric Association, 2013).

The "Alternative DSM-5 Model for Personality Disorders" provides another description of this disorder (American Psychiatric Association, 2013). It is described as instability of self-image, goal-striving, interpersonal relating, and affects accompanied by impulsivity, hostility, and risk-taking. Characteristic difficulties are noted in identity, self-direction, empathy, and intimacy, as well as hostility, risk-taking, impulsivity, depression, and separation insecurity.

Prototypic Description

These individuals have intense and frustrating relationships which begin with high hopes but predictably degenerate into conflict and disappointments. Because they are terrified of being abandoned, they drive others away with unrealistic demands, relentless anger, and self-fulfilling expectations of abandonment. Real or imagined losses can lead to suicide attempts or self-mutilation. The result is repeated destructive relationships and a fragile sense of self. They may engage in impulsive sexual and aggressive behaviors. Suicide rates are high for such individuals. However, those who survive may find some sense of balance and serenity in midlife (Frances, 2013).

Prevalence

Prevalence of this disorder has been estimated at between 1.6 and 5.9 percent in the general population. In primary care settings the figure is 6 percent, but 10 percent of outpatient settings and 20 percent in inpatient settings (American Psychiatric Association, 2013).

Conceptualizations of the Borderline Personality Disorder

Psychodynamic Case Conceptualization

Kernberg (1975) targets the rapprochement sub-phase of Mahler's separation-individuation developmental theory as the point of fixation for borderline pathology. At this phase children lack object constancy and thus cannot integrate the good and bad aspects of themselves or their mothers. Neither can they separate from the mother, since they have yet to internalize a whole, soothing internalized usage of her that sustains them during her physical absence. Kernberg points to a disturbance in the mother's emotional availability during the rapprochement sub-phase, which is attributable to the constitutional excess of aggression in the child, to maternal problems with parenting, or both.

Masterson (1976) and Masterson and Klein (1989) implicate the rapprochement sub-phase but emphasize the mother's behavior rather than the child's aggression. Typically a borderline herself, the mother is deeply conflicted about her children growing up and becoming their own person. Thus, these children receive the message that if they grow up, something awful will happen to them and/or to their mothers, and that remaining dependent is the only way of maintaining the maternal bond. This prospect of separation and individuation thus provokes "abandonment depression" in borderlines. No integration between a rewarding object unit and a withdrawing object unit is possible at this rapprochement sub-phase, accounting for the symptom of the borderline syndrome.

Adler's (1985) understanding of borderline pathology is influenced by Kohut (1971, 1977) and Fraiberg (1969) and is based on a deficit rather than a conflict model, as with Kernberg. Inconsistency in maternal behavior and availability results in the borderline's failure to develop a "holding-nothing" internalized object. This accounts for feelings of emptiness, depressive tendencies, and oral rage. Furthermore, the borderline individual has difficulty summoning up internal images of the natural nurturing figure in stressful situations. This cognitive deficit of evocative memory suggests a regression to developmental age of between 8 and 18 months. These inadequate resources leave the borderline prone to fragmentation of the self, which is accompanied by profound emptiness called "annihilation panic."

Mentalization Approach. Bateman and Fonagy's (2007) mentalization approach to Borderline Personality Disorder is rooted in object relations and attachment theory. Sometimes referred to as "mentalizing," this is the process by which individuals interpret their own subjective cognitions, behaviors, and emotions, as well as those of others. The ability to mentalize is believed to arise as a function of childhood development by age 4. Rather than an automatic consequence of maturation, it is dependent on the quality of an individual's early object relationships. Interactions with the primary caregiver, usually the mother, act as the foundation from which individuals make sense of their mental states and interpersonal interactions. To fully develop this capacity, infants must have a stable, affectionate, safe, and attentive adult to mirror their experiences. Bateman and Fonagy suggest that those with borderline personality lack the ability to interpret mental states and accurately understand their relationships due to psychological trauma in early or late childhood. Neglect, abuse, and incongruent emotional mirroring all lead to insecure/hypersensitive attachments and poor self-regulation.

Transference-Focused Psychotherapy Approach. Clarkin, Yeomans, and Kernberg (2015) subscribe to a similar etiology for Borderline Personality Disorder in their approach, called Transference-Focused Psychotherapy (TFP). Grounded in object relations theory, Clarkin et al. theorize that the specific symptoms of BPD result from a lack of identity integration and incoherence between an individual's experience and understanding of self and others. This unintegrated psychological state is called identity diffusion. Those with Borderline Personality Disorder rely on defensive strategies that distort reality, such as dissociation and splitting. The result of these cognitive distortions is that negative or aggressive affects are not seen as coming from within but from outside the self, leading to feelings of helplessness, anger, and insecurity. Transference-Focused Psychotherapy conceptualizes psychological structure as the product of early interactions with caregivers, which are internalized as the individual develops. In the case of BPD, this process is interrupted by traumatic and/or inconsistent relationships with caregivers. The absence of an integrated self leads to chronic distress and feelings of emptiness for which borderline individuals impulsively act out in an attempt to relieve their discomfort.

Biosocial Case Conceptualization

Millon and Davis (1996) view the borderline's lack of a clear, coherent sense of identity as central to the pathogenesis of this disorder. He believes that identity confusion and/or diffusion is the result of biopsychosocial factors that combine to impair a coherent sense of identity. Because of this central deficit, poor coordinated actions, overmodulated affects, poorly controlled impulses, and a failure of consistent effort result. Thus, the borderline individuals are dependent on others for protection and reassurance, and are hypersensitive to loss or separation of these supports. Based on this research, Millon (1981) and Millon and Everly (1985) contend that the borderline syndrome is essentially more severe and regressed variants of the Dependent, Histrionic, or passive-aggressive personality disorders. They describe three subtypes of this disorder.

Borderline-dependent individuals tend to exhibit a passive infantile pattern and possess family histories of low energy levels. This pattern evokes parental warmth and overprotection, and they subsequently form strong attachments and dependency to a single caregiver, which ultimately restricts their opportunity to learn the necessary skills of social independence and self-efficacy. This sets the stage for rejection by those on whom they have come to rely.

Borderline-histrionic individuals more often possess family histories characterized by high autonomic reactivity, and they exhibit hyperresponsiveness as a result of exposure to high levels of stimulation. Parental control tends to be exercised by contingent reinforcement patterns for which these children feel competent and accepted only if their behavior is explicitly approved by others, and thus they "perform" to secure support, attention, and nurturance.

Borderline-passive aggressive individuals tend to have exhibited "difficult child" (Thomas & Chess, 1977) temperaments. As irritable, difficult-to-soothe infants they likely received inconsistent responses from their caregivers, caring at times, harried and frustrated at others, and even withdraw. They might have been products of broken homes, and likely had a parent who modeled the erratic, vacillating, passive aggressive behavior they display as adults.

Cognitive-Behavioral Case Conceptualization

Three common cognitive behavioral case conceptualizations have been described: Cognitive Therapy, Schema Therapy, and Dialectical Behavior Therapy.

Cognitive Therapy. According to Beck (2015; Beck et al., 1990), three basic assumptions are noted in those with this personality disorders: "I am powerless and vulnerable"; "I am inherently unacceptable"; and "the world is dangerous and malevolent"(Arntz, 2015; Pretzer, 1988). Because of their inherent belief, they are helpless in a hostile world; without a source of security they vacillate between autonomy and dependence without being able to rely on either. In addition, borderlines tend to display "dichotomous thinking," the tendency to evaluate experiences in mutual exclusive categories, all good or all bad, success or failure, trustworthy or deceitful. The combination of dichotomous thinking and basic assumptions are the basis of borderline emotion and behavior, including acting-out, self-destructive behaviors.

Schema Therapy. Young (1990; Young et al., 2003) describes a schema-focused conceptualization of this disorder. The basic premise is that "early maladaptive schemas" develop during childhood and result in maladaptive behavior patterns that reinforce these schemas. These schemas include the abandonment/loss schema "I'll be alone forever. No one would love me or want to be close to me if they really got to know me," and the emotional deprivation schema "No one is ever there to meet my needs, to be strong for me, to care for me."

Dialectical Behavior Therapy. Linehan (1987, 2015) describes a behavioral conceptualization of this disorder. The basic premise is that inadequate emotional regulation and an invalidating environment predispose an individual to this disorder. In addition, there is an invalidating environment "in which communication of private experience is met by erratic, inappropriate, and extreme responses. In other words, the expression of private experience is not validated; instead, it is often punished, and/or trivialized" (Linehan, 1993, p. 49). Linehan (1993) contends that a poor fit between a difficult child and an invalidating environment fosters the development of this disorder. The borderline pattern is believed to be physiologically based and reinforced by experiences with significant others who discount their emotional experiences. Subsequently, borderline individuals develop little or no skill in emotion regulation. In short, the combination of intense emotional responses, inadequate emotional regulation skills, and an invalidating environment predispose an individual for unrelenting crisis, for which these individuals are unable to effectively cope.

Interpersonal Case Conceptualization

Structural Analysis of Social Behavior Approach. Benjamin's (2003a) approach to case conceptualization Structural Analysis of Social Behavior posits that individuals with Borderline Personality Disorder typically grew up in a family marked by a chaotic, soap-opera lifestyle. Without these dilemmas, life was experienced as hollow, boring, and empty. Whether these chaotic dramas were blatant or sequestered from public view, the borderline-to-be played a central role, resulting in the impulsivity, mood instability, and unpredictable characteristic of life without constancy. The developmental histories of these individuals often included traumatic abandonment experiences, the isolation of which was typically marked by physical and/or sexual abuse. This abuse-laden aloneness became inexorably linked with the notion that the borderline-to-be was a bad person. These abuse experiences "taught" the individual to shift from idealization to devaluation. And, to the extent that sexual abuse experiences were painful, they set the stage for self-mutilation, as pleasure became confused with pain during such episodes. Family norms dictated that autonomy was bad, while dependency and sympathetic misery with the family were good. As such movement toward independence, competence, or happiness elicited self-sabotage. Furthermore, young borderline individuals learned from their families that misery, sickness, and debilitation draw forth love and concern from others. The adult consequence is that the borderline-disordered individuals believe that caregivers and lovers secretly love misery. In short, there is a morbid fear of abandonment and a wish for protective nurturance particularly from a lover or caregiver. Initially, friendly dependency on the nurturer gives way to hostile control when the caregiver or lover fails to deliver enough. Borderline individuals believe that significant others secretly like dependency and neediness, and a vicious introject attacks the self in the face of any signs of success or happiness. Treatment based on this model is called Interpersonal Reconstructive Therapy (Benjamin, 2003b, 2007).

Interpersonal Psychotherapy Approach. A related interpersonal conceptualization of this disorder is an adaptation of Interpersonal Psychotherapy, which was originally developed for treatment of chronic depression or Dysthymic Disorder, called Persistent Depressive Disorder in DSM-5 (Weissman, Markowitz, & Klerman, 2000, 2007). In this adaptation, Borderline Personality Disorder is characterized as a mode-inflected condition similar to chronic depression but punctuated by sporadic, ineffective outbursts of anger and impulsivity (Markowitz, Bleiberg, Pessin, & Skodol, 2007).

Integrative Case Conceptualization

The following integrative formulation provides a biopsychosocial explanation for how this personality is likely to have developed and how it is maintained. Biologically, borderlines can be understood in terms of the three main subtypes: borderline-dependent, borderline-histrionic, and borderline-passive aggressive. The temperamental style of the borderline-dependent type is that of the passive infantile pattern (Millon, 1981). Millon hypothesized that low autonomic nervous system reactivity plus an overprotective parenting style facilitates restrictive interpersonal skills and a clinging relational style. On the other hand, the histrionic subtype was more likely to have a hyperresponsive infantile pattern. Thus, because of high autonomic nervous system reactivity and increased parental stimulation and expectations for performance, the borderline-histrionic pattern was likely to result. Finally, the temperamental style of the passive aggressive borderline was likely to have been the "difficult child" type noted by Thomas and Chess (1977). This pattern plus parental inconsistency marks the affective irritability of the borderline-passive aggressive personality.

Psychologically, borderlines tend to view themselves, others, the world, and life's purpose in terms of the following themes. They view themselves by some variant of the theme "I don't know who I am or where I'm going." In short, their identity problems involve gender, career, loyalties, and values, while their self-esteem fluctuates with each thought or feeling about their self-identity. Borderlines tend to view their world with some variant of the theme "People are great, no they are not"; "Having goals is good, no it's not"; or, "If life doesn't go my way, I can't tolerate it." As such they are likely to conclude: "Therefore keep all options open. Don't commit to anything. Reverse roles and vacillate thinking and feelings when under attack." The six defensive operations utilized by the Borderline Personality Disordered individuals are denial, splitting, primitive idealization, projective identification, omnipotence and devaluation (Shulman, 1982).

Socially, predictable patterns of parenting and environmental factors can be noted for the Borderline Personality Disorder. Parenting style differs depending on the subtype. For example, in the dependent subtype, overprotectiveness characterizes parenting, whereas in the histrionic subtype a demanding parenting style is more evident, while an inconsistent parenting style is more noted in the passive aggressive subtype. But, because the borderline personality is a syndromal elaboration and deterioration of the less severe Dependent, Histrionic, or passive aggressive personality disorders, the family of origin in the borderline subtypes of these disorders is likely to be much more dysfunctional, increasing the likelihood the child will have learned various self-defeating coping strategies. The parental injunction is likely to have been "If you grow up and leave me, bad things will happen to me [parent]."

This borderline pattern is confirmed, reinforced, and perpetuated by the following individual and systems factors. Diffuse identity, impulsive vacillation, and self-defeating coping strategies lead to aggressive acting out, which leads to more chaos, which leads to the experience of depersonalization, increased dysphoria, and/or self-mutilation to achieve some relief. This leads to further reconfirmation of their beliefs about self and the world, as well as reinforcement of the behavioral and interpersonal patterns (Sperry, 2015).

Table 5.2 summarizes the characteristic features of this disorder.

TABLE 5.2 Characteristics of Borderline Personality Disorder

Triggering Event(s)	Expectation of meeting personal goals and/or maintaining close relationships
Behavioral Style	Impulsivity Acting out behaviors Helpless, empty "void"
Interpersonal Style	Fear of abandonment Unstable, intense relationships Alternates between extremes of idealization and devaluation
Cognitive Style	Inflexible, rigid thinking Failure to learn from experience External loss of control
Affective Style	Emotionally reactive and dysregulated Inappropriate, intense anger Extreme lability of mood and affect
Attachment Style	Disorganized
Temperament	*Dependent type:* passive infantile pattern—low autonomic nervous system reactivity *Histrionic type:* hyperresponsive infantile pattern—high autonomic reactivity *Passive-Aggressive type:* "difficult" infantile pattern—affect irritability
Parental Injunction	"If you grow up, bad things will happen to me [parent]." Overprotective or demanding or inconsistent parenting
Self-View	"I don't know who I am or where I'm going." Identity problems involving gender, career, loyalties, and values Self-esteem fluctuates with current emotion
World-View	"People are great, no they're not. Having goals is good, no it's not. If life doesn't go my way, I can't tolerate it. Don't commit to anything."
Maladaptive Schemas	Abandonment, defectiveness, abuse/mistrust, emotional deprivation, social isolation, insufficient self-control
Optimal Criteria	Frantic efforts to avoid real or imagined abandonment

Assessment of Borderline Personality Disorder

Several sources of information are useful in establishing a diagnosis and treatment plan for personality disorders. Observation, collateral information, and psychological testing are important adjuncts to the patient's self-report in the clinical interview. This section briefly describes some characteristic observations that the clinician makes and the nature of the rapport likely to develop in initial encounters with specific personality-disordered individuals. Characteristic response patterns on various objective (i.e. MMPI-2 and MCMI-IV) and projective tests (i.e. Rorschach and TAT) are also described.

Interview Behavior and Rapport

Interviewing Borderline Personality-Disordered individuals presents a special challenge because of their instability and ambivalence. Instability or lability is noted in their moods, goals, and rapport with the clinician. Instability regarding rapport is handled by empathically focusing on it. This is done by directing the discussion, keeping the discussion on track, and curbing diversions and outbursts. Asking open-ended questions is preferable to seeking precise answers to closed-ended pointed questions (Ackley et al., 2011). Instability is also processed by separating it as a pathological part that needs to be explored. Since it also affects rapport, the clinician must continually acknowledge its presence and effect. The result is that these patients become less defensive and more willing to disclose, thus furthering rapport.

Dealing with ambivalence requires confronting their contradictions while at the same time exhibiting and understanding their ambivalent feelings. Therapeutic confrontation illustrates their splitting and projective identification and moderates overidealization or devaluation. It further helps these individuals realize that their ambivalence results from perceived lack of support and understanding of mother, which they allow to profoundly influence their sense of well-being (Othmer & Othmer, 2002).

Psychological Testing Data

The Minnesota Multiphasic Personality Inventory (MMPI-2), the Millon Clinical Multiaxial Inventory (MCMI-IV), the Rorschach Psychodiagnostic Test, and the Thematic Apperception Test (TAT) can be useful in diagnosing the Borderline Personality Disorder as well as the borderline personality style (Groth-Marnat, 2009).

On the MMPI-2, elevations on scales 2 (Depression), 4 (Psychopathic Deviate), and 8 (Schizophrenia) are common (Graham, 2012). Scales O (Social Introversion) and K (Correction) tend to be high, and F (Frequency) is typically low. If emotional dysregulation—particularly of anger—is prominent, scale 6 (Paranoia) will be high. Although relatively rare, 2–6 (Depression-Paranoia) 6–2 profile is associated with borderline pathology (Meyer, 1995).

On the MCMI-IV, elevation on scale C (Borderline) is most likely and concurrent elevation on scale 8A (Negativistic—passive aggressive) is also likely (Millon et al., 2015). Elevations on such clinical scales as A (Generalized anxiety disorder), H (Somatic symptom disorder), N (Bipolar I disorder), and/or D (Dysthymia Disorder) can be expected (Choca & Denburg, 1997).

On the Rorschach, illogical and confabulated combinations (i.e., "A horse's head with two sea horses growing out of his ears" for Card 10) are common (Singer & Larsen, 1981; Swiercinsky, 1985). Such responses are most likely on cards 10.9 and 2.

On the TAT, "primitive splitting" may be noted in characters that are judged as all bad, (i.e., devils), in characters wherein only one side of the personality is admitted to or portrayed, or when good-bad characteristics are juxtaposed incongruously. Separation anxiety themes, extreme portrayals of affect, and acting out rather than delayed gratification themes are not uncommon (Bellak, 1997).

Treatment Approaches and Interventions

Treatment Considerations

Included in the differential diagnosis of the Borderline Personality Disorder are these other Axis II personality disorders: Passive Aggressive, Histrionic, Dependent, and Schizotypal personality disorders. The most common Axis I syndromes associated with the personality disorder are Generalized Anxiety Disorder, Panic Disorder, and Dysthymia. In addition, other syndromes may be Brief Reactive Psychoses, Schizoaffective Disorder, Hypochondriasis, or the Dissociative Disorders, especially Psychogenic Fugue.

The Borderline Personality Disorder (DBT) may be the most common Axis II presentation seen in both the public sector and in private practice. It can be among the most difficult and frustrating conditions to treat. Clinical experience suggests that it is important to assess the individual for overall level of functioning and treatment readiness in making decisions about treatment approaches, modalities and strategies. The Borderline Personality Disorder is the most researched of all the personality disorders. To date, several randomized controlled treatment studies have been published. An evaluation of seven controlled trials of DBT concluded that DBT met the criteria for a well-established treatment according to the American Psychological Association's Division 12 Task Force for empirically supported therapies (Lynch, Trost, Salsman & Linehan, 2007).

Individual Psychotherapy

Many consider individual psychotherapy to be the cornerstone of treatment for the Borderline Personality Disorder. Although there are widely divergent opinions on the appropriateness or efficacy of the various individual psychotherapeutic approaches, there is consensus on some general principles. Waldinger (1986) describes five points of consensus on treating the borderline personality. First, the therapist must be active in identifying, confronting, and directing the patient's behaviors during sessions. Second, a stable treatment environment must be afforded in terms of setting and maintaining limits and boundaries, scheduling, payment of fees, and role expectations of patient and clinician. Third, connection between the patient's actions and feelings needs to be established. Fourth, self-destructive behavior must be made ungratifying. And, fifth, careful attention must be paid to countertransference feelings.

Regardless of the specific psychotherapeutic approach utilized, the literature indicates that treatment of the borderline patient is difficult, countertransference problems are common, and the results are uneven (Gunderson, 1989). Some borderline patients experience negative therapeutic reaction and others untoward effects of individual psychotherapy. In some instances, these patients should not be afforded individual treatment. Frances et al. (1984) offer the "no treatment option" and offer specific criteria for its use. Nevertheless, when treatment is indicated, attention to the patient's needs and expectations for treatment and efforts to match and tailor treatment are essential in maximizing treatment outcomes.

This section describes various psychodynamic, cognitive-behavioral, and interpersonal approaches.

Psychodynamic Psychotherapy Approaches

Here is a brief outline of various psychodynamic approaches to the borderline personality: psychoanalytic psychotherapy, supportive psychotherapy, and short-term dynamic psychotherapy.

Psychoanalytic Psychotherapy. There are basically two psychoanalytic opinions regarding the treatment of the borderline patients based on the role of early interpretation and the management of negative transference. One view is that confrontation must occur early in the course of treatment and that interpretation of primitive transference be made in here-and-now situations. The other view is that the early interpretation of aggressive theme is ineffective and possibly disruptive. Kernberg (1984) and Masterson (1976), among others, espouse the first view, while Chessick (1982) and Buie and Adler (1982) and others advocate the second. Nevertheless, both views agree that personality reconstruction is the goal of treatment, requiring three or more sessions a week for a minimum of four years.

Masterson (1976) and Masterson and Klein (1989) have elegantly described the psychotherapeutic process with borderline patients. Supportive psychotherapy is differentiated from reconstructive psychotherapy. The goal of reconstructive psychotherapy is to work through the abandonment depression—feelings of depression, anger and rage, fear, guilt, passivity and helplessness, emptiness, and void that follow a recent experience of separation and loss—associated with the original separation-individuation phase. This leads to the achievement of ego autonomy and the transformation of split object relations into whole object relations and the split ego into a whole ego. Three stages of psychotherapy are noted by Masterson: the testing phase in which confrontation, where the clinician utilizes communicative matching to support the patient's emerging individuation, is the principal technique, the working-through phase and the separation phase.

The expected outcome of such treatment is not only reduction in impulsive behavior and other regressive reactions to stressors, but also improved stability in interpersonal relationships. Such personality reconstruction allows the individual to function normally or on a neurotic level (Gunderson, 1989).

Mentalization Based Treatment. Based on the work of Bateman and Fonagy (2007, 2010), Mentalization Based Treatment (MBT) is intended to help borderline patients develop the capacity to accurately identify and respond to the subjective mental states of themselves and others. This includes helping patients maintain a stable sense of self and appropriate level of arousal. The originators of this treatment maintain that MBT is not a unique therapy model, but rather a therapeutic stance intended to achieve a specific goal. As such, MBT permits the use of many different techniques that may be found in other treatments.

Two important aspects of Mentalization Based Treatment are the therapeutic stance and mentalizing the transference between the patient and therapist. The therapeutic stance encompasses a number of factors, including therapist humility derived from "not knowing"; patience in understanding differences in perspective between therapist and patient; validating and accepting different perspectives; actively seeking to understand the patient's experience by asking questions; not searching for explanations; and clarifying when something is unclear.

In this method of treatment, the primary vehicle for change is the relationship between therapist and patient. Bateman and Fonagy do not focus on transference interpretation to increase the patient's insight, as is common in other psychodynamic therapy approaches. They assert that the ability to benefit from interpretation requires a level of mentalizing capacity that borderline patients typically do no possess. Rather, MBT uses the transference relationship to encourage patients to focus their attention on another individual's mind and examine their own perceptions. Mentalizing the transference is accomplished in six steps: validation of the patient's transference with the therapist; exploration of events which generated the transference; accepting enactment on the part of the therapist; collaborating with the patient to develop an interpretation; offering an alternative perspective; and monitoring the patient's reaction to the process. A randomly controlled trial comparing outpatient mentalizing-based treatment and structured clinical management for Borderline Personality Disorder found that borderline patients in the MBT group experienced a steeper reduction in problems such as suicide attempts and hospitalizations (Bateman & Fonagy, 2009).

Transference Focused Psychotherapy. Clarkin, Cain, and Livesey (2015) developed transference focused psychotherapy (TFP) with the goals of improving behavioral control, increasing self-reflection, and cultivating affect regulation skills in borderline patients. This is accomplished through the relationship between the therapist and patient, as in Mentalization Based Treatment. Transference focused psychotherapy is a highly structured, manualized, evidence-based approach to the treatment of Borderline Personality Disorder. Therapy sessions are 45 minutes long and are held two times a week. During the first year of treatment, the primary goal is to contain parasuicidal behaviors and other forms of self-destructive acting out. The ultimate goal of TFP is identity integration.

Techniques include contracting and limit-setting, along with exploring the patient's inner world in the here-and-now transference relationship. The treatment contract is especially important for this type of treatment, as this structure provides a safe context in which the patient's patterns may manifest and gives the therapist a way to explore the meaning behind deviations from the contract. In transference focused psychotherapy, interpretation is seen as the means by which integration occurs.

Supportive Psychotherapy. From a dynamic perspective, supportive psychotherapy is less intensive and regressive than psychoanalytic psychotherapy or psychoanalysis. The goals of supportive therapy with borderline individuals are principally to improve their adaptation to daily life and reduce their self-destructive responses to interpersonal stressors (Kernberg, 1984).

The basic techniques of supportive psychotherapy consist of exploring the patient's primitive defenses in the here-and-now for the purpose of helping them achieve control by nonanalytic means, and fostering a better adaptation to reality by helping them become more aware of the disorganizing affect of their defensive operations. Manifest and suppressed transferences—rather than unconscious and repressed transferences—are explored and utilized for classification of related interpersonal problems faced by the patient (Kernberg, 1984).

Such supportive psychotherapy is utilized commonly with moderate and lower functioning borderline outpatients. Typically, sessions are scheduled weekly and may continue for several years. The results of the Menninger Outcome Study suggest that supportive treatment is able to bring about the basic personality changes that were expected only from reconstructive dynamic psychotherapy (Wallerstein, 1986). So, despite Kernberg's (1984) characteristic of supportive psychotherapy as "a treatment of last resort," supportive psychotherapy is a potent intervention.

Klein (1989a) describes two types of supportive treatment for lower functioning borderlines. In the first, confrontive psychotherapy, the treatment process involves confronting resistances that maintain maladaptive behaviors until they become ego-dystonic. A therapeutic alliance takes the place of transference acting out. Treatment also involves the implementation of adaptive modes of dealing with underlying affects, such as new patterns replacing previous self-destructive behaviors and defenses. Unlike reconstructive psychotherapy, this approach does not facilitate the patient working through abandonment depression. The goals of this therapy are limited to increasing the patient's capacity to work to achieve some consistency in interpersonal relationships.

Klein (1989a) also describes an approach to "counseling" with very low functioning borderline patients. This approach is the treatment of choice for patients with a history of repeated early abuse, neglect or separation trauma, or repeated, severe psychiatric regressive episodes, or a history of repeating life-threatening suicidal or homicidal actions. The goal of this treatment is to reduce anger, anxiety, and depressive affects that persistently interfere with the patient's capacity to function adaptively. The counselor serves as an auxiliary ego for the patient and utilizes a combination of such techniques as reality testing, encouragement, direction, problem solving, and medication.

Short-Term Dynamic Psychotherapy. While it was previously assumed that borderline patients were unfit for short-term dynamic psychotherapy, it now appears that short-term and time-limited approaches have some utility with selective patients. In as few as 10 to 20 sessions, treatment can be focused on specific relational or situational problems. And, because there is such a specific focus, the likelihood of a regressive transference developing is limited. This approach may be suitable for borderline patients who present with concerns about being engulfed, overwhelmed, or too dependent. It may also be useful for those who have a history of terminating more regressive treatment. Furthermore, it may serve as a springboard for moving into long-term therapy.

Klein (1989b) describes a short-term treatment protocol for borderline patients. The goals are containment—they come to recognize, control, and contain their propensity to act out; learning—emerging affects that covered their defenses can and must be verbalized rather than acted out; and adaptation—they channel their energies associated with these affects into adaptive and sublimated behavior and expressions. This short-term approach follows Masterson's model, except that the frequency of sessions is limited and confrontation is the principal technique utilized, although clarification, interpretation, and communicative matching are sometimes needed. Sessions are scheduled only once or twice a week for a year or less, and day-to-day problems of adaptation and healthy defenses are the focus of treatment.

Research Support for Psychodynamic Interventions. There are now some empirical studies supporting the clinical value and utility of dynamically oriented therapy with Borderline Personality Disorder. In one study, individuals treated with an approach based on self-psychology and who remained in treatment for two years appeared to have profited from therapy (Meares, Stevenson, & Comerford, 1999; Stevenson & Meares, 1992). Because it was a post-hoc, naturalistic study with a waiting list control group for comparison, it cannot be certain that the results can be attributed to this dynamic approach.

A random controlled study of a psychoanalytically oriented approach to treatment in a partial hospitalization study has also been reported (Bateman & Fonagy, 1999, 2001). The treatment was intensive and extensive and consisted of weekly psychoanalytic psychotherapy, thrice-weekly group analytic psycho-therapy, weekly psychodrama and expressive therapy, and a weekly community meeting, along with mediation management. Whether positive treatment out-comes could be attributed to the specific structure and milieu of the partial hospitalization program itself, or to the psychodynamic approach utilized by therapists in the program, is unclear.

A structured, manualized approach, specifically designed for treating Borderline Personality Disorder and called "Transference Focused Psychotherapy," appears promising. This approach focuses on affect-laden themes in the current patient-therapist relationship. These include containment of self-destructive and suicidal behaviors, various ways of sabotaging treatment, and the identification and recapitulation of significant object relations patterns. This uncontrolled trial showed markedly decreased hospitalizations, day hospital treatment, and very low drop out rate (Clarkin, Foelsch, Levy, Hull, Delaney, & Kernberg, 2001).

Cognitive Behavior Therapy Approaches

Cognitive Therapy. According to Beck et al. (1990), the Cognitive Therapy approach has significant advantages over other approaches in the treatment of Borderline Personality-Disordered individuals. Basically, completion of Cognitive Therapy is possible in 18 to 30 months (Freeman et al., 1990), as compared to psychoanalytical-oriented therapies, which typically require five to seven years (Masterson, 1981).

Establishing a collaborative working relationship is the very challenging first step in the treatment process. Since trust and intimacy are major issues for these individuals, taking a collaborative, strategic approach based on guided discovery is suggested. Explicitly acknowledging and accepting the individual's difficulty in trusting the therapist, communicating clearly, assertively, and honestly, following through on agreements, and behaving in a consistently trustworthy manner provides the individual with evidence on which trust can be based. Furthermore, setting limits including specifying a treatment contract is advised. An initial focus in concrete behavioral goals is useful in reducing the impact of the borderline individual's difficulty with intimacy and trust. Many of these individuals find it less threatening to work on issues for which little introspec-tion is required, and where the focus is on behavior rather than on feelings or thoughts. Not surprisingly, a major focus in Cognitive Therapy is changing maladaptive schema. Borderline individuals here believe that the world is a dangerous place, that they are helpless, and that they are inherently flawed in a way that inevitably leads to rejection and abandonment by others. It is suggested that these beliefs must be gradually challenged by "chipping away" at them, by testing expectancies against previous experience, by developing behavioral experiences to test expectancies, and developing new competencies and coping skills. These individuals must learn to challenge dichotomous thinking both during and between sessions, as decreased dichotomous thinking often results in decreased mood liability and impulsivity. Behavioral interventions, such as self-instructional training (Meichenbaum, 1977), may be useful in further reducing self-destructive impulsive behaviors.

Noncompliance with treatment is not an uncommon problem with borderline individuals, and often the reason is fear of change. Since they assume the world is dangerous and they have a low tolerance for ambiguity, they find change— including growth in the course of treatment—threatening. Addressing change openly, examining risks and benefits, planning changes as a series of small steps, and not pressing for change too quickly are recommended. Fears about termination of treatment evoke abandonment and rejection issues, which must be carefully addressed. In summary, the Cognitive Therapy of Borderline Personality-Disordered individuals begins by developing a collaborative working relationship of trust and then focuses on modulating moods, impulses, and behavior with cognitive-behavioral methods, setting the stage so that basic schemas such as abandonment, defectiveness, incompetence, and mistrust can be modified and changed.

In line with Turkat's (1990) formulation that the basic issue for borderlines is problem-solving deficiencies, Turkat proposes a treatment methodology involving several strategies. They are basic problem-solving training, concept formation training, categorization management, and processing speed management.

Dialectical Behavior Therapy. The defining feature of this treatment approach is its emphasis on dialectics, the reconciliation of opposites. The basic dialectic for therapists working with DBT clients is accepting their behaviors, thoughts, and affects in the moment while simultaneously encouraging them to change. Accordingly, DBT treatment requires "moment to moment changes in the use of supportive acceptance versus confrontation and change strategies. This emphasis on acceptance as a balance to change flows directly from the integrative of a perspective drawn from Eastern (Zen) practice with Western Psychological practice" (Linehan, 1993, p. 19).

Linehan (1993, 2015) specified four primary modes of treatment in DBT: individual therapy; group-based skills training, telephone contact, and therapist consultation. Group therapy and other modes of treatment may be added at the discretion of the therapist.

The individual therapist is the primary therapist and the main work of therapy is carried out in the individual therapy sessions. Individual therapy is conceptualized as having three stages: beginning, middle, and end (Marra, 2005). Essential components of individual therapy from a DBT perspective include: dialectical analysis and coaching clients to think dialectically about their own situation; validation of the client's feelings, thoughts and experiences; balancing emotion-focused and solution-focused coping; prompting improved shifting of attention from internal to external cues; teaching new psychological coping skills, and non-pejorative interpretation of the client's behavior and affect.

Skills training is usually carried out in a group context, ideally by someone other than the individual therapist. In the skills training groups clients are taught skills considered relevant to the particular problems of personality-disordered individuals. There are four groups of skills: core mindfulness skills, interpersonal effectiveness skills, emotion modulation skills, and distress tolerance skills. Each of these skills targets key style/temperament overmodulations. However, it is possible to accomplish skills training in the context of individual therapy with select clients (Marra, 2005).

Telephone contact with the therapist after hours is offered, not as psychotherapy but rather to help and support in clients to find alternatives to self-injury and for relationship repair when the client believes she damaged her relationship with her therapist and wants to rectify it prior to the next session.

DBT therapists are encouraged to participate regularly in therapist consultation groups. These groups provide both emotional support for therapists dealing with difficult clients, as well as for ongoing training in DBT methods.

Following an initial period of pre-treatment involving assessment, commitment and orientation to therapy, DBT consists of three stages of treatment.

1   This stage focuses on reducing parasuicidal and suicidal behaviors, therapy interfering behaviors and behaviors that comprise quality of life. It also focuses on developing the necessary skills to resolve these problems. Skills training is usually carried out in a group context, ideally by someone other than the individual therapist. In the skills training groups clients are taught skills considered relevant to the particular problems of personality-disordered individuals. There are four groups of skills: core mindfulness skills, interpersonal effectiveness skills, emotion modulation skills, and distress tolerance skills.

2   This stage deals primarily with difficult problems of living, including treatment of posttraumatic stress-related issues when present. Much of this work is done in individual sessions.

3   The focus of this stage is on self-esteem and individual treatment goals. The targeted behaviors of each stage are brought under control before moving on to the next phase. In particular, posttraumatic stress-related problems such as those related to childhood sexual abuse are not dealt with directly until stage 1 has been successfully completed. Therapy at each stage is focused on the specific targets for that stage, which are arranged in a definite hierarchy of relative importance. These include: decreasing suicidal behaviors, decreasing therapy interfering behaviors, decreasing behaviors that interfere with the quality of life, increasing behavioral skills, decreasing behaviors related to posttraumatic stress, improving self-esteem, and individual targets negotiated with the client.

The core strategies in DBT are "validation" and "problem solving." Attempts to facilitate change are surrounded by interventions that validate clients' behavior and responses in relation to the client's current life situation, and that demonstrate an understanding of their difficulties and suffering. Problem solving focuses on the establishment of necessary skills. Other treatment modalities include contingency management, cognitive therapy exposure based therapies, and medication. Because parasuicidal, suicidal, and other forms of acting-out behaviors are common with BPD individuals, contingency management is commonly employed in each stage of treatment.

The provision of DBT therapy is easier to accomplish in an inpatient, partial hospitalization, or residential treatment setting than in private practice. The reason is that, as described by Linehan (1993), DBT is best implemented with a treatment team in which one therapist provides psychosocial skill training, another provides individual therapy, others can provide a consultation function, and the therapists have access to a therapist consultation group for support.

Marra (2005) has offered suggestions for adapting DBT treatment in private practice settings. While he recommends that skills training be provided by another therapist, he offers guidelines when that is not possible. Nevertheless, he encourages therapists in private practice who want to use DBT to have regular contact with a psychotherapy consultant as a substitute for involvement in a therapist consultation group. The purpose of such consultation is to clarify diagnosis, treatment plans and specific interventions with another professional who can offer a fresh perspective, confront the therapist's interpretation of data and situations, and warn of potential boundary violations.

Cognitive Coping Therapy. This is an active, directive, didactic, and structured cognitive behavioral approach for treating personality-disordered individuals (Sharoff, 2002). It is a complete and self-contained approach to treatment which begins with assessing an individual's coping skills—in terms of skill chains, subskills, and microskills—and then increasing skill competence in targeted areas as needed. Five key skill areas with representative treatment modalities include: *cognitive skills*—problem solving, self-instruction training, and self-management; *emotion skills*—emotional containment and compartmentalization; *perceptual skills* —perspective taking, thought stopping, and psychological distance taking; *physiological skills*—meditation and relaxation training; and *behavior skills*— communication and assertiveness training. Sharoff (2002) describes a detailed protocol, and case example, for using this structured approach with Borderline Personality Disorder.

Schema Therapy. Schema Therapy is an elaboration of cognitive therapy that has been developed by Young (1994, 1999; Young et al., 2003) specifically for personality disorders, and other difficult individual and couples problems. Schema Therapy involves identifying maladaptive schemas and planning specific strategies and interventions. Four main strategies are cognitive, experiential, behavioral, and the therapeutic relationship itself. Cognitive restructuring, modification of maladaptive schemas, is an important cognitive strategy, but is combined with imagery exercises, empathic confrontation, homework assignments, and "limited reparenting," i.e., a form of corrective emotional experience (Young, 1999; Young et al., 2003).

Maladaptive schemas typically associated with Borderline Personality Disorder are: *abandonment,* i.e., the belief that significant others will not or cannot provide reliable and stable support; *defectiveness*—the belief that one is defective, bad, unwanted, or inferior in important respects; *mistrust/abuse*—the belief that others will abuse, humiliate, cheat, lie, manipulate, or take advantage; *emotional*—the belief that one's desire for emotional support will not be met by others; *social isolation*—the belief that one is alienated, different from others, or not part of any group; and *insufficient self-control*— the belief that one is incapable of self-control and frustration tolerance (Bernstein, 2002). Young et al. (2003) provide a detailed treatment protocol for utilizing the schema-focused approach with Borderline Personality Disorder.

Other Cognitive-Behavioral Interventions. Smucker (1999) describes a cognitive behavioral approach that incorporates guided imagery to focus directly on images and affects associated with early childhood abuse in borderline individuals. This approach developed out of Smucker's experience working with severely traumatized borderline individuals who often met criteria for Post-Traumatic Stress Disorder and had failed in previous treatments.

Interpersonal Approach

Benjamin (2003a, 2007) has written extensively about this approach. In her view, psychotherapeutic interventions with Borderline Personality-Disordered individuals are best planned and evaluated in terms of whether they enhance collaboration, facilitate learning about maladaptive patterns and their roots, block these patterns, enhance the will to change, or effectively encourage new patterns.

Benjamin offers a number of observations on facilitating collaboration. She insists that therapists offer these individuals a contract for strength building rather than in enabling regression. A collaboration based on strength building must emphasize in sessions as well as in phone calls or in the clinic lobby that the mutual goal is to build on strengths so these individuals can pull themselves back together. The collaboration must be against "it," their destructive pattern(s). Healthy collaboration further requires that transference and countertransference disasters be avoided through firm physical and verbal boundaries. Benjamin cautions that the treatment approach she advocates is not appropriate for individuals who are unable to agree to a contract in strength building.

Borderline individuals need to learn to recognize that perceived abandonment sets off a chain of self-destructive patterns. These individuals are likely to relinquish self-mutilation, self-sabotage, and homicidal or suicidal acting out if they can "divorce" their internalized abusive attachment figures. Essentially, they must give up the desire to be affirmed by these internalized representations. This occurs by developing a dislike of those figures, or by developing a superseding attachment to someone more constructive, such as the clinician. Once these tasks are achieved, the focus of treatment shifts to facilitating new learning. The basic goal is learning how to give and take autonomy while remaining friendly.

Interpersonal Reconstructive Therapy (IRT). IRT was developed by Benjamin (2003b, 2007) for the treatment of this disorder. Like many other treatments for Borderline Personality Disorder, IRT conceptualizes the problem as one of inadequate attachment to caregivers in early development. Problem patterns are categorized according to the Structural Analysis of Social Behavior (SASB), a method developed by Benjamin. Behaviors are described according to the focus (on other, self, or self as if by other), affiliation (placed on a love-hate axis), and interdependence (placed on an emancipate-control axis). The borderline patient's behavior towards the therapist is classified in the IRT system as either "Regressive Loyalist," or "Red," when the patient is engaging in old, destructive patterns; or "Growth Collaborator," or "Green," when the patient responds to the therapist in new, effective ways. Red and Green remain in conflict throughout the course of treatment until finally the Growth Collaborator becomes dominant in the patient's mind. There are five stages in Interpersonal Reconstructive Therapy: establishing collaboration between therapist and patient; learning about old patterns of behavior, such as where they originate and what purpose they serve; blocking destructive patterns; increasing the will to change; and learning new patterns. As with other treatments with personality reconstruction as the goal, IRT is a long-term form of therapy that may span multiple years.

Group Therapy

Data on the efficacy of group therapy for the treatment of personality disorders is rather "soft." There are many case reports and even a few controlled studies, but no randomized clinical trials, except for the Borderline Personality Disorder. There are numerous case reports and clinical trials, and even one randomized clinical trial reported on group treatment with Borderline Personality-Disordered individuals. What's more, there is general consensus that group therapy, under specified conditions, has enormously therapeutic efficacy. This section will review both dynamic and behavioral group approaches as well as highlight some representative research studies.

The psychodynamic group literature on borderline personality begins in the 1950s. There is general consensus that group dynamic therapy can be a useful adjunct to individual dynamic therapy, but that it cannot be the only treatment (Day & Semrad, 1971; Horowitz, 1980; Hulse, 1958; Slavson, 1964). Horowitz (1980) cautions that borderline patients require individual psychotherapy to support them throughout group engendered stress and to integrate the affects the groups provokes in them. Furthermore, without individual psychotherapy premature termination from group therapy is likely. On the other hand, Pines (1975) contends that concurrent dynamic individual psychotherapy is not necessary, because the group process of itself is a potent holding environment capable of containing primitive impulses and projections. Horowitz (1977) also contends that the individual psychotherapist not function as the group therapist in order to reduce the possibility of jealousy and fantasies of favoritism among other group members.

Most writing on dynamic group therapy for borderline patients prefer heterogeneous to homogenous groups. They insist that borderline patients are more effectively treated in groups consisting of higher functioning individuals with neuroses and other personality disorders (Day & Semrad, 1971; Horowitz, 1977; Stone & Weissman, 1984). There is, however, outcome research that supports the use of homogeneous groups wherein all patients have Borderline Personality Disorder diagnoses (Finn & Shakir, 1990; Linehan et al., 1991; O'Leary, Tunrer, Gardner & Cowdry, 1991).

The advantages of dynamic group therapy include "dilution of intense transference" (Horowitz, 1980), which results from the presence of multiple transferential objects, instead of the single all-encompassing individual clinician. Rage is instead diluted and directed toward other group members. Borderline patients also find it easier to accept feedback and confrontation from group peers than from a therapist. Groups also provide many opportunities to understand and master such borderline defenses as splitting and projective identification.

There are some disadvantages and difficulties with group treatment of borderline patients. First, these patients may be easily scapegoated because of their primitive manner of expression. Second, they may feel deprived amidst the competition of other group members for the group leader's nurturance. And, they may maintain a certain distance in the group because of their privacy attachment to their individual psychotherapist (Gabbard, 2014).

Dynamically oriented groups with borderlines tend to span the continuum from ego psychology (Finn & Shakir, 1990; O'Leary et al., 1991) to self-psychology (Harwood, 1992).

Behavioral group therapies for borderline patients focus less on underlying explanations from the symptomatic behavior, and more helping these patients acquire the specific skills necessary to control their affects, reduce their cognitive distortions and projective identifications, and find alternatives to self-destructive behaviors. Linehan (1987, 1993, 2015) provides a manual-guided strategy for the treatment of self-destructive behavior and impulsivity called "dialectical behavior therapy." Although geared primarily to chronically parasuicidal borderline females, the treatment strategies and interventions have applicability to higher functioning individuals. The group session employs didactic, shell training, and behavioral rehearsal techniques directed at dependency and other interpersonal patterns, as well as improving affect tolerance. These twice-weekly sessions for one year are complemented with weekly individual counseling.

There is some noteworthy research with borderlines in group treatment that will be briefly highlighted. Nehls (1991; Nehls & Diamond, 1993) reports process and outcome data on group therapy of borderline patients in homogeneous treatment format. The group format was highly structured, though group members defined their own treatment goals. Patient outcomes included decreased depression and hostility, which was associated largely with two interventions: providing and seeking information. Dick and Wooff (1986) reported data on a time-limited dynamic group therapy with heterogeneous groups containing a number of borderline patients. The group met daily for 12 weeks. The one year post-group follow-up showed an 82 percent reduction in the use of psychiatric services compared to a control group of untreated patients. Three-year follow-up showed the gains had been maintained. Finally, Linehan et al. (1991) examined parasuicidal female borderline patients randomly assigned to dialectical behavior therapy groups or to traditional community treatment for a one-year period. Those in behavioral groups had fewer incidents of parasuicide, were more likely to remain in individual therapy, and had fewer inpatient psychiatric days as compared to those in traditional treatment. Follow up measures two years after this initial study, as well as subsequent studies, indicated that DBT was an effective treatment and gains were maintained over time (Linehan, 1993, 2015). Another randomly controlled trial in which DBT was compared to general psychiatric management found that both forms of treatment were equally effective in treating borderline personality disorder (McMain et al., 2009).

A manual-guided approach called Relationship Management Psychotherapy is a time-limited group approach. This form of therapy allows borderline patients to choose their own treatment and requires those who threaten self-harm or act in aggressive ways to be expelled from the inpatient program for 24 hours. It has been compared with open-ended individual dynamic psychotherapy in a randomized clinical trial (Clarkin, Marziali, & Munroe-Blum, 1991). Hoch, O'Reilly and Carscadden (2006) compared the mean annual outcome rates for 27 patients consecutively enrolled in a relationship management therapy program from 1998 to 2000. They found significant reductions in the use of restraint, staff observation, self-harm, and days of inpatient treatment.

Marital and Family Therapy

Families of borderline patients often exhibit severe pathology, which may be of etiological significance. Parents of borderline patients have high incidence of affective disorders, alcoholism, antisocial personality disorder, and Borderline Personality Disorder or traits. The parental relationship is usually characterized by neglect and overprotectiveness. Family therapy can be useful, and in some instances necessary, in maintaining borderline patients in outpatient psychotherapy. This is particularly the case when borderline patients remain financially and/or emotionally dependent on their parents.

Family therapy with borderlines has been developed along at least three theoretical lines. The first is the psychodynamic, particularly in terms of object relations and systems theory. Everett, Halperin, Volgy and Wissler (1989) have the most complete discussion of this approach in their book *Treating the Borderline Family: A Systemic Approach*. They specify the following treatment goals: (1) increasing the family's ability to reduce the systemic splitting process; (2) increasing family members' capacities for owning split-off objects and moving toward interacting with others as a "whole person"; (3) reducing oppositional and stereotypic behavior of all family members; (4) "resetting" external boundary for both unclear and intergenerational systems; (5) "resetting" internal boundary for spousal, parent-child, and sibling subtypes; and (6) permitting a clearer alliance between the parents and limiting reciprocal intrusiveness of children and parents. Five treatment strategies for accomplishing these goals in an outpatient family treatment setting are: developing and maintaining a therapeutic structure; reality testing in the family; interactional disengagement; intervening in the intergenerational system; and solidification of the marital alliance and sibling subsystem.

Another treatment orientation is the structural family approach developed by Minuchin (1974). Schane and Kovel (1988) describe severe borderline pathology in terms of a spousal subsystem that is internally overinvolved and contemporarily distant and disengaged from the family system. In effect, borderline females have a systems equivalent of object splitting wherein family subsystems are organized around dichotomous extremes: collusion and sabotage; loyalty and scapegoating; inclusion and rejection; nurturance and neglect; and symbiosis and abandonment. It is this structural pattern of family interaction that is the focus of systemic change. Lachkar (1992) provides an extensive discussion of an integrated object relations and self-psychology approach to the marital treatment of the borderline patient. She provides a detailed treatment protocol and several case reports illustrating this method.

A third option is the Relationship Enhancement Therapy approach for borderline families and couples. Relationship Enhancement was developed by Guerney (1977) and integrates social skills training, psychodynamic principles, and interpersonal therapy techniques. Since borderline patients have major deficits in self-differentiation and communication, Relationship Enhancement's focus on skill building in some areas seems promising with couple and family settings, particularly for mild to moderately dysfunctional borderline patients (Harman & Waldo, 2001; Waldo & Harman, 1993). The clinician functions largely as a coach to develop the necessary relational skills, usually in two-hour sessions. Waldo and Harmon (1993) report a case of time-limited intervention that was successful. A 12-month follow-up showed that the changes had been maintained. These authors also describe and illustrate the use of two therapists working conjointly with couples in which one partner presents with Borderline Personality Disorder (Waldo & Harman, 1998). The fundamental principles of relationship enhancement therapy are further discussed in Accordino, Keat, and Guerney

(2003), as well as a case study of an adolescent with serious mental illness and substance dependence.

Lachkar (1999) offers additional insight into the treatment of couples in which one partner has a borderline personality structure while the other partner presents with a narcissistic pattern. Solomon (1999) also addresses the treatment of the borderline-narcissistic couple from a somewhat different psychoanalytic perspective.

Medication

Medication is commonly used in the treatment of this disorder. Usually the treatment targets are affective instability, interpersonal sensitivity, impulsivity, aggressivity, transient psychotic episodes, and self-harming behavior. Lithium and carbamazepine have targeted affective instability, while serotonergic agents have been effective with impulsivity and aggressivity. Serotonergic agents, like fluoxetine and sertraline, are effective for reducing the interpersonal sensitivity and reactivity (Reich, 2002). For those with rejection sensitivity, and a history of good treatment compliance, a trial of an MAOI (monoamine oxidase inhibitor) can be considered if all other approaches have failed. Serotonergic agents have some efficacy in lower functioning histrionic individuals who exhibit impulsivity and affective instability (Reich, 2002). Transient psychotic episodes, including mild thought disorders and dissociation, are best addressed with atypical antipsychotics instead of traditional neuroleptics, which have the risk of tardive dyskinesia. Finally, for self-harming behavior, trials of SSRIs have been helpful. If not, an adjunctive trial of naltrexone can be considered, if necessary (Reich, 2005).

In recent years, quetiapine (Seroquel) has become the most commonly prescribed medication for Borderline Personality Disorder probably because it reduces various symptoms such as anxiety, presumably because it has a sedating effect. It is an antipsychotic medication that is generally well tolerated. That means it has few adverse effects and specifically has low potential for extrapyramidal (tremor and stiffness) symptoms. However, it can cause weight gain (Diamond, 2009). Very well-designed research has been reported that confirms what clinicians have known for some time. In a randomized controlled trial it was found that low-dose quetiapine (150 mg/day) was effective in reducing the overall severity of symptoms in those with Borderline Personality Disorder. Most improvement was noted in verbal and physical aggression, but less on impulsivity and depression (Black et al., 2014).

There are some potential complications or disadvantages with pharmacotherapy in the treatment of borderline individuals. First is the matter of noncompliance related either to side effects or to secondary gain. Medications can serve as leverage to control the prescribing clinician or other caregivers. Demands for frequent changes in dosage or type of medication, overdosing, and failure to take the medication prescribed are all means of transference acting out. Second, borderline individuals may appear to others to have improved from medication but report they feel worse, or vice versa. Gunderson (1989) suggested that this apparent paradox may ensue to the extent that the individual believes that symptomatic improvement will result in undesirable consequences, such as loss or abandonment of dependent gratifications.

Combined and Integrated Treatment Approaches

There is considerable consensus that combined treatment is essential, or at least preferable, for borderline pathology, given its severity and apparent treatment resistance. Clearly, differences exist between the prognosis and treatability of the high functioning borderline (i.e., GAF over 65) and the low functioning borderline (i.e., GAF below 45). Reports of treatment success using only traditional individual psychoanalytic psychotherapy may be possible with the highest functioning borderline individual, but are not likely with lower functioning borderline individuals. In line with the basic premise of this book, the lower the patient's functioning and motivation and readiness for treatment, the more treatment must be integrated and combined.

The most common recommendation for combined treatment is to prescribe both individual therapy and group therapy. There is currently no consensus on which theoretical approaches to combine or whether both should be combined or sequenced. The earliest recommendation of combined treatment was by Tacbacnik (1965), who advocated concurrent dynamic individual psychotherapy and dynamic group therapy. On the other hand, Horowitz (1977, 1980) advocates sequencing dynamic group and individual therapy in which the group experience prepares the patient to productively utilize individual therapy. Clarkin et al. (1991) also recommend combined individual and group modalities, but favor individual behavior treatment with long-term manual-guided group treatment.

Others recommend combining individual therapy and family therapy. These include Kernberg (1984), who describes the indications for concurrent as well as sequential utilization of these modalities.

Berger (1987) recommends combined psychotherapy and pharmacotherapy because these individuals are difficult to treat with only one modality. He notes that combined treatment can be complicated by the borderline's tendency to idealize one treatment and negate the other. Koenigsberg (1993) offers a very thoughtful review of combining medications and psychotherapy, highlighting the indications and contraindications for this treatment decision. He also describes the complications inherent in combined treatment strategy but believes these can be addressed by special structuring of treatment, attention to countertransference issues, and vigilance for splitting. Koenigsberg contends that combining medication and psychotherapy has considerable value for seriously symptomatic patients, those prone to treatment noncompliance or to intractable affective storms and psychotic regression. Bellino and associates (Bellino, Rinaldi, & Bogetto, 2010) found that combined therapy with antidepressants and interpersonal psychotherapy was more effective than single pharmacotherapy alone in the treatment of borderline patients. Further examination by these researchers revealed that patients with more severe psychopathology had a better chance to improve with this combined treatment (Bellino, Bozzatello, & Bogetto, 2015).

Lazarus (1985), the developer of Multimodal Therapy, endorses the combined use of several modalities, concurrently or sequential, for a variety of difficult patients, including borderline individuals. Vaccani (1989) describes treating the alcohol-abusing Borderline Personality Disorder with psychotherapy, family therapy, group therapy, and Alcoholics Anonymous meetings. Nehls and Diamond (1993) describe the modalities for lower functioning borderlines in a community-based setting. The modalities that are coordinated and continuous include: individual therapy, group therapy, medication, drug and alcohol services, psychosocial rehabilitation, crisis intervention, and crisis houses.

It is now generally accepted that an integrated treatment model is best suited to address personality disorders (Clarkin, Cain, & Livesley, 2015; Livesley, 2012). While there exist some significant differences between the various treatment models developed for borderline personality disorder, certain elements common to all of them that contribute to treatment success have been identified. Perhaps the most important of these is the cultivation and maintenance of a positive therapeutic relationship between therapist and patient. This comprises five main elements regardless of orientation or model: cultivating emotional awareness; structuring treatment; being responsive; supervision or team involvement and support; and exploring ruptures in the relationship (McMain, Boritz, & Leybman, 2015).

6

DEPENDENT PERSONALITY DISORDER

Individuals with dependent personalities present with a pervasive pattern of dependency and submissiveness. They tend to be excessively passive, insecure, self-sacrificing, and nonassertive individuals who become overly dependent on one or more persons for guidance and support (Bornstein, 2012). Despite the fact that it is one of the least studied personality disorders (Simon, 2009), treatment of the Dependent Personality Disorder can be highly effective and successful.

This chapter describes a framework for the assessment and effective treatment of this disorder. It includes sections on diagnosis, psychological assessment, case conceptualization, and treatment interventions. It begins with background information on the disorder as well as a DSM-5 description and a prototypic description of this disorder. The section on case conceptualization provides five common clinical formulations of this disorder: psychodynamic, biosocial, cognitive-behavioral, interpersonal, and an integrative conceptualization of this disorder. Several treatment approaches, modalities, and intervention strategies are also described. These include individual psychotherapy, group therapy, marital and family therapy, medication, and integrative and combined treatment.

Description of the Dependent Personality Disorder

The Dependent Personality Disorder can be recognized by the following descriptors and characteristics: style vs. disorder; triggering event; behavioral style, interpersonal style, cognitive style, affective style, attachment style, and optimal diagnostic criterion.

Style vs. Disorder. The dependent personality can be thought of as spanning a continuum from healthy to pathological, with the dependent personality style

TABLE 6.1 Comparison of Dependent Personality Style and Disorder

Personality Style	*Personality Disorder*
When making decisions they are comfortable seeking out the opinions and advice of others, but ultimately make their own decisions.	Unable to make everyday decisions without an excessive amount of advice or reassurance from others; allows others to make the most of their important decision.
Carefully promote harmony with important persons in their life through being polite, agreeable, and tactful.	Agrees with people even when they believe they are wrong, because of fear of being rejected.
Although they respect authority and prefer the role of team member, they can initiate and complete tasks on their own.	Has considerable difficulty initiating projects or doing things on their own.
Thoughtful and good at pleasing others. Occasionally, they will endure personal discomfort in accomplishing a good deed for the key people in their lives.	Volunteers to do things that are unpleasant or demeaning in order to get other people to like them.
Tend to prefer the company of one or more individuals to being alone.	Feels uncomfortable or helpless when alone, or goes to great lengths to avoid being alone.
Tend to be strongly committed to relationships and work hard to sustain them.	Feels devastated or helpless when close relationships end, and frequently preoccupied with fears of being abandoned.
Can take corrective action in response to criticism.	Easily hurt by criticism or disapproval.

at the healthy end and the Dependent Personality Disorder at the pathological end. Table 6.1 compares and contrasts differences between the dependent style and the disorder.

The two case examples following further illustrate differences between the Dependent Personality Disorder—Ms. C.—and the dependent personality style—Mr. B.

Triggering Event. The typical situation, circumstance, or event that most likely triggers or activates the characteristic maladaptive response of the Dependent Personality Disorder (Othmer & Othmer, 2002), as noted in behavioral, interpersonal, cognitive, and affective styles, is "expectations of self-reliance and/or being alone."

Behavioral Style. The behavioral style of dependent personalities is characterized by docility, passivity, and nonassertiveness.

CASE STUDY: DEPENDENT PERSONALITY DISORDER

Ms. C. is a 38-year-old, single woman with panic symptoms that had begun approximately three years earlier. Once the panic attacks began, Ms. C. moved back into her parents' home and has become nearly totally housebound, fearing that "panic could strike any time." She described both of her parents as caring, concerned, and "my best friends," on whom she is overly reliant. She looks to them to support her financially and emotionally, and to make decisions for her. Ms. C. has also become progressively habituated to the Valium that she was prescribed for panic symptoms.

CASE STUDY: DEPENDENT PERSONALITY STYLE

Mr. B. has been a social worker at a foster care agency for the past seven years. He finds his job fulfilling and is well liked by the other staff members, as well as the children and prospective parents with whom he works. He is a very concerned, caring, and gentle person. A year earlier, he had begun dating Sandra, one of the pediatricians who consults to the agency. Their relationship has been happy and fulfilling for both of them, probably because of Mr. B.'s efforts. He cannot get over the fact that a doctor would be interested in being with him, and he expresses his appreciation in numerous ways. He cannot spend enough time with her, or do enough things for her. He idealizes her, makes every effort to make her feel comfortable and secure, and regularly seeks her opinions and advice. Yet he insists that he has a mind of his own; after much deliberation and soul-searching, he bought an expensive sports car even though Sandra thought it was extravagant.

Interpersonal Style. In interpersonal relations, they tend to be pleasing, self-sacrificing, and clinging, and constantly require the assurance of others. Their compliance and reliance on others lead to a subtle demand that others assume responsibility for major areas of their lives.

Cognitive Style. The cognitive style of dependent personalities is characterized by suggestibility. They easily adopt a Pollyannaish attitude toward life. Furthermore, they tend to minimize difficulties, and because of their naiveté are readily persuadable and others easily take advantage of them. In short, this style of thinking is uncritical and unperceptive.

Affective Style. Their emotional or affective style is characterized by insecurity and anxiousness. Because they lack self-confidence, they experience considerable discomfort at being alone. They tend to be preoccupied with the fear of abandonment and of the disapproval of others. Their mood tends to be one of anxiety or fearfulness, as well as having a somber or sad quality.

Attachment Style. The preoccupied attachment dimension is characterized by a sense of personal unworthiness and a positive evaluation of others. These individuals tend to be very externally oriented in their self-definitions. This Preoccupied Attachment Style is common in individuals with Dependent Personality Disorder (Lyddon & Sherry, 2001).

Optimal Diagnostic Criterion. Of all the diagnostic criteria for the Dependent Personality Disorder, one has been found to be the most useful in diagnosing this disorder. The belief is that, by beginning with this criterion, the clinician can test for the presence or absence of the criterion and more quickly diagnose the personality disorder (Allnutt & Links, 1996). The optimal criterion for this disorder is: needs others to assume responsibility for most major areas of his or her life.

DSM-5 Description

Individuals with this personality disorder are characterized by an excessive and unremitting need to be cared for and cling to others because of their fear of separation. They constantly seek the advice and reassurance of others when making decisions. More than anything, they want others to take responsibility for most major areas of their lives. Not surprisingly, they seldom express disagreement with others for fear they will lose their support and approval. Because they lack confidence in their own judgment and ability, they have difficulty starting projects and doing things on their own. These individuals will even engage in actions that are difficult and unpleasant in order to receive support and caring from others. Because of unrealistic fears of being unable to take care of themselves, they feel helpless or uncomfortable when faced with being alone. When a close relationship is about to end, they immediately seek out another caring and supportive relationship. Finally, they become preoccupied with fears of being left to take care of themselves (American Psychiatric Association, 2013).

Prototypic Description

A prototype is a brief description that captures the essence of how a particular disorder commonly presents. Prototypic descriptions are useful and convenient and clinicians commonly rely on them rather than lists of behavioral criteria or core beliefs (Westen, 2012). Here is a common prototypic description of the Dependent Personality Disorder: These individuals feel inadequate, weak, and needy. They don't take very good care for themselves. They find it nearly impossible to make their own decisions, and they don't feel good about being alone. Their neediness makes them submissive and subservient. So they are more than willing to put others' needs and views above their own. Basically, they will do whatever it takes to get others to care for them, to give them affection, and give direction to their lives (Frances, 2013).

Prevalence

Prevalence of this disorder has been estimated at between 0.49 and 0.6 percent in the general population (American Psychiatric Association, 2013). In clinical settings, estimates are that it is found in 1.4 to 47 percent of patients (Torgersen, 2012).

Conceptualizations of the Dependent Personality Disorder

Psychodynamic Case Conceptualization

Early psychoanalytic writers posited that dependent personalities were formed in the oral phase of psychosexual development. Contemporary formulations view the development of dependency as a function of parental—particularly maternal—overinvolvement and intrusiveness throughout all phases of development. These individuals often present histories of parental reward for maintaining loyalty, and subtle parental rejection whenever they attempted separation and independence. They would react with crying and clinging behavior, while being immobilized by fear and dread of abandonment. Their submissive stance is the result of multiply determined unconscious factors. Gabbard (1990) notes that dependent personalities typically seek to be cared for by others because of their underlying anxiety, which often masks aggression. Dependency thus may be viewed as a compromise formation defending against hostility. Furthermore, dependent behavior can also be used to avoid reactivation of past traumatic experiences.

Biosocial Case Conceptualization

Millon and Everly (1985) speculate that dependent personalities exhibited fearful, withdrawing, or sad temperaments as infants. Accordingly, such behaviors were likely to elicit overly protective behavior from caretakers. Millon (1981) notes that these dependent individuals tend to have ectomorphic (thin and frail) or endomorphic (heavy and cumbersome) body types, which contribute to low energy thresholds and a lack of physical vigor.

Environmental factors such as parental overprotection, competitive deficits, and social-role programming appear to interact with these biological predispositions, resulting in the dependent personality pattern. Parental overprotection often precludes the development of autonomous coping behavior, such as assertiveness, problem solving, and decision making. Hend, Baker, and Williamson

(1991) report that families of individuals with Dependent Personality Disorders are characterized by low expressiveness and high control, as compared with families in clinical and normal control groups, which is indicative of the pervasive reinforcement of dependent behavior. Outside the parental relationship, these children often experience social humiliation and doubts about their efficacy in interpersonal situations. Through such repeated experiences, they learned, particularly as adolescents, that it is better to remain submissive than to strive to be competitive. Furthermore, cultural and social norms seem to reinforce passive dependent behavior patterns among women and endomorphically and ecto-morphically built men. Finally, dependent personality patterns are self-perpetuating through reinforcement of dependent behaviors; avoidance of growth-promoting activities, that is, those that might be challenging, threatening, or anxiety-producing; and self-detraction, by which they not only convince others that they are inferior, defective, and incapable of independence, but also themselves (Millon & Davis, 1996).

Cognitive-Behavioral Case Conceptualization

According to Beck (2015), the dependent personality is rooted in basic assumptions about the self and the world. Typically, they view themselves as inadequate, weak, helpless, incompetent, and needy. They view others as strong, nurturing, supportive, and able to care for them. Related beliefs include needing the assistance of strong and caring individuals in order for them to survive and to make decisions for them. They also are convinced that they must remain close to and not displease such individuals. Not surprisingly, such beliefs are reflected in their main strategy or pattern of subordinating themselves and pleasing others (Beck, 2015; Brauer & Reinecke, 2015).

Therefore these individuals are likely to conclude that they must rely on someone else who is stronger and more adequate to take care of and protect them. For this security they pay a considerable price. First, they must relinquish responsibility and subordinate their own needs. Second, they must relinquish opportunities to learn such skills as assertiveness, decision making, and problem solving. Finally, they must contend with fears of rejection and abandonment if their clinging relationship ends. The main cognitive distortion of such dependent individuals is dichotomous thinking with respect to independence (Brauer & Reinecke, 2015). For example, they believe that they are both totally connected to another and dependent or totally alone and independent, with no gradation between. Also, they believe that things are either "right" or "wrong," and that there is either "absolute success" or "absolute failure." Another cognitive dis-tortion observed among dependent personalities is "catastrophizing," particularly regarding relationships. Common cognitive distortions are: "I never would be able to do that," "I can't," and "I'm too dumb to do that."

Turkat (1990) suggests a behavioral formulation for this disorder that centers on a pervasive fear of decision making and an inability to act assertively. Since these individuals have not previously learned either of these skills, these become basic therapeutic tasks, after their overwhelming anxiety is effectively managed.

Interpersonal Case Conceptualization

According to Benjamin (2003a), persons with Dependent Personality Disorder experienced sufficient caring and attention as infants to enable them to bond with others. They also learned to rely on others, and expect that others will be there to meet their needs. However, the parents of potential dependent-disordered individuals did not wean this level of nurturing when it was developmentally appropriate to do so. Subsequently, these individuals learned compliant dependent behavior, as well as to avoid autonomy at all costs. As a result, they developed poor self-concepts by default, and as adults continue to view themselves as inadequate and overly tolerant of the blaming of others. Because they have not learned to take care of self and life's demands, they must depend on others. Since they have limited coping resources, they must tolerate abuse, which is the price of the needed caretaking. Typically, dependent individuals-in-training were mocked by peers and siblings for their incompetence. As a result, their feelings of inadequacy and incompetence were reinforced and reconfirmed. In short, these individuals are characterized by marked submissiveness to a dominant other person, who presumably will provide unending nurturance and guidance. Such a relationship is maintained even if it means tolerating abuse, since dependent-disordered individuals believe themselves to be incompetent and unable to survive without the dominant other.

Integrative Case Conceptualization

The following integrative formulation provides a biopsychosocial explanation for how this personality is likely to have developed and how it is maintained. Biologically, these individuals are characterized by a low energy level. Their temperament is usually described as melancholic. As infants and young children they were characterized as fearful, sad, or withdrawn.

Psychologically, they can be understood and appreciated in terms of their view of themselves, their world-view, and their life goal. The self-view of these individuals tends to be a variant of the theme "I'm nice, but inadequate (or fragile)." Their view of self is self-effacing, inept, and self-doubting. Their view of the world is some variant of the theme "Others are here to take care of me, because I can't do it for myself." Their life goal is characterized by some variant of the theme "Therefore, cling and rely on others at all cost."

The social features of this personality disorder can be described in terms of parental, familial, and environmental factors. The dependent personality is most likely to be raised in a family in which parental overprotection is prominent. It is as if the parental injunction to the child is "I can't trust you to do anything right (or well)." The dependent personality is likely to have been pampered and overprotected as a child. Contact with siblings and peers may engender feelings of unattractiveness, awkwardness, or competitive inadequacy, especially during the preadolescent and adolescent years. These can have a devastating impact on the individual and further confirm the individual's sense of self-deprecation and doubt.

This personality is reinforced and becomes self-perpetuating by a number of factors: a sense of self-doubt, an avoidance of competitive activity, and particularly by the availability of self-reliant individuals who are willing to take care of and make decisions for the dependent person in exchange for the self-sacrificing and docile friendship of the dependent personality (Sperry, 2015).

Table 6.2 summarizes the characteristics of this disorder.

TABLE 6.2 Characteristics of Dependent Personality Disorder

Triggering Event(s)	Expectations of self-reliance and/or being alone
Behavioral Style	Docile, passive, insecure, and submissive Lacks assertiveness Self-doubting and lacks self-confidence
Interpersonal Style	Pleasing, clinging, and compliant Requires reassurance to make decisions Abdicates responsibility to others Avoids disagreements Self-abasing to receive the support of others Urgently seeks new relationships when one ends
Cognitive Style	Suggestible and pollyannaish
Affective Style	Pleasant and anxious, timid, or sad when stressed
Temperament	Low energy level; fearful, sad or withdrawn, melancholic
Attachment Style	Preoccupied
Parental Injunction	"You can't do it by yourself."
Self-View	"I'm nice, but inadequate (or fragile)."
World-View	"Others are here to take care of me, because I can't do it myself."
Maladaptive Schemas	Defectiveness; self-sacrifice; approval-seeking
Optimal Diagnostic Criterion	Needs others to assume responsibility for most major areas of his or her life

Assessment of Dependent Personality Disorder

Several sources of information are useful in establishing a diagnosis and treatment plan for personality disorders. Observation, collateral information, and psychological testing are important adjuncts to the patient's self-report in the clinical interview. This section briefly describes some characteristic observations that the clinician makes and the nature of the rapport likely to develop in initial encounters with specific personality-disordered individuals. Characteristic response patterns on various objective (i.e., MMPI-2 and MCMI-IV) and projective (i.e., Rorschach and TAT) tests are also described.

Interview Behavior and Rapport

In the initial interview, individuals with Dependent Personality Disorders will commonly wait for the clinician to initiate the conversation. After an opening statement by the clinician, these patients can present an adequate description of their current situation, but then will retreat to silence. Predictable comments are: "I don't know what to say. I've never seen a therapist before," or "Ask me questions so I'll know what's important to talk about." When the clinician responds and asks other questions, the cycle may repeat itself. Nonetheless, interviewing these individuals can be enjoyable, and establishing rapport is relatively easy. After some initial anxiety, they will begin to trust the clinician and the therapeutic process. So long as the clinician provides pleasant advice and support, and shows empathy for their indecisiveness and failures, the interview flows smoothly. However, when the clinician attempts to explore the detriments engendered by their submissiveness, they become uncomfortable and want support. If the dependency is not pursued with an empathic ear, they will change therapists. If pursued sympathetically, they will cooperate and meet their clinician's expectations. They answer questions to the point and will clarify and elaborate on demand. They can tolerate abrupt transitions and will allow deep feelings to be probed. But they cannot tolerate confrontation and interpretation of their dependency (Othmer & Othmer, 2002).

Psychological Testing Data

The Minnesota Multiphasic Personality Inventory (MMPI-2), the Millon Clinical Multiaxial Inventory (MCMI-IV), the Rorschach Psychodiagnostic Test, and the Thematic Apperception Test (TAT) can be useful in diagnosing Dependent Personality Disorder, as well as the dependent personality style or trait (Groth-Marnat, 2009).

On the MMPI-2, the most likely profile is the 2–7/7–2 (Depression-Psychasthenia), which characterizes individuals who are passive, dependent, and docile. A high 3 (Hysteria) scale is common, as is a mildly elevated K (Correction) scale (Graham, 2012). Passivity and naiveté are reflected in a high L (Lie) scale, while the F (Frequency) scale is in the average range. Acceptance of the stereotypical female role is reflected by a low scale 5 (Masculinity-Femininity). Lack of resistance to coercion from authority shows in a low 4 (Psychopathic Deviate) scale. A low scale 9 (Hypomania) reflects passivity and lack of initiative (Meyer, 1995).

On the MCMI-IV a high score on scale 3 (Dependent) would be anticipated (Millon et al., 2015). An elevation on scale A (Generalized Anxiety Disorder) is common, particularly when these individuals feel insecure about placing their welfare in the hands of others (Choca & Denburg, 1997).

With regard to the Rorschach, if dependent personalities feel accepted by the examiner and believe that the examiner expects a high number of responses, they will produce an extensive record. Otherwise, fewer than average responses can be expected. Most common are A (Animal), M (Human Movement), and P (Popular) responses. Finally, C (Color) tends to be used more often than F (Form) in determining responses (Meyer, 1995).

Generally speaking, the TAT responses of dependent personalities are not particularly distinctive. However, themes of dependency and compliance are common on card 2 (Bellak, 1997).

Treatment Approaches and Interventions

Treatment Considerations

The differential diagnoses for this personality disorder include the Histrionic Personality Disorder and the Avoidant Personality Disorder. Common symptom diagnoses that are associated with the Dependent Personality Disorder include the anxiety disorders, particularly Simple Phobia and Social Anxiety Disorder, and Panic Disorder. Other common DSM-5 disorders include Conversion Disorder, and Somatic Symptom Disorder. The experience of loss of a supportive person or relationship can lead to a number of affective disorders, including Persistent Depressive Disorder and Major Depressive episodes. Finally, because Dependent Personality Disorders can have lifelong training in assuming the "sick role" they are especially prone to the Factitious Disorders.

In general, the long-range goal of psychotherapy with a dependent personality is to increase the individual's sense of independence and ability to function interdependently. At other times, the therapist may need to settle for a more modest goal. That is, helping the individual become a "healthier" dependent personality. Treatment strategies typically include challenging the individual's convictions or dysfunctional beliefs about personal inadequacy, and learning ways in which to increase assertiveness. A variety of methods can be used to increase self-reliance. Among these are providing the dependent person directives and opportunities for making decisions, being alone, and taking responsibility for his or her own well-being (Sperry, 2015).

Individual Psychotherapy

For the various individual psychotherapeutic modalities, there are reports of successful treatment for Dependent Personality Disorder. Although no large case series or controlled treatment trials have yet to be published, several case reports suggest that positive treatment outcomes are common. Treatment tends to be shorter and less difficult than for other personality disorders, such as the Borderline, Narcissistic or Antisocial personality disorders.

Psychodynamic Psychotherapy Approaches

A central purpose of psychodynamic psychotherapy is to help patients cope better with previous separations and object losses. Patients enter therapy with the unconscious wish to reinstate earlier relationships and bring them to a more satisfactory resolution. Accordingly, the clinician comes to symbolize the object losses, and therapy succeeds if the clinician becomes a better object than the objects of the patient's childhood. The clinician gratifies certain fundamental wishes that the parent-object did not adequately gratify, as well as provides a more reasonable and benign model for identification. If therapy is a success, the internalization of the objects will be more positive and less laden with anger and guilt, thereby making separation a genuine maturational event (Strupp & Binder, 1984). A major dilemma in the psychotherapy with patients with Dependent Personality Disorder is that they do not readily relinquish the new object, and tend to cling tenaciously to the clinician.

In this form of resistance, the patient leans dependently on the clinician as an end in itself, rather than as a means to an end. Thus, as therapy unfolds, these patients may forget what complaint or symptom brought them into treatment, and their only purpose becomes the maintenance of their attachment to the clinician. Dreading termination, they tend to experience a reexacerbation of their initial symptoms. They will endeavor to make the clinician collude in their avoidance of making decisions or asserting themselves in the hope of continuing their dependency. The clinician, however, must frustrate these wishes and prompt independent thoughts and actions in these patients. By conveying that the anxiety produced by this frustration is tolerable and productive, the clinician encourages the patient toward achieving insight and independence (Gabbard, 1994).

In long-term psychodynamic psychotherapy, the emergence of a dependent transference toward the clinician is thus promoted, which is then dealt with in a way to promote emotional growth. Patients are told that extra sessions may be allowed early in therapy, particularly during periods of heightened anxieties. This assurance of readily available support aids in developing a trusting relationship with and transferring dependent wishes onto the clinician. The clinician must encourage patients to express feelings and wishes and to bear the anxiety of making decisions dealing with episodes of anxiety and accepting pleasurable experiences.

Furthermore, the clinician will need to clarify and interpret the transference elements, as well as support the patients in finding more self-reliant ways of coping when they plead with the clinician to take a more directive role in their lives. During the final stage of therapy, the clinician gradually increases the level of expectation for self-initiated behavior and autonomous decision making. The clinician reinforces the patient's increased ability to cope with crises without extra sessions and to self-soothe and self-manage episodes of heightened anxiety. This requires resolution of the patient's wish to be dependent and instead to accept a more self-reliant position in the therapeutic relationship (Hill, 1970). Finally, it should be noted that individuals with Dependent Personality Disorder commonly create countertransference problems in their clinicians related to dependency conflicts. Thus clinicians must anticipate countertransference contempt or disdain toward dependent patients (Gabbard, 1994).

According to Bornstein (2012), Western society's demands to become autonomous and self-sufficient result in a series of implicit rules and restrictions placed on individuals during childhood. Ambivalence about this expectation may result in both conscious and unconscious conflicts about the "unacceptable" desire for dependency. Bronstein suggests that psychoanalytic psychotherapy is particularly well-suited to address this conflict, with the goal being to make individuals consciously aware of it and open to change. Luborsky and Crits-Cristoph (1990) developed the Core Conflictual Relationship Theme (CCRT) method to resolve dependency dynamics and conflicts. The main element of the CCRT method is an in-depth analysis of the patient's relationships. This included wishes, fears, and intentions; the other person's response; and the patient's reaction. The therapist also creates a supportive "holding environment" within the therapeutic relationship to minimize anxiety and defensiveness while working through dependency-related transference and countertransference.

Time-Limited Dynamic Psychotherapy. Kantor (1992) notes that long-term analytic psychotherapy is arduous and time-consuming, and should be recommended primarily when patients are highly motivated and the dependency is ego-syntonic. Otherwise, the treatment may become interminable because of such resistances as unwillingness to work hard in treatment because this means terminating therapy, which they anticipate will be unbearable. Generally speaking, long-term psychotherapy with motivated patients requires two to four sessions a week over three or more years to work through a dependent transference.

For these and other reasons, time-limited dynamic psychotherapy has been advocated as the treatment of choice for most of these patients (Flegenheimer, 1982; Gunderson, 1989). Knowing at the outset that treatment will end after 12, 16, or 20 sessions means that these patients must confront their deepest anxieties about loss and individuation, as well as their fantasies about unlimited nurturance and timelessness (Mann, 1973). Such time-limited therapies are most likely to succeed when three conditions are present: a circumscribed, dynamic conflict or focus; a patient who can quickly form a therapeutic alliance; and little or no tendency to act out or regress to severe dependency (Luborsky, 1984; Strupp & Binder, 1994). Time-limited therapy is less successful with dependent individuals who have limited ego strengths or greater degrees of separation anxiety (Gabbard, 1994). For such patients, Wallerstein (1986) suggests a supportive treatment approach in which sessions are tapered down to one every few months, provided there is no threat to termination.

Flegenheimer (1982) has critically reviewed six different brief dynamic psychotherapy approaches—those of Sifneos, Alexander, Mann, Malan, Davanloo, and Wolberg. He believes that Mann's, Alexander's, and Wolberg's approaches are tailor-made for the many dependent personality-disordered individuals. Passive, indecisive patients are likely to feel comfortable with the paternalistic stances of Alexander or Wolberg, where the clinician initially takes charge, gives advice, and makes decisions. The approach enables these patients to try new behaviors because they are "told to." The positive response to new behaviors engenders and reinforces those new patterns of behavior. Likewise, more passive dependent patients tend to do well with Mann's approach, wherein a termination date is set at the first session. The dependency of the patient allows the "golden glow" of Mann's first phase of therapy to develop to the fullest, setting the stage for subsequent disillusionment and preparing for a meaningful separation experience.

Mann's (1973) approach requires little modification of the standard analytically oriented approach, and requires the least amount of confrontation of the briefer psychotherapies. Not surprisingly, this rather gentle technique tends not to engender major resistances in dependent patients.

Time-limited approaches are advocated as the starting point for treatment of most dependent patients. For those who have multifocal conflicts or otherwise fail to improve in briefer therapies, longer-term dynamic therapies, supportive therapy, or psychoanalysis would be treatment options.

Cognitive-Behavioral Approaches

Beck et al. (2004) provides an extended description of the cognitive therapy approach with individuals with Dependent Personality Disorder. The basic goal of therapy is increased autonomy and self-efficacy. Autonomy is defined as the capability to act independently of others, along with the capability to develop close and intimate relationships. Because dependent individuals are squeamish about the word "independent" and fear that competence will lead to abandonment, achieving these goals must be accomplished with considerable delicacy. Since these individuals often come to treatment anticipating that clinicians will solve their problems and make their decisions, it is necessary to allow some dependence initially in order to engage them. The structured collaborative nature of cognitive therapy encourages the dependent individual to play an active role in the treatment process, beginning with the agenda and goal setting. The use of guided discovery and Socratic questioning early in treatment helps these individuals to begin to face their own solutions and decisions, reducing overreliance on the therapist and others. As therapy proceeds, progress toward goals can be utilized as powerful evidence to challenge the dependent individual's assumptions of personal helplessness.

Challenging the dichotomous belief about independence—that one is both totally dependent and helpless or totally independent and isolated—helps to modify the distorted notion that autonomy is a commitment to total alienation. Besides challenging and disputing automatic beliefs and maladaptive schemas concerning dependency and helplessness, therapists are encouraged to utilize behavioral methods such as assertiveness training and behavioral experiments, as well as to modify the very structure of therapy.

This modification can be accomplished in several ways, such as by gradually changing to a group format or concurrent individual and group therapy, "weaning" sessions by scheduling them less frequently toward the end of the therapy, or setting a specific termination date early in treatment and focusing therapy as preparation for termination. Since termination typically evokes rejection and abandonment schemas in these individuals, offering the option of one or two booster sessions, late in the course of treatment, following termination can ease the transition. In short, the cognitive treatment of Dependent Personality Disorder begins with a collaborative relationship in which the therapist allows a measure of dependency, which is gradually replaced with guided discovery, and challenges the dichotomy beliefs of independence. As treatment proceeds, schema reconstruction and modification of the structure of treatment, along with behavioral methods, are utilized to achieve treatment goals.

It is particularly important that the therapist monitor his or her thoughts and feelings toward the dependent patient. Therapists may feel the urge to forego thorough evaluation or make other exceptions for these seemingly "pathetic" individuals. In this case, the therapist's directiveness is covertly aiding the patient's pathological pattern and undermining the goal of autonomy. It may be useful for the therapist to create a Dysfunctional Thought Record to determine whether any deviations from protocol are in the interest of the patient or whether they foster continued dependence. Beck et al. (2004) note that dependent patients are more likely than others to report that they have fallen in love with therapists. Therefore, it is of particular importance to avoid "special" treatment.

A more behaviorally oriented approach to this disorder is based on the formulation that the dependent personality is hypersensitive to independent decision making (Turkat, 1990). The corresponding behavioral strategy is bidirectional anxiety management procedures focused on independent decision making. Since individuals with Dependent Personality Disorder are often undersocialized, social skills training may be indicated. Assertive communication and friendship and dating skills are often minimal in lower functioning dependent patients. Fay and Lazarus (1993) offer cognitive-behavioral protocols in assertiveness, friendship, and dating skills. Brauer and Reinecke (2015) recommend that therapists help dependent patients face the sources of their anxiety by developing behavioral skills in a systematic, graduated fashion. This may be accomplished via modeling by the therapist during sessions, *in vivo* practice, and observing others who are more autonomous and assertive.

Cognitive Coping Therapy. Cognitive Coping Therapy is an active, directive, didactic and structured approach for treating personality-disordered individuals (Sharoff, 2002). It is a complete and self-contained approach to treatment which begins with assessing an individual's coping skills—in terms of skill chains, subskills and microskills—and then increasing skill competence in targeted areas as needed. Five key skill areas with representative treatment modalities include: *cognitive skills*—problem solving, self-instruction training and self-management; *emotion skills*—emotional containment and compartmentalization; *perceptual skills*—perspective taking, thought stopping, and psychological distance taking; *physiological skills*—meditation and relaxation training, and *behavior skills*—communication and assertiveness training. Sharoff (2002) describes a detailed protocol (and clinical example) for using this structured approach with a complex and difficult Dependent Personality Disorder case.

Schema Therapy. Schema Therapy is an elaboration of cognitive therapy that has been developed by Young (Young et al., 2003) specifically for personality disorders, and other difficult individual and couples problems. Schema Therapy involves identifying maladaptive schemas and planning specific strategies and interventions. Four main strategies are cognitive, experiential, behavioral, and the therapeutic relationship itself. Cognitive restructuring, modification of maladaptive schemas, is an important cognitive strategy, but is combined with imagery exercises, empathic confrontation, homework assignments, and "limited reparenting," i.e., a form of corrective emotional experience (Young et al., 2003).

Maladaptive schemas typically associated with Dependent Personality Disorder are: *defectiveness*—the belief that one is defective, bad, unwanted, or inferior in important respects; *dependence*—the belief that one is unable to competently carry out everyday responsibilities without considerable help from others; *approval-seeking*—the belief that one must constantly seek to belong and be accepted at the expense of developing a true sense of self; and *self-sacrifice*—the belief that one must meet the needs of others at the expense of one's own gratification (Bernstein, 2002).

Interpersonal Approach

For Benjamin (2003a), psychotherapeutic interventions with persons with Dependent Personality Disorder can be planned and evaluated in terms of whether they enhance collaboration, facilitate learning about maladaptive patterns and their roots, block these patterns, enhance the will to change, and effectively encourage new patterns.

According to Benjamin, those with Dependent Personality Disorder appear to be the ideal patient—at least superficially. They comply with all recommendations and prescriptions, from homework to paperwork and payment. The more authoritative the therapist is, the more the dependent goes along for the ride. However, she notes that the dependent individual's apparent attitude of friendly cooperation actually complicates the development of a collaborative therapeutic alliance and undermines efforts to change. Essentially, eliciting more and better help from clinicians is the agenda for dependent individuals. They see no reason to collaborate with clinicians against their maladaptive pattern of dependency. Therapy may go on forever. The clinician's challenge at the onset of treatment is to engage with the position opposite their usual one: stop submitting, learn about being independent, and separate. Initially, this seems impossible for these individuals because, with their histories of intense enmeshment, they cannot understand what it means to be differentiated. They believe that there are only two options: to control others or to submit to others. Since they believe that controlling represents bossiness, aggressivity, and bullying of others, they reject it in favor of submission. However, if they are helped to understand that separation and competence, rather than control, are the opposite of submission, they can change. Blocking maladaptive patterns in dependent individuals often requires the assistance of their significant others, such as family members. The paradoxical suggestion that others restrict their offers of help at times when dependent individuals are functioning well is a way to reward independent behavior. Such suggestions must be followed with other interventions that change the strong wish to be dependent and strengthen the wish to become more competent and independent.

Essentially, dependent individuals must first recognize their dependent pattern and the high price they pay to maintain it, and then explore alternatives. To the extent that they can collaborate against "it" and face the present-day meaning of this pattern, they may decide to change. As this occurs, the implementation of a new pattern is relatively straightforward. Benjamin points out that standard behavioral techniques such as assertiveness communication and feeling identification and expression can be quite effective.

Group Therapy

Group treatment has been shown to be successful in the treatment of Dependent Personality Disorder. Two considerations are involved in deciding whether group treatment will be an effective format. The first consideration relates to the patient's degree of impairment; where motivation and potential for growth exist, a more interactional psychotherapy group may be indicated. Such a context provides a therapeutic milieu for exploring the inappropriateness of passive dependent behavior and for experimenting with greater assertiveness (Yalom, 1985). However, if dependent traits reflect severe personality impairment or the absence of prosocial behavior such as assertive communication, decision making, and negotiation, an ongoing supportive problem-solving group or a social skills training group might be indicated. The second consideration refers to whether referral should be made to a homogeneous group, with treatment targeted at dependency issues shared by all group members, or a heterogeneous group, where group members have different personality styles or disorders. Frances et al. (1984) provide selection criteria for both types of group formats. Clinical lore suggests that dependent patients tend to get "lost" in heterogeneous groups. Yalom (1995) seems to be describing the dependent personality in his discussion of the "silent patient" in groups. Yet time-limited assertiveness-training groups that are homogeneous and have clearly defined goals have been shown to be very effective (Lazarus, 1981).

Two studies involving the treatment of dependent patients have been reported in the literature. Montgomery (1971) utilized homogeneous group formats for dependent patients who were previously being seen in an individual format in a clinical setting. The patients were described as clinging and dependent, and as expecting magical cures and medication. Engagement within the group provided the patients with the opportunity to redirect their attention-seeking behavior from regressive to more socially adaptive purposes. Montgomery reports that all but three of 30 patients eventually discontinued medication. Sadoff and Collins (1968) reported group therapy for dependent patients who also stuttered. Weekly group treatment, which emphasized dynamic interpretation, was shown to be effective. Positive changes in stuttering and dependency were reported.

Marital and Family Therapy

The professional literature on family therapy interventions with this disorder is almost nonexistent. Harbir (1981) notes that individuals with Dependent Personality Disorder are usually brought to family therapy by their parents. They are frequently older adolescents or young adults between the ages of 20 and 35 who present with a neurotic or psychotic symptom. Harbir describes a proto-typical case of a 29-year-old man with a diagnosis of dependent personality who essentially was totally dependent on his parents for his maintenance. A more functional younger sister had moved out on her own the previous year. Although he did some part-time work at home for his father, he neither made his own meals, cleaned his own room, nor washed his own clothes. He was content to live the rest of his life with his parents, if they would permit it. There was no clear-cut presenting problem, other than the identified patient's unwillingness to work outside the home. Clearly, the son, mother, and father were deeply en-meshed, although the son was much more dependent on the mother than the father, and vice versa. Structural techniques were employed by the clinician to decrease the intensity of the mother-child interaction. Essentially, various tasks were prescribed that encouraged the father and son to form a separate relationship.

Tasks that encouraged social activities outside the family also were prescribed. Since the son had developed few peer relationships, these tasks initially were quite difficult for both the son and his parents.

After one year of family treatment, the son was able to emancipate sufficiently and could work and socialize outside the home. Could these results have been accomplished in individual therapy? Perhaps, but it was not likely in that time frame, and without some cooperation from the parents. Changing the enmeshed family relationship tends to be anxiety-provoking for all parties, and thus there is considerable resistance from other family members when only one member of the family is in therapy.

Very little has been published on marital therapy with persons with Dependent Personality Disorder. Malinow (1981) notes that dependent patients can function adequately if their marital partners consistently meet their needs, but typically become symptomatic and impaired when that support is withdrawn or withheld. Turkat (1990) believes that it is useful to engage the cooperation of the marital partner in treatment for two reasons: (1) because of the negative impact on the relationship as the dependent individual becomes less anxious and more independent, and (2) because the patient's progress can be facilitated if the partner collaborates in accomplishing the treatment goals. Barlow and Waddell (1985) describe a time-limited couples group for the treatment of agoraphobia. Most of the symptomatic partners exhibited features of the dependent personality. In group, the nonsymptomatic partners took the roles of "coach" and "confidant," collaborating on treatment goals. Taking on these roles meant relinquishing the role in which they reinforced their partner's agoraphobia and dependency. During the course of this 10-session treatment protocol, not only did panic and agoraphobia symptoms remit, but the marital relationship shifted from dependency to more interdependency.

A common marital relational pattern is the dependent/narcissistic couple in which one partner presents with Dependent Personality Disorder and the other partner presents with Narcissistic Personality Disorder. Nurse (1998) provides a detailed rationale and treatment protocol for working with such couples based on Millon's theory of personality disorders (Millon & Davis, 1996).

Links, Stockwell, & McFarlane (2004b) examined couples therapy for patients with Dependent Personality Disorder and identified two dimensions of dependency that determine whether or not patients benefit from this type of intervention. They provide details surrounding two cases to represent each dimension. The first focuses on interpersonal dependency that results from insecure attachment. Links et al. note that this couple failed to benefit from couples therapy because of an enmeshed relationship. The second dimension involves a lack of assertiveness and self-confidence in the dependent individual. These deficits result in a crisis within the relationship that may successfully be addressed in the context of couples therapy. The authors maintain that it is imperative to determine which dependence dimension predominates to evaluate the appropriateness of couples therapy.

Beck et al. (2004) explain that treatment geared towards increasing the autonomy and assertiveness of the dependent individual may result in upsetting his or her spouse. Oftentimes, the significant others of those with Dependent Personality Disorder enjoy the unequal balance of the power in the relationship and may see changes to this as a threat. In this case, marital or family therapy can help family members adjust to changes in the identified patient and potentially grow as a unit. If, however, significant others are not willing to accept the changes brought about in treatment, the dependent individual must determine whether or not to end the relationship.

Medication

Currently, there are no psychotropic medications specifically indicated for treating individuals with Dependent Personality Disorder (Silk & Feurino, 2012). Nevertheless, medications are used that target specific troubling symptoms associated with the disorder, such as depression, anxiety, or sleep problems. Generally, these medications are used as an adjunct to psychotherapy and skills training. Because troubling symptoms often respond to medications sooner than most psychological interventions, medications are usually prescribed at the onset of treatment (Sperry, 1995b). Unfortunately, there is little research evidence to provide guidelines for the use of such medications with this disorder (Silk & Feurino, 2012).

Combined/Integrative Treatment Approaches

In many ways, the dependent personality is an "orphan" in the clinical literature, and this certainly is evident in the area of combined and integrative treatment. Another type of combined treatment involves utilizing different modalities simultaneously. Barlow and Waddell's (1985) effort to combine behavior therapy in a group setting with couples was previously described. Not surprisingly, the results of combining modalities are noteworthy. Lazarus (1981, 1985) provides further documentation of the overall efficacy, and cost effectiveness, of multimodal interventions

Little has been written regarding integrative treatment. However, clinical practice is replete with efforts to utilize anxiety-reducing strategies in both dynamic and cognitive therapies. For example, Glantz and Goisman (1990) describe a unique integration of relaxation techniques with object-relations psy-chodynamic psychotherapy with dependent patients. A breath-controlling and progressive muscle-relaxation strategy was used to merge split self-representations in the course of exploration psychotherapy. The technique was introduced after signs of split self-representation had been identified. Patients were taught the technique and it was prescribed as an intersession treatment task. Once they were able to relax adequately in session, they were asked for visual images of first one and then another of the conflicting self-representations. After clear images had been elicited and discussed, they were encouraged to merge the images. Twenty-four of the 27 personality-disordered patients in the study, many of whom were dependent personalities, responded with greater compliance, improved interpersonal relationships, and reduced resistance.

For those with comorbid dependent personality and substance use disorders, Ekleberry (2014) states that participation in self-help programs such as Alcoholics Anonymous (AA) and Narcotics Anonymous (NA) may be helpful; however, she cautions that these individuals may fall prey to aggressive and narcissistic group members.

7

HISTRIONIC PERSONALITY DISORDER

Individuals with histrionic personalities initially appear to be charming, likable, energetic, and seductive, but as time passes they may be viewed as emotionally unstable, immature, and egocentric. While it is noted in males, this personality pattern predominates in females, and typically presents with a caricature of femininity in dress and manner (Blashfield, Reynolds & Stennett, 2012). While treatment of such individuals involves a number of unique therapeutic challenges, it can be highly effective and successful.

This chapter describes a framework for the assessment and effective treatment of this disorder. It includes sections on diagnosis, psychological assessment, case conceptualization, and treatment interventions. It begins with background information on the disorder as well as a DSM-5 description and a prototypic description of this disorder. The section on case conceptualization provides five common clinical formulations of this disorder: psychodynamic, biosocial, cognitive-behavioral, interpersonal, and an integrative conceptualization of this disorder. Several treatment approaches, modalities, and intervention strategies are also described. These include individual psychotherapy, group therapy, marital and family therapy, medication, and integrative and combined treatment.

Description of the Histrionic Personality Disorder

The Histrionic Personality Disorder can be recognized by the following descriptors and characteristics: styles vs. disorders, triggering event, behavioral styles, interpersonal styles, cognitive styles, affective styles, attachment style, and optimal criterion.

Style vs. Disorder. This histrionic personality can be thought of as spanning a continuum from healthy to pathological, wherein the histrionic personality style

TABLE 7.1 Comparison of Histrionic Personality Style and Disorder

Personality Style	Personality Disorder
Enjoys compliments and praise.	Constantly seeks or demands reassurance, approval or praise.
Charming, engaging, and appropriate appearance or behavior.	Inappropriately sexually seductive in appearance and behavior.
Attentive to their appearance and grooming, enjoying clothes, style, and fashion.	Overly concerned with physical attractiveness.
Lively and fun-loving, often impulsive, but can delay gratification.	Expresses emotion with inappropriate exaggeration; self-centered and little tolerance for gratification.
Enjoy being the center of attention, and can rise to the occasion when all eyes are on them.	Uncomfortable in situations where they cannot be the center of attention.
Sensation-oriented, emotionally demonstrative, and physically affectionate. Reacts emotionally but appropriately.	Displays rapidly shifting and shallow expression of emotion.
Utilizes a style of speech which is appropriately global and specific.	Utilizes a style of speech that is excessively impressionistic and lacking in detail.

is on the healthy end and the Histrionic Personality Disorder is on the pathological end. Table 7.1 compares and contrasts the histrionic personality style and disorder.

The following two case examples further illustrate differences between the Histrionic Personality Disorder—Ms. P.—and the histrionic personality style—Mr. M.

CASE STUDY: HISTRIONIC PERSONALITY DISORDER

Ms. P. is a 20-year-old female undergraduate student who requested psychological counseling at the College Health Services for "boyfriend problems." Actually, she had taken a nonlethal overdose of minor tranquilizers the day before coming to the Health Services. She said she took the overdose in an attempt to kill herself because "life wasn't worth living" after her boyfriend had left the afternoon before. She was an attractive, well-dressed woman adorned with makeup and nail polish, which contrasted sharply with the very casual fashion of most coeds on campus. During the initial interview she was warm and charming, maintained good eye contract, yet was mildly seductive. At two points in the interview she was emotionally labile, shifting from smiling elation to tearful sadness. Her ex-boyfriend had accompanied her to the evaluation session and asked to talk to the clinician. He stated the reason he had left the patient was because she made demands on him which he could not meet, and that he "hadn't been able to satisfy her emotionally or sexually." Also, he noted that he could not afford to "take her out every night and party."

CASE STUDY: HISTRIONIC PERSONALITY STYLE

Mr. M. is a 41-year-old literary agent who spent the early years of his career representing nonfiction writers with major publishing houses. He has been quite successful for several years but has also become somewhat disenchanted with his behind-the-scenes efforts. While he has made several of his clients extraordinarily wealthy and famous, he dreamed of the time when he too would be financially independent and in the limelight. When cable TV licenses became available, he sensed the opportunity to fulfill his dream. He would become president of his own station and host his own talk show; after all, he had several high-visibility clients whom he could get to be guests on his show. He set out to garner financing for his plan. With his charming manner and alluring vision, he quickly intrigued several backers and got the station launched. The only problem was, he hadn't thought much about the production side of the enterprise. He quickly arranged interviews for an executive producer. William T. was the fourth person he interviewed. Mr. M. knew as soon as he walked in that he was right for the job, and after a 10-minute interview, William was hired. Mr. M's hunch about both William and the success of the talk show he hosted proved to be right.

Triggering Event. The typical situation, circumstance or event that most likely triggers or activates the characteristic maladaptive response of the Histrionic Personality Disorder Personality Disorder (Othmer & Othmer, 2002), as noted in behavioral, interpersonal, cognitive, and affective styles, is: "opposite sex relationships."

Behavioral Style. The behavioral style is characterized as charming, dramatic, and expressive, while also being demanding, self-indulgent, and inconsiderate. Persistent attention-seeking, mood lability, capriciousness, and superficiality further characterize their behavior.

Interpersonal Style. Interpersonally, these individuals tend to be exhibitionistic and flirtatious in their manner, with attention-seeking and manipulativeness being prominent. They also tend to have empathic deficits, just as Narcissistic Personality-Disordered individuals.

Cognitive Style. The cognitive or thinking style of this personality can be characterized as impulsive and thematic, rather than being analytical, precise, and field-independent. Their tendency is to be nonanalytic, vague, and field-dependent. They are highly suggestible and rely heavily on hunches and intuition. They avoid awareness of their own hidden dependency and other self-knowledge, and tend to be "other-directed" with respect to the need for approval from others. Therefore, they can easily dissociate their "real" or inner self from their "public" or outer self.

Affective Style. Their emotional or feeling style is characterized by exaggerated emotional displays and excitability, including irrational outbursts and temper tantrums. Although they are constantly seeking reassurance that they are loved, they respond with only superficial warmth and charm and are generally emotionally shallow. Finally, they are exquisitely rejection-sensitive.

Attachment Style. The preoccupied attachment dimension is characterized by a sense of personal unworthiness and a positive evaluation of others. These individuals tend to be rather externally oriented in their self-definitions. The Preoccupied Attachment Style is common in individuals with Histrionic Personality Disorder.

Optimal Diagnostic Criterion. Of all the diagnostic criteria for the Dependent Personality Disorder, one criterion has been found to be the most useful in diagnosing this disorder. The belief is that, by beginning with this criterion, the clinician can test for the presence or absence of the criterion and quickly diagnose the personality disorder (Allnutt & Links, 1996). The "optimal criterion" for this disorder is: "uncomfortable in situations in which he or she is not the center of attention."

DSM-5 Description

Individuals with this personality disorder are characterized by an unremitting pattern of attention seeking and emotionality. They tend to be uncomfortable in situations where they cannot be the center of attention. Their emotional reactions tend to be shallow and rapidly shifting. Typically, they draw attention to themselves with the way they dress. Their manner of speech tends to be impressionistic, with few details. These individuals are easily influenced by others or circumstances. They are likely to perceive relationships as more intimate than they really are. They often engage in provocative and inappropriate seductive sexual behavior. Furthermore, they are dramatic and overly exaggerate their emotional expressions (American Psychiatric Association, 2013).

Prototypic Description

A prototype is a brief description that captures the essence of how a particular disorder commonly presents. Prototypic descriptions are useful and convenient and clinicians commonly rely on them rather than lists of behavioral criteria or core beliefs (Westen, 2012). Here is a common prototypic description of the Histrionic Personality Disorder: These individuals are the exhibitionists in life. If they are female, they use charm, physical appeal, and seductiveness to command attention. There is an intensity to their relationships and emotions, but a shallowness at the same time. If they are male, they are more likely to command attention by bragging about a business deal or investment, or their prowess in sports or sex. Their interests and attitudes are easily influenced by what others think and value. They come on strong and seek intimacy quickly. But, such intimacy wears thin quickly, which leaves them feeling unappreciated (Frances, 2013).

Prevalence

Prevalence of this disorder has been estimated at 1.84 percent in the general population (American Psychiatric Association, 2013). In clinical settings, this disorder is the most infrequent in presenting for treatment, with estimates of 1.0 to 22.9 percent (Torgersen, 2012).

Conceptualizations of the Histrionic Personality Disorder

Psychodynamic Case Conceptualizations

Gabbard (1990) argues that the Histrionic Personality Disorder needs to be distinguished from the Hysterical Personality Disorder. The latter has a central place in the tradition of psychoanalytic thinking and refers to a higher functioning healthier group of patients than the group characterized by DSM-IV criteria. Histrionic females typically lack maternal nurturance and turn to their fathers for gratification of their dependence needs. They learn that they can gain their father's attention through flirtatious and exhibitionistic displays of emotion. As she matures she learns she must repress her genital sexuality to remain "daddy's little girl." Similarly, histrionic males will have also experienced maternal deprivation and turned to their fathers for nurturance. If their father is emotionally unavailable, they may develop a passive, effeminate identification or hypermasculine one in reaction to anxiety about effeminacy. He may not become homosexual, but his heterosexual relationships are means of reassuring himself relative to underlying genital inadequacy. These men will be disappointed with all women, since they cannot measure up to mother. Some will choose a celibate lifestyle to maintain their loyalty to their mother, while others will indulge in macho behavior such as bodybuilding and Don Juanism, i.e., compulsive seduction of women, to reassure themselves they are "real men" (Kellerman & Burry, 1989).

Biosocial Case Conceptualizations

Millon (1981) and Millon and Davis (1996) note that individuals with Histrionic Personality Disorders often display a high degree of emotional lability and responsiveness during infancy and early childhood, which they attribute to low excitability thresholds for limbic and posterior hypothalamic nucleus. However, environmental factors seem to play the major role in the development of this pathology. Millon and Everly (1985) list three such factors: parental reinforcement of attention-seeking behavior; histrionic parental role models; and reinforcement of interpersonally manipulative behavior. In effect, as children these individuals learned to employ cuteness, charm, attractiveness, and seduction to secure parental reinforcement. Furthermore, this disorder is self-perpetuated through short-lived relationships, preoccupation with externals, and massive repression. Specifically, by sealing off and repressing aspects of their inner worlds, histrionic individuals deny themselves opportunities to develop psychologically.

Cognitive-Behavioral Case Conceptualizations

Beck (2015) describes a cognitive therapy view of the Histrionic Personality Disorder based on specific underlying assumptions and cognitive distortions. Two underlying assumptions are posited: "I am inadequate and unable to handle life by myself" and "I must be loved by everyone to be worthwhile." Believing they are incapable of caring for themselves, histrionic individuals actively seek the attention and approval of others and expect others to take care of them and their needs. Believing they must be loved and approved by others promotes rejection sensitivity. Finally, feeling inadequate and desperate for approval, they are under considerable pressure to seek attention by "performing" for others. These beliefs also give rise to a thinking style characterized as impressionistic, global, and unfocused, which is not conducive to a differentiated sense of self (Sungar & Gunduz, 2015). Not surprisingly, this global, exaggerated thinking style engenders common cognitive distortions (Beck, 2015), such as dichotomous thinking, overgeneralization, and emotional reasoning.

Taking a more behavioral tack, Turkat (1990) differentiates the Histrionic Personality Disorder in two types: the controlling type in which the basic motivation is achieving total control through the use of manipulative and dramatic ploys; and the reactive type in which the basic motivation is seeking reassurance and approval. Turkat does not believe the controlling type is amenable to behavior treatment. Unable to read others' emotions and interventions accurately, these individuals remain shallow, self-centered, and uncomfortable when immediate reinforcement is not immediately forthcoming from others. In short, they suffer from a primary deficit in empathy.

Interpersonal Case Conceptualizations

For Benjamin (2003a), persons with Histrionic Personality Disorder were likely to be loved for their good looks and entertainment value, rather than for competence or personal strength. They learned that physical appearance and charm could be used to control important others. The household of histrionic personalities tended to be a shifting stage. Unpredictable changes stemmed from parental instability, possibly associated with alcohol or substance use. The chaos in these families was more likely to be dramatic and interesting rather than primitive and life-threatening, as with borderline personalities. On the other hand, the help-seeking histrionic subtypes were likely to be nurtured for being ill. They learned that complaints and disabilities were an effective way to elicit warm concern. Along with encouragement of denial, these families rewarded sickness. Finally, they exhibit a strange fear of being ignored, together with a wish to be loved and taken care of by important others, who can be controlled through charm or guile. In short, a friendly trust is accompanied by a secretly disrespectful agenda of forcing delivery of the desired nurturance and love. Inappropriate seductive behaviors and manipulative suicide attempts exemplify such coercions.

Integrative Case Conceptualization

The following integrative formulation provides a biopsychosocial explanation for how this personality is likely to have developed and how it is maintained. Biologically and temperamentally, the histrionic personality is characterized by a high energy level and emotional and autonomic reactivity. Millon and Everly (1985) noted that histrionic adults tended to display a similarly high degree of emotional lability and responsiveness, as they did in infancy and early childhood. Their temperament then can be characterized as hyperresponsive and externally oriented for gratification.

Psychologically, they can be understood and appreciated in terms of their view of themselves, their world-view, and their life goal. The self-view of the histrionic will be some variant of the theme "I am sensitive and everyone should admire and approve of me." The world-view will be some variant of "Life makes me nervous so I am entitled to special care and consideration." Life goal is some variant of the theme "Therefore, play to the audience, and live in the moment."

In addition to biological and psychological factors, social factors such as parenting style and injunction, and family and environmental factors, influence the development of the histrionic personality. The parental injunction for the histrionic personality involves reciprocity: "I'll give you attention, if you do X." A parenting style that involves minimal or inconsistent discipline helps ensure and reinforce the histrionic pattern. The histrionic child is likely to grow up with at least one manipulative or histrionic parent who reinforces the child's histrionic and attention-seeking behavior. Finally, the following sequence of self- and system

TABLE 7.2 Characteristics of Histrionic Personality Disorder

Behavioral Style	Self-dramatization
	Suggestibility
	Charming and excitement-seeking
Interpersonal Style	Needs to attract others' attention
	Seductive or provocative interactions
	Exhibitionistic and/or flirtatious
	Misreads intimacy of relationships
Cognitive Style	Impulsive
	Thematic, field-dependent
	Impressionistic style of speech
Affective Style	Rapidly shifting, shallow expression of emotions
	Exaggerated emotional display
Temperament	Hyperresponsive infantile pattern
	Externally oriented for gratification
Attachment Style	Preoccupied
Parental Injunction	"I'll give you attention when you do what I want."
Self-View	"I need to be noticed."
World-View	"Life makes me so nervous, so I'm entitled to special care and consideration."
Maladaptive Schemas	Approval-seeking; emotional deprivation; defectiveness
Optimal Diagnostic Criterion	Is uncomfortable in situations in which he or she is not the center of attention

perpetuants are likely to be seen in the Histrionic Personality Disorder: denial of one's real or inner self; a preoccupation with externals; the need for excitement and attention-seeking, which leads to a superficial charm and interpersonal presence; and the need for external approval. This, in turn, further reinforces the dissociation and denial of the real or inner self from the public self, and the cycle continues (Sperry, 2015).

Table 7.2 summarizes these characteristics.

Assessment of Histrionic Personality Disorder

Several sources of information are useful in establishing a diagnosis and treatment plan for personality disorders. Observation, collateral information, and psychological testing are important adjuncts to the patient's self-report in the clinical interview. This section briefly describes some characteristic observations that the clinician makes and the nature of the rapport likely to develop in initial encounters with specific personality-disordered individuals. Characteristic response patterns on various objective (i.e., MMPI-2 and MCMI-III) and projective tests (i.e., Rorschach and TAT) are also described.

Interview Behavior and Rapport

Interviewing Histrionic Personality-Disordered individuals can be enjoyable but, at the same time, challenging. Initially these individuals may be more interested in admiration and approval than in a therapeutic relationship. Rapport, therefore, may be difficult to establish. Exaggerated emotionality, vagueness, superficiality, and phoniness are common in the first encounter. With a male clinician, histrionic females may be flirtatious and seductive, but with a female clinician they are more likely to engage in a power struggle. To elicit sufficient information to complete a diagnostic evaluation usually requires the clinician to overcome their vagueness and dramatic exaggerations. Open-ended and unstructured questions are not useful, since these individuals easily become sidetracked. It is preferable to pursue a main theme, such as a work problem or an interpersonal conflict, and elicit concrete examples, while curbing rambling and contradictions. Confronting contradictions typically results in anger and loss of rapport. Instead, express empathy and encouragement. It is predictable that, when they feel empathy and understanding is slipping away, they will return to dramatization (Othmer & Othmer, 2002).

Psychological Testing Data

The Minnesota Multiphase Personality Inventory (MMPI-2), the Millon Clinical Multiaxial Inventory (MCMI-II), the Rorschach Psychodiagnostic Test, and the Thematic Apperception Test (TAT) can be useful in diagnosing the Histrionic Personality Disorder as well as the Histrionic Personality Style or trait (Groth-Marnat, 2009).

On the MMPI-2, the 2–3/3–2 (Depression-Hysteria) profile is most commonly found. When clinically distressed these individuals are likely to have elevations on 2 greater than 7OT. If not, scale 3 will be more elevated. The 3–4/4–3 (Hysteria-Psychopathic deviant) and 4–9/9–4 (Psychopathic Deviant-Hypermania) patterns are also noted in these individuals (Graham, 2012). Scales 4, 7 (Psychasthenia), and 8 (Schizophrenia) may also be moderately elevated, with scale 4 reflecting their tendency to be overdramatic and self-absorbed, while self-doubt and anxiety raise the 7 score, and impulsive emotionality elevates the 8. Scale 5 is also likely to be elevated in males—but quite low in females—reflecting the association of hysteria with traditional feminine role behavior (Meyer, 1995).

On the MCMI-IV, an elevation on scale 4A (Histrionic) is expected (Millon et al., 2015). Because these individuals are attention-seekers, scales 1 (Schizoid) and 2 (Avoidant) tend to be very low, while H (Somatic symptom disorder) may be high, since somatization can be used as an attention-getting device, as can N

(Bipolar I disorder) (Choca & Denburg, 1997).

On the Rorschach, these individuals provide a low number of responses, as well as a low number of W (Whole), M (Human Movement), C (Pure Color), and shading (Y, YF or T) responses. Occasionally, these individuals will give a "blood" response to a color card (Meyer, 1995).

On the TAT, these individuals typically produce stories containing dependency and control themes. Their stories may also become personalized, generating some affective display. Occasionally, blocking occurs on cards with sexual or aggressive percepts. Rarely, primitive splitting may be noted in characters that are all good or all bad on incongruous juxtapositions (Bellak, 1997).

Treatment Approaches and Interventions

Treatment Considerations

The differential diagnosis of the Histrionic Personality Disorder includes the Narcissistic Personality Disorder and the Dependent Personality Disorder. It also includes the Histrionic-Borderline Disorder, which is a decompensated version of the Histrionic Personality Disorder. Also, Millon (1981) describes a Histrionic-Antisocial Personality Disorder. Associated symptom diagnoses include: Persistent Depressive Disorder, Social Anxiety Disorder, and Obsessive Compulsive Disorder. In addition, Major Depression and Bipolar disorders are common in the decompensated Histrionic Personality Disorder.

The treatment of the Histrionic Personality Disorder may present a considerable challenge for clinicians. For the purposes of this discussion, we will limit ourselves to some general considerations about treatment goals, limits, and medications. General treatment goals include helping the individual integrate gentleness with strength, moderating emotional expression, and encouraging warmth, genuineness, and empathy. Because the histrionic personality can present as dramatic, impulsive, seductive, and manipulative with potential for suicidal gestures, the clinician needs to discuss the matter of limits early in the course of therapy regarding professional boundaries and personal responsibilities. Some histrionic personalities, particularly those that bear some resemblance to "hysteroid dysphoria," may respond to certain antidepressants. Otherwise, unless a concurrent acute psychotic or major depressive episode is present, psychotherapy is the principal mode of treatment (Sperry, 2015).

Individual Psychotherapy

This section will briefly review the major psychotherapeutic approaches for treating the Histrionic Personality Disorder in an individual psychotherapy format. Later sections will describe other treatment formats, such as group therapy, couples therapy, and pharmacotherapy. The individual treatment approaches are:

psychodynamic psychotherapy, cognitive-behavioral therapy, and interpersonal psychotherapy.

Psychodynamic Psychotherapy Approach

Gabbard (1990) is quite optimistic about the responsiveness of higher functioning individuals with Histrionic Personality Disorder to psychoanalytically oriented psychotherapy. He reports that such individuals readily develop a therapeutic alliance and perceive the therapist as helpful. On the other hand, Gabbard believes that treatment with lower functioning individuals with this personality disorder should employ therapeutic strategies utilized for the Borderline Personality Disorder.

Winer and Pollock (1989) indicate the basic dynamic in all presentations of the Histrionic Personality Disorder is the excessive, unresolved effort to have all of their needs met by someone else. The general goal of dynamically oriented therapies is to examine the origins of the pattern and explore the neurotic strategies—seductiveness, temper tantrums, charm, or logical thinking—these individuals employ in order to fulfill their needs.

The classical psychoanalytic method emphasizes therapist neutrality and abstinence, and requires that the patient have sufficient ego strength to regress in a controlled manner. The transference that develops is analyzed with mutative interpretations, and presumably lends to enduring personality change. Thus, proper handling of transference, particularly erotic transference, is important. Gabbard (1990) notes that mishandling of erotic transference is probably the most frequent cause of treatment failure with these individuals. However, with more disturbed and unstable Histrionic Personality-Disordered individuals, transference distortions require that resolving transference distortions by interpretation be undertaken with great caution. In fact, some (Havens, 1976; Khan, 1975) suggest that erotic transference not be allowed to develop too firmly or to be interpreted. Rather, counterprojective techniques are advised. These are direct or subtle, verbal or nonverbal responses which communicate to the patient that the therapist is not a transference figure of childhood (Havens, 1976).

Horowitz and Lerner (2010) have more recently identified three phases of the psychodynamic treatment of Histrionic Personality Disorder: therapist interventions to increase state stability and reduce crises; increasing connection with others and eliminating obstacles to personality growth; and increasing self-coherence and developing intimacy with a sense of integrity. Psychodynamic psychotherapy with histrionic patients has also been examined by Fernandez (2010) in a single-case study involving a 25-year-old female psychology student. This treatment, consisting of couch analysis four times per week, was deemed to be a failure. While the patient had good capacity for insight and provided rich material to process in sessions, she frequently missed appointments or arrived late. This manner of resistance is common for histrionic patients seeking attention, and ultimately derailed the therapy process. O'Donohue, Fowler, and Lilienfeld (2007) note that the effectiveness of psychodynamic psychotherapy specifically for Histrionic Personality Disorder has not been demonstrated in controlled studies.

Brief Dynamic Psychotherapy

While long-term psychoanalytically-oriented psychotherapy is considered the mainstay of dynamic treatment (Quality Assurance Project, 1991), time-limited individual psychotherapy may also be quite useful, particularly with higher functioning histrionic individuals. The approaches of Malan (1976) and Sifneos (1972, 1984) seem quite promising. The short-term-anxiety-provoking psycho-therapy (STAPP) approach developed by Sifneos may be a particularly "good fit" for higher functioning histrionic individuals who present with satisfactory impersonal relationships psychological mindedness, the ability to easily engage and interact with a therapist, and a circumscribed presenting complaint. On the other hand, Mann's (1973, 1984) time-limited approach, which requires patients to quickly engage and disengage from therapy "without suffering unduly," may pose considerable difficulty for these individuals who characteristically develop intense and sticky transference with the therapist (Chodoff, 1989). Winston and Pollack (1991) describe Brief Adaptive Psychotherapy (BAP) as particularly effective with histrionic individuals. BAP has an ego psychological orientation, which focuses on maladaptive patterns of beliefs and behaviors. The maladaptive pattern is thoroughly assessed as its underlying elements are explored in detail, with particular attention on transference and resistance.

Cognitive Analytic Therapy (CAT) (Ryle, 2004) is another time-limited model of psychodynamically oriented treatment that has been used for personality disorders. It consists of a narrative reformulation and the sequential diagrammatic reformulation (SDR). Patients receive 24 weekly sessions and four follow-up sessions spread out over a six-month period. Following the first three assessment sessions, personality patients are read a letter from the therapist that reformulates the origins of their distress and identifies target problems and procedures. In Kellet's (2007) single-case study with a woman diagnosed with histrionic personality disorder, these were: the need to be noticed; pacing of relationships; focus on physical appearance; and trust issues. The SDR was developed over the next four sessions. This is used to create therapeutic "exits" from the problem roles and behaviors identified in the SDR. These included, among others, less self-criticism, interacting with others without wearing makeup or "provocative" clothes, and learning to tolerate not being the center of attention. Cognitive Analytic Therapy ends with a "goodbye letter" jointly formulated by the patient and therapist to summarize achievements, prepare for future obstacles, and address any feelings of abandonment related to the termination of therapy.

Cognitive Therapy Approaches

According to Beck et al. (2004), Cognitive Therapy is particularly appropriate in treating Histrionic Personality-Disordered individuals provided they remain in treatment. Although usually cooperative and motivated for therapy, the histrionic's global, diffuse thinking style is quite different from the systematic, structural nature of Cognitive Therapy. Thus, these individuals initially find treatment difficult and frustrating, as they learn to focus attention on a single issue at a time and then monitor their thoughts and feelings. There are a number of necessary conditions for successful cognitive treatment of this disorder. Since these individuals are generally dependent and demanding in relationships, their use of collaborative and guided discovery is particularly well suited. Taking an active role and utilizing questioning is quite helpful in stemming the histrionic individual's view of clinicians as rescuers and saviors. Setting limits that are clear and firm, while rewarding assertive requests within these limits and demonstrating care in other ways, is another necessary condition of treatment. The next condition is establishing treatment goals. These goals must be meaningful and perceived as urgent by these individuals and be specific and concrete enough that short-term as well as long-term benefits can become realities. This counters the histrionic individual's tendency to set broad, vague, noble-sounding goals. An important key to keeping these individuals in therapy is achieving one or more of the specific, short-term goals that were collaboratively established.

The mainstay of treatment with these individuals involves: challenging automatic thoughts; the self-monitoring of cognition, which is helpful in controlling their impulsivity; and the restructuring, modification, and interpretation of maladaptive schemas. Challenging their most basic assumptions such as "I am inadequate and have to rely on others to survive" is aided by cognitive-behavioral methods such as assertion, problem solving, and behavioral experiments, which can increase their self-efficacy and help them feel more competent. Another central belief that must be modified is that the loss of a relationship is always disastrous. Fantasizing about the reality of what would happen if a relationship would end, and recalling how they survived before that relationship began, can help these individuals "decatastrophize" their beliefs about rejection. The behavioral approach with the "controlling type" of histrionic personality (Turkat, 1990) has not been shown to be effective (Turkat, 1990; Turkat & Maisto, 1985). The "reactive type" is more amenable to change, specifically with empathy training. Turkat (1990) describes this intervention, which consists of social skills training in active listening, paraphrasing, and reflection. The goal is to teach these patients to focus increasingly on others' needs and feelings. Role-playing with video feedback has been particularly effective. The use of dramatic behavioral experiments and training in problem-solving skills are also advocated by Beck et al. (1990).

Sungar and Gunduz (2015) outline several treatment goals that may be used, depending on individual patient needs. The first of these is affect awareness and regulation skills. This is intended to help histrionic patients improve frustration tolerance and learn new, more adaptive behaviors in order to reduce the frequency of dramatic or aggressive behavior. The second possible treatment goal is to confront fears about rejection and decatastrophize ideas about loss of approval or attention. This can be accomplished by separating the patient's behaviors from the "self," so that any criticisms are not taken as attacks to self-worth that require defensiveness. Sungar and Gunduz also point to the goal of social and communication skills development in the treatment of Histrionic Personality Disorder. This includes building empathy, active listening, and being a good audience member rather than being at the center of the stage. The final goal is increasing self-sufficiency, problem-solving skills, and a sense of identity without dependence on others' approval.

In short, effective Cognitive Therapy approach to the Histrionic Personality Disorder will be systematic and structural—including firm limit setting and specific treatment goals—and include cognitive (disputation of automatic thoughts and schemas, restructuring of basic maladaptive beliefs and schemas) as well as behavioral methods.

Schema Therapy. Schema Therapy is an elaboration of cognitive therapy that has been developed by Young (Young et al., 2003) specifically for personality disorders, and other difficult individual and couples problems. Schema Therapy involves identifying maladaptive schemas and planning specific strategies and interventions. Four main strategies are cognitive, experiential, behavioral, and the therapeutic relationship itself. Cognitive restructuring, modification of maladaptive schemas, is an important cognitive strategy, but is combined with imagery exercises, empathic confrontation, homework assignments, and "limited reparenting," i.e., a form of corrective emotional experience (Young et al., 2003).

Maladaptive schemas typically associated with Histrionic Personality Disorder include: *emotional deprivation*—the belief that one's desire for emotional support will not be met by others; *defectiveness*—the belief that one is defective, bad, unwanted, or inferior in important respects; and *approval-seeking*—the belief that one must constantly seek to belong and be accepted at the expense of developing a true sense of self (Bernstein, 2002).

Interpersonal Approach

For Benjamin (2003b), psychotherapeutic interventions with Histrionic Personality-Disordered individuals can be planned and evaluated in terms of whether they enhance collaboration, facilitate learning about maladaptive patterns and their roots, block these patterns, enhance the will to change, and effectively encourage new patterns.

Benjamin notes that to establish a therapeutic alliance facilitating collaboration with the histrionic individual based on knowledge of the basic pattern, wishes, and fears of that individual. It is essential that the therapist communicate warmth and competent support while not reinforcing the histrionic's dependent, needy position. The working contract is with the individual's observing ego, while the "enemy" is the damaging pattern. A major task of beginning treatment is transforming the histrionic's view of treatment as making fantasies come true to a place where personal development can be facilitated. Thus, treatment interventions can be evaluated on the basis of whether or not they accomplish this. If an intervention results in more demanding dependency, then it has failed to achieve the aforementioned goals.

Facilitating collaboration with the histrionic patient is no easy task. Gender dynamics can play a particularly important role. For example, female therapists may have difficulty communicating the accepting warmth and support so desired by the female histrionic patient because of the latter's dim view of the therapist's competence. Male therapists will have an easier time establishing the therapeutic contract—at least at first. Regardless of gender, therapists must be clear in their boundaries and intentions for their relationship with the histrionic patient. The therapy relationship is for the needs and learning of the patient, not the therapist. Benjamin notes it should be clear that the therapist's salary or fees are enough to meet his or her needs in this relationship, and that it is not a social relationship. This challenges the marriage fantasy commonly held by histrionic patients.

The task of learning to recognize patterns is complicated in that histrionic individuals have not sufficiently developed an observing ego to help them to recognize and reflect on patterns. In fact, they've come to believe that if they become competent, they would be left alone and no one would care for them. Establishing stability is tantamount to losing their identity. While the female histrionic can internalize the female clinician's modeling of benign and constructive examination of patterns, the male clinician must help the individual look at her fears that if she becomes competent the clinician will conclude that she is unattractive and stop treatment.

Next, the clinician focuses the histrionic individual's attention on potentially destructive patterns of acting out based on underlying fears and wishes. By providing gentle challenges, the clinician protects these individuals from their own past. The goal is to expand options and enhance awareness in light of what is being learned about patterns. The therapist doesn't block patterns with advice giving as much as reviewing options. Developing the will to change patterns is enhanced if these patterns can be uncovered and clearly connected in an experiential way to the past. This often facilitates the individual's "decision" to give up the goals that drive the patterns. Finally, Benjamin advocates traditional techniques from other approaches that can be utilized to build new patterns and ways of functioning, once the "unconscious underbrush" has been cleared away. Warmth, active listening, and support, are keys to successful therapy. The therapist must remain a loyal and optimistic ally in treatment.

Group Therapy

The literature on the histrionic personality is quite interesting with regard to treatability of this disorder in group settings. There are clear warnings in the older psychoanalytic literature about the impact of these patients on other group members. Slavson (1939) cautioned that their changeability and unpredictability would engender stress and anxiety in a group. Thus, he believed these patients should be treated only in individual therapy. On the other hand, contemporary clinicians like Gabbard (1990, 1994) contend that histrionic patients who are appropriate for individual dynamic psychotherapy are also appropriate for dynamic group psychotherapy. In fact, Gabbard finds these patients are highly valued by other group members for their ability to express affects directly, and because of their concern for other group members. Rutan, Stone, and Shay (2014) provide a detailed analysis of a mixed diagnosis psychodynamic therapy group with a histrionic member. They draw attention to the strong negative reactions these individuals can have on the group facilitator and fellow members, as well as the benefits of having the histrionic patient's honesty.

The group treatment format has a number of advantages over individual treatment. First, a group setting frustrates the wish and demand these patients have for the exclusive attention of the therapist which now must be undeniably inevitably challenge the approval-seeking posture of these patients. Thus, the risk of an eroticized transference developing is relatively small in contrast with individual therapy.

Second, their global cognitive style and associated defenses of repression and denial can be more effectively treated in a group setting. Group members will confront the distorted manner in which histrionic patients view themselves and others by their style, omission of details, and focus on affects over thought.

Finally, histrionic patterns tend to form positive maternal transference and expect the group to make up for the maternal nurturance they missed as children (Gabbard, 1990). While this transference is particularly challenging for the clinician in individual therapy, it is considerably "diluted" in a group treatment format.

Relatively little has been published about the effectiveness of group treatment of histrionic patients. But one study is encouraging. Cass, Silvers, and Abrams (1972) reported a behavioral group treatment that significantly modified inappropriate passivity, manipulativeness, and acting out, replaced by more effective assertive interpersonal behavior.

The question of indication and contraindication has been addressed by some writers. Halleck (1978) notes that histrionic patients who cannot participate in a group process without monopolizing or disrupting it should be excluded. Similarly, Gabbard (1990) cautions that individuals might still be candidates for group therapy if they are concurrently in individual psychotherapy. Scheidlinger and Porter (1980) indicate that combined treatment—individual plus group therapy—may be the treatment of choice for such histrionic patients.

Marital and Family Therapy

There are no reports of family therapy, per se, with histrionic patients. However, there are a number of case reports on marital therapy with these patients. Typically, the marriage consists of an obsessive-compulsive husband and a histrionic wife, wherein the obsessive-compulsive spouse tends to assume increasing responsibility while the histrionic spouse becomes increasingly helpless (Berman, 1983). Treatment may be sought following some primitive outburst, which can include some threat of self-destructive behavior, typically during separation or divorce. The loss of a stable dependent figure is a major stressor for the histrionic patient, who may exhibit aggressive attention-seeking behavior, increased affective display and seductiveness, and/or possibly promiscuity, in an effort to make the other spouse jealous, etc. (Harbir, 1981).

The general goal of treatment is to facilitate changing this pattern in both spouses. This is better accomplished in a couple's therapy format rather than in individual session. Harbir (1981) offers a treatment protocol for couples wherein divorce and child custody are issues.

Nichols (1996) describes the interactional patterns and symptomatology of individuals with Histrionic Personality Disorder and Antisocial Personality Disorder in close interpersonal relationships as well as a suggested treatment plan protocol and strategies for dealing with such couples in a therapeutic context.

An integrative marital therapy approach involving dynamic, cognitive-behavioral, and systemic interventions is described by Sperry and Maniacci (1996) for couples in which one partner presents with Histrionic Personality Disorder and the other with Obsessive-Compulsive Personality Disorder. Three phases of the treatment process are discussed and illustrated: establishing a therapeutic alliance, restoring balance to the couple relationship, and modifying individual partner dynamics. The first two phases involve conjoint couples sessions, while much of the third phase involves individual sessions (Sperry & Maniacci, 1996).

Links, Stockwell, and McFarlane (2004a) point to the apparent paradox of the histrionic/obsessive-compulsive couple. Despite the fact that they demonstrate healthier personality styles compared to other personality disorders, they are often more difficult to engage in treatment than those with more severe forms of psychopathology. This paradox is explained by these individuals' particular attachment styles. Couples with histrionic/obsessive-compulsive styles are able to form attachment relationships; however, when their attachment needs are left unsatisfied, they look for compromises or alternatives that can be damaging to the relationship. These include leaving the relationship for another individual or forming triangulated relationship with a third party to maintain stability. Because of these additional options, these individuals may present as more ambivalent about couples therapy or change. As such, the authors point to the importance of evaluating these possibilities when determining the appropriateness of couple's therapy. The specific style of the histrionic/obsessive-compulsive couple are further illustrated by Landucci and Foley (2014). Couples of this composition are polar opposites: spontaneous vs. controlled; vague vs. detailed and rational. These two individuals are said to form one full person when taken together, so it is not surprising that there is often an instant attraction between these opposites. However, these dramatic differences are also the source of conflict. Couples therapists should normalize the belief that the other partner is "crazy" by discussing these dynamics.

Medication

Generally speaking, there are no psychotropic medications specifically indicated for treating individuals with Histrionic Personality Disorder (Silk & Feurino, 2012). Histrionic Personality-Disordered individuals may exhibit anxiety disorders, depressive disorders, or somatoform symptoms. Nevertheless, medications are used that target specific troubling symptoms associated with the disorder, such as depression, anxiety, or sleep problems. Generally, these medications are used as an adjunct to psychotherapy and skills training. Because troubling symptoms often respond to medications sooner than most psychological interventions, medications are usually prescribed at the onset of treatment (Sperry, 1995b). Unfortunately, there is little research evidence to provide guidelines for the use of such medications (Silk & Feurino, 2012). However, there appears to be an exception. One variant of the histrionic personalities, called "hysteroid dysphoria," has responded to certain antidepressant agents, specifically Parnate and Nardil (Liebowitz & Klein, 1981).

Combined/Integrative Treatment Approach

The basic premise of the book is that symptomatic and lower functioning personality disordered individuals are less likely to respond to single treatment approach or modality. Since personality disorders are biopsychosocial phenomena (Pies, 1992), combined or integrative, tailored treatment is indicated, particularly for the more symptomatic and severe presentations. Stone (1993) advocates combined treatments, wherein two or more approaches or modalities are utilized concurrently or in tandem.

Previously, it was mentioned that combining individual psychotherapy with group therapy concurrently was indicated for histrionic patients who monopolized or were disruptive in group settings (Scheidlinger & Porter, 1980). It has also been noted that behavioral techniques may be integrated with psychodynamic or a cognitive approach. Finally, medications may be a useful adjunct to psychotherapy, either concurrently or in tandem, if specific Axis I or Axis II symptoms or trait clusters are prominent.

Horowitz (1997) discusses guidelines for the psychotherapeutic treatment for the Histrionic Personality Disorder that integrates cognitive and psychodynamic principles and methods. This personality disorder is formulated in terms of levels: states of mind, defensive control processes, and schemas. A phase-oriented treatment plan is linked to these three formulation levels. Specific psychotherapeutic guidelines for each of these phases are described.

Dorfman (2000) provides a case study with a 49-year-old histrionic woman who sought treatment for severe depression, anxiety, and problems with her boyfriend. The time-limited nature of the treatment included elements from a combination of models with three specific treatment goals. First, the therapist dealt with acute emotional distress by developing a supportive and empathic therapeutic relationship to help the patient contain and modulate her emotions. Second, a combination of cognitive challenges, communication skills training, and insight-oriented interpretations of the patient's childhood addressed her distorted self-concept and maladaptive style. Finally, the treatment focused on developing the confidence necessary to resume appropriate functioning at work and achieve some degree of independence.

8

NARCISSISTIC PERSONALITY DISORDER

Individuals with narcissistic personalities tend to be grandiose, entitled, and self-centered. They are often impulsive and anxious, have ideas of grandiosity and "specialness," become quickly dissatisfied with others, and maintain superficial, exploitative interpersonal relationships (Ronningstam, 2012). While treatment of such individuals involves a number of unique therapeutic challenges, it can be highly effective and successful.

This chapter describes a framework for the assessment and effective treatment of this disorder. It includes sections on diagnosis, psychological assessment, case conceptualization, and treatment interventions. It begins with background information on the disorder as well as a DSM-5 description and a prototypic description of this disorder. The section on case conceptualization provides five common clinical formulations of this disorder: psychodynamic, biosocial, cognitive-behavioral, interpersonal, and an integrative conceptualization of this disorder. Several treatment approaches, modalities, and intervention strategies are also described. These include individual psychotherapy, group therapy, marital and family therapy, medication, and integrative and combined treatment.

Description of the Narcissistic Personality Disorder

The Narcissistic Personality Disorder can be recognized by the following descriptors and characteristics: style vs. disorder, triggering event(s), behavioral style, interpersonal style, cognitive style, affective style, attachment style, and optimal diagnostic criterion.

Style vs. Disorder. The narcissistic personality is quite common in western culture particularly among certain occupations and professions such as law, medicine, entertainment and sports, and politics. The narcissistic personality can be thought of as spanning a continuum from healthy to the pathological, with the narcissistic personality style on the healthy end and the personality disorder on the pathological end. Table 8.1 compares and contrasts differences between the narcissistic style and disorder.

The following two case examples illustrate the differences between the Narcissistic Personality Disorder—Mr. C.—and the narcissistic personality style— Mr. J.

Although DSM-5 only describes one type or presentation of the Narcissistic Personality Disorder, research describes three types: overt, covert, and the malignant (Caligor, Levy, & Yeomans, 2015). All three types are highly self-absorbed and have little genuine regard for the needs or feelings of others.

Overt Type. This type presents as grandiose and thick-skinned and is the embodiment of DSM-5 criteria. These individuals are characterized by overt

TABLE 8.1 Comparison of Narcissistic Personality Style and Disorder

Personality Style	Personality Disorder
Although emotionally vulnerable to negative assessments and reaction of others, they can handle these gracefully.	Reacts to criticism with feelings of rage, stress, or humiliation (even if not expressed).
Shrewd in dealing with others, utilizing the strengths and advantages of others to achieve their own goals.	Interpersonally exploitive, taking advantage of others to achieve his or her own ends.
Can energetically sell themselves, their ideas, and their projects.	Grandiose sense of self-importance.
Tend to be able competitors who love getting to the top and enjoy staying there.	Believe their problems are unique and understood only by other special people.
Can visualize themselves as the best or most accomplished in their field.	Preoccupied by fantasies of unlimited success, power, brilliance, beauty, or ideal love.
They believe in themselves, their abilities, and their uniqueness, but do not demand special treatment or privilege.	Have a sense of entitlement and unreasonable expectations of especially favorable treatment.
Accept accomplishments, praise, and admiration gracefully and with self-possession.	Require constant attention and admiration.
Possess a keen awareness of their thoughts and feelings, and have some awareness of those of others.	Lack of empathy; inability to recognize and experience how others feel.
Expect others to treat them well at all times.	Preoccupied with feelings of envy.

CASE STUDY: NARCISSISTIC PERSONALITY DISORDER

Mr. C. is a 41-year-old male who presented for therapy after his wife of six years threatened to leave him and because his employer was pressuring him to resign his position as a sales executive for a condominium project. Apparently, Mrs. C. had told her husband that he loved himself "a hundred times more than you love me." Mr. C. dismissed this by saying he needed to buy $600 suits because his job demanded that he look his best at all times and that he was "tall, dark, handsome, and sexy—all any woman could want in a man." Mr. C. denied that he used scare tactics, exaggerated claims, or other pressure-selling techniques with customers. "Sure, I'm a bit aggressive, but you don't get into the 'Millionaire's Club' by being a wimp." He added that his employer would "go belly-up without me," and that he was too important to be dismissed for such petty reasons.

CASE STUDY: NARCISSISTIC PERSONALITY STYLE

Mr. J. is chairman of his state's democratic party and caucus. Throughout most of his career, he had been incredibly successful and effective. He is extroverted, witty, and charming interpersonally, and astute, visionary, and effective in mobilizing support for his party's political agenda. However, in graduate school a political science professor had criticized a first draft of his Master's thesis, evaluating his arguments as weak and conclusions only partially substantiated by the research cited. Prior to this, he had held the professor in high esteem, but questioned the professor's competence after this criticism. Nevertheless, he swallowed his pride and reworked the thesis according to the professor's suggestion and graduated. A short time after graduation, Mr. J. lost his first job as a speech writer for a state senator because the opinions and conclusions cited in his drafts were not sufficiently well documented. Fortunately, Mr. J. took these lessons to heart and found others to research his own speeches when he ran for office. Mr. J. recognized that this was not one of his strengths and could delegate it while focusing on his real strengths, which were envisioning policy and political agendas and galvanizing support for them.

grandiosity, attention-seeking, entitlement, arrogance, and little observable anxiety. They can be socially charming, despite being oblivious to the needs of others, and are interpersonally exploitative. The problem is that they have a fragile sense of self that is predicated on maintaining a self-view that they are exceptional. Because genuine engagement can result in the painful realization that others have attributes that they lack, these individuals engage in superficial relationships and seek out external feedback that supports this grandiose self-definition (Levy, 2012).

Covert Type. This type presents as vulnerable, "fragile" and thin-skinned. These individuals are characterized as inhibited, manifestly distressed, hypersensitive to the evaluations of others, while chronically envious and evaluating themselves in relation to others. Interpersonally they tend to be shy, outwardly self-effacing, and hypersensitive to slights, but are covertly or secretly grandiose and jealous. Unlike the overt type, these tend to withdraw from social situations (Levy, 2012).

Malignant Type. This type is also referred to as "malignant narcissism" (Kernberg, 1984). These individuals are characterized by the typical symptoms of Narcissistic Personality Disorder, as well as prominent antisocial behavior, paranoid features, and sadism toward others. They may engage in chronic lying, intimidation, and financial or interpersonal secondary gains which maintain their malignant pattern (Caligor et al., 2015).

Triggering Event. The typical situation, circumstance, or event that most likely triggers or activates the characteristic maladaptive response of the Narcissistic Personality Disorder (Othmer & Othmer, 2002), as noted in behavioral, interpersonal, cognitive, and affective styles, is: "evaluation of self."

Behavioral Style. Behaviorally, narcissistic individuals are seen as conceited, boastful, and snobbish. They appear self-assured and self-centered, and they tend to dominate conversation, seek admiration, and act in a pompous and exhibition-istic fashion. They are also impatient, arrogant, and thin-skinned or hypersensitive.

Interpersonal Style. Interpersonally, they are exploitive and use others to indulge themselves and their desires. Their behavior is socially facile, pleasant, and endearing. However, they are unable to respond with true empathy to others. When stressed, they can be disdainful, exploitive, and generally irresponsible in their behavior.

Cognitive Style. Their thinking style is one of cognitive expansiveness and exaggeration. They tend to focus on images and themes rather than on facts and issues. In fact, they take liberties with the facts, distort them, and even engage in prevarication and self-deception to preserve their own illusions about themselves and the projects in which they are involved. Their cognitive style is also marked by inflexibility. In addition, they have an exaggerated sense of self-importance and establish unrealistic goals of power, wealth, and ability. They justify all of this with their sense of entitlement and exaggerated sense of their own self-importance.

Affective Style. Their emotional or affective style is characterized by an aura of self-confidence and nonchalance, which is present in most situations except when their narcissistic confidence is shaken. Then they are likely to respond with rage at criticism. Their feelings toward others shift and vacillate between over-idealization and devaluation. Finally, their inability to show empathy is reflected in their superficial relationships, with minimal emotional ties or commitments.

Attachment Style. Individuals with a view of others that is negative and a self-view that vacillates between positive and negative exhibit a composite fearful-dismissing style of attachment. They tend to view themselves as special and entitled, but are also mindful of their need for others who can potentially hurt them. Accordingly, they use others to meet their needs while being wary and dismissive of them. The fearful-dismissing attachment style is common in individuals with this disorder.

Optimal Diagnostic Criterion. Of all the diagnostic criteria for the Antisocial Personality Disorder, one has been found to be the most useful in diagnosing this disorder. The belief is that, by beginning with this criterion, the clinician can test for the presence or absence of the criterion and more quickly diagnose the personality disorder (Allnutt & Links, 1996). The optimal criterion for this disorder is: has a grandiose sense of self-importance.

DSM-5 Description

Individuals with this personality disorder are characterized by an unremitting pattern of self-centeredness and grandiosity. More specifically, they have an exaggerated sense of their own abilities and achievements. They may have a constant need for attention, affirmation, and praise. Typically, they believe they are unique or special and should only associate with others of the same status. They are likely to have persistent fantasies about attaining success and power. These individuals can exploit others for personal gain. A sense of entitlement and the expectation of special treatment are common. They may come across as snobbish or arrogant. They appear to be incapable of showing empathy for others. In addition, they can be envious or think that others are envious of them (American Psychiatric Association, 2013).

The "Alternative DSM-5 Model for Personality Disorders"—in Section III—better reflects the emerging research on Narcissistic Personality Disorder (Ronningstam, 2011). The updated definition of Narcissistic Personality Disorder includes "variable and vulnerable self-esteem, with attempts at regulation through attention and approval seeking, and either overt or covert grandiosity" (American Psychiatric Association, 2013, p. 767). This definition includes additional styles of narcissism that were not in DSM-IV-TR. In Section III of the DSM-5, vulnerability of self-esteem is now emphasized as a core feature of Narcissistic Personality Disorder and recognizes the covert type. In contrast, Section II of the DSM-5 emphasizes the dimension of grandiosity and only includes the overt type.

Prototypic Description

A prototype is a brief description that captures the essence of how a particular disorder commonly presents. Prototypic descriptions are useful and convenient and clinicians commonly rely on them rather than lists of behavioral criteria or core beliefs (Westen, 2012). Here is a common prototypic description of the Narcissistic Personality Disorder: These individuals are the center of their worlds. They believe and act as if they are special in every way. They can be showoffs and name-droppers. Without a doubt, they are legends in their own minds. There is no limit to their sense of self-importance and entitlement. They are haughty, high-handed, and superior, and expect others to show deference and admiration. They seldom recognize the needs, concerns, or feelings of others. Not surprisingly, they experience disappointments and anger when others fail to live up to their highly unrealistic expectations (Francie, 2013).

Prevalence

Prevalence of this disorder has been estimated at between 0.6 and 6.2 percent of the general population (American Psychiatric Association, 2013). In clinical settings, estimates are that it is found in 2.3 to 35.7 percent of patients (Torgersen, 2012).

Table 8.2 summarizes the characteristics of this disorder.

Conceptualizations of the Narcissistic Personality Disorder

Psychodynamic Case Conceptualizations

Freud (1914/1976) described the original psychoanalytic formulation of narcissistic personality. For Freud, parental overevaluation or erratic, unreliable caretaking in early life were factors disrupting the development of object love in the child providing. As a result of this fixation or arrest at the narcissistic phase of development, Freud posited that narcissists would be unable to form lasting relationships. In other words, the etiology of the Narcissistic Personality Disorder is that it is the outcome of insufficient gratification of the normal narcissistic needs of infancy and childhood. The contrary hypothesis is that the disorder stems from narcissistic overgratification during childhood and, because of this fixation, interferes with the normal maturation and integration of the superego, leading to difficulties in regulation of self-esteem (Fernando, 1998). Another common belief is that the disorder arises from faulty parenting or disturbed object relations. Imbesi (2000) suggests this hypothesis is the common etiology of most personality disorders and instead proposes that the caretaker's failure to provide optimal frustrating experiences necessary to foster the development of a more realistic self-image in the child is the etiology of the narcissistic personality.

TABLE 8.2 Characteristics of Narcissistic Personality Disorder

Triggering Event(s)	Evaluation of self
Behavioral Style	Sense of entitlement Arrogant, thin-skinned Self-assured and pompous
Interpersonal Style	Requires excessive admiration Lacks empathy Envies or feels envied Arrogant and haughty Exploits others
Cognitive Style	Cognitive expansiveness and exaggeration Takes liberties with facts Impatient, persistent, and inflexible
Affective Style	Self-confident Narcissistic rage
Temperament	Active and responsive Special talents and early language development
Attachment Style	Fearful and dismissing
Parental Injunction	"Grow up and be wonderful, for me."
Self-View	"I'm special and unique, and I'm entitled to extraordinary rights and privileges whether I've earned them or not."
World-View	"Life is a banquet table to be sampled at will. People owe me admiration and privilege. Therefore, I'll expect and demand this specialness."
Maladaptive Schemas	Entitlement; defectiveness; emotional deprivation; insufficient self-control; unrelenting standards
Optimal Diagnostic Criterion	Has grandiose sense of self-importance

In the past two decades the formulations of the narcissistic personality by Kohut and Kernberg have become the dominant models. Kohut (1971, 1977) believed the narcissistic is developmentally arrested at the stage which requires specific responses from individuals in their environment to maintain cohesive selves, i.e., the structures of the grandiose self and the idealized parental image are not integrated. He described the formulation of self-object transferences—both mirroring and idealizing—that recreate the situation with parents that was not fully successful during childhood. When such responses are not forthcoming (an empathic deficit), the narcissistic is prone to fragmentation of the self (narcissistic injury).

Unlike Kohut, who worked with high functioning professionals in psychoanalysis, Kernberg (1975, 1984) based his conceptualization of narcissistic pathology on his work with inpatients as well as outpatients. He views the narcissist's grandiosity and exploitation as evidence of oral rage, which he believes results from the emotional deprivation caused by an indifferent and covertly spiteful mother figure. Concurrently, some unique attribute, talent, or role provides the child with a sense of being special, which provides an emotional escape valve in a world of perceived threat or indifference. Thus, grandiosity and entitlement shelter a "real self" that is "split off," i.e., outside consciousness. Parenthetically for Kernberg, the real self contains strong but unconscious feelings of envy, deprivation, fear, and rage. Finally, Kernberg (1975) views the defensive structure of the narcissist as remarkably similar to the borderline, differentiating the two on the basis of their integrated but pathological grandiose self.

Biosocial Case Conceptualizations

According to Millon and Everly (1985), the Narcissistic Personality Disorder primarily arises from environment factors, since the role of biogenic factors is unclear. The principal environmental factors are parental indulgence and overvaluation, learned exploitive behavior, and only-child status. Essentially then, children are pampered and given special treatment by the parents such that they learn to believe the world revolves around them. They become egotistical in their perspectives and narcissistic in their expressions of love and emotion. Not surprisingly, they come to expect special treatment from others outside the home. When special treatment is not forthcoming, the children experiment with demanding and exploitive tactics and subsequently develop considerable skill in manipulating others so as to receive the special consideration they believe they deserve. At the same time they come to believe that most others are inferior, weak, and exploitable. Furthermore, Millon (Millon & Davis, 2000; Millon & Everly, 1985) indicate that parental overindulgence is particularly likely with only children. Finally, the narcissistic pattern is self-perpetuated through their illusion of their superiority, a lack of self-control manifested by their disdain for situations and persons that do not support their exalted beliefs, deficient social responsibility, and the self-reinforcement of the narcissistic pattern itself.

Cognitive-Behavioral Case Conceptualizations

According to Beck (2015), the key feature of this disorder is self-aggrandizement. Individuals with this disorder can be characterized by specific core, conditional, and instrumental beliefs. Their *core beliefs* include deserving special treatment and dispensations because of their specialness. They also include believing that they are not bound by the rules and social conventions that govern others. Their *conditional beliefs* are that others should be punished if they do not recognize their special status, and that to maintain their special status others must be subservient to them. Their *instrumental belief* is to continually strive to demonstrate their superiority. Underlying these various beliefs are their beliefs about self and the world. These individuals tend to view themselves as special, superior, entitled to special favors and treatment, and vulnerable to loss of status. They view others as inferior but also potential admirers, who recognize their superiority and grandiosity. Not surprisingly, such beliefs are reflected in their main strategy or pattern of seeking prestige, power, position, and wealth as a way of reinforcing their image of superiority. If necessary, they will use manipulation and guile to achieve these goals (Beck, 2015; Behary & Davis, 2015).

Specific schemas characterize this disorder. The central schema is the superior/special schema which develops from direct and indirect messages from parents, siblings, and significant others as well as by experiences that mold beliefs about personal uniqueness and self-importance. The schema of being superior can be shaped by flattery, indulgence, and favoritism. Similarly, the schema of being special can be shaped by experiences of rejection, limitations, exclusion, or deficits. The common denominator for such beliefs about self is that the individual perceives himself or herself as different from others in significant ways (Behary & Davis, 2015).

Taking a more behavioral tack, Turkat (1990), differentiates this disorder into three types: the self-centered impulsive type, the ruthless impression-management type, and the acceptance-oriented impression-management type. Of these, he considers the last type to have the best therapeutic prognosis. Nevertheless, he formulates each type as behavioral manifestations of an impulse control deficit that is learned in early childhood. Specifically, these individuals learned to seek reinforcers without having to work for them. This resulted in their development as self-indulgent, egocentric, and impulsive individuals. Individuals with the second and third types focus on creating a favorable impression on others. However, they are unable to maintain close relationships because, while they have excellent skills at reading superficial cues, they have empathic deficits (Turkat, 1990).

Interpersonal Case Conceptualizations

For Benjamin (2003a), a person with Narcissistic Personality Disorder typically was raised in an environment of selfless not contingent love and adoration. Unfortunately this adoration was not accompanied by genuine self-disclosure. As a result the Narcissistic-Personality-Disorder-to-be learned to be insensitive to others' needs and views. The adoring parent is likely to have been consistently differential and nurturant to the narcissistic-in-training. As a result, the adult narcissist held the arrogant expectation that others will continue to provide these emotional supplies. Along with this nurturance and adoration is the ever-present threat of a fall from grace. As such the narcissistic individual who is simply "normal" and ordinary creates unbearable disappointment for the parent(s). Thus, the burden of being special or perfect can be overwhelming for the narcissistic individual. Since this individual's self-concept derives from an internalization of unrealistic adoration and nurturance, the substitution of criticism or disappointment for love can be particularly devastating. Thus, the narcissistically-disordered individual can "dish it out," but is not well-equipped to "take it." In short, there is extreme vulnerability to criticism or being ignored, together with a strong wish for love, support, and admiration from others. Noncontingent love and presumptive control of others is expected and even demanded. If support is withdrawn, or lack of perfection is evident, the self-concept degrades into severe self-criticism. Totally devoid of empathy, these individuals tend to treat others with contempt and rage if their demand for entitlement fails.

Integrative Case Conceptualizations

The following integrative formulation provides a biopsychosocial explanation for how this personality is likely to have developed and how it is maintained. Biologically narcissistic personalities tend to have hyperresponsive temperaments (Millon, 1981). As young children they were viewed by others as being special in terms of looks, talents, or "promise." Often as young children they had early and exceptional speech development. In addition, they were likely keenly aware of interpersonal cues.

Psychologically, the narcissists' view of themselves, others, the world, and life's purpose can be articulated in terms of the following themes: "I'm special and unique, and I am entitled to extraordinary rights and privileges whether I have earned them or not." Their world-view is a variant of the theme "Life is a banquet table to be sampled at will. People owe me admiration and privilege." Their goal is "Therefore, I'll expect and demand this specialness." Common defense mechanisms utilized by the narcissistic personality involve rationalization and projective identification.

Socially, predictable parental patterns and environmental factors can be noted for the narcissistic personality. Parental indulgence and overevaluation characterize the narcissistic personality. The parental injunction was likely: "Grow up and be wonderful—for me." Often they were only children, and, in addition, may have sustained early losses in childhood. From an early age they learned exploitive and manipulative behavior from their parents. This narcissistic pattern is confirmed, reinforced, and perpetuated by certain individual and systems factors. The illusion of specialness, disdain for others' views, and a sense of entitlement lead to an underdeveloped sense of social interest and responsibility. This, in turn, leads to increased self-absorption and confirmation of narcissistic beliefs (Sperry, 2015; Sperry & Mosak, 1996).

Assessment of Narcissistic Personality Disorder

Several sources of information are useful in establishing a diagnosis and treatment plan for personality disorders. Observation, collateral information, and psychological testing are important adjuncts to the patient's self-report in the clinical interview. This section briefly describes some characteristic observations that the clinician makes and the nature of the rapport likely to develop in initial encounters with specific personality-disordered individuals. Characteristic response patterns on various objective (i.e. MMPI-2 and MCMI-IV) and projective tests (i.e., Rorschach and TAT) are also described.

Interview Behavior and Rapport

Interviewing Narcissistic Personality-Disordered individuals is singularly different than interviewing other personality-disordered individuals. Throughout the interview, these individuals give clinicians the impression that the interview has only one purpose: to endorse their self-promoted importance (Othmer & Othmer, 2002). These individuals typically present as self-assured, pretentious, and unwilling to adapt to the basic cultural differences customary to the patient role. They behave as though they are indifferent to the clinician's perspective. As long as the clinician plays the expected role, they are idealized as a marvelous clinician. However, confronting their grandiosity early in the treatment process will inevitably lead to rage and possibly premature termination. They prefer open-ended questions, which permit them extended descriptions of their many talents, accomplishments, and future plans. Rapport is established after a considerable period of mirroring and soothing. Typical clinician countertransferences in the initial interviews are boredom, frustration, and anger. To the extent the clinician can patiently wait through this period of mirroring, the work of confronting and interpreting the grandiosity of the disordered individual can begin.

Psychological Testing Data

This section describes typical themes and patterns noted for the narcissistic personality on the Minnesota Multiphasic Personality Inventory (MMPI-2), the Millon Clinical Multiaxial Inventory (MCMI-IV), the Rorschach Psychodiagnostic Test, and the Thematic Apperception Test (TAT). This data has been useful in diagnosing the Narcissistic Personality Disorder as well as the narcissistic personality style or trait.

On the MMPI-2, a 4–9 (Psychopathic Deviant-Hypomania) profile or an elevation on scale 4 is most likely. Since they develop only superficial relationships, a low score on 0 (Social Introversion) might also be noted (Graham, 2012). And, since they often fit stereotypic sexual roles, scale 5 (Masculinity-Femininity) may be low particularly in narcissistic males. If they also tend to be suspicious or irritable, an elevation on scale 6 (Paranoia) may be noted (Meyer, 1995).

On the MCMI-IV, elevation on scale 5 (Narcissistic) is expected. Scales 4A (Histrionic), 6A (Antisocial), and 6B (Sadistic) could also be elevated. During periods of stress, elevations on P (Paranoid) and PP (Delusional Disorder) may be noted. Since these individuals are averse to admitting psychic distress or personal weakness, elevations on scales A (Generalized Anxiety Disorder) and D (Dysthymia disorder) and S (Schizotypal) are not likely (Choca & Denburg, 1997).

On the Rorschach, these individuals are likely to produce records with a high number of C (Pure Color) and CF (Color Form) responses. They seldom respond directly to Shading (Y, YF, or FY) but often make texture (T, TF, or FT) responses. Responses that reflect the ornate, the exotic, or the expensive are characteristics of narcissism (Shafer, 1954).

On the TAT, these individuals tend to avoid the essential features of the cards and thus their stories may be void of meaningful content. Cards that demand a response to potentially anxiety-producing fantasy, such as 13 MF, may yield a superficially avoidant story or are with blatant shocking or lewd content (Bellak, 1997).

Treatment Approaches and Interventions

Treatment Considerations

Included in the differential diagnosis of the Narcissistic Personality Disorder are the following personality disorders: Histrionic Personality Disorder, Antisocial Personality Disorder, and Paranoid Personality Disorder. The most common concurrent symptom disorders are Anxiety Disorders, Persistent Depressive Disorder, Somatic Symptom Disorders, and Delusional Disorders.

The efficacy of psychotherapeutic and psychopharmacological treatment approaches for Narcissistic Personality Disorder has not been systematically or empirically investigated (Caligor et al., 2015). Clinical practice guidelines for the disorder have yet to be formulated, and psychopharmacological intervention is often symptom-driven. Regardless of severity, the grandiosity and defensiveness that characterize Narcissistic Personality Disorder make engagement in any form of psychotherapy difficult (Ronningstam, 2011).

Treatment recommendations for the narcissistic personality are currently based on clinical experience and theoretical formulations (Caligor et al., 2015). In the absence of empirically supported treatments for this disorder, it is common practice to utilize efficacious treatments for similar disorders, typically with treatment modifications based on theoretical and clinical rationales regarding differences in the disorders (Levy, 2012). These include empirically supported treatments for Borderline Personality Disorder that have adaptations for narcissistic personality such as mentalization-based therapy (Allen & Fonagy, 2006), transference-focused psychotherapy (Stern, Yeomans, & Diamond, 2012), and schema-focused psychotherapy (Young et al., 2003). All three treatments target psychological capacities thought to underlie and organize descriptive features of Narcissistic Personality Disorder. Dialectical behavioral therapy (Linehan, 2015) is another option for those with significant self-destructive behaviors.

Individual Psychotherapy

Alone, or in conjunction with group or marital and family therapy, individual psychotherapy is viewed by many as the basic treatment of choice for individuals with Narcissistic Personality Disorder. Indeed, some have agued that this disorder and psychotherapy itself are both products of the modern world's intense focus on the self (Lasch, 1991). Because of their empathic deficit and proclivity to devalue others, psychotherapy with these individuals can be very trying: giving little, treating others shabbily, and demanding much tends to frustrate the natural inclination of therapists to respond empathically. And, although the literature is divided over whether to utilize either confrontation or mirroring techniques, both approaches must be part of the therapist's armamentarium. Generally speaking, higher functioning narcissistic personalities eventually do well in psychotherapy, as their sense of entitlement gives way to emulation. On the other hand, lower functioning narcissistic personalities have fewer of the necessary personality assets and relational skills for changing, and unless the therapeutic process addresses these deficits, these individuals may predictably leave treatment precipitously to avoid the humiliation of admitting how ill-equipped they are to achieve realistic treatment goals. Psychodynamic, cognitive behavioral, and interpersonal approaches are briefly described.

Psychodynamic Psychotherapy Approaches

This section will briefly outline the various psychodynamic approaches: psycho-analysis, psychoanalytic psychotherapy, supportive psychotherapy, and brief psychoanalytic psychotherapy.

Psychoanalysis. Although Freud (1914/1976) was not optimistic about the treatability of the narcissistic personality, Kernberg (1984) and Kohut (1971) believe that higher functioning Narcissistic Personality-Disordered individuals are particularly suited for psychoanalysis. Kernberg views the core of the disorder as involving anger, envy, and distorted self-sufficiency, and so emphasizes an active interpretation and confrontation of the individual's defenses. Kohut, on the other hand, views the core of the disorder as stunted development of the grandiose self. As such, he emphasizes that through the establishment of self-object transference, both mirroring and idealizing, missing element of the self structure can be added. When a correct empathic interpretation is made, the individual reintegrates by way of the reestablishment of the self-object transference—cohesion—and the disappearance of figmentation. In short, then, Kernberg's goal of psychoanalysis is to effect a significant personality change so that envy and rage no longer overwhelm the individual and lead to a protective need to withdraw to a self-sufficient position. For Kohut, the goal is to heal the individual's incomplete self-structure and increase self-esteem through transmuting internalization, i.e., taking in of missing functions from the self-object analyst. The process of psychoanalysis for both Kohut and Kernberg is expected to take several years, since significant personality change is the goal. Kernberg (2010) maintains that psychoanalysis is preferable for higher functioning narcissistic patients, as cognitive-behavioral or supportive modalities may successfully reduce symptoms but do not address the unconscious dynamics behind them. However, he states that psychoanalytically oriented psychotherapy is contraindicated for overwhelming negative prognostic indicators.

Psychoanalytic Psychotherapy. In what he calls expressive psychotherapy, Kernberg (1984) describes a modified psychoanalytic treatment as an alternative to psychoanalysis and supportive psychotherapy. In expressive psychotherapy the therapeutic effort focuses on the negative transference in which early manifestations of anger toward the therapist are explored and interpreted. Also included are the defenses of splitting, projection, and projective identification. Masterson (1981) and Rinsley (1982) further emphasize the value of this approach in the development of a therapeutic alliance. Masterson also emphasizes the importance of exploring the individual's exquisite sensitivity to the therapist's empathic failures and the importance of therapeutically exploring this vulnerability. Although Kohut did not describe a psychotherapeutic treatment of the Narcissistic Personality Disorder, Goldberg (1973) and Chessick (1985) have shown that self-object transference does become established in psychotherapy and can be interpreted in light of Kohut's approach. Goldberg (1989) describes the use of the mirroring and idealizing, and the twinship transference, in a self-psychology approach to the narcissistic patient.

Psychoanalytically oriented psychotherapy of narcissistically disordered individuals typically involves one to three sessions a week for two or more years. Kantor (1992) offers a number of proactive suggestions for use in the course of psychotherapy. Among them is the use of predictive interpretation. He points out how painful therapy will be, as the individual feels forced to abandon their entitlement and grandiosity. Such forewarning of the individual is less likely to leave therapy precipitously.

The idea of dependence on another person for help is anathema to the narcissistic individual. Kernberg (2010) notes that this dependence is often seen as humiliating, and the narcissist's defense mechanisms are activated in order to protect against this feeling. Individuals may attempt to wrest control of the treatment from the therapist by engaging in "self-analysis." They treat therapists as "vending machines" of interpretations, accepting those with which they agree and rejecting others. Narcissistic patients may alternatively compete with and idealize their therapists, both of which are intended to create distance and assume control. Treatment is filled with feelings of envy and hostility on the part of the patient. These may manifest in attempts to seduce the therapist or self-injurious behaviors intended to destroy the legitimacy of the therapist's role. As such, psycho-analytically oriented psychotherapy with narcissistic individuals must account for these particular defenses.

Supportive Psychotherapy. According to Kernberg (1984), supportive psychotherapy emphasizes an avoidance of working with the negative transference, and instead focuses on supporting the individual in developing expanding ego functions, skills, and capacities. According to Kernberg, rapid symptomatic improvement is more likely in supportive psychotherapy than in more expressive approaches. The reader is referred to Kernberg's (1984) chapter on "Supportive Psychotherapy" for an extended discussion of treatment goals and techniques. Kantor (1992) recommends palliation as the goal of supportive psychotherapy, wherein the disordered narcissistic personality is maintained while reducing or eliminating its destructive sequelae. He recommends a number of palliative strat-egies, such as teaching the individual to become a better narcissist. For instance, Kantor shows the individual how excessive self-adoration actually interferes with the ability to receive more realistic, wanted, and needed adoration from others.

Brief Psychoanalytically Oriented Psychotherapy. Not surprisingly, the least explored treatment modality of the psychodynamic therapies of Narcissistic Personality Disorder are the shorter-term and brief approaches. Until recently, a self-deficit disorder like the narcissistic personality was considered unamenable to any but long-term treatment. However, as economic realities collide with ideology, this view may be changing somewhat. Kernberg (1984) describes a short-term crisis intervention for Narcissistic Personality Disorder until the individual is ready and motivated for long-term treatment. Lazarus (1982) and Binder (1979) report utilizing a brief approach for increasing the individual's self-esteem and self-cohesion, again as preparation for longer-term treatment.

Klein (1989b) describes a shorter-term treatment which is not a preparation for longer-term therapy. Admittedly, the goals are not ego repair, but are more limited. The goals are learning—increased awareness and anticipation of personal vulnerability to injury, shame, and disappointment; containment—increased ability to modulate affects, especially narcissistic rage; and adaptation—seriously taking into account those aspects of reality previously ignored and their destruc-tive consequences. Interpretation of narcissistic vulnerability and clarification of the need for containment of defensive devaluation and withdrawal are the cornerstones of this approach. Klein, a colleague of Masterson, describes two selection criteria. An acute interruption of narcissistic "supply lines" (i.e., inter-personal rejection or disappointment) results in narcissistic injury amenable to a substitute "supply line" (i.e. the therapist's mirroring). Second, when the nar-cissistic injury milieus makes conscious a persistent vulnerability (often experienced as depression or somatic preoccupation) and these individuals are motivated to learn more adaptive ways of managing their environment. Klein specifically excludes individuals who present or are referred with chronic, nonspecific, vague or ego-syntonic symptoms from his brief approach. He describes a course of time-limited treatment (i.e., six months) with a young male, which effected symptom relief and circumscribed improvement in functioning. Oldham and Skodol (2000) describes a 24-session treatment strategy that he describes as a dynamically informed directive approach with limited, focused treatment goals. Marmar and Freeman (1988) also describe a brief dynamic approach, as does Trujillo (2013).

Cognitive-Behavioral Therapy Approaches

Cognitive Therapy. Beck et al. (2004) provide an in-depth discussion of the Cognitive Therapy approach to Narcissistic Personality-Disordered individuals. Early in the course of therapy with these individuals, three treatment objectives must be met: developing a collaborative working relationship, socializing the individuals to the cognitive theory and model of treatment, and agreeing on treatment goals. Narcissistic individuals often arrive to treatment somewhere between pre-contemplation and contemplation in a stance that is opposed to change. Even while experiencing distress, these individuals are ambivalent about accepting help or examining their own thoughts and behaviors, because this may activate their core negative belief of inferiority. Forming a collaborative relationship is challenging, in that narcissistic individuals are deeply invested in being special and superior, and usually have a limited capacity for working collaboratively. These self-protective strategies can easily provoke strong reactions in the therapist, such as annoyance, anxiety, defensiveness, or lapses in judgment. Establishing and maintaining firm treatment guidelines and limits, in a neutral, matter-of-fact tone, is necessary. It should be pointed out that sticking to an agreed-upon agenda allows the therapist to more effectively address the narcissistic individual's important concerns. Similarly, the therapist can approach other counterproductive behaviors in therapy by appealing to the individual's self-interest. With these particular individuals, it is important to offer praise and support for their strengths in order to meet their expectations for the relationship and keep them engaged in treatment. Of course, this must be done strategically to reinforce desired behaviors without contributing to problem ones.

Because disclosing shortcomings and weaknesses is alien to the narcissist's style, behavioral interventions are usually easier to implement earlier in treatment, since they require less self-disclosure than most cognitive techniques. The rhythm of treatment with narcissistic individuals alternates focus among increasing responsibility for behavior, decreasing cognitive distortions and dysfunctional affects—such as rage reactions—and, developing healthier attitudes and beliefs. The challenge of treatment with these individuals is to tailor treatment for the three components of grandiosity, hypersensitivity to criticism, and emphatic deficits. Cognitive techniques are useful in revising a distorted self-view, particularly with dichotomous, black-white thinking. Furthermore, magical restructuring methods wherein a realistic and pleasure fantasy replaces a grandiose one are useful.

Systematic desensitization and role reversal can be used to address hypersensitivity. Working with empathy deficits is a major focus of treatment and involves several techniques. After bringing these deficits to the attention of the individual, emotional schemas related to the feelings and reactions of others are activated, usually through role plays including role reversal. Then alternative ways of relating to others can be discussed, and new statements of belief, such as "others' feelings count too," are formulated. The use of significant others in therapy—such as in couples sessions—has been found useful in developing and practicing empathy and in reinforcing changes, as well as helping the significant other cope more effectively with the narcissistic individual.

According to Behary and Davis (2015), five key treatment goals are: recognize maladaptive coping modes and weaken their predominance; build affect regulation skills, emphasizing tolerance of frustration and imperfection; increase respect and empathy for others; increase attunement to natural strengths rather than contingent self-worth; and increase role involvement and appropriate reciprocity. The ultimate purpose of these goals is not to create homogenous individuals who are unfalteringly loving and tolerant; rather, it is to allow narcissistic individuals the capacity to be more flexible and adaptive manner.

In summary, cognitive therapy with the Narcissistic Personality Disordered individual can be most challenging, nevertheless, they can make significant changes. Beck indicates that the best predictors of success are the degree of narcissism and the therapist's ability to withstand the individual's demands for approval and special treatment. Positive treatment outcomes are likely to the extent that (1) a collaborative working relationship is established, (2) limits are set and maintained regarding the control of therapy and special treatment, (3) schemas of grandiosity, hypersensitivity and empathy are changed, and (4) associated behaviors and affects are modulated.

Schema Therapy. Schema Therapy is an elaboration of cognitive therapy that has been developed by Young (1999) specifically for personality disorders, and other difficult individual and couples problems. Schema Therapy involves identifying maladaptive schemas and planning specific strategies and interventions. Four main strategies are cognitive, experiential, behavioral, and the therapeutic relationship itself. Cognitive restructuring, modification of maladaptive schemas, is an important cognitive strategy, but is combined with imagery exercises, empathic confrontation, homework assignments, and "limited reparenting," i.e., a form of corrective emotional experience (Young, 1999).

Maladaptive schemas typically associated with Narcissistic Personality Disorder include: *entitlement*—the belief that one is superior to others and not bound by the rules and norms that govern normal social interaction; *emotional deprivation*—the belief that one's desire for emotional support will not be met by others; *defectiveness*—the belief that one is defective, bad, unwanted, or inferior in important respects; *unrelenting standards*—the belief that striving to meet unrealistically high standards of performance is essential to be accepted and to avoid criticism; and *insufficient self-control*—the belief that one is incapable of self-control and frustration tolerance (Bernstein, 2002). Young et al. (2003) provide a detailed treatment protocol for treating Narcissistic Personality Disorder.

Interpersonal Psychotherapy

For Benjamin (2003b) psychotherapeutic interventions with Narcissistic Personality-Disordered individuals can be planned and evaluated in terms of whether they enhance collaboration, facilitate learning about maladaptive patterns and their roots, block these patterns, enhance the will to change, and effectively encourage new patterns. As with other interpersonal psychotherapy applications, the success of interventions aimed at treating Narcissistic Personality Disorder should be evaluated in terms of their impact on the patient and not the therapist's intention. This means the occurrence of rage, angry withdrawal from the therapist, or regal autonomy signal that an error has been made. Any subtle suggestion of blame may elicit problem patterns.

Facilitating collaboration with narcissistic individuals is rooted in accurate, consistent empathy. Consistent empathy provides the affirmation and soothing needed to learn self-regulation through the experience of being accurately mirrored, able to internalize this empathic affirmation of self. Another important aspect of collaboration involves the individual's learning to tolerate his or her faults. This is facilitated through modeling, as the therapist acknowledges mistakes or error, such as an occasional minor lapse in understanding the individual. In therapy, narcissistic individuals must learn to recognize and block the patterns of entitlement, grandiosity, and envy of others' success. Gentle confrontations embedded in strong support are utilized for this purpose. Benjamin considers this a fragile practice, one that may easily result in a hurt narcissistic individual abandoning treatment. To accomplish this successfully, the therapist must master the delicate art of pushing the edge of awareness without destroying the therapeutic relationship. Couples therapy can be useful in the recognition and blocking of maladaptive patterns.

Once these individuals understand their maladaptive patterns and choose to relinquish the quest for unattainable or maladaptive goals, new learning is relatively easy. According to Benjamin, the basic focus of interpersonal learning is empathy. Empathy can effectively be taught in couples therapy. Role-playing and other empathy training approaches can be particularly useful. Benjamin contends that, when utilizing role-playing, it is important that a collaborative and benign use of the individual's exact words and inflections be employed, as inexact mirroring can elicit rage and withdrawal.

Group Therapy

There is growing literature in the treatment of Narcissistic Personality-Disordered individuals in group therapy formats. Many of the recent reports are based on object relations and/or self-psychology approaches (Leszcz, 1989). Outcome research demonstrates that group therapy is as effective as any other therapy in treating the Narcissistic Personality Disorder (Alonso, 1992). A number of factors contribute to the effectiveness of groups with this personality disorder. First, peer rather than therapist feedback is likely to be more acceptable to the individual. Second, transference is likely to be less intense than in individual therapy. Working through intense affects is more possible because of the individual's positive attachments within the group and because of peer group scrutiny of the individual's disavowed affects. Third, group membership provides the narcissist individual with three unique needs: mirroring of needs, objects for idealization, and opportunities for peer relationships (Grotjahn, 1984). Finally, the group provides individuals with opportunities to increase their capacity to empathize with others, as well as enhance self-esteem and self-cohesion.

Most of the recent reports suggest that groups consisting exclusively of narcissistic individuals can have successful therapeutic outcomes. Alonso (1992) notes that, while narcissistic pathology undermines the usual forces that lead to group cohesion, a properly run group can function as a container for splitting and oscillation of self-love and hate. She also notes that a high drop-out rate is common in groups for Narcissistic Personality-Disordered individuals, with up to 50 percent of the individuals dropping out in ongoing—rather than time-limited—groups. Alonzo recommends intermittent individual therapy focused on helping individuals remain in the group. Horowitz (1987) describes the indication and contraindications for group treatment of narcissistic individuals. He notes four indications: demandingness, egocentrism, social isolation and withdrawal, and socially deviant behavior. Even though these traits may be taxing to both therapist and group members, Horowitz believes individuals with such traits are quite amenable to group treatment. Stone and Whiteman (1980) note that attention to the unique needs of the individual might warrant a deemphasis on interpretations geared to the entire groups, with a focus on an individual members' needs or capacities that are different from that of the group. Finally, Rutan et al. (2014) maintain that group therapy does not provide narcissistic individuals with the safety of individual psychotherapy. The presence of others triggers fears of non-responsiveness and, as such, presents a serious danger to the self. Groups provide an opportunity for narcissistic individuals to face their difficulties *in vivo*, gaining valuable reparative experiences in self-other interactions. While all group members may suffer narcissistic injury from time to time, it is important to distinguish between the narcissistic needs of all individuals and the pathology of this disorder.

Marital and Family Therapy

The early family therapy literature emphasized the treatment of adolescents in families with severe narcissistic pathology (Berkowitz et al., 1974; Shapiro, 1982). Typically, such families identify the adolescent as the patient and project onto him or her their own devalued view of themselves. Not surprisingly, when the adolescent attempts to separate and individualize, the parent's rage and projections intensify. In a family therapy format, the therapist functions to contain displaced, projected, and acted-out impulses and affects. Furthermore, the therapist must acknowledge, work through, and redirect these responses and so provide the family an opportunity to restore previously severed communication and mutual support during this critical phase of adolescent development.

More recent applications of family therapy to Narcissistic Personality Disorder involve entire family systems for one or both parents/spouses. Jones (1987) advocates a family systems approach to the narcissistic family. He suggests several strategies, particularly, determining the dilemma the family faces regarding change by analyzing the metaphorical themes that paradoxically bind the family to resist change. Subsequently, the therapist must join—rather than challenge or confront —the family's resistance. Such an empathic relationship is useful in understanding how resistance can be lowered. Usually, family sessions are scheduled weekly for 90 minutes with all family members. Such family treatment has been described as up to or more than a year's duration.

Considerably more has been published about marital therapy with the narcissistic spouse or couple. Berkowitz (1985) has described a couples therapy protocol based on Kohut's view of narcissistic vulnerability, self-object needs, and projective identification. The couple is seen conjointly in weekly sessions—usually 75–90 minutes—with the goal of "owning" projections and internalizing needed self-object functions. Lachkar (1986, 1992) describes a common spousal bond: the narcissistic dominated by mirroring needs, and the others by fears of abandonment. She describes a psychoanalytic treatment approach—combining both object relations theory and self-psychology—in which the therapist functions as a self-object so that the exhibitionistic/bonding expectations can become channeled into more realistic goals. Therapy is envisioned as involving three developmental phases: fusion, separation, and interaction. It should be noted that Lachkar views conjoint marital therapy as a precursor to individual psychotherapy or psychoanalysis of one or both spouses. Furthermore, she adds that, in conjoint work, the therapeutic alliance must be joined with the spouse who is predominantly narcissistic because of their tendency to flee, isolate, and withdraw from therapy.

Solomon (1989) describes marital therapy wherein one or both spouses meet criteria for the Narcissistic Personality Disorder. Elucidating a self-psychology perspective of narcissism in marriage, she described a conjoint treatment protocol wherein marital therapy session functions as a "holding environment." Furthermore, she believes that distorted conscious and unconscious communication is central to marital conflict and its resolution. Finally, she describes the therapist's empathic self as the basic tool of treatment. Masterson and Orcutt (1989) describe a conjoint approach to working with the narcissistic couple.

Relationship Enhancement Therapy. This approach has recently been adapted to couples therapy with narcissistic spouses (Snyder, 1994). Relationship enhancement therapy is a unique blending of object relationship theory, social learning theory, interpersonal theory, and system theory, which provides a psychoeducational format for incorporating skills training in either an individual psychotherapy or conjoint couples therapy.

Relationship enhancement couples therapy focuses on the learning and application of four core interpersonal skills: empathy; effective expression; discussion—mode switching between empathic and expressor roles; and problem solving/conflict resolution. The therapist explains, demonstrates, and coaches each skill in the conjoint session, and the spouse then practices these skills during and between sessions with progressively difficult issues. Not surprisingly, the empathic skills and the subjective aspect of the expressor skill are notably deficient for the narcissistically vulnerable couple. Furthermore, the therapist provides a "holding" environment" in which narcissistic vulnerability is minimally acted out and instead is experienced and addressed productively. As a result, both spouses learn to express feelings with less risk of shaming the other and more ability to empathize with the feelings of the other spouse that previously evoked defensive reactions. Snyder (1994) provides a detailed case example of this promising approach.

There have been a number of recent developments in couples therapy wherein one or both partners present with narcissistic personality issues or the full-blown personality disorder. Kalojera et al. (1998) provide a detailed rationale and treatment strategy for approaching such couples from a self-psychology perspective that incorporate systemic dynamics. These authors present a useful flowchart of the process of relational work with such couples and a detailed case example illustrating the application of this approach.

Lachkar (1999) offers additional insight into the psychoanalytic treatment of couples in which one partner has a narcissistic personality structure, while the other partner presents with a borderline personality pattern or meets criteria for the Borderline Personality Disorder. Solomon (1999) also addresses the treatment of the narcissistic-borderline couple from a somewhat different psychoanalytic perspective. This line of research has been continued by Landucci and Foley (2014). They note that the therapist's job in working with the narcissistic-borderline couple is to assist the couple in understanding how their dysfunctional interactions replay developmental problems and do not necessarily signal problems in the relationship itself. Therapist empathy and the ability to contain the narcissistic partner's rage enable the other partner to feel safe in the session and thereby rekindle the developmental process for both. Another common relational pattern is the dependent/narcissistic couple. Nurse (1998) provides a detailed rationale and treatment protocol for working with such couples based on Millon's theory of personality disorders (Millon & Davis, 1996).

Medication

Currently, there are no psychotropic medications specifically indicated for treating individuals with Narcissistic Personality Disorder (Silk & Feurino, 2012). Nevertheless, medications are used that target specific troubling symptoms associated with the disorder, such as depression, anxiety, or sleep problems. Generally, these medications are used as an adjunct to psychotherapy and skills training. Because troubling symptoms often respond to medications sooner than most psychological interventions, medications are usually prescribed at the onset of treatment (Sperry, 1995b). Unfortunately, there is little research evidence to provide guidelines for the use of such medications with this disorder (Silk & Feurino, 2012).

Combined/Integrative Treatment Approaches

As noted in the opening chapter of this book, there is seldom a single treatment of choice, be it specifically method—i.e., mirroring—or general approach—i.e., psychoanalysis—that can ensure positive treatment outcomes with personality-disordered individuals. Rather, depending on the individual's overall level of functioning, temperamental patterns, defensive style, and skill deficits, a focused, specific, and sequentially coordinated tailored treatment protocol is usually necessary to accomplish treatment goals and objectives in a timely matter and fashion. Pincus, Wright, and Cain (2014) describe narcissistic grandiosity and narcissistic vulnerability in the context of psychotherapy, with links to the previous discussion of overt and covert narcissism. Symptoms of social anxiety, depression, and suicidality often drive narcissistic individuals into treatment-seeking relief, and addressing these with a combined/integrative treatment strategy is particularly useful. Roche, Pincus, Lukowitsky, Ménard, and Conroy (2013) also provide an integrative approach to the assessment of this disorder.

9

OBSESSIVE-COMPULSIVE PERSONALITY DISORDER

Individuals with obsessive compulsive personalities often present as inhibited, stubborn, perfectionistic, judgmental, overconscientious, rigid, and chronically anxious. They tend to avoid intimacy and experience little pleasure from life. They may be successful, but at the same time can be indecisive and demanding (Samuels & Costa, 2012). All of these factors can impede personal change. However, despite a number of unique therapeutic challenges, it can be highly effective and successful. Furthermore, although there are some similarities, this disorder differs from the Obsessive Compulsive Disorder, which is characterized by ritualistic compulsions and obsessions (Samuels & Costa, 2012).

This chapter describes a framework for the assessment and effective treatment of this disorder. It includes sections on diagnosis, case conceptualization, psychological assessment, and treatment interventions. It begins with background information on the disorder as well as a DSM-5 description and a prototypic description of this disorder. The section on case conceptualization provides five common clinical formulations of this disorder: psychodynamic, biosocial, cognitive-behavioral, interpersonal, and an integrative conceptualization of this disorder. Several treatment approaches, modalities, and intervention strategies are also described. These include individual psychotherapy, group therapy, marital and family therapy, medication, and integrative and combined treatment.

Description of the Obsessive-Compulsive Personality Disorder

The Obsessive-Compulsive Personality Disorder can be recognized by the following descriptors and characteristics: style vs. disorder, triggering event(s), behavioral style, interpersonal style, cognitive style, affective style, attachment style, and optimal diagnostic criterion.

Style vs. Disorder. The obsessive compulsive personality can be thought of as spanning a continuum from healthy to pathological, with the obsessive personality style on the healthy, and the Obsessive-Compulsive Personality Disorder on the pathological end. Table 9.1 compares and contrasts differences between the obsessive compulsive style and disorder.

TABLE 9.1 A Comparison of the Obsessive-Compulsive Personality Style and Disorder

Personality Style	Personality Disorder
Desires to complete tasks and projects without flaws or errors.	Perfectionism that interferes with task completion.
Takes pride in doing all job or tasks well, including the smallest details of it.	Preoccupation with details, rules, lists, order, organization, or schedules to the extent that the major point of the activity is lost.
Tends to want things to be done "just right" and in a specific manner, but has some tolerance for things being done.	Unreasonable insistence that others submit exactly to their way of doing things, or unreasonable reluctance to allow others to do things because of the conviction that they will not do them correctly.
Dedicated to work and working hard and capable of intense, single-minded effort.	Excessive devotion to work and productivity to the exclusion of leisure activities and friendships (not accounted for by obvious economic necessity).
Carefully considers alternatives and their consequences in making decisions.	Indecisive: decision making either avoided, postponed, or prolonged (but not due to excessive need for advice or reassurance from others).
Tends to have strong moral principles and strongly desires to do the right thing.	Overconscientious, scrupulous, and inflexible about matters of morality, ethics, or values.
No-nonsense individuals who do their work without much emotional expenditure.	Restructured expression of affection.
Generally, careful, thrifty, and cautious, but able to share from their abundance.	Lack of generosity in giving time, money, or gifts when no personal gain is likely to result.
Tend to save and collect objects and is reluctant to discard objects that have, formerly had or someday may have sentimental value for them.	Unable to discard worn-out or worthless objects even when they have no value.

The following case examples further illustrate the differences between the personality disorder—Mr. Z.—and the personality style—Mr. C.

CASE STUDY: OBSESSIVE-COMPULSIVE PERSONALITY DISORDER

Mr. Z. is a 39-year-old male business executive who wanted to begin a course of psychotherapy because his "whole world was closing in." He gave a history of long-standing feelings of dissatisfaction with his marriage, which had worsened in the past two years. He described his wife's increasing demands for time and affection from him, which he believed was a weakness she had. His professional life also had become conflicted when his partner of 10 years wanted to expand their accounting firm to another city. Mr. Z. believed this proposal was fraught with dangers and had come to the point of selling out his share of the business to his partner. He knew he had to make some decisions about his marriage and his business, but found himself unable to do so. He hoped therapy would help with these decisions. He presented as neatly dressed in a conservative three-piece blue suit. His posture was rigid and he spoke in a formal and controlled tone with constricted affect. His thinking was characterized by preoccupation with details and was somewhat circumstantial.

CASE STUDY: OBSESSIVE COMPULSIVE PERSONALITY STYLE

Mr. C. is a 41-year-old assistant vice president of personnel for a public utility. He rose through the ranks because of his loyalty and accomplishments above and beyond the call of duty. Because of his thoroughness and attention to detail, he has saved his corporation nearly $3 million in the past two years on insurance and health benefits for the employees of the utility. Most evenings, Mr. C. takes a briefcase of work home with him. Although he didn't really mind this intrusion into his family life, his wife of 18 years did. Accordingly, they've reached an agreement that Mr. C. will spend at least two hours with his wife and three kids before turning to his briefcase.

Triggering Event. The typical situation, circumstance, or event that most likely triggers or activates the characteristic maladaptive response of the Obsessive-Compulsive Personality Disorder (Othmer & Othmer, 2002), as noted in behavioral, interpersonal, cognitive, and affective styles, is: "authority; unstructured situations, and/or demands of intimate and close relations."

Behavioral Style. Behaviorally, this disorder is characterized by perfectionism. Individuals with this disorder are likely to be workaholics. In addition to dependability, they tend to be stubborn and possessive. They tend to be indecisive and procrastinating.

Interpersonal Style. Interpersonally, these individuals are exquisitely conscious of social rank and status and modify their behavior accordingly. That is, they tend to be deferential and obsequious to superiors, and haughty and autocratic to subordinates and peers. They can be doggedly insistent that others do things their way without an appreciation or awareness of how others react to this insistence. At their best they are polite and loyal to the organizations and ideals they espouse.

Cognitive Style. Their thinking style can be characterized as constricted and rule-based. They have difficulty establishing priorities and perspective. They are "detail" people and often lose sight of the larger project. In other words, they "can't see the forest for the trees." Their indecisiveness and doubts make decision making difficult. Their mental inflexibility is matched by their nonsuggestible and unimaginative style, suggesting they have a restricted fantasy life. Like passive aggressive individuals, obsessive compulsive individuals have conflicts between assertiveness and defiance, and pleasing and obedience, but for different reasons.

Affective Style. Their affective or emotional style is characterized as grim and cheerless. They have difficulty with the expression of intimate feelings such as warmth and tenderness. They tend to avoid the "softer" feelings, although they may express anger, frustration, and irritability quite freely. This grim, feeling-avoidant demeanor shows itself in stilted, stiff relationship behaviors.

Attachment Style. The preoccupied attachment dimension is characterized by a sense of personal unworthiness and a positive evaluation of others. These individuals tend to be very externally oriented in their self-definitions. This preoccupied attachment style is common in individuals with Obsessive-Compulsive Personality Disorder.

Optimal Diagnostic Criterion. Of all the diagnostic criteria for the Dependent Personality Disorder, one has been found to be the most useful in diagnosing this disorder. The belief is that, by beginning with this criterion, the clinician can test for the presence or absence of this criterion and more quickly diagnose the personality disorder (Allnutt & Links, 1996). The optimal criterion for this disorder is: shows perfectionism that interferes with task completion.

DSM-5 Description

Individuals with this personality disorder are characterized by an unremitting pattern of perfectionism, orderliness, and control instead of flexibility, openness, and efficiency. They are overly preoccupied with details, rules, and schedules. Their perfectionism interferes with completing tasks due to their overly strict standards. They are overly devoted to work and productivity to the exclusion of leisure activities and friendships. When it comes to matters of values, morality, or ethics, these individuals are inflexible, scrupulous, and overconscientious. Often, they are unable to discard worn-out or worthless objects that have no sentimental value. They will not delegate tasks or work with others unless it can be on their terms. Not surprisingly, these individuals are also rigid and stubborn. Finally, they are misers with money, and it is hoarded in the event of future catastrophes (American Psychiatric Association, 2013).

The "Alternative DSM-5 Model for Personality Disorders" provides another description of this disorder (American Psychiatric Association, 2013). It is described as difficult in establishing and maintaining close personal relationships, associated with perfectionism, restricted emotional expression, and inflexibility. Characteristic difficulties are noted in identity, self-direction, empathy, and intimacy, as well as restricted affect, intimacy avoidance, perseveration, and rigid perfectionism.

Prototypic Description

A prototype is a brief description that captures the essence of how a particular disorder commonly presents. Prototypic descriptions are useful and convenient and clinicians commonly rely on them rather than lists of behavioral criteria and core and instrumental beliefs (Westen, 2012). Here is a common prototypic description of the Obsessive-Compulsive Personality Disorder: These individuals are perfectionists and unyielding control freaks. They cannot rest until they get every detail exactly right. Because they insist that others can never be careful or competent enough, they never delegate or trust important matters to others. Their lives are controlled by schedules, rules, and rigid routines. Because of their scrupulous attention to details and their projects, they cannot relax, be spontaneous, or enjoy close and intimate relationships. They are unusually tight with money, feelings, and affection. They make it clear they must always have their way, or else (Frances, 2013).

Prevalence

Prevalence of this disorder has been estimated at between 2.1 and 7.9 percent in the general population (American Psychiatric Association, 2013). In clinical settings, estimates are that it is found in 2.8 to 34.6 percent of patients (Torgersen, 2012).

Conceptualizations of Obsessive-Compulsive Personality Disorder

Psychodynamic Case Conceptualizations

Early psychoanalytic writers formulated the obsessive compulsive personality as a regression from the Oedipal phase to the anal phase of development. Because of a punitive superego, the obsessive compulsive individual was observed to employ intellectualization, isolation of affect, undoing, development and reaction formation as defenses. Presumably, these individuals experienced difficulty expressing aggression as a result of power struggle with maternal figures over toilet training.

However, contemporary writers formulate this pattern much broader than anal fixation. As children, these individuals were not sufficiently valued or loved by their caretakers and subsequently developed overwhelming doubt. Salzman (1980) believes the obsessive pattern is basically a device for preventing any thought or feeling that could produce shame, loss of pride or status, or a feeling of deficiency or weakness, irrespective of whether the feelings are hostile, sexual, or otherwise. He views obsessive compulsivity as a neurotic strategy, which protects these individuals from exposure of any thoughts or feelings that could endanger their physical or psychological existence. This overriding need to control their inner and outer world requires these individuals to lead overly structured and manageable lives. They tend to maintain doubts, are willing to make commitments, and strive for perfection. Thus, it is necessary for them to know everything to predict the future and prepare for every exigency. To maintain the fiction of perfection, they must never make an error or admit any deficiency. Furthermore, their tendency to procrastinate is related to their tendency to doubt as a means of guaranteeing their omniscience when life forces a decision or choice. As such, they are deeply ambivalent, which allows them to maintain security, but at the price of productivity and positive feelings and attitudes. These individuals find both anger and dependency consciously unacceptable and so defend against these feelings with defenses like reaction formation and isolation of affect as well as differential and obsequious behaviors. Intimacy poses major concerns for these individuals, who fear being overwhelmed by powerful wishes to be taken care of, while also experiencing the frustration of those wishes along with the fear of being out of control. In addition, these individuals harbor the secret conviction that, if they could become perfect, they would finally receive the parental approval and esteem they missed in early life. Finally, psychodynamic writers have noted the unique cognitive style of obsessive compulsive individuals (Horowitz, 1988; Horowitz et al., 1984; Shapiro, 1965), as characterized by drivenness, careful attention to detail, lack of spontaneity, and ruminative thinking.

Biosocial Case Conceptualization

To date there is no research evidence that biological predisposing factors underlie this disorder (Millon & Davis, 1996). Nonetheless, clinical observations suggest that many obsessive compulsive individuals display an anhedonic temperament (Millon, 1981) and tend to be the first-born in their families of origin (Toman, 1961). Certain environmental factors may be etiologic: parental overcontrol, learned compulsive behavior, and responsibility training. Rather than being overprotective, parents of obsessive compulsive individuals overcontrol with firmness and punitiveness. This attempt to prevent their children from causing trouble for themselves or others, is punitive when the child misbehaves or fails to meet expectations. These children learn compulsive behavior directly and indirectly within the family matrix. They learn to avoid punishment by accepting and meeting the demands and expectations of perfectionistic and punitive parents. Furthermore, they learn compulsivity by imitating the compulsive behaviors modeled by one or both parents. As a result, they do not develop the ability to generate options and explore alternatives and thus fail to function autonomously. Obsessive compulsive individuals are regularly exposed to conditions that teach them to overvalue a sense of responsibility to others. They are taught to feel guilt when these responsibilities are not met, and shame when they act impulsively or even playfully. Instead they learn to be polite, pleasing and loyal to superiors. These influences typically yield individuals who are hard-driving, perfectionistic, polite, pleasing and who lead rather restrictive, tentative, colorless lives.

This obsessive compulsive pattern is self-perpetuated through an interaction of cognitive and behavioral rigidity, strict adherence of roles, regulations and social convention, and a tendency to be highly self-critical. While their cognitive rigidity serves to reduce anxiety associated with flexibility and ambivalence, they tend to lead overstructured, one-sided lives. Self-criticism serves to keep them in line, while striving for perfection reduces opportunities for risk-taking and adventure.

Cognitive-Behavioral Case Conceptualizations

Beck (2015) identified the core beliefs or schemas held by obsessive compulsive individuals: perfectionism and control. The perfectionism schema involves beliefs such as: "To be worthwhile I must avoid making mistakes because to make a mistake is to fail which would be intolerable," and "If the perfect course of action is unclear, it is better to do nothing." The control schema involves beliefs such as: "I must be perfectly in control of myself and my environment, because loss of control is intolerable and dangerous," "Without my rules and rituals, I'll collapse into an inert pile," and "Magical rituals or obsessive ruminations prevent the occurrence of catastrophes." Typically, they view themselves as responsible and accountable for most everything in their lives. At the same time they believe they are inadequate, helpless, or defective. They view others as incompetent, careless, and less concerned about matters than they are. Related beliefs include needing rules and regulations in order to survive. Because of their beliefs about control and perfection, should they fail at a task, they are likely to conclude that they must be failures and worthless. Not surprisingly, such beliefs are reflected in their main strategy or pattern of exercising maximum control over themselves and others through the use of directiveness, coercion, and disapproval (Beck, 2015; Simon, 2015).

Guidano and Liotti (1983) provide a similar but different cognitive formulation which involves three maladaptive schemas. They are: perfectionism, the need for certainty, and the belief that there is an absolute correct solution for human problems. Guidano and Liotti note that these individuals received mixed, contradictory messages from at least one parent. They also describe typical automatic thoughts of obsessive compulsive individuals. "I need to get this assignment done perfectly," "I have to do this project myself or it won't be done right," "That person misbehaved and should be punished," and "I should keep these old reports because I might need them some day." In addition to these schemas and automatic thoughts, individuals with this personality pattern often utilize the cognitive distortions of dichotomous thinking and magnification or catastrophizing.

Turkat (1990) and Turkat and Maisto (1985) suggest a behavioral formulation of this pattern. These individuals are noted to have been reared in families that emphasized productivity and rule-following at the expense of emotional expressivity and interpersonal relationships. Accordingly, these individuals did not acquire adequate levels of empathy skills or skills in interacting with others on an emotional basis.

Interpersonal Case Conceptualizations

According to Benjamin (2003a), persons diagnosed with Obsessive-Compulsive Personality Disorder were likely raised in an atmosphere of unreasonable and relentless coercion to perform correctly and follow rules regardless of personal cost. As a consequence, the obsessive compulsive individual has an unbalanced devotion to perfection of self and others. These parents typically held extremely high expectations for self-control and perfection, and not only punished their children for not being perfect, but gave them little or no reward for success. Subsequently, these children focused primarily on avoiding mistakes and self-criticism by trying hard to be good and right. Furthermore, there tended to be little warmth in these households. Laughter, hugging, holding, and other signs of affection were seldom, if ever, modeled. Expression of feelings was considered dangerous. The adult consequence of their lack of warmth and demand for perfection is social correctness, albeit inaccessibility of feelings. Finally, there is a fear of making mistakes and a penchant for rule-following. A quest for order underlies blame and inconsiderate control of others with control alternating with blind obedience to authority of principle. This stance is supported by excessive self-discipline, feeling avoidance, self-criticism, as well as neglect of the self.

Integrative Case Conceptualizations

The following integrative formulation provides a biopsychosocial explanation for how this personality is likely to have developed and how it is maintained. Biologically, these individuals were likely to have exhibited an anhedonic temperament as children. Not surprisingly, first-born children have a greater propensity for developing a compulsive style than other siblings.

Psychologically, these individuals view themselves, others, the world, and life's purpose in terms of the following themes. They tend to view themselves with some variant of the theme "I'm responsible if something goes wrong, so I have to be reliable, competent, and righteous." Their world-view is some variant of the theme "Life is unpredictable and expects too much." As such, they are likely to conclude, "Therefore, be in control, right, and proper at all times."

Socially, predictable patterns of parenting and environmental conditioning are noted for this personality. The parenting style they experienced could be characterized as both consistent and overcontrolled. As children they were trained to be overly responsible for their actions and to feel guilty and worthless if they were not obedient, achievement-oriented, or "good." The parental injunction to which they were most likely exposed was "You must do and be better to be worthwhile."

This obsessive compulsive pattern is confirmed, reinforced, and perpetuated by a number of factors: exceedingly high expectations plus harshly rigid behavior and beliefs, along with a tendency to be self-critical, lead to rigid rule-based behavior and avoidance of social, professional, and moral unacceptability. This in turn further reconfirms the harshly rigid behaviors and beliefs of this personality pattern (Sperry, 2015).

Table 9.2 summarizes the characteristics of this disorder.

Assessment of Obsessive-Compulsive Personality Disorder

Several sources of information are useful in establishing a diagnosis and treatment plan for personality disorders. Observation, collateral information, and psychological testing are important adjuncts to the patient's self-report in the clinical interview. This section briefly describes some characteristic observations that the clinician makes and the nature of the rapport likely to develop in initial encounters with specific personality-disordered individuals. Characteristic response patterns on various objective (i.e., MMPI-2 and MCMI-IV) and projective (i.e., Rorschach and TAT) tests are also described.

TABLE 9.2 Characteristics of Obsessive-Compulsive Personality Disorder

Triggering Event(s)	Demands of authority figures; unstructured situations, and/or demands of intimate and close relations
Behavioral Appearance	Perfectionistic and righteous Workaholic Dependable, reliable, and overly conscientious Indecisive and procrastinates
Interpersonal Behavior	Devotion to tasks or work limits relationships Unwillingness to delegate or collaborate Rigid and stubborn Judgmental Autocratic to subordinates but deferential to superiors Polite and loyal
Cognitive Style	Constricted—rule-based Inflexibility Unimaginative
Affective Style	Grim and cheerless Feeling avoidance
Temperament	Irritable, difficult, or anxious
Attachment Style	Preoccupied
Parental Injunction Self-View	"You must do/be better to be worthwhile." "I'm responsible if something goes wrong."
World-View	"Life is unpredictable and expects too much. Therefore, be in control, be right and proper and don't make mistakes."
Maladaptive Schemas	Unrelenting standards; punitiveness; emotional inhibition
Optimal Diagnostic Criterion	Shows perfectionism that interferes with task completion

Interview Behavior and Rapport

The obsessive compulsive's dynamics of circumstantiality, perfectionism, and ambivalence make interviewing these individuals difficult and challenging. Their preoccupation with, and focus on, details and need for control leads to a seemingly endless struggle about words, issues, and who is in charge without being able to develop an atmosphere of understanding and cooperation. Open-ended questions lead them to confusion. Instead they want more focused questions, but interpret them too narrowly when this kind of question is asked. They may bring a notebook of their medical history, diet, and exercise pattern, or even dreams, expecting to review these details with you. And, while they may admit that affects and feelings are associated with the details, they are unwilling to admit the value of expressing those affects, much less talking about them. Their ambivalence is difficult to over-come, since they cannot accept others' assurances that their problems are solvable or that they can tolerate less control in their lives.

The clinician's expression of empathy is problematic for them, since they insist they are objective and have no feelings. Thus, they are perturbed at the expression of empathy and reject it as irrelevant. They may insist that their problems, not their suffering, are important. Yet, their problems are unsolvable! The only thera-peutic leverage for the clinician is to attempt to get and keep this individual in touch with their anger and other feelings. But, this is difficult, as they will attempt to defend or deny affects, and put forth even more obstructive obsessive thinking to neutralize such therapeutic leverage. Needless to say, forming a therapeutic alliance is difficult and the interview often consists of aborted attempts, frustrations, and struggles (Othmer & Othmer, 2002).

Psychological Testing Data

The Minnesota Multiphase Personality Inventory (MMPI-2), the Millon Clinical Multiaxial Inventory (MCMI-IV), the Rorschach Psychodiagnostic Test, and the Thematic Apperception Test (TAT) can be useful in diagnosing the Compulsive Personality Disorder as well as the personality style (Groth-Marnat, 2009).

On the MMPI-2 there is likely to be a moderately high K (Correction) scale. Since individuals with obsessive compulsive features are not inclined to self-disclosure, they seldom leave elevated profiles. However, scales 1 (Hypo-chondriasis) and 3 (Hysteria) tend to be elevated. If physical complaints are the focus of the distress, scale 1 may be particularly elevated. An elevation on scale 9 (Hypomania) usually reflects the degree to which these individuals are autocratic and dominant in interpersonal relationships. Since scale 7 (Psychasthenia) reflects obsessionalism, elevation of this scale usually indicates a complaining and querulous attitude in them (Graham, 2012; Meyer, 1995).

On the MCMI-IV, a high score on scale 7 (Compulsive) is likely (Millon et al., 2015). Elevations on scale A (anxiety) are not likely, since these individuals tend to express anxiety somatically, thus scale H is likely to be elevated (somatic symptom disorder) (Choca & Denburg, 1997).

On the Rorschach test, there is likely to be an emphasis on Dd (Unusual Detail) and D (Common Detail) responses. Also, a high F+% (Form Plus) and fewer W (Whole) response and color-based responses. Obsessive compulsive individuals tend to describe some responses in overly specific detail and make criticisms of the ink blots (Meyer, 1995).

The TAT stories of these individuals tend to be lengthy, with a variety of themes. Sometimes the primary theme is lost amid the detailing of their response. This is particularly likely on card 2 and 13 MF (Bellak, 1997).

Treatment Approaches and Interventions

Treatment Considerations

Included in the differential diagnosis of this disorder is the Dependent Personality Disorder, and the so-called Passive Aggressive Personality Disorder. Common symptom diagnoses that are associated with the Dependent Personality Disorder include the Anxiety Disorders, particularly Simple Phobia, Social Anxiety Disorder, and Panic Disorder. Other common DSM-5 disorders include Conversion Disorders and Somatic Symptom Disorders.

The Obsessive Compulsive Disorder (OCD) has a long tradition of treatment dating back to Freud's case of the "Rat Man" and Adler's "Case of Mrs. A." Note that OCD is a symptom disorder, while the Obsessive-Compulsive Personality Disorder is personality disorder. Since the "Rat Man" exhibited both Axis I and II disorders, many who have read Freud's account of this case and its treatment have incorrectly assumed that both disorders are the same and are treated the same. They are not the same disorder, but in about one third of cases both disorders have been shown to be present (Jenike, Baer, & Minichiello, 1998; Phillips & Stein, 2015). When both disorders are present together, treatment has been shown to be much more challenging than if only OCD is present.

The goals of treatment include increased cognitive constriction and increased feeling expression, so that a more reasonable balance can be obtained between thoughts and feelings. Treatment strategies for the Obsessive-Compulsive Personality Disorder usually involve long-term, insight-oriented therapy. Unlike the Obsessive Compulsive Disorder, where antidepressants plus behavior therapy can result in amelioration of obsessions and compulsions in a relatively short period of time, the Obsessive-Compulsive Personality Disorder does not lend itself to short-term treatment outcomes. However, psychodynamic and cognitive behavioral intervention both appear to be effective. Medication is usually not needed with this disorder if the restitution of the accompanying symptom disorder is attainted (Sperry, 2015).

Individual Psychotherapy

Psychodynamic Psychotherapy Approach

The therapy of the obsessive compulsive patients involves exposing the patient's extreme feelings of insecurity and uncertainty. As they come to identify their neurotic structure as a defense against recognizing these weaknesses, they can begin to develop a more adaptive security system. At the outset of treatment, these patients are unable to abandon their obsessive compulsive defense, fearing unspeakable consequences. However, as their self-esteem grows and awareness of their strengths increases, they are able to take the risks of abandoning these patterns and are thus freer to function more productively. The goal of therapy is to switch from impossible expectations for self and others to more realistic achievable ones. In short, these individuals come to learn that by relinquishing their rigid, inflexible patterns of control and protection, they can actually feel more productive as well. Doing psychodynamically oriented psychotherapy with obsessive compulsive patients requires a number of modifications. The modification involves the clinician's level of activity. The clinician must be active from the beginning through the end of treatment. Clinician passivity, according to Salzman (1980), can lead only to interminable analysis and an atmosphere of confusion. Specifically, free association, and a tendency to endless detail and circumstantiality must be controlled and limited. Because of these patients' need for perfection, they tend to qualify and quantify their descriptions, which, rather than clarifying, confuses and obfuscates. The free association process tends to defeat its own purpose. Thus, the clinician must be active to prevent this tangentiality and distraction by attempting to interrupt the irrelevances and avoidances. Of course the major avoidance is affects. While these patients may talk about feelings and emotions, and even about transference and countertransference, they assiduously avoid the expression of affect. The clinician must, therefore, focus on real feelings and their expression, and limit intellectual discussion of affects.

Another modification from traditional analytic methods involves a focus on recent events. While obsessive compulsive individuals can discuss anger and hostile behavior associated with past events, they find it very difficult to disclose tender impurities and feelings with recent and here-and-now experiences. Such tender impulses and feelings are viewed as threatening and dangerous, and Salzman (1980) contends this is the essence of obsessive compulsive defenses. It is the failure to express these feelings, rather than their hostile behavior, that initiated retaliatory behavior from others, which in turn stirs up their wrath and hostile responders.

Finally, the usual instruction to forgo major decisions during the course of therapy must be modified. Because of their fear of making mistakes, such instruction can serve to reinforce their pathological pattern. Rather, risk-taking and decision making must be promoted. The techniques for dealing with their indecisiveness are clarification and interpretation of their need for absolutes and certainties. If dream material is utilized, the emphasis must be in the here-and-now, and dream content treated as data dealt with in the same manner as their other therapeutic material.

The outcome goal of treatment is that these individuals achieve some degree of balance and compromise, and, instead of needing to be superhuman, be able to function as fallible human persons. Because of their anticipatory anxiety, termination issues abound with these patients. It must be clearly understood by both patients and clinicians that anxiety episodes will occur throughout life, and that continuation in therapy is no guarantee against life's distress.

A related goal is superego modification, so much that these patients can accept that their wish to transcend such feelings as anger, lust, and dependency are doomed to failure, and must be integrated rather than disowned. Gabbard (1994) notes that such changes occur through detailed interpretation of conflicts around aggression, sexuality, and dependence.

There is a consensus that long-term psychodynamic treatment is needed with these patients. This is because of their constricted emotionality and their vulnerability to deflation of self-esteem under their rigid exterior. Treatment typically lasts two to three years of one or two sessions per week. The prevailing wisdom is that dynamic psychotherapy, with the ancillary support of medication and behavioral interventions, is effective (Salzman, 1989).

Schanche, Stiles, McCullough, Svartberg, and Nielsen (2011) provide a useful discussion of Cluster C personality disorders from a psychodynamic perspective, including commentary on treatment for Obsessive-Compulsive Personality Disorder.

Time-Limited Supportive-Expressive Therapy

Supportive-expressive therapy was provided to individuals with both obsessive compulsive and Avoidant Personality-Disordered individuals. Those with Obsessive-Compulsive Personality Disorder lost their personality disorder diagnosis in a significantly shorter period of time than those with Avoidant Personality Disorder. While both groups responded to this time-limited therapy on measures of personality disorder, depression, anxiety, general functioning, and interpersonal problems, those with Obsessive-Compulsive Personality Disorder no longer met Axis II criteria within the first 17 sessions (Barber, Morse, Krakauer, Chittams, & Crits-Christoph, 1997).

Cognitive-Behavioral Therapy Approaches

Which cognitive behavioral approach and treatment targets have the best treatment outcomes with Obsessive-Compulsive Personality Disorder? Unfortunately, no randomly controlled trials have been published to date which offer the clinician usable and reliable guidelines. Bailey (1998) describes and critiques the two most common cognitive approaches: Young's schema-focused approach and Beck's more traditional approach. Kyrios (1999) describes several cognitive-behavioral treatment targets in treating Obsessive-Compulsive Personality Disorder. These include targeting dysfunctional cognitions, restricted behavioral repertoires, negative affective dispositions, and issues related to attachment and identity. Until research-based guidelines are forthcoming, a careful assessment of client and situational attributes and clinician judgment must continue to guide treatment decisions.

Cognitive Therapy Approach. Beck et al. (2004) provide an extended discussion of the Cognitive Therapy approach with Obsessive-Compulsive Personality-Disordered individuals. The general outcome goal in working therapeutically with these individuals is helping them modify and restructure their maladaptive schemas that underlie behaviors and effects. Establishing a collaborative working relationship is the first task of therapy. This can be quite difficult for these individuals because of their rigidity, feeling avoidance, and tendency to minimize the importance of interpersonal relationships. Therefore, rapport is based on the individual's respect for the therapist's competence and the belief that the therapist will be respecting and helpful. Efforts to develop a closer emotional relationship early in treatment may result in premature termination. However, Strauss et al. (2006) conducted a nonrandomized trial of cognitive therapy for Obsessive-Compulsive Personality Disorder and Avoidant Personality Disorder and found that stronger early therapeutic alliances predicted more improvement in symptoms. Even ruptures in the relationship later in therapy may be used as learning experiences if they are managed properly. As such, there are both risks and rewards to early investments in the alliance with these clients. It is also essential to introduce the obsessive compulsive individual to the cognitive theory of emotion early in the course of therapy, as well as establishing therapeutic goals. Usually these involve presenting problems. After collaboratively establishing these, they are ranked in the order they are to be addressed. A given problem is monitored between sessions with the Dysfunctional Thought Record, which includes the situation as well as the feelings and thoughts about when the problem occurred. The record is reviewed at the next session, which is the basis for discussing automatic thoughts and the assumptions or schemas underlying the thoughts. In this collaborative relationship, the individual can identify and understand the negative consequences of the schema and ways of refuting them. This process of cognitive disputation and restructuring is particularly useful and well received by obsessive compulsive individuals because of its structured and problem-centered, here-and-now focus.

Several specific strategies and techniques have been found to be particularly useful with these individuals as adjunctive to cognitive therapy. Setting an agenda, prioritizing problems, utilizing problem-solving and thought-stopping techniques are effective with issues of rumination, procrastination, and indecisiveness. Salzman (1989) reports that flooding, desensitization, response prevention, and satiation training have been used in treating this disorder. Relaxation training is useful with anxiety and psychosomatic symptoms, while behavioral experiments can be used instead of direct disputation of maladaptive beliefs. Because of their difficulty in attending to their emotions and those of others, empathy training and role reversal have been used effectively. In sum, Obsessive-Compulsive Personality Disorder is a challenging but very treatable disorder. With collaboration, cognitive restructuring, and systematic application of cognitive and behavioral strategies and techniques, the obsessive compulsive individual's automatic thoughts and schemas, that underlie their maladaptive behavior and affects, can be effectively modified and changed.

Turkat (1990) concludes that behavioral modification alone is not sufficient for effective treatment outcomes with most of these patients. Turkat's treatment regimen involved social skills training to increase pleasure and emotion-related experience and to decrease their overcommitment to work. He note that, while these patients would agree with the clinical formulation and treatment plan, most would not agree to undergo the training. Turkat and Maisto (1985) report similar experience, leading them to conclude that behavior modification alone was not effective for Obsessive-Compulsive Personality Disorder.

Simon (2015) identifies four main goals in the cognitive treatment of OCPD: educating the patient about the role of perfectionism in the development and maintenance of symptoms; testing the rigidity of long-held rules and routines by evaluating whether or not they are working; evaluating the automatic thoughts, underlying assumptions, and core beliefs that maintain perfectionism; and, finally, linking all of the above goals to work and interpersonal relationships to develop more targeted treatment goals.

Schema Therapy. Schema Therapy is an elaboration of cognitive therapy that has been developed by Young (Young et al., 2003) specifically for personality disorders, and other difficult individual and couples problems. Schema Therapy involves identifying maladaptive schemas and planning specific strategies and interventions. Four main strategies are cognitive, experiential, behavioral, and the therapeutic relationship itself. Cognitive restructuring, modification of maladaptive schemas, is an important cognitive strategy, but is combined with imagery exercises, empathic confrontation, homework assignments, and "limited reparenting," i.e., a form of corrective emotional experience (Young et al., 2003).

Maladaptive schemas typically associated with this disorder include: *unrelenting standards*—the belief that striving to meet unrealistically high standards of performance is essential to be accepted and to avoid criticism; *punitiveness*—the belief that others should be harshly punished for making errors; and *emotional inhibition*—the excessive inhibition of spontaneous action, feeling, or communication (usually to avoid disapproval by others), feelings of shame, or losing control of one's impulses (Bernstein, 2002).

Interpersonal Approach

For Benjamin (2003a), psychotherapeutic interventions with Obsessive-Compulsive Personality-Disordered individuals can be planned and evaluated in terms of whether they enhance collaboration, facilitate learning about maladaptive patterns and their roots, block these patterns, enhance the will to change, and effectively encourage new patterns.

Because of the centrality of control in their lives, obsessive compulsive individuals find collaboration difficult. These individuals are often inconsistent in their attitudes about control of the therapy, sometimes wanting to take control, and other times wanting the clinician to take it. Benjamin suggests breaking through a potential power struggle by describing their typical patterns of control, submission, and self-control, and their opposites—affirmation, disclosure, and self-affirmation—and how and why the obsessive compulsive patterns developed. She notes that these individuals quickly grasp—intellectually—the idea of friendly differentiation as the opposite of hostile control, and will develop an interest in collaboration. After this shared goal of openness and warmth has been established, they can begin working in experiencing feeling and changing their relational behaviors. Not surprisingly, the work of learning to let go is not easy.

As these individuals begin seeking connections between early life experiences and present difficulties, they must be helped to develop compassion and empathy for themselves as children. Benjamin notes that couples therapy is a particularly potent format for learning about and changing maladaptive patterns in obsessive compulsive individuals. Dealing with control and power struggles between partners is aided by reframing and paradoxical injunctions. A paradoxical use of their preference for rule-following would involve the clinician "ordering" the obsessive compulsive individual to collaborate with the partner to develop "rules" for dealing with the problematic relational issues.

Therapeutic efforts to block maladaptive patterns should be targeted to power struggles, feeling avoidance and perfectionism. With regard to perfectionism, undercutting the need to reach perfection through control usually results in anger reduction. As the obsessive compulsive individual no longer needs to make others perfect, there is no need to be angry at them; similarly, with the anxiety that comes from fear of not reaching perfection. Since the individuals do not need to be perfect to survive, they no longer need to be anxious about not being perfect. As these individuals come to understand the origins of their quest for perfection, and compare their early life situations with the present, they are better able to relinquish their past neurotic strivings. Developing empathy for the self as a child and for the parent at that distant time can strengthen their will to give up their maladaptive patterns.

Cognitive therapy is particularly useful in modifying their constricted cognitive style and self-criticism. Likewise, insight can increase the probability these individuals will become more comfortable with fallibility and ordinariness. Benjamin concludes that both insight and transference are important parts of the process of change for obsessive compulsive individuals. A caring, benevolent relationship with the therapist as a trustworthy caregiver who accurately responds to the individual's needs enhances the insight. However, she cautions that treating this disorder, as with the other personality disorders, is a long-term process with no easy short cuts.

Group Therapy

Because a major deficit of the obsessive compulsive personality is the inability to share tenderly and spontaneously with others, group treatment has particular advantages with such patients. Nonetheless, there are certain complications, because of these patients' tendency to competitiveness and control of situations. Yalom (1995) uses the description "monopolist" to refer to this obsessive compulsive pattern in group therapy. They can easily dominate a group with their rambling and excessive speech patterns. They may find the affective atmosphere in a psychotherapy group particularly overwhelming at first, resulting in either further isolation or detached intellectualization. The group leader may need to intervene and to avoid unnecessary power struggles. If this is achieved, these patients may be able to vicariously model the emotional expressiveness of other group members.

Actually, group therapy offers a number of advantages over individual therapy, as the obsessive compulsive personality pattern tends to make the dyadic therapy process tedious, difficult, and unrewarding, particularly during the inevitable "constipated" period of treatment when clinicians commonly err with premature interpretations or behavioral prescriptions (Salzman, 1980; Wells, Glickauf-Hughes, & Buzzell, 1990).

A group format can diffuse intensity of the patient's impact, particularly in a heterogeneous group (Frances et al., 1984). Group treatment can also reduce transference and countertransference traps, because patients are more likely to accept feedback from peers without the same power struggle that often accompanies feedback from the clinician (Gabbard, 1994). Furthermore, group therapy propels these patients into having problems rather than just talking about them (Alonso & Rutan, 1984). Rutan et al. (2014) also echo this notion from a psychodynamic perspective. Their review suggests that group therapy is particularly helpful for those with strict or otherwise problematic superegos. These individuals may use the group members to offset the intensity of transference found in individual therapy, allowing them to work on issues without this disruption.

Wells et al. (1990) note the following contraindications for group therapy for these patients. They are severe depression or strong suicidal potential, impulsive dyscontrol, strong paranoid propensities, acute crisis, difficulty in establishing trust, fear of relinquishing obsessive compulsive defenses, the need to establish superiority, and the use of "pseudo insight" to avoid dealing with both hostile and tender feelings.

These authors have described a unique group approach combining interpersonal and psychodynamic principles based on the premise that this personality disorder arises from the unsuccessful resolution of the developmental tasks of autonomy vs. shame and doubt. The process of treatment involves six goals: (1) modifying cognitive style; (2) augmenting decision making and action taking; (3) modifying harsh superego; (4) increasing comfort with emotional expression; (5) resolving control issues; and (6) modifying interpersonal style.

Marital and Family Therapy

The professional literature in this area is particularly limited; however, some of the dynamics and treatment discussed regarding group therapy are relevant in a family treatment context.

Harbir (1981) notes that Obsessive-Compulsive Personality-Disordered individuals typically enter family treatment because close family members are angry with their rigidity, procrastination, constricted affect, perfectionism, and somber or joyless outlook. The spouse of an obsessive compulsive individual may threaten divorce if the individual does not change. Often, such a threat of separation or divorce is the only motivation for treatment. The anxiety of the complaining spouse may be the only leverage for treatment, and the clinician may need to work with that spouse to deal more effectively with the other spouse's obsessive compulsive personality pattern. Harbir adds that it is not uncommon for an obsessive compulsive individual to marry an individual with a histrionic personality.

Salzman (1989) cautions that obsessive compulsive patients who are particularly anxious may not be able to participate in family therapy until their anxiety has been sufficiently ameliorated in individual psychotherapy or combined psychotherapeutic and psychopharmacological treatment. Even when excessive anxiety is not a particular concern, these patients are often tyrants in family sessions. They may immobilize other family members to such an extent that treatment is jeopardized. The use of structural and strategic intervention directed at redistributing power may be particularly advantageous in such situations (Minuchin, 1974).

Regarding treatment outcomes, no controlled research studies have been published. However, Minuchin (1974) and Haley and Hoffman (1976) have reported favorable outcomes with family therapy interventions with obsessive compulsive personalities and particularly those with permanent eating disorders. Harbir (1981) and Perry, Francis, and Clarkin (1990) present a case example of marital therapy wherein one partner exhibits an obsessive compulsive personality and the other a histrionic personality. This case is quite instructive with regard to treatment strategy and technique.

An integrative approach involving dynamic, cognitive-behavioral, and systemic interventions is described for couples in which one partner presents with Obsessive-Compulsive Personality Disorder and the other with Histrionic Personality Disorder. Three stages of the treatment process are discussed and illustrated: establishing a therapeutic alliance, restoring balance to the couple's relationship, and modifying individual partner dynamics. The first two phases involve conjoint couples sessions, while much of the third phase involves individual sessions (Sperry

& Maniacci, 1996). This particular relationship configuration is also addressed by Landucci and Foley (2014), who state that the spontaneity and liveliness of the histrionic partner provides the obsessive compulsive individual with a welcome break from his or her mundane routines.

For additional commentary on family therapy with Obsessive-Compulsive Personality Disorder, refer to Benjamin (2003b). She notes that many disorders are the result of patients' desire to gain the approval of a critical parent. This dream of reconciliation is rarely realized as a clinical goal, however. The likelihood of the patient's own internalizations or the family members themselves undermining the process is high. Rather, Benjamin suggests that family therapy may accomplish change only when the obsessive-compulsive patient gives up this fantasy.

Medication

Currently, there are no psychotropic medications specifically indicated for treating this personality disorder (Silk & Feurino, 2012). Nevertheless, medications are used that target specific troubling symptoms associated with the disorder, such as depression, anxiety, or sleep problems. Generally, these medications are used as an adjunct to psychotherapy and skills training. Because troubling symptoms often respond to medications sooner than most psychological interventions, medications are usually prescribed at the onset of treatment (Sperry, 1995b). Because antidepressants have been effective in the treatment of obsessive compulsive disorder, it was expected that these medications might also reduce the symptoms of this personality disorder. However, there is no evidence to support this expectation. Furthermore, there is little research evidence even to provide guidelines for the use of any medications with this disorder (Silk & Feurino, 2012).

Combined/Integrative Treatment Approach

Salzman (1989) elegantly makes the case for a combined/integrated approach to the treatment of the Obsessive Compulsive Disorder, particularly for the more severe cases. He argues that the various treatment modalities and approaches are supplementary rather than mutually exclusive.

Combining treatment should follow a protocol. Since high levels of anxiety or depression may limit participation in psychotherapy, an appropriate medication trial may be useful at the onset of treatment. If rituals or obsessions are prominent, specific behavior interventions—such as response prevention, exposure, habituation, and thought stopping (Salkovskis & Kirk, 1989) are indicated. The basic dynamics of perfectionism, indecisiveness, and isolation of affect are best reached by psychotherapeutic approaches. The decision to choose an individual, group, or a marital modality, or a combination of modalities, is best based on severity of the disorder, the particular treatment target, and specific contraindications.

For instance, where isolation of affect and perfectionism manifest primarily as rambling speech pattern, integrative group therapy approach, such as described by Wells, et al. (1990), may greatly delimit resistance and subsequent counter-transference so common in dynamic treatment formats. Where indecisiveness is a prominent issue, modelling and other behavioral methods, as well as role playing might be incorporated in individual treatment formats. In general, the more severe the disorder, the more treatment needs to be tailored and multimodal.

Salzman (1989) concludes that a true understanding and appreciation of the obsessive compulsive personality "requires an integration of psychodynamic, pharmacologic, and behavior therapies, because the resolution of the disabling disorder demands cognitive clarity plus behavioral and physiologic alterations. Each modality alone deals with only a piece of the puzzle. A therapist who can combine all these approaches will be the most effective" (Salzman, 1989, p. 2782).

Developmental Therapy. Developmental approaches to therapy focus on fostering optimal functioning. For individuals with obsessive-compulsive personality style who seek to develop beyond the adequate level of functioning, the current endpoint of therapy, a developmental-focused therapy utilizes a variety of interventions to facilitate this process and goal. Various developmental approaches have been proposed (Blocher, 2000; Cortright, 1997; Sperry, 2002). A protocol for conducting developmental therapy for individuals with Obsessive-Compulsive Personality is described and illustrated by Sperry (2002).

Manduchi and Schoendorff (2012) provide a case study of a 36-year-old mother of three undergoing Functional Analytic Psychotherapy (FAP) for a diagnosis of Obsessive-Compulsive Personality Disorder with borderline features. This type of treatment involves using the therapist's in-the-moment private experiences regarding the client to promote changes in behavior. It is an integrative approach that may include exploration of past significant relationships as well as the practice of new interpersonal skills in the session. This is accomplished through the analysis of three types of Clinically Relevant Behaviors (CRBs). CRB1s are behaviors that are directly observable in session and linked to client reports of outside-of-session problems; CRB2s are in-session behaviors that represent improvements over CRB1s; finally, CRB3s are the client's functional explanations for his or her behavior, including antecedents and consequences.

10

PARANOID PERSONALITY DISORDER

Individuals with paranoid personalities are aloof, emotionally cold individuals who display unjustified suspiciousness, hypersensitivity, jealousy, and a fear of intimacy. In addition they can be grandiose, rigid, contentious, and litigious. Because of their hypersensitivity to criticism and tendency to project blame on others, they tend to lead isolated lives and are often disliked by others (Hopwood & Thomas, 2012). Paranoid Personality Disorder can be thought of as a paranoid spectrum disorder ranging from this personality disorder through the delusional disorder to paranoid schizophrenia. The distinguishing feature of this personality disorder from others on the spectrum is the lack of clear-cut delusions, hallucination, or other psychotic features.

This chapter describes a framework for the assessment and effective treatment of this disorder. It includes sections on its description, case conceptualizations, assessment, and treatment interventions. It begins with background information on the disorder as well as a DSM-5 description and a prototypic description of this disorder. The section on case conceptualizations provides five common clinical formulations of this disorder: psychodynamic, cognitive-behavioral, interpersonal, biosocial, and an integrative conceptualization of this disorder. Several treatment approaches, modalities, and intervention strategies are also described. These include individual psychotherapy, group therapy, marital and family therapy, medication, and integrative and combined treatment.

Description of the Paranoid Personality Disorder

The Paranoid Personality Disorder can be recognized by the following descriptors and characteristics: style vs. disorder, triggering event(s), behavioral style, interpersonal style, cognitive style, affective style, attachment style, and optimal diagnostic criterion.

Style vs. Disorder. The paranoid personality can be thought of as spanning a continuum from healthy to the pathological, with the paranoid personality style on the healthy end and the Paranoid Personality Disorder on the pathological end. Table 10.1 compares and contrasts differences between the paranoid personality style and disorder.

The following two cases further illustrate differences between the Paranoid Personality Disorder—Mr. W.—and the paranoid personality style—Ms. L.

TABLE 10.1 Comparison of the Paranoid Personality Style and Disorder

Personality Style	Personality Disorder
Self-assured and confident in their ability to make decisions and take care of themselves.	Reluctant to confide in others because of unwarranted fear that the information will be used against them.
Good listeners and observers, keenly aware of subtlety, tone, and multiple levels of meaning.	Reads hidden meanings or threats into benign remarks or events, i.e., suspects that a neighbor put out trash early to annoy them.
Take criticism rather seriously without becoming intimidated.	Bears grudges or is unforgiving of insults or slights.
Place a high premium on loyalty, fidelity, working hard to earn and maintain loyalty, and never taking it for granted.	Questions, without justification, the fidelity of spouse or sexual partner, friends, and associates.
Careful in dealings with other people, preferring to size up individuals before entering into relationships with them.	Expects, without sufficient basis, to be exploited or harmed by others.
Are assertive and can defend themselves without losing control and becoming aggressive.	Easily slighted and quick to react with anger or to counterattack.

CASE STUDY: PARANOID PERSONALITY DISORDER

Mr. W. is a 53-year-old male referred for psychiatric evaluation by his attorney to rule out a treatable psychiatric disorder. Mr. W. had entered into five lawsuits in the past two and one-half years. His attorney believed that each suit was of questionable validity. Mr. W. was described as an unemotional, highly controlled male who was now suing a local men's clothing store "for conspiring to deprive me of my consumer rights." He contends that the store manager had consistently issued bad credit reports on him. The consulting psychiatrist elicited other examples of similar concerns. Mr. W. had long distrusted his neighbors across the street and regularly monitors their activity, since one of his garbage cans disappeared two years ago. He took an early retirement from his accounting job one year ago because he could not get along with his supervisor, whom he believed was faulting him about his accounts and paperwork. He contends he was faultless. On examination, Mr. W.'s mental status is unremarkable except for constriction of affect and for a certain hesitation and guardedness in his response to questions.

CASE STUDY: PARANOID PERSONALITY STYLE

Ms. L. is a 46-year-old tax attorney for a major corporation. Although she had been reluctant to leave her private law practice, the corporation had courted her for several years. They really needed a skilled and successful female to round out their legal team. They made her an offer she couldn't refuse, and after ensuring that she could maintain sufficient independence in the job, she accepted. Although she had a loose reporting relationship to the chief counsel and two corporate vice-presidents, from the beginning Ms. L. maintained cordial but somewhat distant relationships with them. She attended only those meetings and social gatherings that were absolutely required. She kept small talk to a minimum and went about her work with a single-minded vigor that others came to respect, although they couldn't quite understand her style of relation. When others began to question her standoffish manner, she replied she was hired "to be a competent litigator, not a social butterfly." In the courtroom she was an awesome sight: cool, calm, and collected. She was totally in charge of examining and cross-examining witnesses, and in her opening and closing statements. No stone was left unturned and no verbal or nonverbal cue was missed. She instinctively went for the "juggler," as her peers would say, and seldom lost a judgment. There was never a question about her worth or loyalty to the corporation, and, in time, her peers and superior came to accept her unique style.

Triggering Event. The typical situation, circumstance, or event that most likely triggers or activates the characteristic maladaptive response of the Paranoid Personality Disorder (Othmer & Othmer, 2002), as noted in behavioral, interpersonal, cognitive, and affective styles, is: "close interpersonal relationships and/or personal queries."

Behavioral Style. Behaviorally, paranoid individuals are resistive of external influences. They tend to be chronically tense because they are constantly mobilized against perceived threats from their environment. Their behavior also is marked by guardedness, defensiveness, argumentativeness, and litigiousness.

Interpersonal Style. Interpersonally, these individuals tend to be distrustful, secretive, and isolative. They are deeply suspicious of others' motives. They are also intimacy-avoiders by nature, and repudiate nurturant overtures by others.

Cognitive Style. Their cognitive style is characterized by mistrusting preconceptions. They carefully scrutinize every situation, and scan the environment for "clues" or "evidence" to confirm their preconceptions rather than objectively focus on data. Thus, while their perception may be accurate, their judgment often is not. The paranoid personalities' prejudices mold the perceived data to fit their preconceptions. Thus, they tend to disregard evidence that does not fit their preconceptions. When under stress their thinking can take on a conspiratorial or even delusional flavor. Their hypervigilance and need to seek evidence to confirm their beliefs lead them to have a rather authoritarian and mistrustful outlook on life.

Affective Style. Their emotional or affective style is characterized as cold, aloof, unemotional, and humorless. In addition, they lack deep sense of affection, warmth, and sentimentality. Because of their hypersensitivity to real or imagined slights, and their subsequent anger at what they believe to be deceptions and betrayals, they tend to have few, if any, friends. The two emotions they experience and express with some depth are anger and intense jealousies.

Attachment Style. Individuals with a fearful attachment style exhibit a sense of personal unworthiness combined with an expectation that other people will be rejecting and untrustworthy. They trust neither their own internal cognitions or feelings nor others' intentions. While they believe themselves to be special and different from others, they guard against threats and unexpected circumstances, since they cannot trust that others will protect them. This fearful attachment style is common in individuals with Paranoid Personality Disorder.

Optimal Diagnostic Criterion. Of all the diagnostic criteria for the Dependent Personality Disorder, one has been found to be the most useful in diagnosing this disorder. The belief is that, by beginning with this criterion, the clinician can test for the presence or absence of the criterion and more quickly diagnose the personality disorder (Allnutt & Links, 1996). The optimal criterion for this disorder is: suspects, without sufficient basis, that others are exploiting, harming, or deceiving him or her.

DSM-5 Description

Individuals with this personality disorder are characterized by an unremitting pattern of distrust and suspicion and interpret others' motives as harmful. Without sufficient basis, they suspect that others are exploiting, harming, or deceiving them. They are obsessed with unfounded doubts about the loyalty of friends and associates. Because of their unfounded fears, they are reluctant to confide in others. They are likely to interpret otherwise benign remarks and situations as threatening and dangerous. Not surprisingly, they are unforgiving of slights, insults, and injuries.

These individuals are quick to react angrily or to counterattack when they believe that their character or reputation is being attacked. They are likely to continually suspect, without justification, that their spouse or sexual partner is unfaithful (American Psychiatric Association, 2013).

Prototypic Description

A prototype is a brief description that captures the essence of how a particular disorder commonly presents. Prototypic descriptions are useful and convenient and clinicians commonly rely on them rather than lists of behavioral criteria and core and instrumental beliefs (Westen, 2012). Here is a common prototypic description of the Paranoid Personality Disorder: These individuals grew up believing that the world is dangerous and that others—particularly those closest to them—are never to be trusted. They are constantly checking to make sure that no one takes advantage of them, makes fun of them, or plots against them. Convinced that it will be used against them, they will not share their thoughts or feelings. They hold on to grudges, never forget a slight, nor pass up a chance for revenge.

Prevalence

Prevalence of this disorder has been estimated at between 2.3 and 4.4 percent in the general population (American Psychiatric Association, 2013). In clinical settings, estimates are that it is found in 4.2 to 27.6 percent of patients (Torgersen, 2012).

Conceptualizations of the Paranoid Personality Disorder

Psychodynamic Case Conceptualizations

Psychoanalytic formulations of the paranoid personality focus on the phenomenon of projection. Essentially, paranoid individuals inaccurately perceive in others that which is true of them, and, as by projecting unacceptable feelings and impulses onto these experience reduction of anxiety and distress (Shapiro, 1965).

The self-representation of the paranoid personality involves the coexistence of a special, entitled grandiose self with a weak, worthless, inferior polar opposite (Gabbard, 1990). Developmentally, individuals with Paranoid Personality Disorder are likely to have grown up in an atmosphere charged with criticism, blame, and hostility, and to have identified with a critical parent. Identification with such critical parents suppresses these individuals' feelings of inadequacy and ensures the continuing importance of the mode of criticalness in the development and functioning of the personality. Through their identifications paranoid individuals learn hypervigilance, suspiciousness, and blaming. Hypervigilance and suspiciousness prevent self-criticism, while blaming—considered an identification with the aggressor—serves to erase possible experience of humiliation (Kellerman & Burry, 1989).

Paranoid individuals focus on seeing imperfection in the world around them. This externalization permits a denial of any personal imperfection. Essentially, paranoid individuals feel inferior, weak, and ineffective; thus, grandiosity and specialness are allowed to be understood as a compensatory defense against feelings of inferiority (Gabbard, 1990).

The primary defense mechanisms of this disorder are, then, projection and projective identification. In addition to externalizing threats with projection, projective identification additionally serves to control others in the environment by binding them to paranoid individuals in pathological ways. This need to control others reflects low self-esteem, which is at the heart of the Paranoid Personality Disorder. Basically, it sensitizes these individuals to concerns about all passive surrender to all impulses and to all persons (Shapiro, 1965). Finally, rationalization, reaction formation, and displacement are secondary defense mechanisms.

In short, the need to criticize the world and external objects allows paranoid individuals to maintain an anxiety-free existence in the face of personal imperfections and a grave sense of inadequacy. Profound inferiority feelings are projected onto the "inferior" world, which is then related to in a consistently critical manner. The self can be then viewed as "good" and "badness" split off and projected outward.

Cognitive-Behavioral Case Conceptualizations

According to Beck (2015), individuals with paranoid personality are distrustful of others in most circumstances. They are identifiable by their characteristic core, conditional, and instrumental beliefs. Their *core beliefs* include: "Other people can't be trusted," "Others have ulterior motives (or bad intentions) toward me," and "Others are deceptive, and are out to hurt or undermine me." Their *conditional belief* is that, if they are not careful, others will abuse, manipulate, or take advantage of them, and that if others act friendly it is only because they have an ulterior motive. Their *instrumental belief* is to be on guard, look for hidden meaning, trust no one, and don't get taken in. Underlying these various beliefs are their beliefs about self and the world.

These individuals typically view themselves as righteous and mistreated by others. They tend to view others as devious, treacherous, manipulative, and discriminatory. They may believe that others form secret coalitions against them. Based on belief that others are against them, these individuals are driven to be hypervigilant and on guard. Their strategy is to be wary, vigilant, and counterattack. When they confront their "adversaries," they often provoke the hostility that they believed already existed (Renton & Mankiewicz, 2015).

From a more behavioral perspective, Turkat (1990) contends there is no single formulation for this disorder. However, hypersensitivity to criticism is characteristic. Such individuals receive early training to be frightened at what others think of them. These individuals also learn that they are different than others, and that they must not make mistakes. As a result of these two beliefs, paranoid individuals become overly concerned about the evaluations of others, constrained to conform to parental expectations, and hypersensitive to others' evaluation. This, of course, often interferes with acceptance by their peers. Eventually, they are humiliated and ostracized by their peers, in part because they lack the interpersonal skills necessary to overcome this ostracism. Consequently, they excessively engage in ruminating about their isolation and mistreatment by others. From this, they conclude that the reason for this rejection and persecution is because they are special and others are jealous of them. Accordingly, they act in ways to avoid negative evaluations from others, but these attempts lead them to act differently, which invites social criticism. In their isolation they brood about their predicament, which engenders persecutory and grandiose thoughts, which further maintain their social isolation. Accordingly, these individuals are caught in a vicious cycle that perpetuates the disorder (Turkat, 1990).

Interpersonal Case Conceptualizations

According to Benjamin (2003a), persons diagnosed with Paranoid Personality Disorder were likely to have experienced sadistic, controlling, and degrading parenting. Typically abused children themselves, parents of paranoid-disordered individuals believed that children are basically evil or bad, require containment, and deserve retribution. Family loyalty was a basic value, and sharing family secrets with others was not tolerated. The adult consequences of such harsh upbringing is that paranoid-disordered individuals expect attack and abuse even from those close to them. As children they were harshly punished for dependency, and even attached when they were sick, hurt, or cried. As a result, they learned not to cry, not to ask for help even if injured or sick, and not to trust anyone. Subsequently, as adults they tend to avoid intimacy unless they can control their partner. Often these individuals were subjected to covert as well as overt invidious comparisons within the family, and later among peers. They learned that mistakes and hurts were seldom forgotten and that grudges were long-lasting. Not surprisingly, paranoid individuals are exquisitely sensitive and angry about exclusion, slights, and even whispering. They tend to be keenly aware of any inequalities in punishments or privileges, and they are likely to sustain grudges for long periods. Furthermore, as children they were rewarded for competence in helping the family, while "staying out of the way." While they were given permission and support to do well, they were degraded and humiliated for venturing out of an assigned area. They came to believe that being a good and lovable person was outside their reach. Subsequently, as adults they can function competently and independently but are interpersonally withdrawn. Their expectation of not being acknowledged inspires fear, resentment, and alienation. Finally, they constantly fear that others will attack, blame, or hurt them, while they continue to wish that others will affirm and understand them. Not expecting to be affirmed, they angrily withdraw and tightly control themselves and, if they perceive attack, will reflexively counterattack.

Biosocial Case Conceptualizations

In a marked departure from other formulations of Paranoid Personality Disorder, Millon (Millon & Davis, 1996) and Millon and Everly (1985) conceive of the Paranoid Personality Disorder as a severe form of character pathology. More specifically, Millon and Everly describe it as syndromal continuation of three less severe personality disorders: Narcissistic, Antisocial, or Compulsive. Based on their clinical research, individuals with paranoid personalities develop in one of these three syndromal patterns based on their unique biogenic and environmental histories. The narcissistic variation of the paranoid disorder is largely shaped by parental overvaluation and indulgence. As a result, these individuals fail to adequately learn interpersonal responsibility, cooperation, and interpersonal skills. They are often perceived by others as selfish and egotistical. Furthermore, lack of parental controls can give rise to grandiose fantasies of success, power, beauty, or brilliance. As a result they tend to be rejected and humiliated by their peers. These interpersonal rebuffs are followed by increased fantasy and isolation from which a propensity for paranoia emerges.

The antisocial variant of the paranoid personality exhibits high levels of activation and impulsive high-energy temperaments. The principal environmental determinant seems to be harsh parental treatment. Consequently, they develop a deep, abiding mistrust of others and manifest a strong self-directedness and arrogance. Because of their tendency to reject both parental and social controls, they also develop an aggressive, impulsive, hedonistic lifestyle. Anticipating the attacks of others, paranoid-antisocial individuals react irrationally and vindictively. Since they are unable to cope directly with perceived threats, they often erupt in overt hostility.

Individuals with the paranoid-compulsive pattern have developmental histories quite similar to the Obsessive-Compulsive Personality Disorder. However, they exhibit more irrationally rigid and inflexible behavior (Millon & Everly, 1985). These three versions of the paranoid disorder appear to be self-perpetuated by their own rigidity and suspiciousness. By ascribing slanderous and malevolent motives to others, paranoid individuals remain in a defensive and vindictive posture most of the time. Furthermore, keeping distance from others fosters the maintenance of their illusion of superiority, which allows a self-fulfilling pattern: as they expect others to be hostile and malevolent, others often become so.

Integrative Case Conceptualizations

The following integrative formulation provides a biopsychosocial explanation for how this personality is likely to have developed and how it is maintained. Biologically, a low threshold for limbic system stimulation and deficiencies in inhibitory centers seem to influence the behavior of the paranoid personality. The underlying temperament can best be understood in terms of the subtypes of the paranoid disorder. Each of three subtypes are briefly described in terms of their underlying temperament, and correlative parental and environmental factors. In the narcissistic type, a hyperresponsive temperament and precociousness, parental overvaluation and indulgence, as well as the individual's sense of grandiosity and self-importance, probably result in deficits in social interest and limited interpersonal skills. The antisocial type of the paranoid personality is likely to possess a hyperresponsive temperament. This, plus harsh parental treatment, probably contributes to the impulsive, hedonistic, and aggressive style of this type. In the compulsive type, the underlying temperament may have been anhedonic. This, as well as parental rigidity and overcontrol, largely accounts for the development of this type. Finally, a less common variant is the paranoid-passive aggressive type. As infants, the individuals usually demonstrated the "difficult child" temperament, and later temperament characterized by affective irritability. This, plus parental inconsistency, probably accounts in large part for the development of this type (Millon, 1981).

Psychologically, paranoid individuals view themselves, others, the world, and life's purpose in terms of the following themes. They tend to view themselves by some variant of the theme "I'm special and different. I'm alone and no one likes me because I'm better than others." Life and the world are viewed by some variant of the theme "Life is unfair, unpredictable and demanding. It can and will sneak up and harm you when you are least expecting it." As such, they are likely to conclude: "Therefore, be wary, counterattack, trust no one, and excuse yourself from failure by blaming others." The most common defensive mechanism associated with the paranoid disorder is projection.

Socially, predictable patterns of parenting and environmental factors can be noted for this disorder. For all the subtypes the parental injunction appears to be: "You're different. Don't make mistakes." Paranoid Personality-Disordered individuals tend to have perfectionistic parents who expose these children to specialness training. This, plus the parental style that has been articulated for the subtypes of the disorder and parental criticism leads to an attitude of social isolation and hypervigilant behavior. To make sense of the apparent contradiction between being special and being ridiculed, the children creatively conclude that the reason they are special and that no one likes them is because they are better than other people. This explanation serves the purpose of reducing their anxiety and allowing them to develop some sense of self and belonging.

This paranoid pattern is confirmed, reinforced, and perpetuated by the following individual and systems factors: a sense of specialness, rigidity, attributing malevolence to others, blaming others, and misinterpreting motives of others leads to social alienation and isolation, which further confirms the individual's persecutory stance (Sperry, 2015; Sperry & Mosak, 1996).

Table 10.2 summarizes the characteristics of this disorder.

TABLE 10.2 Characteristics of Paranoid Personality Disorder

Triggering Event(s)	Close interpersonal relationships and/or personal queries
Behavioral Appearance	Guarded and defensive Resists external influence Hypervigilant and chronically tense
Interpersonal Behavior	Distrustful and suspicious of others Reluctance to confide Bears grudges and blames Counterattacks for perceived slights Hypersensitive to slights and criticism
Cognitive Style	Tends to disregard evidence to the contrary Quick to rationalize and hold to preconceptions
Affective Style	Restricted affect, but easily provoked Aloof and humorless Jealous and envious
Temperament	Narcissistic type: active, hyperresponsive Compulsive type: irritable Passive-Aggressive type: affective irritability
Attachment Style	Fearful
Parental Injunction	"You're different. Keep alert. Don't make mistakes."
Self-View	"I'm so special and different. I'm alone and no one likes me, because I'm better than others."
World-View	"Life is unfair, unpredictable, and demanding. It will sneak up and harm you. Therefore, be wary, counter-attack, trust no one, and excuse yourself from failure by blaming others."
Maladaptive Schemas	Abuse/mistrust; defectiveness
Optimal Diagnostic Criterion	Suspects, without sufficient basis, that others are exploiting, harming, or deceiving him or her

Assessment of Paranoid Personality Disorder

Several sources of information are useful in establishing a diagnosis and treatment plan for personality disorders. Observation, collateral information, and psychological testing are important adjuncts to the patient's self-report in the clinical interview. This section briefly describes some characteristic observations that the clinician makes and the nature of the rapport likely to develop in initial encounters with specific personality-disordered individuals. Characteristic response patterns on various objective (i.e., MMPI-2 and MCMI-IV) and projective (i.e., Rorschach and TAT) tests are also described.

Interview Behavior and Rapport

Interviewing Paranoid Personality-Disordered individuals is a delicate challenge. Rapport with them is hampered by their pervasive belief that others will harm and exploit them. Therefore, they screen all questions for conspiratorial content and hidden meaning, and assume that any kindness shown by the clinician is a clever maneuver to take advantage of their weakness. Similarly, they cannot allow themselves to relax in the interview, fearful that easing up would make them too vulnerable, and so they justify their suspiciousness and hypervigilance. They can easily confront others, but will not tolerate being confronted. Smooth transitions from topic to topic are essential. Any abruptness may be experienced as an unjustified attempt to trap them, which could lead to anger, counterattack, or termination of the interview (Ackley et al., 2011; Othmer & Othmer, 2002).

Psychological Testing Data

The Minnesota Multiphase Personality Inventory (MMPI-2), the Millon Clinical Multiaxial Inventory (MCMI-IV), the Rorschach Psychodiagnostic Test, and the Thematic Apperception Test (TAT) can be useful in diagnosing the Compulsive Personality Disorder as well as the Obsessive Compulsive Personality style (Groth-Marnat, 2009).

On the MMPI-2, an elevation on the 6 scale (Paranoia) is common. However, since these individuals tend to be hyperalert about being perceived as paranoid, this scale may be greatly elevated (Graham, 2012). These individuals are easily irritated at the MMPI's forced choice format as well as the self-disclosure required of many of the items (Meyer, 1995). Scales 3 (Hysteria) and 1 (Hypochondriasis) and K (Correction) tend to be high in these individuals, reflecting their use of denial and projection, their inclination to focus on somatic concerns, and their need to present a facade of adequacy (Graham, 2012).

On the MCMI-IV, elevation on scale 6B (Sadistic) and P (Paranoid) are expected (Millon et al., 2015). Since this personality pattern often overlaps with the antisocial, the narcissistic, and the passive aggressive, elevations are likely on scales 6A (Antisocial), 5 (Narcissistic), and 8A (Negativistic-passive aggressive) (Choca & Denburg, 1997).

On the Rorschach, these individuals produce records that are generally constricted, but characterized by more P (Popular) and A (Animal) responses than C (Pure color) and M (Human Movement) responses. These individuals typically resent ambiguous stimuli and so respond to the test with condescending criticism and flipping of cards, and a focus on D (Detail) responses. Occasionally they reject cards or refuse to continue with the examination (Meyer, 1995).

On the TAT, suspiciousness may characterize their stories. This is particularly likely to occur on cards 9, G, F, 11, and 16 (Bellak, 1997).

Treatment Approaches and Interventions

Treatment Considerations

Included in the differential diagnosis of this disorder are the following personality disorders: Antisocial, Narcissistic, and Obsessive Compulsive. The most common symptom disorders associated with the Paranoid Personality Disorder are Generalized Anxiety Disorder, Panic Disorder, and Delusional Disorder. If a Bipolar Disorder is present, an irritable manic presentation is likely. Decompensation into schizophrenic reaction is also likely. When this occurs, the paranoid and catatonic subtypes are most likely to be present (Sperry, 2015).

Until recently, the prognosis for treatment of the Paranoid Personality Disorder was considered guarded. Today, more optimism prevails in achieving specific treatment goals, such as increasing the benignness of perception and interpretation of reality, and increasing trusting behavior. Several psychotherapeutic and psychoeducation interventions are useful in accomplishing these goals. Medication may be useful in decreasing anxiety associated with loss of control. To date, no controlled treatment outcomes studies have been completed for the Paranoid Personality Disorder (Crits-Christoph & Barber, 2002).

Individual Psychotherapy

Psychodynamically Oriented Psychotherapy

Patients with paranoid personalities tend to be individuals who lead reasonably adaptive and productive lives and, not surprisingly, are responsive to psychodynamic psychotherapy. Meissner (1978) contends, however, that their treatment is not easy but requires empathy, patience, and a great deal of sensitivity to their vulnerabilities. Meissner contends that the treatment process must be slowly paced, with limited, long-term goals. Three treatment principles characterize such treatment (Meissner, 1978, 1986).

First, a meaningful therapeutic alliance must be established and maintained. The therapeutic alliance requires the patient have a certain degree of trust in the clinician, which is considerably difficult for paranoid patients. The clinician's empathic responsiveness and willingness to serve as a container for a range of negative affects is essential. The clinician must avoid responding defensively, nor challenge the patient's perception of events or of the clinician. Instead, the clinician asks for more details and empathizes with the patient's perceptions and affects. Most importantly, the clinician must resist the countertransference tendency to be rid of indescribable projection by deflecting them back to the patient with predictive interpretations (Epstein, 1984). In short, the patient must come to view the clinician as a benign, disinterested, but friendly, helper (Salzman, 1980).

Second, the essential treatment strategy is to convert paranoid manifestations into depression and work through the underlying mourning. Gradual undermining of paranoid defenses and attitudes leads to the emergence of a depressive core in which the patient's inner sense of weakness, defectiveness, vulnerability, and powerlessness comes into focus. This is accomplished through the techniques of counterprojection and "creative doubt" (Meissner, 1986). Depressive elements are worked through in the transference, which allows them to begin the process of mourning their frustrated learning and disappointments with early objects.

Third, the clinician must respect the patient's fragile and threatened sense of autonomy and work toward building and reinforcing it in the therapeutic relationship. A commitment to openness, honesty, and confidentiality means that all decisions must be explored with the patient, and the ultimate choice must be the patient's. This even applies to decisions about medication, if when and if they are indicated (Meissner, 1989).

Since these patients tend to be resistant, provocative and contentious, countertransference issues cannot be underestimated. Behind their defensiveness and arrogance are narcissistic vulnerability, core feelings of shame and humiliation, and passive longing for dependence. Thus, these patients attempt to counter their anxieties by "turning the tables" and making the clinician feel vulnerable, humiliated, and helpless. Clinicians may react with annoyance, impatience, confrontation and argumentation. Or, they may experience frustration, discouragement and victimization. These reactions must be monitored, their impact on therapy analyzed, and efforts to rebalance the therapeutic alliance initiated (Meissner, 1989). Examples of these kinds of exchanges can be found in Williams (2010).

Metacognition-oriented therapy provides another treatment for personality disorders based on individual narrative and interpretation. Its goal is to progressively promote awareness of problems in subjective experience and schemas driving social behavior (Salvatore, Russo, Russo, Popolo, & Dimaggio, 2012). Therapists elicit patients' autobiographies, or narrative episodes, to identify the influences and theories behind their problems. This also includes work intended to develop the skills to understand the minds of others. The authors present a case study of an eight-month, ongoing course of metacognition-oriented treatment with a 31-year-old female law student diagnosed with Paranoid Personality Disorder and delusional disorder.

A similar type of psychotherapy used for Paranoid Personality Disorder is based on Dialogical Self Theory (DST), which examines the inner dialog between different parts, or voices, of the self (Dimaggio, Catania, Salvatore, Carcione, & Nicolo, 2006).

Brief Psychodynamic Psychotherapy

Long-term psychodynamically oriented psychotherapy involves two or more sessions per week for three or more years. However, since Paranoid Personality-Disordered individuals do not easily engage in the therapeutic process, they may have reluctance to such intensive long-term work. On the other hand, receptivity for treatment has increased during crisis period, usually the experience of acute anxiety or depression. Shorter-term therapy that is more crisis-oriented might be a preferable way of beginning treatment. Such crisis-focused short-term therapy could be a prelude to longer-term treatment.

Malan (1976) and Balint, Ornstein, and Blaint (1972) describe short-term psychotherapy with acute paranoid difficulties. While these treatments were effective with reactive paranoid presentations, it may not be for the enduring presentations, more typical of the Paranoid Personality Disorder. Currently, there are no published reports of completed successful treatments of Paranoid Personality Disorder in the context of brief dynamic psychotherapy.

Cognitive Analytic Therapy (CAT) (Ryle, 2004) is another time-limited model of psychodynamically oriented treatment that has been used for personality disorders. It consists of a narrative reformulation and the sequential diagrammatic reformulation (SDR). Patients receive 24 weekly sessions and four follow-up sessions spread out over a six-month period. Following the first three assessment sessions, personality patients are read a letter from the therapist that reformulates the origins of their distress and identifies target problems and procedures. Kellett and Hardy (2014) conducted a mixed-methods single-case study with a 36-year-old male diagnosed with Paranoid Personality Disorder. The six target complaint measures were as follows: suspiciousness; hypervigilance; dissociation; conspiracy; questioning; and anxiety. Cognitive Analytic Therapy ends with a "goodbye letter" jointly formulated by the patient and therapist to summarize achievements, prepare for future obstacles, and address any feelings of abandonment related to the termination of therapy. Results showed that five out of the six measures identified at the onset of treatment were extinguished during the treatment phase. The patient also attributed his changes to the CAT method.

Cognitive-Behavioral Therapy Approaches

Cognitive Therapy Approach. Beck et al.(2004) provide an extended discussion of the Cognitive Therapy approach with Paranoid Personality-Disordered individuals. The initial phase of treatment can be exceedingly stressful for paranoid individuals in that participating in treatment requires self-disclosure, trusting another, and acknowledging weakness, all of which they experience as being quite dangerous. This stress can be reduced by focusing initially on less sensitive issues or by discussing issues directly, i.e., talking about how "some individuals" experience and react to such situations, or by beginning with a more problem-solving approach and behaviorally focused interventions on presenting problems. Such strategies, as well as giving the individual more than the usual amount of control over scheduling appointments or the content of sessions, can facilitate development of a collaborative working relationship wherein they will feel less distrustful, coerced, and vigilant. Trust can be engendered by explicitly acknow-ledging and accepting the individual's difficulty in trusting the therapist. As this becomes evident and gradually demonstrated through trustworthiness and actions, it provides the evidence on which trust can be based.

A guided discovery approach when working on treatment goals will reveal the manner in which their paranoid pattern contributes to their problems, facilitating collaborative work on their distrust of others, feelings of vulnerability, and desire for retribution, rather than the therapist insisting that these issues be directly addressed. As treatment progresses to working on specific goals, emphasis should shift to increasing the individual's sense of self-efficacy before attempting to modify interpersonal behaviors, automatic thoughts, or schemas. Developing an increased awareness of another's point of view, and learning a more assertive approach to interpersonal conflict, are other common treatment goals with these individuals. The use of traditional cognitive behavioral techniques such as assertive communication training and behavioral rehearsal are commonly employed to reverse the provocation of hostile reactions from others that previously confirmed the paranoid individual's view of self and others. In instances where hypervigilance and ideas of reference are particularly resistant, the information-processing social skills intervention strategy described by Turkat and Maisto (1985) can be exceptionally useful.

The treatment goals are to decrease sensitivity to criticism, and modify social behavior. Social skills training consists of instructional role-playing, behavioral rehearsal, and videotaped feedback. The patient is taught to attend to more appropriate social stimuli; to interpret that information more accurately; to attack, criticize, or single out the patient; and to receive others' feedback in a nondefensive way and utilize it constructively (Turkat, 1990). Turkat and Maisto (1985) present a detailed case report illustrating these treatment strategies.

Williams (1988) provides a detailed case report of time-limited cognitive therapy with a substance-depressed college student who also met criteria for Paranoid

Personality Disorder. The patient was distressed about poor interpersonal relations and drug use, and was quite intelligent and motivated for therapy. Noteworthy about Williams' treatment protocol is that only 11 sessions were available and needed to achieve three treatment goals: reduce depressive symptoms, less threatening perceptions of the world, and other people; and increase skills in being more relaxed and comfortable with others. Cognitive restructuring and progressive muscle relaxation were the principal intervention strategies. The six-month follow-up showed that all gains had been maintained. Williams concludes that brief cognitive therapy may be particularly well suited for the Paranoid Personality Disorder. Renton and Mankiewicz (2015) identify three key treatment goals for the treatment of any Cluster A disorder: elicit trust in therapy by exploring ambivalence and respecting the individual's independence and boundaries; explore the influence of unhelpful beliefs about others in key social contexts while developing alternative, functional beliefs; and experiment with new social behaviors not based on suspicion and mistrust. They provide a case study of a 27-year-old female accountant diagnosed with Paranoid Personality Disorder.

In short, the Cognitive Therapy approach to working with paranoid individuals focuses considerable effort on carefully developing a work collaborative relationship, and increasing the individual's sense of self-efficacy early in treatment. It utilizes cognitive techniques and behavioral experiments to directly challenge the individual's remaining paranoid beliefs late in therapy.

Schema Therapy. Schema Therapy is an elaboration of cognitive therapy that has been developed by Young (1999; Young et al., 2003) specifically for personality disorders, and other difficult individual and couples problems. Schema Therapy involves identifying maladaptive schemas and planning specific strategies and interventions. Four main strategies are cognitive, experiential, behavioral, and the therapeutic relationship itself. Cognitive restructuring, modification of maladaptive schemas, is an important cognitive strategy, but is combined with imagery exercises, empathic confrontation, homework assignments, and "limited reparenting," i.e., a form of corrective emotional experience (Young, 1999; Young et al., 2003).

Maladaptive schemas typically associated with Paranoid Personality Disorder include: *mistrust/abuse*—the belief that others will abuse, humiliate, cheat, lie, manipulate, or take advantage; *defectiveness*—the belief that one is defective, bad, unwanted, or inferior in important respects; and *approval-seeking* (Bernstein, 2002).

Interpersonal Approach

For Benjamin (2003a), psychotherapeutic interventions with Paranoid Personality-Disordered individuals can be planned and evaluated in terms of whether they enhance collaboration, facilitate learning about maladaptive patterns and their roots, block these patterns, enhance the will to change, and effectively encourage new patterns.

Benjamin notes that the major treatment problem with paranoid individuals is establishing a collaborative therapeutic relationship. To the extent that collaboration occurs, paranoia disappears. Accustomed to being abused and humiliated, paranoid individuals view therapists as critical and judgmental, look for "slip-ups," and want them to leave. Patience and kindness without hints of coercion, criticism, or appeasement are essential for a considerable period during the early stages of therapy. Benjamin provides an excerpt from a session with a woman hospitalized with delusional disorder, suspicious type, that illustrates the effectiveness of this kind of respectful, caring curiosity.

As treatment proceeds, they must learn that their expectations of attack and abusive control stem from past experiences. As such, they can begin appreciating that these expectations are not always appropriate in the present, and that hostility begets hostility. Furthermore, they must come to understand that their defenses of control, avoidance, and anticipatory relation will elicit attack and alienation in others. Benjamin advocates the use of "verbal holding" as an antidote to their original abuse. Accurate empathy, genuine affirmation of accomplishments, and understanding constitute verbal holding. At the same time, therapists need to gently but firmly confront provocations. Since confrontation is likely to be threatening to them, therapists must carefully balance affirmation with confrontation. The goal here is for proactive criticism, and these individuals to learn the meaning of feedback and that their feelings of vulnerability and fearfulness do not "prove" that others, including therapists, are attacking them.

Benjamin's discussion of blocking maladaptive patterns in paranoid individuals includes strategies for dealing with various crises, such as aborting or redirecting rageful outbursts at therapists, dealing with homicidal threats, and abuse of their children. She believes that the therapist's honesty, caring, calmness, attentiveness, and clear commitment to resolving conflicts are extremely useful to paranoid individuals in crisis. Benjamin finds that the wish to relinquish patterns of alienation, hostile control, carrying grudges, and fearfulness do not develop until these individuals feel safe to do otherwise. As therapy proceeds, they are helped to lessen their enmeshment with early controlling, attacking figures. As they can see that they are acting like a hated parent, they may become interested in becoming different.

Once safer bases are established with significant others and/or with their therapist, they can begin channeling their anger in a direction that encourages separation from earlier destructive patterns and beliefs. Finally, to the extent that therapeutic collaboration develops, considerably new learning about trust, giving and receiving positive and negative feedback from and to others, and thinking more benignly about people and life circumstances, has already taken place. As these are mastered, any residual learning that remains by the last stage of therapy is relatively easy to implement. For paranoid individuals at the last stage of treatment, excursions into the social world further the idea that friendly approaches elicit friendly reaction which can be slightly frightening but also exhilarating.

Group Therapy

Because of their hypersensitivity, suspiciousness, and tendency to misinterpret comments of others, Paranoid Personality-Disordered individuals tend to avoid group therapy and other forms of group treatment. Similarly, the paranoid tendency to be accusatory, self-righteous, obstinate, hostile, and evasive has been a contraindication to heterogeneous intensive group therapy (Frances et al., 1984; Vinogradov & Yalom, 1989; Yalom, 1985).

On the other hand, higher functioning paranoid patients who can maintain a degree of self-awareness and are able to tolerate a group confrontation of their paranoid distortion, may derive considerable benefit from participation in an established group that is sufficiently cohesive and tolerant of divergent opinions (Meissner, 1989). Rutan et al. (2014) provide an example of a patient sharing about, but not acting upon, his paranoid fantasies about the group facilitator's vacation being a covert attempt to get away from him. The patient connected this abandonment fantasy to being the only child in his family to be given up for adoption.

Marital and Family Therapy

There is relatively little published literature on therapy with the paranoid personality, per se. Nonetheless, either treatment modality can be used alone or concurrently with individual therapy. Meissner (1989) indicates that family therapy might be combined sometime during the course of long-term individual psychotherapy. Family therapy might be indicated for the paranoid adolescent whose family dynamics and interaction patterns interfere with or contribute to the patient's difficulties.

Harbir (1981) details some general principles for couples therapy for the paranoid personality. He notes that paranoid features often lead to severe marital dysfunction. The paranoid partner's hypersensitivity, joyless intensity, hyper-vigilance, extreme mistrust, and jealousy cause considerable suffering for their partner. Nevertheless, the nonparanoid partner also causes suffering, because their actions often exacerbate the paranoid condition. Typically, nonparanoid spouses react passively and secretively when accused or criticized. The more they withdraw and are evasive, the more their paranoid partner becomes suspicious and mistrustful. Therefore, the clinician who is treating a married paranoid patient in individual therapy should consider concurrent couples therapy or, at least, a conjoint session with the nonparanoid partner to modify the marital interaction pattern that seems to be maintaining the psychopathology.

The goal of marital therapy is to enhance the positive growth of the couple by reducing the personality pathology of either or both partners. Harbir (1981) reports that paranoid patients can progress in couples therapy despite the inevitable issues of trust and confidentiality. The clinician needs to be constantly aware of the paranoid partner's close monitoring of the clinician's behavior. These patients invariably become angry if they perceive the clinician taking sides, or become jealous of the clinician's relationship with their partner. Thus, the clinician, just as in individual psychotherapy, must be open and forthright about the specific therapeutic process and their rationale. Once a therapeutic alliance has been established, the clinician can support the nonparanoid spouse to confront and challenge the constant mistrust of the paranoid partner. An angry response can be expected at first, but the paranoia will start decreasing. Obviously, such confrontation is only prescribed when the patient has adequate impulsive control and has not been violent. Harbir describes a detailed case example of conjoint couples therapy involving a paranoid spouse. The treatment involves two stages and illustrates Harbir's therapy approach.

Benjamin (2003a) also comments on the role of family in the treatment of this disorder. Damage caused by the controlling and attacking figures found in early life may be challenged by the rehabilitative presence of a spouse or child involved in sessions. The paranoid individual may come to see that their hostile behavior resembles that of their abuser, which can spark a desire to be different. She discusses the implications of child abuse by the paranoid individual at length, including the unintended effect of mandatory reporting laws that can lead to premature termination of treatment.

Medication

Currently, there are no psychotropic medications specifically indicated for treating this personality disorder (Silk & Feurino, 2012). Nevertheless, medications are used that target specific troubling symptoms associated with the disorder, such as depression, anxiety, or sleep problems. Generally, these medications are used as an adjunct to psychotherapy and skills training. Because troubling symptoms often respond to medications sooner than most psychological interventions, medications are usually prescribed at the onset of treatment. Since antipsychotic medications are somewhat effective in paranoid schizophrenia, it was hoped that these medications would likewise be useful in the treatment of this personality disorder. Unfortunately, evidence does not support this hope. Furthermore, there is little research evidence to provide guidelines for the use of such medications (Silk & Feurino, 2012).

Combined/Integrative Treatment Approaches

There are sufficient data to suggest that the Paranoid Personality Disorder is no longer untreatable, as was previously believed, but can be successfully treated. Although treatment with psychodynamic and cognitive-behavioral approaches is considered long term, there has been at least one report of successful time-limited treatment (Williams, 1988). Currently, there is little published data on integrating and tailoring treatment with this disorder. Nevertheless, clinical experience shows that an integrative treatment approach probably can maximize therapeutic outcomes while decreasing the length of treatment.

Conceptualizing Paranoid Personality Disorder as having temperament and characterological dimensions, it appears that the dynamic approaches are particularly effective with the characterological dimensions, but less effective with the temperament/style dimension. It seems that cognitive restructuring and the behavioral-information processing approach (Turkat & Maisto, 1985) are particularly effective with modifying the paranoid's cognitive style of hyper-vigilance. The cognitive-behavioral approach is also useful with constricted affects. The interpersonal approach (Benjamin, 2003a) seems particularly effective in reducing blame and hypersensitivity to criticism. Thus, integrating dynamic, cognitive-behavioral, and interpersonal approaches could have a synergistic effect on changing both temperamental and characterological dimensions of this disorder. It also appears that combining treatment modalities should increase treatment efficacy and cost-effectiveness, especially for the more severe presentations of this disorder. The most obvious combined treatment involves the concurrent or sequential use of family, marital, or group therapy with individual psychotherapy. Also quite promising is the combination of medication, i.e., pimozide or serotonin reuptake inhibitors when they are indicated, with individual psychotherapy.

11

SCHIZOID PERSONALITY DISORDER

Individuals with schizoid personalities tend to be reclusive and have little desire or capacity for interpersonal relationships, primarily because they derive little pleasure from such relationships. Yet, they can perform well if left alone. For instance, they can be effective nightwatchmen and security guards. Nevertheless, they have little emotional range, they daydream excessively, and appear to be humorless and aloof (Hopwood & Thomas, 2012).

This chapter describes a framework for the assessment and effective treatment of this disorder. It includes sections on its description, case conceptualization, assessment, and treatment interventions. It begins with background information on the disorder as well as a DSM-5 description and a prototypic description of this disorder. The section on case conceptualization provides five common clinical formulations of this disorder: psychodynamic, biosocial, cognitive-behavioral, interpersonal, and an integrative conceptualization of this disorder. Several treatment approaches, modalities, and intervention strategies are also described. These include individual psychotherapy, group therapy, marital and family therapy, medication, and integrative and combined treatment.

Description of the Schizoid Personality Disorder

Schizoid Personality Disorder can be recognized by the following descriptors and characteristics: style vs. disorder, triggering event(s), behavioral style, interpersonal style, cognitive style, affective style, attachment style, and optimal diagnostic criterion.

Style vs. Disorder. The schizoid personality can be thought of as spanning a continuum from healthy to pathological, with the dependent personality style at the healthy end and the Schizoid Personality Disorder at the pathological end.

TABLE 11.1 Comparison of Schizoid Personality Style and Disorder

Personality Style	Personality Disorder
Exhibit little need of companionship and are most comfortable alone	Neither desire nor enjoy close relationships, including being part of a family; have one or no close friends or confidants other than first-degree relatives.
Tend to be self-contained, not requiring interaction with others in order to enjoy experiences or live their lives.	Nearly always choose solitary activities.
Even-tempered, dispassionate, calm, unflappable, and rarely sentimental.	Rarely, if ever, claim or appear to experience strong emotion, such as anger or joy.
Little driven by sexual needs, and, while they can enjoy sex, do not suffer in its absence.	Little if any desire to have sexual experiences with another person.
Tend to be unswayed by either praise or criticism and can confidently come to terms with their own behavior.	Indifferent to the praise and criticism of others; display constricted affects, e.g., is aloof, cold, and rarely reciprocates gestures or facial expressions, such as smiles or nods.

Table 11.1 compares and contrasts differences between the dependent style and the disorder.

The following case examples further illustrate the differences between the Schizoid Personality Disorder—Mr. Y.—and the schizoid personality style—Mr. P.

CASE STUDY: SCHIZOID PERSONALITY DISORDER

Mr. Y. is a 20-year-old freshman who met with the director of the Introductory Psychology course program to arrange an individual assignment in lieu of participation in the small-group research project course requirement. He told the course director that, because of a daily two-hour commute each way, he "wouldn't be available for the research project," and that he "wasn't really interested in psychology and was only taking the course because it was required." Upon further inquiry, Mr. Y. disclosed that he preferred to commute and live at home with his mother, even though he had the financial resources to live on campus. He admitted he had no close friends nor social contacts, and preferred being a "loner. " He had graduated from high school with a "B" average, but did not date or participate in extracurricular activities, except the electronics club. He was a Computer Science major, and "hacking" was his only hobby. Mr. Y's affect was somewhat flattened and he appeared to have no sense of humor and failed to respond to attempts by the course director to make contact through humor. There was no indication of a thought or perceptual disorder. The course director arranged for an individual project for the student.

CASE STUDY: SCHIZOID PERSONALITY STYLE

Mr. P. is a 28-year-old and six-year veteran of the US Department of the Interior. He has been a forest ranger since graduating from college. While in school, he excelled in the classroom, but was considered a loner by others. Unlike most of his classmates, he didn't pledge a fraternity, feeling he really needed to live in a place that was quiet and distraction-free. Mr. P. enjoyed his work and has received commendations for it. A year ago, he was offered a promotion to field supervisor, which he turned down, since it would have required him to have regular voice or face-to-face contact with up to 10 forest rangers who would report to him. Mr. P had befriended a college friend, with whom he roomed for three years and continues to have occasional contact. He has never considered marriage or family, so he has little interest in dating.

Triggering Event. The typical situation, circumstance, or event that most likely triggers or activates the characteristic maladaptive response of the Schizoid Personality Disorder (Othmer & Othmer, 2002), as noted in behavioral, interpersonal, cognitive, and affective styles, is: "close interpersonal relationships."

Behavioral Style. The behavioral pattern of schizoids can be described as lethargic, inattentive, and occasionally eccentric. They exhibit slow and monotonal speech and are generally nonspontaneous in both their behavior and speech.

Interpersonal Style. Interpersonally, they appear to be content to remain socially aloof and alone. These individuals prefer to engage in solitary pursuits, they are reserved and reclusive, and rarely respond to others' feelings and actions. They tend to fade into the social backdrop and appear to others as "cold fish." They do not involve themselves in group or team activity. In short, they appear inept and awkward in social situations.

Cognitive Style. Their style of perceiving, thinking and information processing can be characterized as cognitively distracted. That is, their thinking and communication can easily become derailed through internal or external distraction. This is noted in clinical interviews when these patients have difficulty organizing their thoughts, are vague, or wander into irrelevance such as the shoes certain people prefer (Millon, 1981). They appear to have little ability for introspection, nor ability to articulate important aspects of interpersonal relationships. Their goals are vague and appear to be indecisive.

Affective Style. Their emotional or affective style is characterized as being humorless, cold, aloof, and unemotional. They appear to be indifferent to praise and criticism, and they lack spontaneity. Not surprisingly, their rapport and ability to empathize with others are poor. In short, they have a constricted range of affective response.

Attachment Style. Individuals with a dismissing attachment style are characterized by a sense of self that is worthy and positive, as well as a low and negative evaluation of others, which typically manifests as mistrust of others. Because they believe they are emotionally self-sufficient while others are emotionally unresponsive, they dismiss the need for friendship and contact with others. This Dismissing Attachment Style is common in individuals with Schizoid Personality Disorder (Lyddon & Sherry, 2001).

Optimal Diagnostic Criterion. Of all the diagnostic criteria for the Dependent Personality Disorder, one has been found to be the most useful in diagnosing this disorder. The belief is that, by beginning with this criterion, the clinician can test for the presence or absence of the criterion and more quickly diagnose the personality disorder. The optimal criterion for this disorder is: neither desires nor enjoys close relationships, including being part of a family (Allnutt & Links, 1996).

DSM-5 Description

Individuals with this personality disorder are characterized by an unremitting pattern of detachment from others and restricted emotional expression. They do not desire nor enjoy close relationships, including family relationships. Except for first-degree relatives, they are unlikely to have close friends or confidants. These individuals typically choose solitary activities, and have little, if any, interest in sexual relations. Not surprisingly, they seem indifferent to the feedback, including criticism, of others. They experience little, if any, pleasure in most activities. Instead, they exhibit emotional coldness, detachment, or flat affect (American Psychiatric Association, 2013).

Prototypic Description

A prototype is a brief description that captures the essence of how a particular disorder commonly presents. Prototypic descriptions are useful and convenient, and clinicians commonly rely on them rather than lists of behavioral criteria and core and instrumental beliefs (Westen, 2012). Here is a common prototypic description of the Schizoid Personality Disorder: These individuals just want to be left alone. Making and maintaining contact with others has little or no meaning and is without pleasure, comfort, or emotion. Accordingly, they live alone, avoid dating, have no real friends, and have jobs that require little or no contact with others. Others consider them awkward, distant, and overly formal in all social contacts. In short, they come across to others as "cold fish."

Prevalence

Prevalence of this disorder has been estimated at between 3.1 and 4.0 percent in the general population (American Psychiatric Association, 2013). In clinical settings, this disorder is the most infrequent in presenting for treatment, with estimates of 0.5 to 5.1 percent (Torgersen, 2012).

Conceptualizations of the Schizoid Personality Disorder

Psychodynamic Case Conceptualizations

The inner world of schizoid individuals appears to be different than their outward appearance. Akhtar (1987) describes them as overtly detached, asexual, self-sufficient, and uninteresting, while covertly emotionally needy, exquisitely sensitive and vulnerable, creative and acutely vigilant. These stark differences represent a splitting or fragmentation of different self-representations that remain integrated. The result is identity diffusion.

Balint (1968) and Nachmani (1984) believe that their difficulty relating to others stems from a deficit—inadequate mothering—rather than from an Oedipal conflict. In short, these individuals base their decision to be isolative on the conviction that, because they failed to receive maternal nurturance and support as infants, they cannot expect or attempt to receive any emotional supplies from subsequent significant figures. Fairburn (1954) views the isolation of schizoid individuals as a defense against a conflict between a wish to relate to others and a fear that their neediness will harm others. Thus, they vacillate between a fear of driving others away by their neediness, and the fear that others will smother or consume them. Consequently, all relationships are experienced as dangerous and must be avoided.

Kellerman and Burry (1989) view this isolation and social distancing as a way of managing anxiety. Schizoid individuals are remote, cool, and aloof, but not necessarily malicious toward others. Typically, schizoid individuals utilize the defenses of repression, suppression, isolation of fantasy affect, displacement, and compensation to ensure distance from others and avoid anxiety.

Biosocial Case Conceptualizations

Millon and Davis (1996) believe the schizoid personality is formed by an interaction of biogenic and environmental factors. Millon and Everly (1985) suggest that a proliferation of dopaminergic postsynaptic receptors in limbic and frontal cortical regions account for the unusual cognitive activity and inhibited emotional responses of schizoid individuals. Along with this excessive parasympathetic nervous system, dampening could account for their apathy, flattened affect, and underresponsiveness. Finally, Millon and Everly note that an ectomorphic—thin and frail—body type, which has been associated with shyness and introversion, is common among schizoid individuals.

Major environmental factors involve parental indifferences and fragmented communication patterns. Families of schizoid individuals are typically characterized by interpersonal reserve, formality, superficiality, and coldness. They tend to communicate in a fragmented, aborted, and circumstantial fashion. Not surprisingly, individuals raised in such environments are likely to be vague, abortive, and circumstantial in all their communications. These disjointed communication patterns tend to be confusing to others and foster misunderstanding, frustration, lack of tolerance, and hostility on the part of others. Schizoid individuals are prone to be isolative and come to believe that others do not understand them. Furthermore, these individuals are usually incapable of correcting the problem.

Their schizoid disorder is perpetuated by social distancing, by having their social isolation reinforced, and by their cognitive and social insensitivity. Their infrequent social activities limit their ability to grow, and their social isolation is frequently reinforced by others who ostracize isolative individuals. Furthermore, their social and cognitive insensitivity tends to oversimplify and make boring a world that is so rich and diverse to others.

Cognitive-Behavioral Case Conceptualizations

According to Beck (2015), individuals with schizoid personality are, for all practical purposes, detached from others. There are characteristic core, conditional, and instrumental beliefs noted in individuals with this disorder. Their *core beliefs* are that they are misfits from life, that relationships take effort and are not worth the trouble, and that they are happier being alone. Their *conditional beliefs* are that if they get too close to others, they will be teased or imposed on by others, and there is no point in trying to connect with others. Their *instrumental beliefs* are don't get involved, say no to others' demands, and leave social situations quickly. Underlying these various beliefs are their beliefs about self and the world.

They typically view themselves as loners and oddballs who don't fit in. They tend to view others as demanding, hostile, and intrusive. Accordingly their basic strategy is to keep their distance from others and avoid contact when others are around. While they may make contact with others as part of their job or meet basic needs, they typically avoid any form of intimacy (Renton & Mankiewicz, 2015).

From the behavioral perspective, Turkat (1990) does not offer a formulation for this disorder. However, it might be that parental indifference, emotional reserve, and little opportunity to develop interpersonal skills contribute to the development of this disorder.

Interpersonal Case Conceptualizations

According to Benjamin (2003a), persons diagnosed with Schizoid Personality Disorder were likely to have been raised in a home that was orderly and formal. While these children's physical and educational needs were met, there was little warmth, play, or social and emotional interaction within the family, or elsewhere, for that matter. The schizoid individual would have modeled social isolation and colorless, unemotional functioning. Such identification with withdrawn parents, leads schizoid individuals to expect little and give little. Though they may be socialized for work, they are not predisposed to intimate contact, and prefer fantasy and solitary advocating instead. In short, they have neither fears of, nor desires for, others. Underdeveloped in social awareness and skills, they can meet social role expectations and employees or even as parents. They may be married but do not develop close, intimate relationships.

Integrative Case Conceptualizations

The following integrative formulation provides a biopsychosocial explanation for how this personality is likely to have developed and how it is maintained. Biologically, the schizoid personality was likely to have had a passive and anhedonic infantile pattern and temperament. Millon (1981) suggested that this pattern results, in part, from increased dopaminergic postsynaptic limbic and frontal lobe receptor activity. Constitutionally, the schizoid is likely to be characterized by an ectomorph body type (fragile and delicate) (Sheldon, Dupertius, & McDermott, 1954).

Psychologically, they view themselves, others, the world, and life's purpose in terms of the following themes. They view themselves by some variant of the theme "I'm a misfit from life, so I don't need anybody. I am indifferent to everything." For schizoid personalities, the world and others are viewed by some variant of the theme "Life is a difficult place and relating to people can be harmful." As such, they are likely to conclude, "Therefore, trust nothing and keep a distance from others and you won't get hurt." Alexandra Adler (1956) further describes these lifestyle dynamics. The most common defense mechanism utilized by them is intellectualization.

Socially, predictable patterns of parenting and environmental factors can be noted in them. Parenting style is usually characterized by indifference and impoverishment. It is as if the parental injunction was "You're a misfit," or "Who are you, what do you want?" Their family pattern is characterized by fragmented communications and rigid, unemotional responsiveness. Because of these conditions, schizoids are grossly undersocialized and develop few if any interpersonal relating and coping skills. This schizoid pattern is confirmed, reinforced, and perpetuated by the following individual and systems factors: Believing themselves to be misfits they shun social activity. This plus social insensitivity leads to reinforcement of social isolation and further confirmation of the schizoid style (Sperry, 2015; Sperry & Mosak, 1996).

Table 11.2 summarizes the characteristic features of this disorder.

TABLE 11.2 Characteristics of Schizoid Personality Disorder

Triggering Event(s)	Close interpersonal relationships
Behavioral Style	Slow and monotonous speech Lethargic and inattentive Nonspontaneous and indifferent
Interpersonal Style	Minimal desire for relationships Chooses solitude over social interaction Lacks confidants Fades into social background Isolative and content to remain aloof
Cognitive Style	Cognitively distracted, easily derailed, and tangential Absent-minded Minimally introspective
Affective Style	Emotionally distant Rarely responsive to another's feelings
Temperament	Passive and anhedonic infantile pattern
Attachment Style	Dismissing
Parental Injunction	"Who are you, what do you want?"
Self-View:	"I'm a misfit from life, so I don't need anybody." "I'm indifferent to everything."
World-View	"Life is a difficult place and can be harmful. Therefore, trust no one and keep distance from others and you won't get hurt."
Maladaptive Schemas	Social isolation; emotional deprivation; defectiveness; subjugation; undeveloped self
Optimal Diagnostic Criterion	Neither desires nor enjoys close relationships, including being part of a family

Assessment of Schizoid Personality Disorder

Several sources of information are useful in establishing a diagnosis and treatment plan for personality disorders. Observation, collateral information, and psychological testing are important adjuncts to the patient's self-report in the clinical interview. This section briefly describes some characteristic observations that the clinician makes and the nature of the rapport likely to develop in initial encounters with specific personality-disordered individuals. Characteristic response patterns on various objective (i.e., MMPI-2 and MCMI-IV) and projective (i.e., Rorschach and TAT) tests are also described.

Interview Behavior and Rapport

Interviewing the Schizoid Personality-Disordered individual can seem like an exercise in futility, given their pervasive emotional withdrawal. They express little or no emotionality even when talking about anxious or depressed feelings. More intelligent individuals with this disorder may complain about anhedonia and may even use the label "depression," but seldom report associated sadness or guilt. Since emotional warmth is absent, it is difficult to judge whether problems or concerns are central to them. Typically, they have one-word or short phrase answers to all questions. Neither open-ended questions, structured questions, nor other interview strategies will change the flow of information or expression of affect. Unlike paranoid individuals, this restricted verbal and emotional expression is not due to self-protectiveness, but rather to emotional and mental emptiness. Rapport usually reflects a willingness to reveal symptoms, problems, and innermost feelings. Since these patients are so impoverished, rapport and engagement may seem impossible with these patients. Long periods of silence are not uncommon. If these patients return for sessions, it usually means they are "connecting" insofar as they know how. Thus, the clinician's persistence, patience, and tolerance for limited verbal interchange may have a therapeutic effect (Ackley et al., 2011; Othmer & Othmer, 2002).

Psychological Testing Data

The Minnesota Multiphase Personality Inventory (MMPI-2), the Millon Clinical Multiaxial Inventory (MCMI-IV), the Rorschach Psychodiagnostic Test, and the Thematic Apperception Test (TAT) can be useful in diagnosing the Schizoid Personality Disorder as well as the schizoid personality style or trait. On the MMPI-2, a normal profile is common for reasonably well-integrated Schizoid individuals. In such instances O (Social Introversion) may be elevated (Lachar, 1974). As these individuals become distressed, a rise in F (Frequency), 2 (Depression), and 8 (Schizophrenia) are likely. Occasionally, a 1–8 (Hypochondriasis-Schizophrenia) "nomadic" profile is noted wherein interpersonal attraction is limited (Graham, 2012).

On the MCMI-IV, an elevation on scale 1 (Schizoid) with low scores on 4A (Histrionic), 5 (Narcissistic), and N (Bipolar-Manic), are likely (Millon et al., 2015).

On the Rorschach, a high percentage of A (Animal) and few C (Color) responses are likely. The overall record tends to be constricted and certain blots may be rejected. Reaction time to many of the cards may be slow. There may be a higher Experience Potential than Experience Actual, and their M (Human Movement) production will be high relative to the overall quality of the protocol (Exner, 1986).

On the TAT, constricted response along with a blindness of theme is common. So also is an impoverished portrayal of story characters (Bellak, 1997).

Treatment Approaches and Interventions

Treatment Considerations

Included in the differential diagnosis of this disorder are the following personality disorders: Avoidant, Schizotypal, and Dependent. The most common symptom disorders likely to be associated with this disorder are: Depersonalization Disorder, Bipolar Disorders, Obsessive-Compulsive Disorder, Somatic Symptom Disorder, Schizophreniform, and Disorganized and Catatonic Schizophrenias.

Schizoid personalities rarely volunteer for treatment unless decompensation is present. However, they may accept treatment if someone, like a family member, demands it. Treatment goals are focused on symptom alleviation rather than on restructuring of personality. Common treatment strategies include crisis management and a consistent and supportive therapeutic interaction. Medications, particularly the antipsychotics, have not been shown to be useful with this disorder (Silk & Feurino, 2012).

Individual Psychotherapy

Some form of individual psychotherapy is indicated for the majority of the schizoid patients. Whether the clinician chooses an active confrontative approach, or cognitive restructuring and social skills training approach, or one that is more supportive, depends on a number of factors, including a patient's psychological-mindedness, resilience, and treatment expectations, the clinician's therapeutic repertoire, and resources for treatment.

This section briefly describes the psychodynamic, cognitive-behavioral, and interpersonal approaches to individual therapy.

Psychodynamic Psychotherapy Approaches

Because the dynamic understanding of both the schizoid and schizotypal personality are inherently similar, Gabbard (1990, 1994) proposes that their treatment is similar. Schizoid patients can be treated effectively with dynamically oriented psychotherapy, both expressive and supportive, depending on their level of functioning and treatment readiness (Gabbard, 1994). The basis for dynamic treatment is not interpretation of conflict, but rather internalization of a therapeutic relationship (Stone, 1985).

Essentially, the clinician's task is to meet the patient's frozen internal object relations by providing a correct emotional experience. The schizoid's style of relatedness results from inadequacies in early relationships with parental figures. As a result, these patients go through life distancing themselves from others. Therapy must therefore provide a new relationship for internalization (Gabbard, 1994). Thylstrup and Hesse (2009) suggest that the schizoid individual's outward emotional detachment from others actually conceals a deep inner longing for closeness. This ambivalence can be addressed within the context of therapy; however, because these patients are unable to adequately articulate their emotional needs, therapists tend to lose interest in them easily. Therapists must pay particular attention to countertransference with these patients, to avoid further alienation. Questions such as "Do I feel like canceling appointments with my socially isolated patient, thinking it won't hurt him or her?" and "Do I find myself wondering if this patient has any problems at all, in spite of clear evidence that he does?" are useful guidelines. The authors present a case study of a 40-year-old unemployed male.

Kavaler–Adler (2004) presents the treatment of this disorder from an object-relations perspective. In this course of psychoanalysis, the schizoid individual is taken through a period of "developmental mourning" in order to grieve the loss of normal development in the separation-individuation process and understand how traumatic early childhood experiences influence current interpersonal problems. The schizoid patient may then work to confront and give up the regret associated with this. She presents a detailed case example of psychoanalysis with a female writer.

Supportive Therapy. Since their basic mode of functioning is non-relational, they find the task of therapy very challenging and difficult. Not surprisingly, they respond to the challenge with silence and emotional distancing. Clinicians need to adopt a permissive, accepting attitude, and must be exceedingly patient with these individuals. It is more helpful to understand silence as a nonverbal form of relating rather than as treatment resistance. By listening with a third ear, the clinician can learn much about these patients. Through projective identification they will evoke certain responses in that clinician that contain valuable diagnostic information regarding the patient's inner world (Gabbard, 1989). Dealing effectively with countertransference issues is critical in working with schizoid patients. Accepting silent nonrelatedness is foreign to the clinician's psychological predisposition and training. Thus, when silence is prolonged, the clinician must guard against acting out and projecting their own self- and object representations into the patient. Accepting the silence, and refraining from interpreting it, legitimizes the patient's private, noncommunicative core self. And, it may be the only viable technique for building a therapeutic alliance (Gabbard, 1989).

The proper pace and depth of therapy is controversial. Bonime (1959) advocates an active, confrontative approach, while Gabbard (1990) and others maintain that a more restrained approach is more respecting and less threatening for these patients.

Supportive techniques can be utilized to encourage the lower functioning schizoid to become more active. For example, the patient is first urged to engage in activities where others are present, but where the patient's participation is minimal, for example, at a sports event. If some level of comfort is achieved, further involvement may be encouraged. Involvement in a computer club, travel tour, or aerobics class risks them attending a sports event, but less than a social gathering or dance class. Kantor (1992) advocates the techniques of "productive substitution" and "modification total push" with these therapeutic tasks. In productive substitution the clinician suggests gratifying replacements for what is missing from the patient's life. Thus, relationships with peers in a therapy group substitutes for the unmarried patient. Using modified total push, the clinician urges the patient to become more socially active. Suggestions are presented tentatively, to test the patient's limits. Problems encountered are brought back into therapy and discussed. Treatment goals and outcomes may be quite limited: the patient may eventually work, albeit in isolation, i.e., as a nightwatchman, may have one or two social friends, and possibly even a long-term relationship with someone who is willing to remain distant companions (Kantor, 1992).

Long-Term vs. Short-Term Dynamic Therapy. Decisions about the type and frequency of dynamic therapy should be based on the patient's level of functioning and motivation and readiness for treatment. Higher functioning schizoid patients who exhibit some depressive symptoms, or some capacity for empathy and emotional warmth, tend to have better outcomes in dynamic psychotherapy (Stone, 1983).

Those patients who are highly motivated for exploratory psychotherapy can make dramatic gains in intense, long-term treatment of two to three sessions per week over several years. On the other hand, long-term supportive psychotherapy is indicated for the majority of schizoid patients who present with major ego deficits and personal eccentricities. The goal of such treatment is improved adaptive functioning in day-to-day living. The frequency of sessions is one to two times per week for the majority of patients (Stone, 1989). Gamache and Diguer (2012) provide a case study of a 34-year-old male with schizoid personality treated for one year using psychodynamic psychotherapy.

Short-term dynamic therapy is indicated for crisis issues and situational difficulties related to job or personal life. It may also serve as follow-up for a previous course of long-term psychotherapy. Not surprisingly, there are no reports of short-term dynamic individual treatment as curative intervention.

Cognitive-Behavioral Therapy Approaches

Cognitive Therapy Approach. Beck et al. (2004) describe the Cognitive Therapy approach to working with Schizoid Personality-Disordered individuals. Since schizoid individuals tend to have limited motivation for social interaction, a principal treatment goal is to establish or increase positions of social interaction, as well as reduce social isolation. These individuals enter treatment largely because of symptomatic Axis I disorders rather than to alter their manner of relating to others. Thus, the initial goal of treatment is a collaborative focus on presenting problems. As this occurs, the therapist can be commenting on the individual's relational patterns, discussing its advantages and disadvantages, and how this pattern affects the presenting problem. The collaborative therapeutic relationship can itself serve as a prototype for other interpersonal relationships, as well as a basis for increasing the individual's range and frequency of interactions outside sessions. After rapport has been established, the therapist can point out the characteristic interaction pattern as well as give feedback on how this impacts other persons. As these individuals develop a greater awareness and understanding of interpersonal relating, they are guided in learning needed social skills and practicing them both within and outside the sessions. Given their lack of expressiveness, routinely soliciting feedback on their level of anxiety should reduce the likelihood of premature termination. Unlike work with other personality disorders where considerable therapeutic leverage and motivation for change are available, relatively little of either is likely with schizoid individuals besides reason. Accordingly, Freeman et al. (1990) advise therapists to clearly present the rationale for therapy, reasons for acting differently, the advantages and disadvantages of changing behavior, and the concrete gains possible. Presumably this strategy can induce these individuals to change.

Beck et al. (2004) indicate that the following techniques are effective with schizoid individuals. The Dysfunctional Thought Record is not only useful in challenging dysfunctional automatic thoughts, but also in identifying a variety of affects and their subtle graduation in intensity, as well as indicating the reactions of others. Teaching social skills is best done directly through role-playing, *in vivo* exposure, and homework assignments. Helping these individuals become more attentive to, and experience, positive emotions can be facilitated by guided discovery. For example, as these individuals are helped to recognize their over-generalized view of others—"I don't like people"—they can learn to be specific about things they don't like, as well as things they do like about others, after all.

As treatment needs termination, the matter of relapse prevention is discussed. Beck et al. (1990) report that schizoid individuals are very likely to relapse into an isolative lifestyle after termination. Thus they suggest maintaining contact with these individuals through booster sessions. Finally, although treatment with these individuals can be difficult, with persistence it is possible to improve their social skills, frequency of social interaction, and decrease their "strangeness." However, the therapist should anticipate that schizoid individuals are likely to retain some distance and passivity in interpersonal relations after planned termination.

Renton and Mankiewicz (2015) echo the notion that these individuals rarely present for treatment of their own accord, and, if doing so, it is likely to be short-lived and exclusively for the purpose of symptom relief or the resolution of specific problems related to changes in their environment. Therapy rarely extends to the examination and resolution of underlying cognitive factors, and ambivalence about change may be present throughout treatment. If these individuals can acknowledge the connection between their early experiences, maladaptive beliefs, and current problems, then they may be willing to reframe these beliefs.

Schema Therapy. Schema Therapy is an elaboration of cognitive therapy that has been developed by Young (1999; Young et al., 2003) specifically for personality disorders, and other difficult individual and couples problems. Schema Therapy involves identifying maladaptive schemas and planning specific strategies and interventions. Four main strategies are cognitive, experiential, behavioral, and the therapeutic relationship itself. Cognitive restructuring, modification of maladaptive schemas, is an important cognitive strategy, but is combined with imagery exercises, empathic confrontation, homework assignments, and "limited reparenting," i.e., a form of corrective emotional experience (Young, 1999; Young et al., 2003).

Maladaptive schemas typically associated with Schizoid Personality Disorder include: *social isolation*—the belief that one is alienated, different from others, or not part of any group; *defectiveness*—the belief that one is defective, bad, unwanted, or inferior in important respects; *emotional deprivation*—the belief that one's desire for emotional support will not be met by others; *subjugation*—the belief that one's desires, needs, and feelings must be suppressed in order to meet the needs of others and avoid retaliation or criticism; and *undeveloped self*—the belief that one must be emotionally close with others at the expense of full individuation or normal social development (Bernstein, 2002).

Interpersonal Approaches

There is very little in the literature about treatment of this disorder from an interpersonal perspective. For example, Benjamin (2003a) provides no discussion of treatment goals or strategies for the Schizoid Personality Disorder. She notes that these individuals are socially withdrawn, do not desire social connections, and do not suffer from anger, fear, or depression. As such, they have little reason to present for treatment.

Group Therapy

Schizoid patients can profit from group therapy, particularly dynamic group therapy (Azima, 1983). Group therapy offers these patients a socialization experience, involving exposure to and feedback from others in a safe, controlled environment. It is an environment in which new parenting can occur. Here group members can function as a reconstructed family and provide a corrective emotional experience that can counterbalance the schizoid's negative and frightening internal objects (Appel, 1974). As their worst fears are not realized and they feel accepted, these patients gradually become more comfortable with others. Giles and Wienclaw (2008) note that the timing of group therapy is important to consider. They suggest that it is first better to develop a strong therapeutic alliance between the patient and the individual therapist before initiating group treatment, as these individuals generally avoid social contact.

From an object relations perspective, Leszcz (1989) contends that the group functions as a holding environment which provides an opportunity for these patients to be initially involved in a "nonrelated" way while slowly building trust. They do not have to leave their cocoon of self-sufficiency, but can observe how others relate in the groups, how feelings make a difference, how to deal with others related in the groups, and how to deal with negative emotions. The wise group leader will permit this non-related position until this patient is better able to tolerate the ambiguities of the group.

From a systems perspective, Bogdanoff and Elbaum (1978) maintain that the schizoid's isolation is not simply due to a fragile ego, but is also a function of the group's need to maintain that isolation. So, while the schizoid patient may provoke the group to make the schizoid talk, at other times the group effectively silences the schizoid by ragefulness or blaming that frightens the schizoid. Essentially, the schizoid is caught in an interpersonal trap—which they call a "role lock." On the other hand, successful group interaction can occur only when the role lock is broken. If the group is avoiding the schizoid, the therapeutic task is to focus the group's attention on the role lock. The aim is for group members to reveal their contribution of the lock and to relieve pressure on the locked member, and for the locked member to reveal how he or she sees the group process to isolate himself or herself.

From an interpersonal perspective, Yalom (1995) discusses other useful interventions for dealing with role lock. The schizoid is helped to differentiate responses to different group members, to take seriously feelings in the here-and-now, to become more aware of their specific avoidance strategies, and to become more aware of their bodily response. Yalom insists that these goals and strategies are preferable to cathartic methods, which can drive the schizoid from the group. He cautions that this process is slow and that patience is essential for the clinician.

Finally, there seems to be a consensus of sorts, that heterogeneous groups are preferable to homogeneous groups (Bogdanoff & Elbaum, 1978; Leszcz, 1989; Slavik, Sperry, & Carlson, 1992). Spotnitz (1975) suggests that the schizoid patient should be referred to a group that is homogeneous in terms of global functioning, but heterogeneous in terms of personality types.

Marital and Family Therapy

Schizoid patients, particularly males, do not marry, and seldom become self-supporting. They may reside with and become dependent on their families. This can result in a vicious cycle in which limited motivation for social contacts and a job or career leads to interferences and bitterness on the part of the family, which is followed by lowered self-esteem, and an even greater reluctance to leave home (Stone, 1989).

Clinicians working with the schizoid patient still living at home often confront family tension, impatience, and discord arising from differences between parental expectations and the patient's capacities and motivation. Family therapy can be quite effective in addressing these expectational differences, discord, and impatience (Anderson, 1983). Shapiro (1982) describes how the family therapist can function to contain such displaced and projected affects and impulses, and acknowledge, bear, work through, and redirect them. Family treatment can also help family members reestablish more functional communication patterns between schizoid patients and their families.

McCormack (1989) describes a common marital constellation in which schizoid individuals marry borderline individuals. In discussing the treatment of the schizoid spouse, McCormack indicates that the core of the schizoid's difficulty is an overwhelming fear of attachments. Insecurity arises from escalating aggression, because frustration of their dependency needs leads to marital dissatisfaction and discord. Schizoid spouses experience their love as lethal and then abort awareness of these feelings and dependency needs as a defense against them. Thus, they develop and maintain relationships in which they are never fully involved.

The treatment of the schizoid spouse emphasizes clarification and careful interpretation and deemphasizes confrontation. Exploration should involve their narcissistic vulnerability, legitimization of their needs, acknowledgment of the potential risks and gains attached to pursuing them, and the schizoid compromise. McCormack describes the "schizoid compromise" as a means of maintaining relationships that require limited emotional involvement, at the cost of limiting personality development. The clinician needs to acknowledge to these patients that this compromise has been adaptive, but is a stage through which they must pass before facing their fear of genuine, healthy relationships.

Schizoid spouses tend to treat others as they fear being treated, which is frustrating to those wanting an intimate relationship with them. In a conjoint session, the clinician helps both spouses to see that each suffers from difficulties that are both similar to and different from their own and that, though these difficulties are fostered in the marriage relationship, they also exist independent of it.

Couples therapy with the schizoid-borderline relationship may require referral of one spouse for individual therapy, the use of medication, or hospitalization. Long-term couples treatment is usually necessary if the goal is to foster separation and autonomy, increased marital satisfaction, and harmony.

Medication

Currently, there are no psychotropic medications specifically indicated for treating individuals with Schizoid Personality Disorder (Silk & Feurino, 2012). Because some controlled trials indicated that antipsychotics were useful in the treatment of Schizotypal Personality Disorder (Koenigsberg, Woo-Ming, & Siever, 2002), it was hoped that these medications might also be useful with this disorder. Unfortunately, that hope has not been realized. Nevertheless, antipsychotics are still prescribed, but are only likely to be useful if some psychotic decompensation has been noted (Sperry, 1995b). Furthermore, there is little research evidence to provide guidelines for the use of medications with this personality disorder (Silk & Feurino, 2012).

Combined/Integrative Treatment Approaches

Schizoid patients tend to avoid mental health professionals just as they avoid relationships in general. When they do present for help, often at the urging of their family, they have a tendency to prematurely terminate therapy after a short time (Stone, 1989). This means there is only a small window of opportunity to engage these patients in the therapeutic process. Combining treatment modalities and integrating treatment approaches can facilitate both commitment to treatment and positive treatment outcomes.

Gabbard (1994) advocates combining dynamic group therapy with dynamic individual psychotherapy as the treatment of choice for the majority of schizoid patients. However, he cautions that many of these patients will recoil at the recommendation for group therapy, even feeling betrayed by their clinician. Thus, Gabbard suggests that, prior to making a group referral, fantasies about the group experience need to be explored and worked through. Stone (1989) also recommends combining individuals and group modalities. However, he proposes a developmental approach in which the patient first forms a stable dyadic relationship with the clinician and then proceeds to group therapy with the same clinician. In both instances, the combined treatment is concurrent.

As noted earlier, McCormack (1989) makes the case for combining marital therapy with individual therapy, particularly when there is considerable splitting and projective identification. Combining family therapy and individual therapy has advantages, particularly if the schizoid patient is financially dependent on the family and/or resides with the family. Family can greatly influence the patient's continuation in individual and/or group treatment.

Armstrong (2002) describes schizoid personality features in substance abusers. He echoes others when he suggests that these are individuals who want to relate, but whose social anxiety stands in the way of this. Substance abuse is one way in which these individuals actively isolate themselves from others while medicating their intense feelings. For these dually diagnosed individuals, the addition of treatments targeted at changing substance use behaviors, such as Motivational Interviewing, may be helpful.

Slavik et al. (1992) advocate both combining treatment modalities and integrating treatment approaches. They indicate the utility of concurrent individual and group treatment. And they describe how an Adlerian approach can be integrated with an object relations theory approach, social skills training, hypnosis, and psychodrama depending on the patient's style, needs, and expectations. These authors believe that the Schizoid Personality Disorder is eminently treatable, and that these patients are largely untreatable because clinicians have not found sufficient ways to engage and encourage them in the change process.

12

SCHIZOTYPAL PERSONALITY DISORDER

Individuals with schizotypal personalities share some features of the schizoid personality. In addition, they are characterized by eccentric behavior and peculiar thought content. Typically, they describe strange intrapsychic experiences, think in odd and unusual ways, and are difficult to engage. Yet, none of these features reach psychotic proportions. It has been suggested that the schizotypal personality is one of the schizophrenic spectrum disorders, because schizophrenia occurs with increased frequency in family members of the schizotypal individual (Kwapil & Barrantes-Vidal, 2012).

This chapter describes a framework for the assessment and effective treatment of this disorder. It includes sections on its description, case conceptualization, assessment, and treatment interventions. It begins with background information on the disorder as well as a DSM-5 description and a prototypic description of this disorder. The section on case conceptualization provides five common clinical formulations of this disorder: psychodynamic, biosocial, cognitive-behavioral, interpersonal, and an integrative conceptualization of this disorder. Several treatment approaches, modalities, and intervention strategies are also described. These include individual psychotherapy, group therapy, marital and family therapy, medication, and integrative and combined treatment.

Description of the Schizotypal Personality Disorder

The Schizotypal Personality Disorder can be recognized by the following descriptors and characteristics: style vs. disorder; triggering event(s); behavioral style; interpersonal styles; cognitive style; affective style; attachment style; and optimal diagnostic criterion.

Style vs. Disorder. The schizotypal personality can be thought of as spanning a continuum from healthy to pathological, wherein the schizotypal personality

TABLE 12.1 Comparison of Schizotypal Personality Style and Disorder

Personality Style	Personality Disorder
Tend to be tuned into and sustained by their own feelings and beliefs.	Ideas of reference; suspicious or paranoid ideation; inappropriate or constricted affect.
Keen observation of others, and are particularly sensitive to how others react to them.	Excessive society anxiety, e.g., extreme discomfort in social situations involving unfamiliar people.
Tend to be drawn to abstract and speculative thinking.	Odd beliefs or magical thinking, influencing behavior and inconsistent with subculture with norms, e.g., superstitiousness, belief in clairvoyance, telepathy, or "sixth sense."
Receptive and interested in the occult, extrasensory, and the supernatural.	Unusual perceptual experiences, e.g., illusions, sensing the presence of a force or person not actually there (e.g., "I felt as if my dead mother were in the room with me").
Tend to be indifferent to social convention, and lead interesting and odd unusual lifestyle.	Odd or eccentric behavior or appearance, e.g., unkempt, unusual mannerisms, talks to self, speech.
Usually are self-directed and independent, requiring few close relationships.	No close friends or confidants (or only one) other than first-degree relatives.

style is closer to the healthy end and the schizotypal personality is on the pathological end. Table 12.1 compares and contrasts the schizotypal personality style and disorder.

The following two case examples further illustrate the differences between the Schizotypal Personality Disorder—Ms. R.—and the schizotypal personality style—Ms. S.

CASE STUDY: SCHIZOTYPAL PERSONALITY DISORDER

Ms. R. was a 41-year-old single female who was referred to a community mental health clinic by her mother because Ms. R. had no interests, friends, or outside activities and was considered by neighbors to be an "odd duck." Her father had recently retired, and because of a limited pension the parents were having difficulty in making ends meet, since Ms. R. had been living with them for the past eight years after she had been laid off from an assembly-line job she had held for about 10 years. The patient readily admitted she preferred to be alone but denied that this was a problem for her. She believed that her mother was concerned about her because of what might happen to the patient after her parents' deaths. Ms. R. was an only child who had graduated from high school with average grades, but had never been involved in extracurricular activities while in school. She had never dated, and mentioned she had a female friend whom she had not talked with in four years. Since moving back with her parents, she stayed in her room preoccupied with books about astrology and charting her astrological forecast. On examination, she was an alert, somewhat uncooperative female appearing older than her stated age, with moderately disheveled hair and clothing. Her speech was monotonal and deliberate. She maintained poor eye contact with the examiner. Her thinking was vague and tangential, and she expressed a belief that her fate lay in "the stars." She denied specific delusions or perceptual abnormalities. Ms. R's affect was constricted, except for one episode of anger when she thought the therapist was being critical.

CASE STUDY: SCHIZOTYPAL PERSONALITY STYLE

Ms. S. is a 37-year-old acquisitions editor for a large publisher. Her primary responsibility is to review proposals and manuscripts in science fiction and the occult to determine if her company should publish them. She finds her job fascinating and energizing, particularly since her boss has allowed her to work from home four days out of five. She has great difficulty in working a typical 9:00 to 5:00 workday, as she prefers to sleep days and work at night. When reviewing a submitted manuscript, she literally tries to put herself into the plot by imagining herself as the heroine and enhances the effect by donning appropriate clothing, burning incense, and playing suitable background music. She refers to Mark as her "soulmate" rather than a boyfriend. They do not actually date, since he lives in another city. But they spend long hours on the phone and "let their spirits commune" the rest of the time. Occasionally, they meet each other at various science fiction, UFO, and *Star Trek* conventions.

Triggering Event. The typical situation, circumstance, or event that most likely triggers or activates the characteristic maladaptive response of the Schizotypal Personality Disorder (Othmer & Othmer, 2002), as noted in behavioral, interpersonal, cognitive, and Affective styles, is: "close interpersonal relationships."

Behavioral Style. Behaviorally, schizotypals are noted for their eccentric, erratic, and bizarre mode of functioning. Their speech is markedly peculiar without being incoherent. Occupationally, they are inadequate, either quitting or being fired from jobs after short periods of time. Typically, they become drifters, moving from job to job and town to town. They tend to avoid enduring responsibilities and in the process lose touch with a sense of social propriety.

Interpersonal Style. Interpersonally, they are loners with few, if any, friends. Their solitary pursuits and social isolation may be the result of intense social anxiety, which may be expressed with apprehensiveness. This apprehensiveness doesn't diminish with familiarity, and is associated with paranoid features rather than negative self-appraisal. If married, their style of superficial and peripheral relating often leads to separation and divorce in a relatively short period of time. Their lives tend to be marginal, and they gravitate toward jobs that are below their capacity or demand little interaction with others.

Cognitive Style. The cognitive style of schizotypals is described as scattered and ruminative, and is characterized by cognitive slippage. Presentations of superstitiousness, telepathy, and bizarre fantasies are characteristic. They may describe vague ideas of reference and recurrent illusions of depersonalizing, derealizing experiences without the experience of delusions of reference, or auditory or visual hallucinations.

Affective Style. Their affective style is described as cold, aloof, and unemotional with constricted affect. They can be humorless and difficult individuals to engage in conversation, probably because of their general suspicious and mistrustful nature. In addition, they are hypersensitive to real or imagined slights.

Attachment Style. Individuals with an "other-view" that is negative and a "self-view" that vacillates between positive and negative exhibit a composite fearful-dismissing style of attachment. They tend to view themselves as special and entitled, but are also mindful of their need for others who can potentially hurt them. Accordingly, they use others to meet their needs while being wary and dismissive of them. This fearful-dismissing attachment style is common in individuals with Schizotypal Personality Disorder.

Optimal Diagnostic Criterion. Of all the stated DSM-IV-TR criteria for the Schizotypal Personality Disorder, one criterion has been found to be the most useful in diagnosing this disorder. The belief is that, by beginning with this criterion, the clinician can test for the presence or absence of the criterion and quickly diagnose the personality disorder (Allnutt & Links, 1996). The "optimal criterion" for this disorder is: "odd thinking and speech: behavior or appearance that is odd, eccentric, or peculiar."

DSM-5 Description

Individuals with this personality disorder are characterized by an unremitting pattern of social and interpersonal deficits with significant discomfort and limited capacity for relationships, as well as by perceptual distortions and eccentric behavior. They experience ideas of reference as well as unusual beliefs and thinking that influence their behavior, and which is inconsistent with their subculture. They also experience unusual perception, such as bodily illusions, and odd speech thinking. These individuals are prone to suspiciousness and paranoid ideation. They exhibit inappropriate or constricted emotions, and behavior that is odd, peculiar, or eccentric. With few exceptions, they lack close friends or confidants, except for first-degree relatives. When they are around others, they experience excessive social anxiety that is not diminished by familiarity and is associated with suspicion and fears (American Psychiatric Association, 2013).

The "Alternative DSM-5 Model for Personality Disorders" provides another description of this disorder (American Psychiatric Association, 2013). It is described as an impaired capacity for relationship and eccentricities in perception, cognition, and behavior associated with distorted self-image and incoherent goals involving suspiciousness and limited emotional expression. Characteristic difficulties are noted in identity, self-direction, empathy, and intimacy, as well as suspiciousness, withdrawal, restricted affect, eccentricity, unusual beliefs and experiences, or cognitive and perceptual dysregulation.

Prototypic Description

A prototype is a brief description that captures the essence of how a particular disorder commonly presents. Prototypic descriptions are useful and convenient, and clinicians commonly rely on them rather than lists of behavioral criteria and core and instrumental beliefs (Westen, 2012). Here is a common prototypic description of the Schizotypal Personality Disorder: These individuals display disorganized behavior and speech and emotional blunting, but not the delusions and hallucinations associated with the diagnosis of schizophrenia. Their characteristic eccentric thinking and behavior, strange beliefs, and unusual perceptual experiences are below the threshold of psychosis. These symptoms have an early onset and usually remain stable throughout life. It is also not uncommon for these individuals to be misdiagnosed as having Asperger's Disorder.

Prevalence

Prevalence of this disorder has been estimated at between 0.6 and 4.6 percent in the general population (American Psychiatric Association, 2013). In clinical settings, it is relatively infrequent, with estimates between 0.6 and 9.1 percent (Torgersen, 2012).

Conceptualizations of the Schizotypal Personality Disorder

Psychodynamic Case Conceptualizations

Gunderson (1988) admits that little is known about the dynamics of the Schizotypal Personality Disorder. Gabbard (1990), among other psychoanalytically oriented writers, believes that, except for a few symptoms suggestive of an attenuated form of schizophrenia, the schizoid personality and the schizotypal personality are inherently similar.

On the other hand, Kellerman and Burry (1989) believe that the dynamics of the two disorders are quite different. They classify the Schizoid Personality Disorder as an emotion-controlled character type—along with the Paranoid and Obsessive-Compulsive personality disorders—while they classify the Schizotypal Personality Disorder as an emotion-avoidant character type—along with the Borderline and Avoidant personality disorders.

Kellerman and Burry believe that schizotypal individuals probably experienced consistent object contact in early childhood. However, their parents failed to provide sufficient emotional closeness and warmth and were probably punitive and critical. These factors probably account for the social hypersensitivity, which serves as a defense against intense social anxiety noted in these individuals. Emotion is generally restricted, but when expressed tends to be inappropriate. These individuals typically utilize a wide variety of defense mechanisms, including projection to externalize fear and anger, preoccupation with magic thinking and intellectualization to reduce emotional overstimulation, and hysterical denial to screen out undesirable social interactions in order to rationalize them.

Biosocial Case Conceptualization

The schizotypal personality is viewed by Millon and Everly (1985) as a syndromal continuation of the Schizoid and Avoidant personality disorders. Thus, the etiological and developmental determinants of the schizotypal disorder will be similar, as in the schizoid and avoidant disorders, but in greater intensity or chronicity. Biogenic factors in the schizotypal schizoid variant include a genetic predisposition at least as reported in one study (Torgerson, 1984). Millon and Everly suggest that schizotypal-schizoid individuals have shown a passive infantile reaction pattern which probably initiated a sequence of impoverished infantile stimulation and consequent parental indifference. Further, they point out that a dampening of the ascending reticular activity system of the limbic system may result in the autostimulation and fantasy of these individuals. Environmentally, a cold and formal family environment combined with fragmented parental communication probably interacts with biogenic factors to produce this personality pattern and disorder. The background of schizotypal-avoidant individuals is somewhat different. Genetically, these individuals are more likely to exhibit a "slow-to-warm-up" temperament (Thomas & Chess, 1977). These individuals tend to be apprehensive, tense, and do not adapt quickly to new situations. Such behavior can precipitate parental tension and derogation, which further aggravates this temperament. Socially, the developmental histories of these individuals typically show parental deprecation as well as peer and sibling humiliation, which results in interpersonal mistrust and lowered self-esteem. Continuation of these derogating and humiliating attitudes eventually leads to self-criticism and self-deprecation.

The schizotypal personality is self-perpetuated by social isolation, over-protection, and self-insulation. While social isolation and overprotectiveness have immediate benefits, in the long run they are counter-productive as they deprive these individuals of opportunities to develop social skills, besides fostering dependency. Furthermore, their tendency toward self-insulation serves to foster and further perpetuate the spiral of cognitive and social deterioration that typifies this disorder (Millon & Davis, 1996).

Cognitive-Behavioral Case Conceptualizations

According to Beck (2015), individuals with schizotypal personality are odd and different from others. There are characteristic core, conditional, and instrumental beliefs noted in individuals with this disorder. Their *core belief* is that the world is uncaring and life is full of powerful forces that cannot be explained. Their *conditional belief* is that if they get close to normal people, they will be rejected; if others view them as different, they will be left alone; and if they use their special gifts, the powers will protect them. Their *instrumental belief* is that being different is protective. Underlying these various beliefs are their beliefs about self and the world. They tend to view themselves as different, special, gifted, or supernaturally attuned. They typically view others as unfriendly and hostile, untrustworthy, and unable to understand their specialness. Accordingly, their basic strategy is to cultivate unusual appearance or mannerisms, keep a distance from others, and use their special gifts or magical powers to protect themselves (Renton & Mankiewicz, 2015).

From a behavioral perspective, Turkat (1990) describes the Schizotypal Personality Disorder, but is unable to provide behavioral formulation for it. Instead, he notes that these individuals tend to be quite diverse in terms of behavioral presentation. This is consistent with the observation that the schizotypal personality is a decompensation of either the avoidant personality or the schizoid personality (Millon & Davis, 2000; Millon & Everly, 1985).

Interpersonal Case Conceptualizations

According to Benjamin (2003a), persons diagnosed with Schizotypal Personality Disorder likely had parents who punished them for allegedly inappropriate customary talking, while their parents did the same. Thus, the absent father severely reprimands the child for not staying home. Essentially, such a parent modeled "mindreading," suggesting that, even though not present, he "knew" something vitally important about the child. The adult consequence of this schizotypal modeling is that the individual imitates this pattern of "knowing" through special means, such as telepathy, mindreading, or "sixth" sense. Parents were also likely to place inappropriate reliance on children for performance of household duties with undue threat and duress. Thus, these children learned that proper behavior and obedience could avert bad outcomes. The adult consequence is the paradoxical tendency to submit to rituals that bring control. Severe abuse, often involving invasion of these children's personal boundaries is common. Furthermore, it also is likely that strong injunctions against leaving the home for peer play or other reasons were levied by the parents. Such prohibitions interfered with the development of social feelings and skills, and reinforced social isolation as well as fantasy and autism. Finally, there is a fear of being attacked and controlled by humiliation. These individuals are prone to hostile withdrawal and self-neglect. Furthermore, they believe they can magically influence—from a distance —circumstances and individuals through telepathy or ritual. Although they may be aware of their aggressive feelings, they usually constrain them.

Integrative Case Conceptualizations

The following integrative formulation provides a biopsychosocial explanation for how the Schizotypal Personality Disorder is likely to develop and be maintained. Because this disorder is a syndromal extension or deterioration of the Schizoid or the Avoidant personality disorders (Millon, 1981), the biological and tempera-mental features of both of these subtypes should be consulted. The schizoid subtype of a schizotypal personality is characterized with a passive infantile pattern, probably resulting from low autonomic nervous system reactivity and parental indifference that led to impoverished infantile stimulation. On the other hand, the avoidant subtype is characterized by the fearful infantile temperamental pattern (Millon, 1981). This probably resulted from the child's high autonomic nervous system reactivity combined with parental criticism and deprecation that was further reinforced by sibling and peer deprecation. Both subtypes of the schizotypal personality have been noted to have impaired eye-tracking motions, which is a characteristic shared with schizophrenic individuals.

Psychologically, the schizotypals view themselves, others, the world, and life's purpose in terms of the following themes. They tend to view themselves by some variant of the theme: "I'm on a different wavelength than others." They commonly experience being selfless, that is, they experience feeling empty, estranged, and disconnected or dissociated from the rest of life. Their world-view is some variant of the theme "Life is strange and unusual, and others have special magical intentions." As such, they are likely to conclude: "Therefore, observe caution while being curious about these special magical intentions of others." The most common defense mechanism utilized by them is undoing, the effort to neutralize "evil" deeds and thoughts by their eccentric, peculiar beliefs and actions.

TABLE 12.2 Characteristics of Schizotypal Personality Disorder

Triggering Event(s)	Close interpersonal relationships
Behavioral Style	Eccentric and peculiar behaviors Odd speech but not incoherent Depersonalization and/or dissociation
Interpersonal Style	May relate to others with similar unusual interests Suspicious of others not in their like-minded group Indifferent to social convention
Cognitive Style	Tangential and scattered thought processing Magical thinking and superstitious
Affective Style	Inappropriate or constricted affect Hypersensitive
Temperament	Schizoid types: passive infantile pattern Avoidance type: fearful infantile pattern
Attachment Style	Fearful and dismissing
Parental Injunction	"You're a strange bird."
Self-View	"I'm on a different wavelength than others."
World-View	"Life is strange and unusual, and others have special magic intentions. Therefore, observe caution while being curious."
Maladaptive Schemas	Alienation; abandonment; dependence; vulnerability to harm
Optimal Diagnostic Criterion	Thinking, speech, behavior, or appearance that is odd, eccentric, or peculiar

Socially, predictable patterns of parenting and environmental factors can be noted for the Schizotypal Personality Disorder. The parenting patterns mentioned previously—the cold indifference of the schizoid subtype or the deprecating and derogatory parenting style and family environment of the avoidant subtype—are noted. In both cases, the level of functioning in the family of origin then would be noted in the Schizoid Personality Disorder or the Avoidant Personality Disorder. Fragmented parental communications are a feature common to both subtypes of the Schizotypal Personality Disorder. The parental injunction is likely to have been: "You're a strange bird" (Sperry, 2015; Sperry & Mosak, 1996).

Table 12.2 summarizes the characteristics of this disorder.

Assessment of Schizotypal Personality Disorder

Several sources of information are useful in establishing a diagnosis and treatment plan for personality disorders. Observation, collateral information, and psychological testing are important adjuncts to the patient's self-report in the clinical interview. This section briefly describes some characteristic observations that the clinician makes and the nature of the rapport likely to develop in initial encounters with specific personality-disordered individuals. Characteristic response patterns on various objective (i.e., MMPI-2 and MCMI-IV) and projective (i.e., Rorschach) tests are also described.

Interview Behavior and Rapport

Interviewing Schizotypal Personality-Disordered individuals usually elicits surprising statements and peculiar ideas. Rapport is hampered as long as they feel the clinician cannot appreciate their experiences. To the extent the clinician is empathic and indicates understanding, they will be more willing to share their secret and autistic world. Unlike the schizoid, these individuals establish rapport easily and are usually willing to respond to all types of questions. The clinician will frequently need to ask for clarification of the impressions and constructions. Empathic listening together with continuation techniques usually suffices in encouraging them to explain their experience. On the other hand, doubting questions or confronting their views will cause them to recoil. More intelligent individuals with this disorder may query the clinicians, wanting to know whether the clinician had had experiences similar to theirs. Handling this situation is more a matter of rapport than an issue of formulating questions more effectively (Ackley et al., 2011; Othmer & Othmer, 2002).

Psychological Testing Data

The Minnesota Multiphase Personality Inventory (MMPI-2), the Millon Clinical Multiaxial Inventory (MCMI-IV), and the Rorschach Psychodiagnostic Test can be useful in diagnosing the Schizotypal Personality Disorder as well as the schizotypal personality style or trait.

On the MMPI-2 a 2–7–8 (Depression-Psychasthenia-Schizophrenia) code is likely among these individuals (Edell, 1987). Scales F (Frequency) and O (Social Introversion) are also likely to be elevated (Graham, 2012).

On the MCMI-IV, elevations on S (Schizotypal), 2A (Avoidant), 7 (Compulsive), and 8A (Negativistic: passive aggressive) can be expected (Choca & Denburg, 1997; Millon et al., 2015).

On the Rorschach, it might be expected that these individuals would respond much like those with Schizoid Personality Disorder. However, the response of schizotypal individuals is more similar to schizophrenics and those with Borderline Personality Disorder than those with Schizoid Personality Disorder (Swiercinsky, 1985).

Treatment Approaches and Interventions

Treatment Considerations

Included in the differential diagnosis of this disorder are three other personality disorders: Schizoid, Avoidant, and Borderline. The most common symptom disorders associated with Schizotypal Personality Disorder are the schizophrenias, particularly the Disorganized, Catatonic, and Residual types. Other disorders noted are the Anxiety Disorders, the Somatic Symptom Disorders, and the Dissociative Disorders.

Individuals with this disorder find it difficult to engage and remain in a psychotherapeutic relationship. Typically, they are on medication and may be referred for adjunctive psychotherapy. Accordingly, the focus of treatment is on "management" rather than on "treatment." Thus, instead of attempting personality restructuring, the realistic treatment goal for the schizotypal personality is to increase the individual's ability to function more consistently, even though on the periphery of society. Specifically, successful management will likely incorporate psychoeducational or social skills training with supportive psychotherapeutic methods. Reid (1989) noted that if these patients can remain in long-term treatment, they may be able to increase their ability to function more consistently and with less disease. He reports that homogeneous groups can occasionally be a useful adjunct to individual treatment. In terms of medication, low-dose neuroleptics have been found to be useful for the schizotypal personality, even in the absence of psychotic features. Yet, it should be noted that medication compliance is a particular problem with this disorder (Sperry, 2015).

Individual Psychotherapy

Psychodynamic Psychotherapy Approaches

Schizotypal Personality-Disordered individuals tend to be treated in office, clinic, and day treatment programs rather than in acute inpatient programs. They may profit from dynamically oriented psychotherapy, both expressive and supportive, depending on their level of functioning and treatment readiness. The basis for dynamic treatment is not interpretation of conflict, but rather internalization of a therapeutic relationship (Stone, 1985).

Essentially, the clinician's task is to "melt" the patient's frozen internal object relations by providing a correct emotional experience. Their style of relatedness results from inadequacies in early relationships with parental figures. As a result these patients go through life distancing themselves from others. Therapy must therefore provide a new relationship for internalization (Gabbard, 2000).

There has been relatively little psychodynamic research about this personality disorder, as noted by Perry, Presniak, and Olson (2013). They conducted a study that evaluated the defense mechanisms used by individuals with various personality disorders during videotaped therapy sessions. With schizotypal individuals, there was the least variance of defense mechanisms among the other disorders. Projection, splitting, passive aggression, and devaluation were the most common defenses used. Defenses specific to Schizotypal Personality Disorder include displacement and fantasy. Individuals with this disorder prefer to deal with others indirectly. Since their basic mode of functioning is nonrelational, they find the task of therapy very challenging and difficult. Not surprisingly, they respond to the challenge with silence and emotional distancing. Clinicians need to adopt a permissive, accepting attitude, and must be exceedingly patient with these individuals. It is more helpful to understand silence as a nonverbal form of relating rather than as treatment resistance. By listening with a third ear, the clinician can learn much about these patients. Through projective identification they will evoke certain responses in the clinician that contain valuable diagnostic information regarding the patient's inner world (Gabbard, 1990). Dealing effectively with countertransference issues is critical in working with schizotypal patients. Accepting silent nonrelatedness is foreign to the clinician's psychological pre-disposition and training. Thus, when silence is prolonged, the clinician must guard against acting out and projecting their own self- and object representations into the patient. Accepting the silence, and refraining from interpreting it, legitimizes the patient's private, noncommunicative core self. It may be the only viable technique for building a therapeutic alliance (Gabbard, 1990).

Long-Term vs. Short-Term Dynamic Therapy. Decisions about the type and frequency of dynamic therapy should be based on the patient's level of functioning and motivation and readiness for treatment. Higher functioning schizotypal patients who exhibit some depressive symptoms, or some capacity for empathy and emotional warmth, tend to have better outcomes in dynamic psychotherapy (Stone, 1983). Similarly, patients with better ego functioning in terms of judgment, reality testing, and cognitive slippage tend to do better than those with poorer ego functioning.

Those patients who are highly motivated for exploratory psychotherapy can make dramatic gains in intense, long-term treatment of two to three sessions per week over several years. On the other hand, long-term supportive psychotherapy is indicated for the majority of schizotypal patients who present with major ego deficits and personal eccentricities. The goal of such treatment is improved adaptive functioning in day-to-day living (Stone, 1989). Mehlum et al. (1991) described a long-term day treatment program for Schizotypal Personality-Disordered individuals based on psychodynamic principles.

Short-term dynamic therapy is indicated for crisis issues and situational difficulties related to job or personal life. It may also serve as follow-up for a previous course of long-term psychotherapy. Not surprisingly, there are few case reports of short-term dynamic individual treatment as curative intervention.

Cognitive-Behavioral Therapy Approaches

Stone (1989) indicates that, for schizotypal patients who aspire to "fit in" better and feel less alienated, corrective experiences may be necessary. Such experiences might include referral to elocution lessons, or a Dale Carnegie course, or accompanying the patient to a clothing store to assist in selecting appropriate apparel for a job interview. Stone has also found videotape feedback useful in pointing out the patient's awkwardness of gait, or gestures. Turkat (1990) recommends that anxiety management and modification of hypersensitivity and hypervigilance also may be necessary, depending on the case formulation.

Cognitive Therapy. Beck et al. (2004) briefly describe the Cognitive Therapy approach to working with Schizotypal Personality-Disordered individuals. Developing a collaborative working relationship is the starting point for treatment with these individuals. Since these individuals hold a number of irrational beliefs about others, the importance of the therapeutic relationship should not be underestimated. Since these individuals desire social relationships and experience distress with social isolation, assisting them in increasing their social support network is an initial treatment goal. Increasing social appropriateness is a related goal. Social skills training as well as the therapist modeling appropriate behavior and speech are effective strategies. In combination with these behavioral strategies, the clinician works collaboratively with the individual to identify automatic thoughts and underlying schemas about social interactions. Role-playing more appropriate behavior then becomes much more meaningful.

Perhaps the most critical aspect of treatment is helping the schizotypal individual seek out objective evidence in the environment to evaluate their thoughts, rather than relying on emotional responses. As they learn to disregard inappropriate thoughts, they are able to consider the consequences that responding emotionally or behaviorally to such thoughts would have, and respond more rationally. The individual's eccentric and magical thoughts are perceived as symptoms, and predesigned coping statements, such as "There I go again. Even though I have this thought, it doesn't mean it's true," are practiced. In addition to guided discovery and direct disputation of maladaptive beliefs, indirect strategies such as encouraging the schizotypal individual to keep track of the predictions they make and the accuracy of these predictions is an effective but less threatening intervention. In addition to focusing on automatic thoughts and schemas, efforts to change the schizotypal's cognitive style are helpful. Since the communication patterns of these individuals tends to be circumstantial and idiosyncratic, collaborative experiments can be set up to modify this style. Furthermore, Beck et al. (1990) note that, provided the therapist has realistic treatment expectations, much can be accomplished, and the collaborative work can be a positive experience, as these individuals are able to control portions of their inappropriate behaviors and thoughts.

Freeman et al. (1990) are not optimistic about the cognitive treatment of schizotypal individuals, indicating that behavioral interventions such as social skills training are initially useful. It is only after these individuals can be more socially appropriate—that is, they begin acting more like schizoid personalities—that their automatic thoughts and cognitive distortions are amenable to cognitive methods.

Renton and Mankiewicz (2015) agree that establishing a collaborative and trusting therapeutic relationship is crucial to the successful treatment of these individuals. Typically, they present for help only when some external crisis forces them to do so. Schizotypal patients often harbor suspicions about the therapist, which may include magical thinking such as having their minds read against their will. Once trust is established and therapeutic goals have been identified, a number of cognitive interventions can be attempted. Developmental conceptualizations may be particularly useful in helping schizotypal individuals see how past events shape the beliefs and rules they currently hold about the world. However, these individuals may resist deeper examination into the origins of their belief systems and commonly terminate therapy once symptom relief is achieved or the presenting situation is resolved.

Schema Therapy. Schema Therapy is an elaboration of cognitive therapy that has been developed by Young (1999) specifically for personality disorders, and other difficult individual and couples problems. Schema Therapy involves identifying maladaptive schemas and planning specific strategies and interventions. Four main strategies are cognitive, experiential, behavioral and the therapeutic relationship itself. Cognitive restructuring, modification of maladaptive schemas, is an important cognitive strategy, but is combined with imagery exercises, empathic confrontation, homework assignments and "limited reparenting," i.e., a form of corrective emotional experience (Young, 1999).

Maladaptive schemas typically associated with Schizotypal Personality Disorder include: *abandonment*—the belief that significant others will not or cannot provide reliable and stable support; *alienation*—the belief that one must meet the needs of others at the expense of one's own gratification; *vulnerability to harm*— the exaggerated fear that imminent catastrophe will strike at any time and that one will be unable to prevent it; and *dependence*—the belief that one is unable to competently deal with everyday responsibilities without considerable help from others (Bernstein, 2002).

Interpersonal Approaches

For Benjamin (2003a) psychotherapeutic interventions with Schizotypal Personality-Disordered individuals can be planned and evaluated in terms of whether they enhance collaboration, facilitate learning about maladaptive patterns, and their roots block these patterns, enhance the will to change, and effectively encourage new patterns.

The therapist facilitates collaboration by deferring to the schizotypal individual's sensitivities. For example, at the beginning of therapy, the therapist may need to be quite tolerant about cancelled appointments and control over the course of sessions. If not allowed to maintain distance and control in this manner, these individuals will quickly terminate. Gradually the therapist should be able to engage these individuals through empathic listening, accurate mirroring, and constancy. As treatment progresses, they may develop sufficient trust and insight to relinquish control by magic and ritual. Unlike parents, clinicians require no caregiving themselves. And, unlike the parents of schizotypals, therapists can be consistent in mainstreaming focus and supportive attention. Such an experience is, therefore, emotionally corrective.

During the course of treatment, schizotypal individuals need to learn that their efforts to take responsibility for abusive situations when they were helpless served to predispose them to magical thinking. Such early experiences led these individuals to assume they had inordinate power and influence. Next, they are helped to recognize when and how they distort reality. At the same time, they are taught new self-talk that can keep them grounded in the here-and-now. Later, they are helped to understand the contribution of early experiences and learning to their unrealistic thoughts. However, for reconstructive changes to occur these individuals must change their wish to magically protect their self and others while maintaining loyalty to early abusers. For example, interpreting suicidal or other fantasies in relation to underlying wishes can lead to fuller awareness, allowing the individual an opportunity for a new choice. Accurate mirroring and empathy can assist these individuals in mobilizing their will to recover and visualize better ways of viewing self, the world, and others. With these individuals, the therapist must remain cautious. There is a fragile balance between allowing the patient to continue to participate in maladaptive behaviors in order to keep them in therapy and blocking them when they occur to promote change. Benjamin is doubtful that major changes in learning patterns will occur, believing that this disorder is genetically mediated.

Group Therapy

Clinical reports of group therapy with schizotypal patients have been limited. Nevertheless, there is sufficient indication these patients may profit from supportive group therapy (Mehlum et al., 1991; Stone, 1989).

A reasonable outcome or goal of group therapy is increased awareness that others harbor fantasies and self-criticisms similar to schizotypals, and that others may find them likable despite their conviction of unlikability. Group therapy may impact such social alienating tendencies as standoffishness and peculiarities of speech. An ongoing heterogeneous group may be able to tolerate some degree of these tendencies. But, beyond the limits of tolerability, these behaviors may so affect either the patient or other group members that therapeutic group process is mollified. Obviously, appropriate selection of which schizotypal patients will benefit from being in a group is an important task of the group leaders (Stone, 1989).

Marital and Family Therapy

Clinical reports of marital or family therapy with schizotypal patients have not yet appeared. In general, schizotypal individuals tend to remain single. Because of their rejection sensitivity or insensitivity to others' feelings, these patients are likely to avoid committed relationships. Not surprisingly, schizotypals who do marry tend to have problems stemming either from insensitivity to the feelings of their partner or from oversensitivity to the partner's behavior. Therefore, in couples therapy, the clinician's first task is to assess the degree of and balance between these two tendencies. Typically, it is easier to assist a hypersensitive partner to respond more appropriately than to help an insensitive partner become more empathic (Stone, 1989).

Family therapy has been identified as a potentially beneficial intervention for adolescents with Schizoid Personality Disorder (Ryan, Macdonald, & Walker, 2013). Because of the shared symptoms with schizophrenia and other schizophrenia spectrum disorders, family education interventions have been adapted to Schizotypal Personality Disorder that enlist family members to support patient recovery. These include family education about the disorder, identification of relapse signs and development of action plans, and communication training to reduce stress within the family.

Medication

Currently, there are no psychotropic medications specifically indicated for treating this personality disorder (Silk & Feurino, 2012). Nevertheless, medications are used that target specific troubling symptoms associated with the disorder, such as depression, anxiety, or sleep problems. Generally, these medications are used as an adjunct to psychotherapy and skills training. Because troubling symptoms often respond to medications sooner than most psychological interventions, medications are usually prescribed at the onset of treatment. These include low-dose neuroleptics, which can be useful in decreasing anxiety associated with loss of control (Sperry, 1995b). In a randomized controlled trial, Risperdal (risperidone), an antipsychotic medication, has been shown to be effective with this disorder (Koenigsberg, Woo-Ming, & Siever, 2002; Silk & Feurino, 2012).

Combined/Integrative Treatment Approaches

Probably because of the impairing nature of this disorder, there is surprisingly little resistance to combining medication with psychological treatments, and tailoring treatment. Liebowitz et al. (1986) suggest beginning individual therapy and medication, where indicated, concurrently. Stone (1992) advocates beginning with medication or a behavioral intervention and adding a dimensional psychotherapy: a blending of supportive, exploratory, cognitive, and behavioral elements to match the concurrent needs and circumstances of the patient. This, of course, represents the epitome of integrated, tailored treatment.

Others have advocated social skills training as an adjunct to supportive psychotherapy (Liebowitz et al., 1986) or combining group therapy with individual dynamic psychotherapy (Gabbard, 1994). Mehlum et al. (1991) report on the combining of several treatment modalities for Schizotypal and Borderline personality-disordered patients: individual psychodynamic psychotherapy, group therapy, community meetings, art therapy, awareness group therapy, and milieu therapy. This unique prospective study of a day treatment program showed that efficacy of this combined treatment approach held up an average of three years later. Major changes were noted in symptom reduction. However, social adjustments and employment were not as robust as with borderline patients. Nathanson and Jamison (2011) present a case study with a 21-year-old US combat infantryman diagnosed with Schizotypal Personality Disorder. His treatment involved selectively reinforcing positive self-statements, social skills training, and anxiety reduction, as well as pharmacological interventions. Ryan, Macdonald, and Walker (2013) note that many individuals with schizophrenia spectrum disorders also abuse cannabis, which can exacerbate psychotic symptoms. To address this issue, they discuss Motivational Interviewing as an effective option.

REFERENCES

Accordino, M. P., Keat II, D. B., & Guerney, Jr., B. G. (2003). Using relationship enhancement therapy with an adolescent with serious mental illness and substance dependence. *Journal of Mental Health Counseling, 25*(2), 152–164.

Ackley, C., Mack, S., Beyer, K., & Erdberg, P. (2011). *Investigative and forensic interviewing: A personality-focused approach.* Boca Raton, FL: CRC Press.

Adler, A. (1956). Problems in psychotherapy. *American Journal of Individual Psychology, 12,* 12–24.

Adler, G. (1985). *Borderline psychopathology and its treatment.* New York: Jason Aronson.

Ainsworth, M. D. S., Blehar, M. C., Waters, E., & Wall, S. (1978). *Patterns of attachment: A psychological study of the strange situation.* Hillsdale, NJ: Erlbaum.

Akhtar, S. (1987). Schizoid personality disorder: A synthesis of developmental, dynamic, and descriptive features. *American Journal of Psychotherapy, 41,* 449–518.

Alden, L. (1989). Short-term structured treatment for avoidant personality disorder. *Journal of Consulting and Clinical Psychology, 57,* 756–764.

Alden, L. (1992). Cognitive-interpersonal treatment of avoidant personality disorder. In P. Keller, S. Heyman (Eds.), *Innovations in clinical practice: A source book. Vol. 11* (pp. 5–22). Sarasota, FL: Professional Resources Exchange.

Alexander, J., & Parsons, B. (1973). Short-term behavioral intervention with delinquent families: Impact on family process and recidivism. *Journal of Abnormal Psychology, 8,* 219–225.

Allen, J., & Fonagy, P. (Eds). (2006). *The handbook of mentalization-based treatment.* New York, NY: Wiley.

Allnutt, S., & Links, P. (1996), Diagnosing specific personality disorders and the optimal criteria. In P. Links (Ed.), *Clinical assessment and management of severe personality disorders* (pp. 21–48). Washington, DC: American Psychiatric Press.

Allport, G. (1937). *Personality: A psychological interpretation.* New York, NY: Holt.

Alonso, A. (1992). The shattered mirror: Treatment of a group of narcissistic patients. *Group, 16,* 210–219.

Alonso, A., & Rutan, J. (1984). The impact of object relations theory on psychodynamic group therapy. *American Journal of Psychiatry, 141,* 1376–1380.

American Psychiatric Association. (2013). *Diagnostic and Statistical Manual of Mental Disorders, Fifth Edition*. Alexandria, VA: Author.

Arntz, A. (2015). Borderline personality disorder. In A. Beck, D. Davis, & A. Freeman (Eds.), *Cognitive therapy of personality disorders* (3rd ed., pp. 366–392). New York, NY: Guilford.

Anderson, C. (1983). A psychoeducational program for families of patients with schizophrenia. In W. McFarlene (Ed). *Family therapy in schizophrenia* (pp. 99–116). New York, NY: Guilford.

Appel, G. (1974). An approach to the treatment of schizoid phenomena. *Psychoanalytic Review, 61,* 99–113.

Armstrong, R. (2002). Schizoid phenomena in substance abusers. *Journal of Addictive Diseases, 21*(3), 73–85.

Azima, F. (1983). Group psychotherapy with personality disorders. In H. Kaplan & B. Sadock (Eds.), *Comprehensive group psychotherapy* (2nd ed., pp. 262–268). Baltimore: Wilkins & Wilkins.

Babiak, P., & Hare, R. (2007). *Snakes in suits: When psychopaths go to work.* New York, NY: Harper.

Bailey, G. (1998). Cognitive-behavioral treatment of obsessive-compulsive personality disorder. *Journal of Psychological Practice, 4,* 51–59.

Balint, M. (1968). *The basic fault: Therapeutic aspects of regression.* London: Tavistock.

Balint, M., Ornstein, P., & Balint, E. (1972). *Focal psychotherapy.* London: Tavistock.

Barber, J., Morse, J., Krakauer, I., Chittams, J., & Crits-Christoph, K. (1997). Change in obsessive-compulsive and avoidant personality disorder following time-limited supportive-expressive therapy. *Psychotherapy, 34,* 133–143.

Barlow, D., & Waddell, M. (1985). Agorophobia. In D. Barlow, (Ed.), *Clinical handbook of psychological disorders: A step-by-step manual.* New York, NY: Guilford.

Bartholomew, K. (1990). Avoidance of intimacy: An attachment perspective. *Journal of Social and Personal Relationships, 7,* 147–178.

Bartholomew, K., & Horowitz, L. (1991). Attachment styles among young adults: A test of a four-category model. *Journal of Personality and Social Psychology, 61,* 226–244.

Bateman, A., & Fonagy, P. (1999). Effectiveness of partial hospitalization in the treatment of borderline personality disorder: A randomized controlled trial. *American Journal of Psychiatry, 156,* 1563–1569.

Bateman, A., & Fonagy, P. (2001). Treatment of borderline personality disorder with psychoanalytically oriented partial hospitalization: An 18-month follow-up. *American Journal of Psychiatry, 158,* 36–42.

Bateman, A., & Fonagy, P. (2007). *Mentalization based treatment: A practical guide.* New York, NY: Oxford University Press.

Bateman, A., & Fonagy, P. (2009). Randomly controlled trial of outpatient mentalizing-based treatment versus structured clinical management for borderline personality disorder. *American Journal of Psychiatry, 166,* 1355–1364.

Bateman, A., & Fonagy, P. (2010). Mentalization based treatment for borderline personality disorder. *World Psychiatry, 9*(1), 11–15.

Beck, A. (2015). Theory of personality disorders. In A. Beck, D. Davis, & A. Freeman, A. (Eds.) *Cognitive therapy of personality disorders* (3rd ed., pp. 19–62). New York, NY: Guilford.

Beck, A. Davis, D., & Freeman, A. (Eds.) (2015) *Cognitive therapy of personality disorders* (3rd ed.). New York, NY: Guilford.

Beck, A., Freeman, A., & associates (1990). *Cognitive therapy of personality disorders.* New York, NY: Guilford.

Beck, A., Freeman, A., Davis, D., & associates (2004). *Cognitive therapy of personality disorders* (2nd ed.). New York, NY: Guilford Press.

Behary, W., & Davis, D. (2015). Narcissistic personality disorder. In A. Beck, D. Davis, & A. Freeman, A. (Eds.), *Cognitive therapy of personality disorders* (3rd ed., pp. 299–324). New York, NY: Guilford.

Beitman, B. (2003). *Integrating psychotherapy and pharmacotherapy: Dissolving the mind-brain barrier.* New York, NY: Norton.

Beitman, B., & Yue, D. (1999). *Learning psychotherapy.* New York, NY: Norton.

Bellak, L. (1997). *The TAT, CAT and SAT in clinical use* (6th ed.). Boston: Allyn & Bacon.

Bellino, S., Rinaldi, C., & Bogetto, F. (2010). Adaptation of interpersonal psychotherapy to borderline personality disorder: a comparison of combined therapy and single pharmacotherapy. *Canadian Journal of Psychiatry, 55,* 74–81.

Bellino, S., Bozzatello, P., & Bogetto, F. (2015). Combined treatment of borderline personality disorder with interpersonal psychotherapy and pharmacotherapy: Predictors of response. *Psychiatry Research, 226,* 284–288.

Bender, D., Morey, L., & Skodol, A. (2011). Toward a model for assessing level of personality functioning in DSM–5, Part I: A review of theory and methods, *Journal of Personality Assessment, 93*(4), 332–346.

Benjamin, L. (1993). *Interpersonal diagnosis and treatment of personality disorders.* New York, NY: Guilford.

Benjamin, L. (2003a). *Interpersonal diagnosis and treatment of personality disorders* (2nd ed.). New York, NY: Guilford.

Benjamin, L. (2003b). *Interpersonal reconstructive therapy: Promoting change in nonresponders.* New York, NY: Guilford.

Benjamin, L. (2007). *Interpersonal reconstructive therapy: An integrative, personality-based treatment for complex cases.* New York, NY: Guilford.

Berger, P. (1987). Pharmacologic treatment for borderline personality disorder. *Bulletin of the Menninger Clinic, 51,* 277–284.

Berkowitz, D. (1985). Self-object needs and marital disharmony. *Psychoanalytic Review, 72,* 229–237.

Berkowitz, D., Shapiro, R., Zinner, J., & Shapiro, H. (1974). Concurrent family treatment of narcissistic disorders in adolescents. *International Journal of Psychoanalysis, 3,* 371–396.

Berman, E. (1983). The treatment of troubled couples. In L. Grinspoon (Ed.), *Psychiatric Updates, Vol. 2.* Washington, DC: American Psychiatric Association.

Bernstein, D. (2002). Cognitive therapy of personality disorders in patients with histories of emotional abuse or neglect. *Psychiatric Annals, 32,* 618–628.

Binder, J. (1979). Treatment of narcissistic problems in time-limited psychotherapy. *Psychiatric Quarterly, 51,* 257–270.

Black, D., Zanarini, M., Romine, A., Shaw, M., Allen, J., & Schulz, S. (2014). Comparison of low and moderate doses of extended-release quetiapine in borderline personality disorder: A randomized, double-blind, placebo-controlled trial. *American Journal of Psychiatry, 171,* 1174–1182.

Blocher, D. (1974). *Developmental counseling.* New York, NY: Wiley.

Blocher, D. (2000). *Counseling: A developmental approach* (4th ed.). New York, NY: Wiley.

Bogdanoff, M., & Elbaum, P. (1978). Role lock: Dealing with monopolizers, isolates, helpful hannahs, and other associated characters in group psychotherapy. *International Journal of Group Psychotherapy, 28,* 247–281.

Bonime, W. (1959). The pursuit of anxiety-laden areas in therapy of the schizoid patient. *Psychiatry, 22,* 239–244.

Bornstein, R. (2012). Dependent personality disorder. In T. Widiger (Ed.), *The Oxford handbook of personality disorders* (pp. 505–526). New York, NY: Oxford University Press.

Bowlby, J. (1973). *Attachment and loss, Vol. 2, Separation.* New York, NY: Basic Books.

Brauer, L., & Reinecke, M. (2015). Dependent personality disorder. In A. Beck, D. Davis, & A. Freeman (Eds.), *Cognitive therapy of personality disorders* (3rd ed., pp. 155–173). New York, NY: Guilford.

Brennan, K., & Shaver, P. (1998). Attachment styles and personality disorders: Their connection to each other and to parental divorce, parental death, and perceptions of parental caregiving. *Journal of Personality, 66,* 835–878.

Brown, E., Heimberg, R., & Juster, H. (1995). Social phobia subtype and avoidant personality disorder: Effects of severity of social phobia impairment and outcome of cognitive behavioral treatment. *Behavior Therapy, 26,* 467–486.

Buie, D., & Adler, G. (1982). The definitive treatment of the borderline personality. *International Journal of Psychoanalysis, 9,* 51–87.

Caligor, E., Levy, K., & Yeomans, F. (2015). Narcissistic personality disorder: Diagnostic and clinical challenges. *American Journal of Psychiatry, 172,* 415–422.

Carlson, J. (2006). *Psychotherapy over time* [DVD]. Washington, DC: American Psychological Association.

Cass, D., Silvers, F. and Abrams, G. (1972). Behavioral group treatment of hysterics. *Archives of General Psychiatry, 26,* 42–50.

Chessick, R. (1982). Intensive psychotherapy of a borderline patient. *Archives of General Psychiatry, 39,* 413–419.

Chessick, R. (1985). *Psychology of the self and the treatment of narcissism.* New York, NY: Jason Aronson.

Choca, J., & Denburg, E. (1997). *Interpretative guide to the Millon Clinical Multiaxial Inventory* (2nd ed.). Washington, DC: American Psychological Association.

Chodoff, P. (1989). Histrionic personality disorder. In T. Karasu (Ed.), *Treatment of psychiatric disorders* (pp. 2727–2735). Washington, DC: American Psychiatric Press.

Clarkin, J., Cain, N., & Livesley, J. (2015). An integrated approach to patients with personality disorders. *Journal of Psychotherapy Integration, 25,* 3–12.

Clarkin, J., Foelsch, P., Levy, K., Hull, J., Delaney, J., & Kernberg, O. (2001). The development of a psychodynamic treatment for patients with borderline personality disorder: A preliminary study of behavior change. *Journal of Personality Disorders, 15,* 487–495.

Clarkin, J., Marziali, E., & Munroe-Blum, H. (1991). Group and family treatment of borderline personality disorder. *Hospital and Community Psychiatry, 42,* 1038–1043.

Clarkin, J., Yeomans, F., & Kernberg, O. (2015). *Transference-focused psychotherapy for borderline personality disorder: A clinical guide.* Washington, DC: American Psychiatric Publishing.

Clinical Psychiatry News. (1991). Better personality disorders therapies foreseen. *Clinical Psychiatry News,* September, p. 26.

Cloninger, C. (2004). *Feeling good: The science of well-being.* New York, NY: Oxford University Press.

Cortright, B. (1997). *Psychotherapy and spirit.* Albany, NY: State University of New York Press.

Costa, P., & McCrae, R. (1990). Personality disorders and the five-factor model of personality. *Journal of Personality Disorders, 4,* 362–371.

Costello, C. (Ed.). (1996). *Personality characteristics of the personality disordered.* New York, NY: Wiley.

Cramer Azima, F. (1983). Group psychotherapy with personality disorders. In H. Kaplan & B. Sadock (Eds.), *Comprehensive group psychotherapy.* Baltimore: Williams & Wilkins.

Crits-Christoph, P., & Barber, J. (2002). Psychological treatment for personality disorders. In P. Nathan & J. Gorman (Eds.), *A guide to treatments that work* (2nd ed., pp. 611–624). New York, NY: Oxford Press.

Davidson, K., Halford, J., Kirkwood, L., Newton-Howes, G., Sharp, M., & Tata, P. (2010). CBT for violent men with antisocial personality disorder: Reflections on the experience of carrying out therapy in MASCOT, a pilot randomized controlled trial. *Personality and Mental Health, 4,* 86–95.

Davidson, K., Tyrer, P., Tata, P., Cooke, D., Gumley, A., Ford, I., et al. (2009). Cognitive behaviour therapy for violent men with antisocial personality disorder in the community: An exploratory randomized controlled trial. *Psychological Medicine, 39,* 569–577.

Day, M., & Semrad, E. (1971). Group therapy with neurotics and psychotics. In H. Kaplan & B. Sadock (Eds.), *Comprehensive group psychotherapy* (pp. 566–580). Baltimore: Williams and Wilkins.

Diamond, R. (2009). *Instant psychopharmacology* (3rd ed.). New York, NY: W. W. Norton.

Dick, B. M., & Wooff, K. (1986). An evaluation of a time-limited programme of dynamic group psychotherapy. *The British Journal of Psychiatry, 148*(2), 159–164.

Dimaggio, G., Catania, D., Salvatore, G., Carcione, A., & Nicolo, G. (2006). Psychotherapy of paranoid personality disorder from the perspective of dialogical self-theory. *Counseling Psychology Quarterly, 19,* 69–87.

Dimaggio, G., D'Urzo, M., Pasinetti, M., Salvatore, G., Lysaker, P. H., Catania, D., & Popolo, R. (2015). Metacognitive interpersonal therapy for co-occurrent avoidant personality disorder and substance abuse. *Journal of Clinical Psychology, 71*(2), 157–166.

Dolan, M., & Park, I. (2002). The neuropsychology of antisocial personality disorder. *Psychological Medicine, 32,* 417–427.

Dorfman, W. I. (2000). Histrionic personality disorder. In H. E. Hersen & M. Biaggio (Eds.), *Effective brief therapies: A clinician's guide* (pp. 355–370). San Diego, CA: Academic Press.

Driscoll, K., Cukrowicz, K., Reardon, M., & Joiner, T. (2004). *Simple treatments for complex problems: A flexible cognitive behavior analysis system approach to psychotherapy.* Mahwah, NJ: Lawrence Erlbaum Associates.

Edell, W. (1987). Relationship of borderline syndrome disorders to early schizophrenia on the MMPI. *Journal of Clinical Psychology, 43,* 163–174.

Eells, T. (2007). Comparing the methods. Where is the common ground? In T. Eells (Ed.), *Handbook of psychotherapy case formulation* (2nd ed., pp. 412–432). New York, NY: Guilford.

Eells, T. (2010). The unfolding case formulation: The interplay of description and inference. *Pragmatic Case Studies in Psychotherapy, 6*(4), 225–254.

Eikenaes, I., Gude, T., & Hoffart, A. (2006). Integrated wilderness therapy for avoidant personality disorder. *Nordic Journal of Psychiatry, 60*, 275–281.

Ekleberry, S. (2014). *Treating co-occurring disorders: A handbook for mental health and substance abuse professionals.* New York, NY: Routledge.

Epstein, L. (1984). An interpersonal-object relations perspective working with destructive aggression. *Contemporary Psychoanalysis, 20*, 651–662.

Erdman, P., & Caffery, T. (Eds.). (2003). *Attachment and family systems: Conceptual, empirical and therapeutic relatedness.* New York, NY: Brunner/Routledge.

Eskedal, G., & Demetri, J. (2006). Etiology and treatment of cluster C personality disorders. *Journal of Mental Health Counseling, 28*, 1–18.

Everett, S., Halperin, S., Volgy, S., & Wissler, A. (1989). *Treating the borderline family: A systematic approach.* Boston: Allyn & Bacon.

Exner, J. (1986). *The Rorschach: A comprehensive system* (2nd ed.). New York, NY: John Wiley.

Fairburn, W. (1954). *An object-relations theory of the* personality. New York, NY: Basic Books.

Fawcett, J. (2002). Schemas or traits and states: Top down or bottom up? *Psychiatric Annals, 32*, 567.

Fay, A., & Lazarus, A. (1993). Cognitive-behavior group therapy. In A. Alonso & H. Willer (Eds.), *Group therapy in clinical practice* (pp. 449–469). Washington, DC: American Psychiatric Press.

Fenichel, O. (1945). *The psychoanalytic theory of the neurosis.* New York, NY: Norton.

Fernandez, S. (2010). Complex case Carmen: Histrionic personality disorder and psychotherapy. *Personality and Mental Health, 4*, 146–152.

Fernando, J. (1998). The etiology of the narcissistic personality disorder. *Psychoanalytic Study of the Child, 53*, 141–158.

Fernbach, B., Winstead, B., & Derlega, V. (1989). Sex differences in diagnosis and treatment recommendations for antisocial personality and somatization disorders. *Journal of Social and Clinical Psychology, 8*(3), 238–255.

Finn, B., & Shakir, S. (1990). Intensive group psychotherapy of borderline patients, *Group, 14*, 99–110.

Fiore, D., Dimaggio, G., Giuseppe, N., Semerari, A., & Carcione, A. (2008). Metacognitive interpersonal therapy in a case of obsessive-compulsive and avoidant personality disorders. *Journal of Clinical Psychology: In Session, 64*, 168–180.

Flegenheimer, W. (1982). *Techniques of brief therapy.* New York, NY: Jason Aronson.

Fossatti, A., Madeddu, F., & Maffei, C. (1999). Borderline personality disorder and childhood sexual abuse: A meta-analytic study. *Journal of Personality Disorders, 13*, 2268–2280.

Fraiberg, S. (1969). Libidinal object constancy and mental representation. *Psychoanalytic Study of the Child, 24*, 9–47.

Frances, A. (2013). *Essentials of psychiatric diagnosis: Responding to the challenge of DSM-5* (rev. ed.). New York, NY: Guilford.

Frances, A., Clarkin, J., & Perry, S. (1984). *Differential therapeutics in psychiatry: The art and science of treatment selection.* New York, NY: Brunner/Mazel.

Freeman, A., Pretzer, J., Fleming, B., & Simon, K. (1990). *Clinical application of cognitive therapy.* New York, NY: Plenum.

Freud, S. (1914/1976). On narcissism: An introduction. *Complete psychological works, standard edition, Vol. 14* (pp. 69–102). London: Hogarth Press.

Gabbard, G. (1989). On "doing nothing" in the psychoanalytic treatment of the refractory borderline patient. *International Journal of Psychoanalysis, 70*, 527–534.

Gabbard, G. (1990). *Psychodynamic psychiatry in clinical practice.* Washington, DC: American Psychiatric Press.

Gabbard, G. (1994). *Psychodynamic psychiatry in clinical practice: The DSM-IV edition.* Washington, DC: American Psychiatric Press.

Gabbard, G. (2000). *Psychodynamic psychiatry in clinical practice* (3rd ed.). Washington, DC: American Psychiatric Press.

Gabbard, G. (2014). *Psychodynamic psychiatry in clinical practice* (5th ed.). Washington, DC: American Psychiatric Press.

Gamache, D., & Diguer, L. (2012). The film enthusiast: Reflections on the treatment of schizoid personality disorder. *Mental Health in Quebec, 37,* 135–155.

Gilbert, S., & Gordon, K. (2012). Interpersonal psychotherapy informed treatment for avoidant personality disorder with subsequent depression. *Clinical Case Studies, 12,* 111–127.

Gilles, G., & Wienclaw, R. (2008). Schizoid personality disorder. In L. Fundukian & J. Wilson (Eds.), *The Gale encyclopedia of mental health* (2nd ed., pp. 990–993). Farmington Hills, MI: The Gale Group.

Glantz, K., & Goisman, R. (1990). Relaxation and merging in the treatment of personality disorders. *American Journal of Psychotherapy, 44,* 405–413.

Glueck, S., & Glueck, E. (1950). *Unraveling juvenile delinquency.* Cambridge, MA: Harvard University Press.

Goldberg, A. (1973). Psychotherapy of narcissistic injuries. *Archives of General Psychiatry, 28,* 722–726.

Goldberg, A. (1989). Self psychology and the narcissistic personality disorders. *Psychiatric Clinics of North America, 12,* 731–739.

Graham, J. (2012). *MMPI-2: Assessing personality and psychopathology* (5th ed.). New York, NY: Oxford University Press.

Graybar, S., & Boutilier, L. (2002). Nontraumatic pathways to borderline personality disorder. *Psychotherapy: Theory/Research/Practice/Training, 39*(2), 152–162.

Greist, J., & Jefferson, J. (1992). *Panic disorder and agoraphobia: A guide.* Madison, WI: Anxiety Disorders Center and Information Centers.

Groth-Marnat, G. (2009). *Handbook of Psychological Assessment* (5th ed.). New York, NY: Wiley.

Grotjahn, M. (1984). The narcissistic person in analytic group psychotherapy. *International Journal of Group Psychotherapy, 30,* 299–318.

Guerney, B. (1977). *Relationship enhancement: Skill-training programs for therapy, problem prevention, and enrichment.* San Francisco: Jossey-Bass.

Guidano, V. and Liotti, G. (1983). *Cognitive processes and emotional disorders.* New York, NY: Guilford Press.

Gunderson, J. (1986). Pharmacotherapy for patients with borderline personality disorders. *Archives of General Psychiatry, 43,* 698–700.

Gunderson, J. (1988). Personality disorders. In A. Nicholi (Ed.), *The new Harvard guide to psychiatry* (pp. 337–357). Cambridge, MA: Harvard University Press.

Gunderson, J., (1989). Borderline personality disorder. In T. Karasu (Ed.), *Treatments of Psychiatric Disorders* (pp. 2749–2758). Washington, DC: American Psychiatric Press.

Gunderson, J. (1996). Introduction to section IV: Personality disorders. In T. Widiger, A. Frances, H. Pincus, R. Ross, M. First, W. Davis, et al. (Eds.), *DSM IV Sourcebook* (pp. 647–664). Washington, DC: American Psychiatric Association.

Gurman, A., & Kniskern, D. (1981). Family therapy outcomes research: Known and unknown. In A. Gorman & D. Kniskern (Eds.), *Handbook of family therapy* (pp 742–776). New York, NY: Brunner/Mazel.

Haley, J. (1978). *Problem solving therapy.* San Francisco, CA: Jossey-Bass.

Haley, J., & Hoffman, L. (1976). *Techniques of family therapy*. New York, NY: Basic Books.

Halleck, S. (1978). *The treatment of emotional disorders*. New York, NY: Jason Aronson.

Harbir, H. (1981). Family therapy with personality disorders. In J. Lion (Ed.), *Personality disorders: Diagnosis and management* (2nd ed.). Baltimore: Williams & Wilkins.

Hare, R., Neumann, C., & Widiger, T. (2012). Psychopathy. In T. Widiger (Ed.), *The Oxford handbook of personality disorders* (pp. 478–504). New York, NY: Oxford University Press.

Harman, M., & Waldo, M. (2001). Family treatment of borderline personality disorder through relationship enhancement therapy. In M. MacFarlane (Ed.), *Family therapy and mental health: Innovations in theory and practice* (pp. 215–235). Binghamton, NY: Haworth Clinical Practice Press.

Harper, R. (2004). *Personality-guided therapy in behavioral medicine*. Washington, DC: American Psychological Association.

Harris, G., & Rice, M. (2006). Treatment of psychopathy: A review of empirical findings. In C. Patrick (Ed.), *Handbook of psychopathy* (pp. 555–572), New York, NY: Guilford.

Harwood, I. (1992). Advances in group psychotherapy and self psychology: An interobjective approach with narcissistic and borderline patients. *Group, 16,* 220–232.

Hatchett, G. (2015). Treatment guidelines for clients with antisocial personality disorder. *Journal of Mental Health Counseling, 37*(1), 15–27.

Havens, J., Cornelius, L., Ricketts, E., Latkin, C., Bishai, D., Lloyd, J., et al. (2007). The effect of a case management intervention on drug treatment entry among treatment-seeking injection drug users with and without comorbid antisocial personality disorder. *Journal of Urban Health, 84*(2), 267–271.

Havens, L. (1976). Discussion: How long the Tower of Babel? *Proceedings of American Psychopathological Association, 64,* 62–73.

Hayes, S., Follette, V. & Linehan, M. (Eds). (2004). *Mindfulness and acceptance: Expanding the cognitive-behavioral tradition*. New York, NY: Guilford.

Hazan, C., & Shaver, P. (1987). Romantic love conceptualized as a attachment process. *Journal of Personality and Social Psychology, 52,* 511–524.

Hend, S., Baker, J., & Williamson, D. (1991). Family environment characteristics and dependent personality disorder. *Journal of Personality Disorders, 5,* 256–263.

Hill, D. (1970). Outpatient management of passive dependent women. *Hospital and Community Psychiatry, 21,* 402–405.

Hoch, J., O'Reilly, R., & Carscadden, J. (2006). Relationship management therapy for patients with borderline personality disorder. *Psychiatric Services 57*(2), 179–181.

Hopwood, C., & Thomas, K. (2012). Paranoid and Schizoid Personality Disorders. In T. Widiger (Ed.), *The Oxford handbook of personality disorders* (pp. 582–602). New York, NY: Oxford University Press.

Horowitz, L. (1977). Group psychotherapy of the borderline. In P. Hartocollis (Ed.), *Borderline personality disorder* (pp. 399–422). New York, NY: International Universities Press.

Horowitz, L. (1980). Group psychotherapy for borderline and narcissistic patients. *Bulletin of the Menninger Clinic, 4,* 181–200.

Horowitz, L. (1987). Indications for group psychotherapy with borderline and narcissistic patients. *Bulletin of the Menninger Clinic, 51,* 248–318.

Horowitz, L. (1997). Psychotherapy of histrionic personality disorder. *Journal of Psychotherapy Practice and Research, 6*(2), 93–107.

Horowitz, M. (1988). *Introduction to psychodynamics: A new synthesis*. New York, NY: Basic Books.

Horowitz, M., & Lerner, U. (2010). Treatment of Histrionic Personality Disorder. In J. F. Clarkin, P. Fonagy, & G. O. Gabbard (Eds.), *Psychodynamic psychotherapy for personality disorders: A clinical handbook* (pp. 289–309). Arlington, VA: American Psychiatric Publishing, Inc.

Horowitz, M., Marmar, C., Krupnick, J., Wilner, N., Kaltreider, N., & Wallerstein, R. (1984). *Personality styles and brief psychotherapy*. New York, NY: Basic Books.

Hulse, W. (1958). Psychotherapy with ambulatory schizophrenic patients in mixed analytic groups. *Archives of Neurology and Psychiatry, 79,* 681–687.

Imbesi, E. (2000). On the etiology of narcissistic personality disorder. *Issues in Psychoanalytic Psychology, 22*(2), 3–58.

Jenike, M., Baer, L., & Minichiello, W. (1998). *Obsessive-compulsive disorders: Theory and management* (3rd ed.). St. Louis, MO: Mosby.

Jones, S. (1987). Family therapy with borderline and narcissistic patients. *Bulletin of the Menninger Foundation, 51,* 285–295.

Kabat-Zinn, J., Massion, A., Kristeller, J., Peterson, L., Fletcher, K., Ebert, L., et al. (1992). Effectiveness of a meditation-based stress reduction intervention in the treatment of anxiety disorders. *American Journal of Psychiatry, 149,* 936–943.

Kagan, J., Resnick, J., & Snidman, N. (1988). Biological basis of childhood shyness. *Science, 240,* 167–171.

Kalojera, I., Jacobson, G., Hoffman, G., Hoffman, P., Raffe, I., White, H., & Leonard-White, L.

(1998). The narcissistic couple. In J. Carlson & L. Sperry (Eds.), *The disordered couple* (pp. 207–238). New York, NY: Brunner/Mazel.

Kantor, M. (1992). *Diagnosis and treatment of the personality disorders*. St. Louis, MO: Ishiyaku EuroAmerica.

Kavaler-Adler, S. (2004). Anatomy of regret: A developmental view of the depressive position and a critical turn toward love and creativity in the transforming schizoid personality. *American Journal of Psychoanalysis, 64*(1), 39–76.

Keller, M., McCullough, J., Klein, D., Arnow, B., et al. (2000). A comparison of nefazodone, the cognitive behavioral analysis system or psychotherapy, and their combination for the treatment of chronic depression. *New England Journal of Medicine, 342,* 1462–1470.

Kellerman, H., & Burry, A. (1989). *Psychopathology and differential diagnosis: Vol. 2, Diagnostic primer*. New York, NY: Columbia University Press.

Kellett, S. (2007). A time series evaluation of the treatment of histrionic personality disorder with cognitive analytic therapy. *Psychology and Psychotherapy: Theory, Research and Practice, 80*(3), 389–405.

Kellett, S., & Hardy, G. (2014). Treatment of Paranoid Personality Disorder with cognitive analytic therapy: A mixed methods single case experimental design. *Clinical Psychology & Psychotherapy, 21*(5), 452–464.

Kellner, R. (1986). Personality disorders. *Psychotherapy and Psychosomatics, 46*(1–2), 58–66.

Kernberg, O. (1975). *Borderline conditions and pathological narcissism*. New York, NY: Jason Aronson.

Kernberg, O. (1984). *Severe personality disorders: Psychotherapeutic strategies*. New Haven, CT: Yale University Press.

Kernberg, O. (2010). Narcissistic personality disorder. In J. Clarkin, P. Fonagy, & G. Gabbard (Eds.), *Psychodynamic psychotherapy for personality disorders: A clinical handbook* (pp. 289–309). Arlington, VA: American Psychiatric Publishing.

Khan, M. (1975). Grudge and the hysteric. *International Journal of Psychoanalysis and Psychotherapy, 4,* 349–357.

Klein, R. (1989a). Diagnosis and treatment of the lower-level borderline patient. In J. Masterson & R. Klein (Eds.), *Psychotherapy of disorders of the self* (pp. 147–168). New York, NY: Brunner/Mazel.

Klein, R. (1989b). Shorter-term psychotherapy of the personality disorders. In J. Masterson & R. Klein (Eds.), *Psychotherapy of disorders of the self* (pp. 90–109). New York, NY: Brunner/Mazel.

Koenigsberg, H. (1993). Combining psychotherapy and pharmacotherapy in the treatment of borderline patients. In J. Oldham, M. Riba, & A. Tasman.(Eds.), *American Psychiatric Press Review of Psychiatry, Vol. 12* (pp. 541–564). Washington, DC: American Psychiatric Press.

Koenigsberg, H., Woo-Ming, A., & Siever, L. (2002). Pharmacological treatment for personality disorders. In P. Nathan & J. Gorman (Eds.), *A guide to treatments that work* (2nd ed., pp. 625–641). New York, NY: Oxford University Press.

Kohut, H. (1971). *The analysis of the self.* New York, NY: International Universities Press.

Kohut, H. (1977). *The restoration of the self.* New York, NY: International Universities Press.

Kristeller, J., & Hallet, B (1999). An exploratory study of meditation-based intervention for binge eating disorder. *Journal of Health Psychology, 4*(3), 357–363.

Kwapil, T., & Barrantes-Vidal, N. (2012). Schizotypal personality disorder: An integrative review. In T. Widiger (Ed.), *The Oxford handbook of personality disorders* (pp. 437–477). New York, NY: Oxford University Press.

Kyrios, M. (1999). A cognitive-behavioral approach to the understanding and of obsessive-compulsive personality disorder. In C. Perris & P. McGorry (Eds.), *Cognitive psychotherapy of psychotic and personality disorders* (pp. 351–378). New York, NY: Wiley.

Lachar, D. (1974). *The MMPI: Clinical assessment and automated interpretation.* Los Angeles: Western Psychological Services.

Lachkar, J. (1986). Narcissistic/borderline couples: Implications for medication. *Conciliation Courts Review, 24,* 31–38.

Lachkar, J. (1992). *The narcissistic/borderline couple: A psychoanalytic perspective on marital treatment.* New York, NY: Brunner/Mazel.

Lachkar, J. (1999). Narcissistic/borderline couples: A psychodynamic approach to conjoint treatment. In J. Carlson & L. Sperry (Eds.), *The disordered couple* (pp. 259–284). New York, NY: Brunner/Mazel.

Landucci, J., & Foley, G. (2014). Couples therapy: Treating selected personality-disordered couples within a dynamic therapy framework. *Innovations in Clinical Neuroscience, 11*(3–4), 29–36.

Lasch, C. (1991). *The culture of narcissism.* New York, NY: Norton.

Lazarus, A. (1981). *The practice of multimodal therapy.* New York, NY: McGraw-Hill.

Lazarus, A. (Ed.). (1985). *Casebook of multimodal therapy.* New York, NY: Guilford.

Lazarus, L. (1982). Brief psychotherapy of narcissistic disturbances. *Psychotherapy: Theory, Research and Practice, 19,* 228–236.

Leszcz, M. (1989). Group psychotherapy of the characterologically difficult patient. *International Journal of Group Psychotherapy, 39,* 311–335.

Levy, K. (2012). Subtypes, dimensions, levels, and mental states in narcissism and narcissistic personality disorder. *Journal of Clinical Psychology, 68,* 886–897.

Liberman, R. P., DeRisi, W. J., & Mueser, K. T. (1989). *Social skills training for psychiatric patients.* Oxford: Pergamon Press.

Liebowitz, M., & Klein, D. (1981). Interrelationship of hysteroid dysphoria and borderline personality disorder. *Psychiatric Clinics of North America, 4,* 67–87.

Liebowitz, M., Stone, M., & Turkat, I. (1986). Treatment of personality disorders. In A. Frances & R. Hales (Eds.), *Psychiatric Update, American Psychiatric Association, Annual Review, Vol. 5* (pp. 356–393). Washington, DC: American Psychiatric Press.

Linehan, M. (1983). *Dialectical behavior therapy for treatment of parasuicidal women: Treatment manual.* Seattle, WA: University of Washington.

Linehan, M. M. (1987). Dialectical behavior therapy: A cognitive behavioral approach to parasuicide. *Journal of Personality Disorders, 1,* 328–333.

Linehan, M. (1993). *Cognitive-behavioral treatment for borderline personality disorder.* New York, NY: Guilford.

Linehan, M. (1994). Acceptance and change. The central dialectic in psychotherapy. In S. Hayes, N. Jacobson, V. Follette, & M. Dougher (Eds.), *Acceptance and change: Content and context in psychotherapy* (pp. 73–86). Reno, NV: Context Press.

Linehan, M. (2015). *DBT skills training manual* (2nd ed.). New York, NY: Guilford.

Linehan, M., Armstrong, H., Suarez, A., Allmon, D., & Heard, H. (1991). Cognitive-behavioral treatment of chronically parasuicidal borderline patients. *Archives of General Psychiatry, 48*(12), 1060–1064.

Linehan, M., Heard, H., & Armstrong, H. (1993). Naturalistic follow-up of a behavioral treatment for chronically parasuicidal borderline patients. *Archives of General Psychiatry 50*(12), 971–974.

Linehan, M., Dimeff, L., Reynolds, S., Comtois, K., Welch, S., Heagerty, P., & Kivlahan, D. (2002). Dialectical behavior therapy versus comprehensive validation therapy plus 12-step for the treatment of opioid dependent women meeting criteria for borderline personality disorder. *Drug & Alcohol Dependence, 67,* 13–26.

Linehan, M., Comtois, K., Murray, A., Brown, M., Gallop, R., Heard, H., ... & Lindenboim, N. (2006). Two-year randomized controlled trial and follow-up of dialectical behavior therapy vs therapy by experts for suicidal behaviors and borderline personality disorder. *Archives of General Psychiatry, 63*(7), 757–766.

Links, P., Stockwell, M., & MacFarlane, M. (2004a). Indications for couple therapy: The paradox of the histrionic/obsessive-compulsive couple. *Journal of Family Psychotherapy, 15*(4), 73–88.

Links, P., Stockwell, M., & MacFarlane, M. (2004b). Is couples therapy indicated for patients with dependent personality disorder? *Journal of Family Psychotherapy, 15*(3), 63–79.

Livesley, W. J. (2012). Integrated treatment: a conceptual framework for an evidence-based approach to the treatment of personality disorder. *Journal of Personality Disorders, 26*(1), 17–42.

Luborsky, L., & Crits-Christoph, P. (1990). *Understanding transference: The Core Conflictual Relationship Theme method.* New York, NY: Basic Books.

Lyddon, W., & Sherry, A. (2001). Developmental personality styles: An attachment theory conceptualization of personality disorders. *Journal of Counseling and Development, 79*(4), 405–414.

Lynch T., & Cuper, P. (2012). Dialectical behavior therapy of borderline and other personality disorders. In T. Widiger (Ed.), *The Oxford handbook of personality disorders* (pp. 785–793). New York, NY: Oxford University Press.

Lynch, T., Trost, W., Salsman, N., & Linehan, M. (2007). Dialectical behavior therapy for borderline personality disorders. *Annual Review of Clinical Psychology, 3,* 181–205.

Mackinnon, R., & Michels, R. (1971). *The psychiatric interview in clinical practice.* Philadelphia: Saunders.

Main, M., Goldwyn, R., & Hesse, E. (1998). Adult attachment scoring and classification system. Unpublished manuscript, University of California at Berkeley.

Main, M., & Solomon, J. (1990). Procedures for identifying infants as disorganized/disoriented during the Ainsworth Strange Situation. In M. T. Greenberg, D. Cicchetti, & E. M. Cummings (Eds.), *Attachment in the Preschool Years* (pp. 121–160). Chicago, University of Chicago Press.

Malan, D. (1976). *The frontier of brief psychotherapy.* New York, NY: Plenum.

Malancharuvil, J. (2012). Empathy deficit in antisocial personality disorder: A psychodynamic formulation. *American Journal of Psychoanalysis, 72*(3), 242–250.

Malinow, K. (1981). Dependent personality. In J. Lion (Ed.), *Personality disorders: Diagnosis and management* (2nd ed., pp. 79–91). Baltimore: Williams & Wilkins.

Manduchi, K., & Schoendorff, B. (2012). First steps in FAP: Experiences of beginning Functional Analytic Psychotherapy therapist with an obsessive-compulsive personality disorder client. *International Journal of Behavioral Consultation and Therapy, 7*(2–3), 72.

Mann, J. (1973). *Time-limited psychotherapy.* Cambridge, MA: Harvard University Press.

Mann, J. (1984). Time-limited psychotherapy. In L. Grinspoon (Ed.), *Psychiatry Update, Vol. 3.* Washington, DC: American Psychiatric Association.

Markowitz, J., Bleiberg, K., Pessin, H., & Skodol, A. (2007). Adapting interpersonal psychotherapy for borderline personality disorder. *Journal of Mental Health, 16,* 103–116.

Marlatt, G. (1994). Addiction, mindfulness and acceptance. In S. Hayes, N. Jacobson, V. Follette, & M. Dougher (Eds.), *Acceptance and change: Content and context in psychotherapy* (pp. 175–197). Reno, NV: Context Press.

Marlatt. G., & Kristeller, J. (1999). Mindfulness and meditation. In. W. Miller (Ed.), *Integrating spirituality into treatment: Resources for practitioners* (pp. 67–84). Washington, DC: American Psychological Association.

Marmar, C., & Freeman, M. (1988). Brief dynamic psychotherapy of post-traumatic stress disorders: Management of narcissistic regression. *Journal of Traumatic Stress, 1,* 323–337.

Marra, T. (2005). *Dialectic behavior therapy in private practice: A practical and comprehensive guide.* Oakland, CA: New Harbinger Publications.

Martin, J. (1997). Mindfulness: A proposed common factor. *Journal of Psychotherapy Integration, 7,* 291–312.

Masterson, J. (1976). *Psychotherapy of the borderline adult: A developmental approach.* New York, NY: Brunner/Mazel.

Masterson, J. (1981). *The narcissistic and borderline disorders.* New York, NY: Brunner/Mazel.

Masterson, J., & Klein, R. (Eds.) (1989). *Psychotherapy of the disorders of the self.* New York, NY: Brunner/Mazel.

McCormack, C. (1989). The borderline/schizoid marriage: The holding environment as an essential treatment construct. *Journal of Marital and Family Therapy, 15,* 299–309.

McCullough, J. (2000). *Treatment for chronic depression: Cognitive behavioral analysis system of psychotherapy.* New York, NY: Guilford.

McCullough, J. (2002). What kind of questions are we trying to answer with our psychotherapy research? *Clinical Psychology: Science and Practice, 9,* 447–452.

McCullough, J., Schramm, E., & Penberthy, J. (2015). *CBASP as a distinctive treatment for persistent depressive disorder: Distinctive features.* New York, NY: Routledge.

McGauley, G., Yakeley, J., Williams, A., & Bateman, A. (2011). Attachment, mentalization, and antisocial personality disorder: The possible contribution of mentalization-based treatment. *European Journal of Psychotherapy & Counseling, 13*(4), 371–393.

McMain, S., Boritz, T., & Leybman, M. (2015). Common strategies for cultivating a positive therapy relationship in the treatment of borderline personality disorder. *Journal of Psychotherapy Integration, 25*(1), 20–29.

McMain, S., Links, P., Gnam, W., Guimond, T., Cardish, R., Korman, L., & Streiner, D. (2009). A randomized trial of dialectical behavior therapy versus general psychiatric management for borderline personality disorder. *American Journal of Psychiatry, 166*(12), 1365–1374.

Meares, R., Stevenson, J., & Comerford, A. (1999). Psychotherapy with borderline personality patients: A comparison between treated and untreated cohorts. *Australian & New Zealand Journal of Psychiatry, 33*, 467–472.

Megargee, E., & Bohn, M. (1979). *Classifying criminal offenders.* Beverly Hills, CA: Sage.

Mehlum, L., Fris, S., Irion, T., Johns, S., Karterud, S., Vaglum, P., et al. (1991). Personality disorders 2–5 years after treatment: A prospective follow-up study. *Acta Psychiatrica Scandinavia, 84,* 72–77.

Meichenbaum, D. (1977). *Cognitive-behavioral modification: An integrated approach.* New York, NY: Plenum.

Meissner, W. (1978). *The paranoid process.* New York, NY: Jason Aronson.

Meissner, W. (1986). *Psychotherapy and the paranoid process.* Northvale, NJ: Jason Aronson.

Meissner, W. (1989). Paranoid personality disorder. In T. Karasu (Ed.), *Treatments of psychiatric disorders* (pp. 2705–2711). Washington, DC: American Psychiatric Press.

Meloy, J. (1988). *The psychopathic mind: Origins, dynamics, and treatment.* Northvale, NJ: Jason Aronson.

Meloy, J., & Yakeley, J. (2010). Psychodynamic treatment of antisocial personality disorder. In J. Clarkin, P. Fonagy, & G. Gabbard (Eds.), *Psychodynamic psychotherapy for personality disorders: A clinical handbook* (pp. 289–309). Arlington, VA: American Psychiatric Publishing.

Messina, N., Farabee, D., & Rawson, R. (2003). Treatment responsivity to cocaine-dependent patients with antisocial personality disorder to cognitive-behavioral and contingency management interventions. *Journal of Consulting and Clinical Psychology, 71*(2), 320–329.

Messina, N., Wish, E., Hoffman, J., & Nemes, S. (2002). Antisocial personality disorder and TC treatment outcomes. *American Journal of Drug and Alcohol Abuse, 28*(2), 197–212.

Meyer, R. (1995). *The clinician's handbook: Integrated diagnostics, assessment, and intervention in adult and adolescent psychotherapy* (4th ed.). Boston: Allyn and Bacon.

Miller, W., & Rollnick, S. (2013). *Motivational interviewing: Helping people change* (3rd ed.). New York, NY: Guilford.

Millon, T. (1981). *Disorders of personality: DSM-III Axis II.* New York, NY: Wiley.

Millon, T. (1990). *Toward a new personology: An evolutionary model.* New York, NY: Wiley.

Millon, T., & Davis, R. (1996). *Disorders of personality: DSM-IV and beyond* (2nd ed.). New York, NY: Wiley.

Millon, T., & Davis, R. (2000). *Personality disorders in modern life.* New York, NY: John Wiley & Sons.

Millon, T., & Everly, G. (1985). *Personality and its disorders: A biosocial learning approach.* New York, NY: Wiley.

Millon, T., Millon, C., Grossman, S., Boice, A., & Sinsabaugh, K. (2015). *MCMI-IV manual.* Minneapolis, MN: Pearson.

Minuchin, S. (1974). *Families and family therapy.* Cambridge, MA: Harvard University Press.

Minuchin, S., & Montalvo, B. (1967). Techniques for working with disorganized low socioeconomic families. *American Journal of Orthopsychiatry, 37*(5), 880.

Mitchell, D., Tafrate, R., & Freeman, A. (2015). Antisocial personality disorder. In A. Beck, D. Davis, & A. Freeman, A. (Eds.), *Cognitive therapy of personality disorders* (3rd ed., pp. 346–365). New York, NY: Guilford.

Montgomery, J. (1971). Treatment management of passive-dependent behavior. *International Journal of Social Psychiatry, 17,* 311–319.

Morey, L., Skodol, A., & Oldham J. (2014). Clinician judgments of clinical utility: A comparison of DSM-IV-TR personality disorders and the alternative model for DSM-5 personality disorders. *Journal of Abnormal Psychology, 123,* 398–405.

Mulder, R. (2012). Cultural aspects of personality disorders. In T. Widiger (Ed.), *The Oxford handbook of personality disorders* (pp. 260–274). New York, NY: Oxford University Press.

Nachmani, G. (1984). Hesitation, perplexity, and annoyance at opportunity. *Contemporary Psychoanalysis, 20,* 448–457.

Nathanson, B., & Jamison, S. (2011). Psychotherapeutic and pharmacologic treatment of schizotypal personality disorder: The heuristic utility of stressing function over form. *Clinical Case Studies, 10*(5), 395–407.

Nehls, N. (1991). Borderline personality disorder and group therapy. *Archives of Psychiatric Nursing, 5,* 137–146.

Nehls, N., & Diamond, R. (1993). Developing a systems approach to caring for persons with borderline personality disorder. *Community Mental Health Journal, 29,* 161–172.

Nichols, W. (1996). Persons with antisocial and histrionic personality disorders in relationships. In F. Kaslow (Ed.), *Handbook of relational diagnosis and dysfunctional family patterns* (pp. 287–299). New York, NY: Wiley.

Nurse, A. (1998). The dependent/narcissistic couple. In J. Carlson & L. Sperry (Eds.), *The disordered couple* (pp. 315–332). New York, NY: Brunner/Mazel.

O'Donohue, W., Fowler, K., & Lilienfeld, S. (2007). *Personality Disorders: Toward the DSM-V.* Thousand Oaks, CA: Sage.

O'Leary, K., Turner, E., Gardner, D., & Cowdry, R. (1991). Homogeneous group therapy or borderline personality disorder. *Group, 15,* 56–64.

Oldham, J., & Skodol, A. (2000). Charting the future of Axis II. *Journal of Personality Disorders, 14,* 17–29.

Ogloff, J., Talevski, D., Lemphers, A., Wood, M., & Simmons, M. (2015). Co-occurring mental illness, substance use disorders, and antisocial personality disorder among clients of forensic mental health services. *Psychiatric Rehabilitation Journal, 1,* 16–23.

Osterbaan, D., van Balkom, A., Spinhoven, P., de Meij, T., & van Dyck, R. (2002). The influence of treatment gain on comorbid avoidant personality disorder in patients with social phobia. *Journal of Nervous and Mental Disease, 190*(1), 41–43.

Othmer, E., & Othmer, S. (2002). *The clinical interview using DSM-IV, Vol. 1, Fundamentals.* Washington, DC: American Psychiatric Press.

Padesky, C., & Beck, J. (2015). Avoidant personality disorder. In A. Beck, D. Davis, & A. Freeman, A. (Eds.), *Cognitive therapy of personality disorders* (3rd ed., pp. 174–202). New York, NY: Guilford.

Parsons, B., & Alexander, J. (1973). Short-term family interventions: A therapy outcome study. *Journal of Abnormal Psychology, 8,* 219–225.

PDM Task Force. (2006). *Psychodynamic diagnostic manual (PDM).* Silver Spring, MD: Alliance of Psychoanalytic Organizations.

Perry, J., Francis, A., and Clarkin, J. (1990). *A DSM-III-R casebook of treatment selection.* New York, NY: Brunner/Mazel.

Perry, J. C., Presniak, M., & Olson, T. (2013). Mechanisms in schizotypal, borderlines, antisocial, and narcissistic personality disorders. *Psychiatry, 76*(1), 32–52.

Phillips, K., & Stein, D., (Eds.). (2015). *Handbook on obsessive-compulsive and related disorders.* Alexandria, VA: American Psychiatric Publishing.

Pies, R. (1992). The psychopharmacology of personality disorders. *Psychiatric Times,* February, 23–24.

Pincus, A., Wright, A., & Cain, N. (2014). Narcissistic grandiosity and narcissistic vulnerability in psychotherapy. *Personality Disorders: Theory, Research, and Treatment, 5*(4), 439–443.

Pines, M. (1975). Group psychotherapy with difficult patients. In L. Wolberg & M. Aronson (Eds.), *Group therapy 1975: An overview.* New York, NY: Stratton Intercontinental Medical Books.

Porcerelli, J., Dauphin, V., Ablon, J., Leitman, S., & Bambery, M. (2007). Psychoanalysis with avoidant personality disorder: A systemic case study. *Psychotherapy: Theory, Research, Practice, Training, 44*(1), pp. 1–13.

Pretzer, J. (1988). Paranoid personality disorder: A cognitive view. *International Cognitive Therapy Newsletter, 4*(4), 10–12.

Quality Assurance Project (1991). Treatment outlines for borderline, narcissistic and histrionic personality disorders. *Australian & New Zealand Journal of Psychiatry, 25,* 392–403.

Regier, D., Boyd, J., Burke, J., Rae, D., Myers, J., Kramer, M., et al. (1988). One-month prevalence in mental disorders in the United States. *Archives of General Psychiatry, 45,* 977–986.

Reich, J. (2002). Drug treatment of personality disorder traits. *Psychiatric Annals, 32*(10), 590–600.

Reich, J. (2005). State and trait in personality disorders. In J. Reich (Ed.), *Personality Disorders: Current Research and Treatments* (pp. 3–20). New York, NY: Routledge.

Reid, W. (1989). *The treatment of psychiatric disorders. Revised for the DSM-III-R.* New York, NY: Brunner/Mazel.

Rennenberg, B., Goldstein, A., Phillips, D., & Chambliss, D. (1990). Intensive behavioral group treatment of avoidant personality disorder. *Behavior Therapy, 21,* 363–377.

Renton, J., & Mankiewicz, P. (2015). Paranoid, schizotypal, and schizoid personality disorders. In A. Beck, D. Davis, & A. Freeman, A. (Eds.), *Cognitive therapy of personality disorders* (3rd ed., pp. 244–275). New York, NY: Guilford.

Rentrop, M., Zilker, T., Lederle, A., Birkhofer, A., & Horz, S. (2014). Psychiatric comorbidity and personality structure in patients with polyvalent addiction. *Psychopathology, 47*(2), 133–140.

Rinsley, D. (1982). *Borderline and other self disorders.* New York, NY: Jason Aronson.

Roche, M., Pincus, A. Lukowitsky, R., Ménard, K., & Conroy, D. (2013). An integrative approach to the assessment of narcissism. *Journal of Personality Assessment, 9*(3), 237–248.

Roemer, L., & Orsillo, S.(2002). Expanding our conceptualization of and treatment for generalized anxiety disorder: Integrating mindfulness/acceptance-based approaches with existing cognitive-behavioral models. *Clinical Psychology: Science and Practice. 9*(1), 54–68.

Ronningstam, E. (2011). Narcissistic personality disorder: A clinical perspective. *Journal of Psychiatric Practice, 17,* 89–99.

Ronningstam, E. (2012). Narcissistic personality disorder: The diagnostic process. In T. Widiger (Ed.), *The Oxford handbook of personality disorders* (pp. 527–548). New York, NY: Oxford University Press.

Rutan, J. S., Stone, W., & Shay, J. (2014). *Psychodynamic group psychotherapy* (5th ed.). New York, NY: Guilford.

Ryan, A., Macdonald, A., & Walker, E. (2013). Treatment of adolescents with schizotypal personality disorder and related conditions: A practice-oriented review of the literature. *Clinical Psychology: Science and Practice, 20*(4), 408–424.

Ryle, A. (2004). The contribution of cognitive analytic therapy to the treatment of borderline personality disorder. *Journal of Personality Disorders, 18*(1), 3–35.

Sadoff, R., & Collins, D. (1968). Passive dependency in sufferers. *American Journal of Psychiatry, 124,* 1127–1136.

Salkovskis, P., & Kirk, J. (1989). Obsessional disorders. In K. Hawton, P. Salkovskis, J. Kirk, & D. Clark (Eds.), *Cognitive behavior therapy for psychiatric problems* (pp. 129–168). Oxford: Oxford University Press.

Salvatore, G., Russo, B., Russo, M., Popolo, R., & Dimaggio, G. (2012). Metacognition-oriented therapy for psychosis: The case of a woman diagnosed with delusional disorder and paranoid personality disorder. *Journal of Psychotherapy Integration, 22*(4), 314–329.

Salzman, L. (1980). *Treatment of the obsessive personality.* New York, NY: Jason Aronson.

Salzman, L. (1989). Compulsive personality disorder. In T. Karasu (Ed.), *Treatment of psychiatric disorders* (pp. 2771–2782). Washington, DC: American Psychiatric Press.

Samuels, J., & Costa, P. (2012). Obsessive-compulsive personality disorder. In T. Widiger (Ed.), *The Oxford handbook of personality disorders* (pp. 566–581). New York, NY: Oxford University Press.

Sanislow, C., da Cruz, K., Gianoli, M., & Reagan, E. (2012). Avoidant Personality Disorder, Traits, and Type. In T. Widiger (Ed.), *The Oxford handbook of personality disorders* (pp. 549–565). New York, NY: Oxford University Press.

Schanche, E., Stiles, T., McCullough, L., Svartberg, M., & Nielsen, G. (2011). The relationship between activating affects, inhibitory affects, and self-compassion in patients with Cluster C personality disorders. *Psychotherapy, 48,* 293–303.

Schane, M., & Kovel, V. (1988). Family therapy in severe borderline personality disorder. *International Journal of Family Psychiatry, 9,* 241–258.

Scheidlinger, S., & Porter, K. (1980). Group therapy combined with individual psycho-therapy. In T. Karasu & L. Bellak (Eds.), *Specialized Techniques in Individual Psychotherapy* (pp. 426–440). New York, NY: Brunner/Mazel.

Schwartz, J., & Begley, S. (2002). *The mind and the brain: Neuroplasticity and the power of mental force.* New York, NY: HarperCollins.

Segal, Z., Williams, J., & Teasdale, J. (2002). *Mindfulness-based cognitive therapy of depression.* New York, NY: Guilford.

Segal, Z., Williams, J., Teasdale, J., & Williams, M. (2004). Mindfulness-based cognitive therapy: Theoretical and empirical status. In S. Hayes, V. Follette, & M. Linehan (Eds.), *Mindfulness and acceptance: Expanding the cognitive-behavioral tradition* (pp. 45–65). New York, NY: Guilford.

Shafer, R. (1954). *Psychoanalytic interpretation in Rorschach testing.* New York, NY: Grune and Stratton.

Shapiro, D. (1965). *Neurotic styles.* New York, NY: Basic Books.

Shapiro, E. (1982). The holding environment and family therapy for acting out adolescents. *International Journal of Psychoanalysis, 9,* 209–226.

Sharoff, K. (2002). *Cognitive coping therapy.* New York, NY: Brunner/Routledge.

Sheldon, W., Dupertius, C., & McDermott, E. (1954). *A guide for somatotyping the adult male at all ages. Atlas of men* (2nd ed.). New York, NY: Harper Brothers.

Shostrum, E. (1976). *Actualizing therapy: Foundations for a scientific ethic.* San Diego, CA: EdITS Publishers.

Shulman, B. (1982). An Adlerian interpretation of the borderline personality. *Modern Psychoanalysis, 7,* 137–153.

Siegel, D. (1999). *The developing mind.* New York, NY: Guilford.

Sifneos, P. (1972). *Short-term psychotherapy and emotional crisis.* Cambridge, MA: Harvard University Press.

Sifneos, P. (1984). The current status of short-term dynamic psychotherapy and its future: An overview. *American Journal of Psychotherapy, 38,* 472–487.

Silk, K., & Feurino, L. (2012). Psychopharmacology of personality disorders. In T. Widiger (Ed.), *The Oxford handbook of personality disorders* (pp. 713–726). New York, NY: Oxford University Press.

Simon, W. (2009). Follow-up psychotherapy outcome of patients with dependent, avoidant and obsessive–compulsive personality disorders: A meta-analytic review. *International Journal of Psychiatry in Clinical Practice, 13,* 153–165.

Simon, K. (2015). Obsessive-compulsive personality disorder. In A. Beck, D. Davis, & A. Freeman (Eds.), *Cognitive therapy of personality disorders* (3rd ed., pp. 203–222). New York, NY: Guilford.

Singer, M. T., & Larson, D. G. (1981). Borderline personality and the Rorschach test. *Archives of General Psychiatry, 38*(6), 693–698.

Skodol, A., Bender, D., Gunderson, J., & Oldham, J. (2014). Personality disorders. In R. Hales, S. Yudofsky, & L. Weiss (Eds.), *The American Psychiatric Publishing Textbook of Psychiatry* (pp. 851–894). Alexandria, VA: American Psychiatric Publishing.

Slavik, S., Sperry, L., & Carlson, J. (1992). The schizoid personality disorder: A review and an Adlerian view and treatment. *Individual Psychotherapy, 7,* 137–154.

Slavson, S. (1939). *Dynamics of group psychotherapy.* New York, NY: Jason Aronson.

Slavson, S., (1964). *A textbook in analytic group psychotherapy.* New York, NY: International Universities Press.

Snyder, M. (1994). Couple therapy with narcissistically vulnerable clients: Using the relationship enhancement model. *Family Journal: Counseling and Therapy for Couples and Families, 2,* 27–35.

Soloff, P., Lynch, K., & Kelly, T. (2002). Childhood abuse as a risk factor for suicidal behavior in borderline personality disorder. *Journal of Personality Disorders, 16*(3), 201–214.

Solomon, M, (1989). *Narcissism and intimacy: Love and marriage in an age of confusion.* New York, NY: Norton.

Solomon, M. (1999), Treating narcissistic and borderline couples. In J. Carlson & L. Sperry (Eds.), *The disordered couple* (pp. 239–258). New York, NY: Brunner/Mazel.

Sperry, L. (1990). Personality disorders: Biopsychosocial descriptions and dynamics. *Journal of Individual Psychology, 46,* 193–202.

Sperry, L. (1995a). *Handbook of diagnosis and treatment of DSM-IV personality disorders.* New York, NY: Brunner/Mazel.

Sperry, L. (1995b). *Psychopharmacology and psychotherapy: Strategies for maximizing treatment outcomes.* New York, NY: Brunner/Mazel.

Sperry, L. (1988). Biopsychosocial therapy: An integrative approach for tailoring treatment. *Journal of Individual Psychology, 44,* 225–235.

Sperry, L. (2000). Biopsychosocial therapy: Essential strategies and tactics. In J. Carlson & L. Sperry (Eds.), *Brief therapy with individuals and couples.* Phoenix, AZ: Zeig, Tucker & Theisen.

Sperry, L. (2002). From psychopathology to transformation: Retrieving the developmental focus in psychotherapy. *Journal of Individual Psychology, 58*, 398–421.

Sperry, L. (2003). *Handbook of diagnosis and treatment of DSM-IV-TR personality disorders* (2nd edition). New York, NY: Brunner-Routledge.

Sperry, L. (2005). Case conceptualization: The missing link between theory and practice. *The Family Journal: Counseling and Therapy for Couples and Families, 13*, 71–76.

Sperry, L. (2006a). *Cognitive behavior therapy of DSM-IV-TR personality disorders: Highly effective interventions for the most common personality disorders* (2nd ed.). New York, NY: Brunner/Mazel.

Sperry, L. (2006b). *Psychological treatment of chronic illness: The biopsychosocial therapy approach.* New York, NY: Brunner/Mazel.

Sperry, L. (2010). *Core competencies in counseling and psychotherapy: Becoming a highly competent and effective therapist.* New York, NY: Routledge.

Sperry, L. (2014). Effecting change: The centrality of the case conceptualization. In L. Sperry & J. Carlson. *How master therapists work: Effecting change from the first through the last session and beyond* (pp. 74–99). New York, NY: Routledge.

Sperry, L. (2015). Personality disorders. In L. Sperry, J. Carlson, J. Duba-Sauerheber, & J. Sperry (Eds.), *Psychopathology and psychotherapy: DSM-5 diagnosis, case conceptualization and treatment* (3rd ed., pp. 27–61). New York, NY: Routledge.

Sperry, L. (in press). Educating the next generation of psychotherapists: Considering the future of theory and practice in Adlerian Psychotherapy. *Journal of Individual Psychology.*

Sperry, L., Brill, P., Howard, K., & Grissom, G. (1996). *Treatment outcomes in psychotherapy and psychiatric interventions.* New York, NY: Brunner/Mazel.

Sperry, L., & Carlson, J. (2014). *How master therapists work: Effecting change from the first to the last session and beyond.* New York, NY: Routledge.

Sperry, L., Gudeman, J., Blackwell, B., & Faulkner, L. (1992). *Psychiatric case formulations.* Washington, DC: American Psychiatric Press.

Sperry, L., & Maniacci, M. (1996). The histrionic-obsessive couple. In J. Carlson & L. Sperry (Eds.), *The disordered couple* (pp. 187–205). New York, NY: Brunner/Mazel.

Sperry, L., & Mosak, H. (1996). Personality disorders. In L. Sperry & J. Carlson (Eds.), *Psychopathology and psychotherapy: From diagnosis to treatment* (2nd ed., pp. 279–336). Washington, DC: Accelerated Development/Taylor & Francis.

Sperry, L., & Sperry, J. (2012). *Case conceptualization: Mastering this competency with ease and confidence.* New York, NY: Routledge.

Sperry, L., & Sperry, J. (2016). *Cognitive behavior therapy of DSM-5 personality disorders* (3rd ed.). New York, NY: Routledge.

Spotnitz, H. (1975). The borderline schizophrenic in group psychotherapy. *International Journal of Group Psychotherapy, 7*, 155–174.

Stern, B., Yeomans, F., & Diamond, D. (2013). Transference-focused psychotherapy (TFP) for narcissistic personality disorder. In J. Ogrodniczuk (Ed.), *Understanding and treating pathological narcissism* (pp. 235–252). Washington, DC: American Psychological Association.

Stevenson, J., & Meares, R. (1992). An outcome study of psychotherapy for patients with borderline personality disorder. *American Journal of Psychiatry, 149*, 144–150.

Stone, M. (1983). Psychotherapy with schizotypal borderline patients. *Journal of the American Academy of Psychoanalysis, 11*, 87–111.

Stone, M. (1985). Schizotypal personality: Psychotherapeutic aspects. *Schizophrenia Bulletin, 11*, 576–589.

Stone, M. (1989). Schizotypal personality disorder. In T. Karasu (Ed.), *Treatment of psychiatric disorders* (pp. 2719–2726). Washington, DC: American Psychiatric Press.

Stone, M. (1992). Treatment of severe personality disorders. In A. Tasman & M. Riba (Eds.), *American Psychiatric Press Review of Psychiatry. Vol. 2* (pp. 98–115). Washington, DC: American Psychiatric Press.

Stone, M. (1993). *Abnormalities of personality: Within and beyond the realm of treatment.* New York, NY: Norton.

Stone, W., & Whiteman, R. (1980). Observation and empathy in group psychotherapy. In L. Wolberg & M. Aronson (Eds.), *Group and Family Therapy.* New York, NY: Brunner/Mazel.

Stone, M., & Weissman, R. (1984). Group therapy with borderline patients. In H. Slavinska (Ed.), *Contemporary perspectives in group psychotherapy.* London: Routledge & Kegan Paul.

Stout, M. (2005). *The sociopath next door.* New York, NY: Broadway Books.

Strauss, J., Hayes, A., Johnson, S., Newman, C., Brown, G., Barber, J., et al. (2006). Early alliance, alliance ruptures, and symptom change in a nonrandomized trial of cognitive therapy for avoidant and obsessive-compulsive personality disorders. *Journal of Consulting and Clinical Psychology, 74,* 337–345.

Stravynski, A., Grey, S., & Elie, R. (1987). Outline of the therapeutic process in social skills training with socially dysfunctional patients. *Journal of Consulting and Clinical Psychology, 55,* 224–228.

Stravynski, A., Marks, I., & Yule, W. (1982). Social skills problems in neurotic outpatients. *Archives of General Psychology, 39,* 1378–1383.

Strupp, H., & Binder, J. (1984). *Psychotherapy in a new key: A guide to time-limited dynamic psychotherapy.* New York, NY: Basic Books.

Sungar, M., & Gunduz, A. (2015). Histrionic personality disorder. In A. Beck, D. Davis, & A. Freeman, A. (Eds.), *Cognitive therapy of personality disorders* (3rd ed., pp. 325–345). New York, NY: Guilford.

Svartberg, M., Stiles, T., & Seltzer, M. (2004). Randomized control trial of the effectiveness of short-term dynamic therapy and cognitive therapy for Cluster C personality disorders. *American Journal of Psychiatry, 161*(5), pp. 810–817.

Swiercinsky, D. (Ed.). (1985). *Testing adults.* Kansas City: Test Corporation of America.

Symington, N. (1980). The response aroused by the psychopath. *International Review of Psychoanalysis, 7,* 291–298.

Tacbacnik, N. (1965). Isolation, transference, splitting and combined treatment. *Comprehensive Psychiatry, 6,* 336–346.

Tarrier, N. (Ed.). (2006). *Case formulation in cognitive behaviour therapy. The treatment of challenging and complex cases.* London, UK: Routledge.

Teasdale, J., Segal, Z. Williams, J., Mark, G., Ridgeway, V., Soulsby, J, et al. (2000). Prevention of relapse/recurrence in depression by mindfulness-based cognitive therapy. *Journal of Consulting and Clinical Psychology, 68,* 615–623.

Thomas, A., & Chess, S. (1977). *Temperament and development.* New York, NY: Brunner/Mazel.

Thylstrup, B.& Hesse, M. (2009). "I am not complaining"—Ambivalence construct in schizoid personality disorder. *American Journal of Psychotherapy, 63*(2), 147–167.

Toman, W. (1961). *Family constellation: Theory and practice of a psychological game.* New York, NY: Springer.

Torgersen, S. (1984). Genetic and nosological aspects of schizotypal and borderline personality disorders: A twin study. *Archives of General Psychiatry, 41,* 546–554.

Torgersen, S. (2009). Prevalence, sociodemographics, and functional impairment. In J. Oldham, J. Skodol, & D. Bender (Eds.), *Essentials of personality disorders* (pp. 83–102), Washington, DC: American Psychiatric Publishing.

Torgersen, S. (2012). Epidemiology. In T. Widiger (Ed.), *The Oxford handbook of personality disorders* (pp. 186–205). New York, NY: Oxford University Press.

Trujillo, M. (2013). Treating pathological narcissism with short term dynamic psychotherapy. In J. Ogrodniczuk (Ed.), *Understanding and treating pathological narcissism* (pp. 269–284). Washington, DC: American Psychological Association.

Turkat, I. (1990). *The personality disorders: A psychological approach to clinical management.* New York, NY: Pergamon.

Turkat, L. & Maisto, S. (1985). Application of the experimental method to the formulation and modification of personality disorders. In D. Barlow (Ed.), *Clinical handbook of psychological disorders* (pp. 503–570). New York, NY: Guilford.

Vaccani, J. (1989). Borderline personality and alcohol abuse. *Archives of Psychiatric Nursing, 3,* 113–119.

Valliant, G., & Perry, J. (1985). Personality disorders. In H. Kaplan & B. Sadock (Eds.), *Comprehensive textbook of psychiatry* (4th ed.). Baltimore: Williams & Wilkins.

Van der Kolk, B. A., Perry, J. C., & Herman, J. L. (1991). Childhood origins of self-destructive behavior. *American Journal of Psychiatry, 148*(12), 1665–1671.

Van Gelder, K. (2010). *The Buddha and the borderline: A memoir.* Oakland, CA: New Harbinger.

Vaughn, B., & Bost, K. (1999). Attachment and temperament: Redundant, independent, or interacting influences on interpersonal adaptation and personality development? In P. Cassidy & P. Shaver (Eds.), *Handbook of attachment: Theory, research and clinical applications* (pp. 198–225). New York, NY: Guilford.

Vinogradov, S., & Yalom, I. (1989). *Concise guide to group psychotherapy.* Washington, DC: American Psychiatric Press.

Wagner, E., & Wagner, C. (1981). *The interpretation of psychological test data.* Springfield, IL: Charles Thomas.

Waldinger, R. (1986). Intensive psychodynamic psychotherapy with borderline patients: An overview. *American Journal of Psychiatry, 144,* 267–274.

Waldo, M., & Harman, M. (1993). Relationship enhancement therapy with borderline personality. *Family Journal, 1,* 25–30.

Waldo, M., & Harman, M. (1998). Borderline personality disorder and relationship enhancement marital therapy. In J. Carlson & L. Sperry (Eds.), *The disordered couple* (pp. 285–298). New York, NY: Brunner/Mazel.

Walker, R. (1992). Substance abuse and B-cluster disorders: Treatment recommendations. *Journal of Psychoactive Drugs, 24,* 233–241.

Wallerstein, R. (1986). *Forty-two lives in treatment: A study of psychoanalysis and psychotherapy.* New York, NY: Guilford.

Walsh, A., & Wu, H. H. (2008). Differentiating antisocial personality disorder, psychopathy, and sociopathy: Evolutionary, genetic, neurological, and sociological considerations. *Criminal Justice Studies, 21*(2), 135–152.

Weeks, G., & L'Abate, L. (1982). *Paradoxical psychotherapy: Theory and practice with individuals, couples, and families.* New York, NY: Brunner/Mazel.

Weissman, M., Markowitz, J., & Klerman, G. (2000). *Comprehensive guide to interpersonal psychotherapy.* New York, NY: Basic Books.

Weissman, M., Markowitz, J., & Klerman, G. (2007). *Clinician's quick guide to interpersonal psychotherapy.* New York, NY: Oxford University Press.

Wells, M., Glickauf-Hughes, C., & Buzzell, V. (1990). Treating obsessive-compulsive personalities in psychoanalytic/interpersonal group therapy. *Psychotherapy, 27,* 366–379.

Westen, D. (2012). Prototypic diagnosis of psychiatric syndromes. *World Psychiatry, 11*(1), 16–21.

Wilberg, T., Karterud, S., Urnes, O., Pedersen, G., & Friis, S. (1999). One-year follow-up of day treatment for poorly functioning patients with personality disorders. *Psychiatric Services, 50*(10), 1326–1330.

Williams, J. (1988). Cognitive intervention for a paranoid personality disorder. *Psychotherapy, 25,* 570–575.

Williams, P. (2010). Psychotherapeutic treatment of Cluster A personality disorders. In J. Clarkin, P. Fonagy, & G. Gabbard (Eds.), *Psychodynamic psychotherapy for personality disorders: A clinical handbook* (pp. 289–309). Arlington, VA: American Psychiatric Publishing.

Winer, J., & Pollock, G. (1989). Psychoanalysis and dynamic therapy. In T. Karasu (Ed.), *Treatments of psychiatric disorders* (pp. 2639–2648). Washington, DC: American Psychiatric Press.

Winston, A., & Pollack, J. (1991). Brief adaptive psychotherapy. *Psychiatric Annals, 21,* 415–418.

Woody, G., McLellan, A.., Luborsky, L., & O'Brien, C. (1985). Sociopathy and psychotherapy outcome. *Archives of General Psychiatry, 42*(11), 1081–1086.

Wright, A., Hallquist, M., Morse, J, Scott, L., Stepp, S., Nolf, K, et al. (2013). Clarifying interpersonal heterogeneity in borderline personality disorder using latent mixture modeling. *Journal of Personality Disorders, 27*(2), 125–143.

Wurmser, L. (1981). *The mask of shame.* Baltimore: Johns Hopkins University Press.

Yalom, I. (1995). *The theory and practice of group psychotherapy* (4th ed.). New York, NY: Basic Books.

Young, J. (1994). *Cognitive therapy for personality disorders: A schema-focused approach* (rev. ed.). Sarasota, FL: Professional Resource Exchange.

Young, J. (1999). *Cognitive therapy for personality disorders: A schema-focused approach* (3rd ed.). Sarasota, FL: Professional Resource Press.

Young, J., Klosko, J., & Weishaar, M. (2003). *Schema therapy: A practitioner's guide.* New York, NY: Guilford.

Young, P. (1990). *Cognitive therapy for personality disorders: A schema-focused approach.* Sarasota, FL: Professional Resource Exchange.

Zanarini, M., Frankenburg, F., Reich, D., & Fitzmaurice, G. (2010). Time to attainment of recovery from borderline personality disorder and stability of recovery: A 10-year prospective follow-up study. *American Journal of Psychiatry, 167,* 663–667.

Zimbardo, P. (1977). *Shyness.* New York, NY: Jove/Berkeley Publishing Group.

Zimmerman, M., Rothschild, L., & Chelminski, I. (2005). The prevalence of DSM-IV personality disorders in outpatients. *American Journal of Psychiatry, 162,* 1911–1918.

INDEX